Methods of Historical Analysis
in Electronic Media

LEA's Communication Series

Jennings Bryant/Dolf Zillmann, General Editors

Selected titles in the series include:

Bucy/Newhagen • Media Access: Social and Psychological Dimensions of New Technology Use

Butler • Television: Critical Methods and Applications, Second Edition

Bryant/Bryant • Television and the American Family, Second Edition

Eastman • Research in Media Promotion

Fisch/Truglio • "G" is for Growing: Thirty Years of Research on Children and Sesame Street

Godfrey • Methods of Historical Analysis in Electronic Media

Sterling/Kittross • Stay Tuned: A History of American Broadcasting, Third Edition

Methods of Historical Analysis in Electronic Media

Edited by

Donald G. Godfrey
Walter Cronkite School of Journalism and Mass Communication
Arizona State University

LAWRENCE ERLBAUM ASSOCIATES, PUBLISHERS
2006   Mahwah, New Jersey   London

Camera ready copy for this book was provided by the author.

Copyright © 2006 by Lawrence Erlbaum Associates, Inc.

Lawrence Erlbaum Associates, Inc., Publishers
10 Industrial Avenue
Mahwah, New Jersey 07430
www.erlbaum.com

Cover design by Kathryn Houghtaling Lacey and Candice Anderson.
Typesetting by Janet Soper, Publication Assistance Center,
College of Public Programs, Arizona State University.

Library of Congress Cataloging-in-Publication Data

Methods of historical analysis in electronic media / edited by Donald G. Godfrey.
    p. cm. — (LEA's communication series)

Includes bibliographical references and index.

ISBN 0-8058-5185-2 (cloth : alk. paper)
ISBN 0-8058-5186-0 (pbk. : alk. paper)
1. Mass media—History—Research Methodology. I. Godfrey, Donald G.
    II. Series.
P91.3.M482005
302.23'072—dc22   2004062910
                                                            CIP

Printed in the United States of America
10 9 8 7 6 5 4 3 2 1

Contents

ABOUT THE AUTHORS

Craig Allen, Associate Professor, Broadcast Journalism Coordinator, Walter Cronkite School of Journalism and Mass Communication, Arizona State University. Allen's most recent books include *The Global Media Revolution and Eisenhower, Mass Media,* and *News Is People*—a local history of national news.

John Armstrong, Assistant Professor, Department of Communication Studies, Furman University. Armstrong has 14 years of professional experience as a television journalist and executive. His research specializations include media history, media law, and policy.

Robert K. Avery, Professor, Department of Communication, University of Utah. Avery is the founding Editor of the journal *Critical Studies in Mass Communication.* His most current work is *A History of Public Broadcasting.*

Mary E. Beadle, Professor, Department of Communication. Dean of the Graduate School, John Carroll University. Beadle specializes in history and international media. Her most recent work is *Indelible Images: Women of Local Television.*

Louise M. Benjamin, Associate Professor, Grady College of Journalism and Mass Communication, Department of Telecommunication, University of Georgia. Benjamin is the former Associate Director, Peabody Awards. She has written numerous articles and chapters on the regulatory history. Her most recent publication, *Freedom of the Air and the Public Interest: First Amendment Rights in Broadcasting to 1935,* was honored with the National Communication Association's Franklin Haiman Award for Distinguished Scholarship in Freedom of Expression.

Marvin J. Bensman, Professor, Department of Communication, University of Memphis. Bensman is the Director of the University of Memphis Radio Archive. His interests include law and new technology. The author of numerous books and articles, his most recent is *The Beginning of Broadcast Regulation in the Twentieth Century.*

Dale Cressman, Assistant Professor, Department of Communication, Brigham Young University. Cressman worked as a news producer and manager at television stations in Indiana, Texas, Wisconsin, and Utah and is authoring a forthcoming biography of Elmer Lower. His research specializations are in broadcast history and biography.

Donald G. Godfrey, Professor, Walter Cronkite School of Journalism and Mass Communications, Arizona State University. Godfrey is the Editor of the *Journal of Broadcasting & Electronic Media.* He has authored more than eight books and numerous articles. His most recent work concerns television pioneers *Philo T. Farnsworth: The Father of Television* and C. Francis Jenkins.

Chuck Howell, Curator, Library of American Broadcasting, University of Maryland. A member of the Academy of Certified Archivists, Howell has contributed to several media-related works, including *Airings: Radio in Society Since 1945* and the *Encyclopedia of Radio.*

Michael C. Keith, Associate Professor, Department of Communication, Boston College. Keith is the former Chair of Education at the Museum of Broadcast Communication. The author of more than 15 books and numerous articles his most recent being *Queer Airwaves.*

Tim Larson, Department of Communication, University of Utah. Larson is the Founder of the Utah Broadcast Archive. Research specializations include broadcasting, cable, integrated marketing and the history of Utah broadcasting.

Rebecca Ann Lind, Associate Professor, Director of Undergraduate Studies, Department of Communication, University of Illinois, Chicago. Lind's research interests include race and gender in the media, new communication technologies, media ethics, journalism, and audience studies. She is the Editor of the Broadcast Education Association's *Membership Directory* and is on the editorial boards of several major academic journals. Her most recent work is *Race/Gender/Media: Considering Diversity across Audiences, Production, and Content.*

Michael D. Murray, Professor, former Chair of the Department of Communication, University of Missouri–St. Louis. Murray is the former John Adams Fellow, University of London and has authored and edited several books on history and teaching. His most recent works are *Mass Communication Education* and the *Encyclopedia of Television News.* He is the current editor of the Review and Criticism section of the *Journal of Broadcasting & Electronic Media.*

Christopher H. Sterling, Professor of Media and Public Affairs and Telecommunication, Associate Dean for Graduate Affairs, George Washington University. Sterling is the founder and editor of *Communication Footnotes* and the former editor of the *Journal of Broadcasting.* Author of more than 15 books, his most recent is *Stay Tuned: A History of American Broadcasting,* 3rd ed.

Kyu Ho Youm, Professor and Jonathan Marshall First Amendment Chair in the University of Oregon School of Journalism and Communication. Youm has published scholarly articles on communication law subjects in a number of major U.S. and international law journals, including *Federal Communications Law Journal* and *Communication Law & Policy.* He is currently serving on the editorial boards of a dozen communication law journals in the United States and abroad.

Preface

This text is about history—broadcast electronic media history and history that has been broadcast. It is about historiography, research written, and research yet to be written. We are discussing research methodologies, suggesting differing approaches, and assessing the history of broadcasting. The purpose of this text is to provide a foundation for historical research in electronic media by addressing the literature and the methods—the traditional and the eclectic methods of scholarship as applied to electronic media. This text provides the scholars of broadcast history with a basic overview of the process and challenges in historical research. It provides traditional historians with suggestions for dealing with a broad range of issues challenging broadcast record. The text remedies the trivial exposure history often receives in introductory research texts.

The authors of each chapter are scholars, nationally and internationally recognized for their contributions to the history of electronic media. The text is divided into 5 parts, and 15 chapters. **Part I: Traditional Historiography** addresses the challenges in the application of the historical method to broadcast history. Chapter 1 describes the value of broadcast history, varied sources, the basic steps in the historical process; and, the apprehension the traditional historian has in utilizing broadcast sources as historical source materials. Chapter 2 discusses historical evidence, the categories of evidence, the rules of handling evidence, and the challenge of separating the facts, myth, and commercial dramatization from historical evidence history. Chapter 3 evaluates oral history and elite interview process and provides ideas for conducting oral history interviews. It also assesses as source materials oral history interviews versus news and documentary interviews. Chapter 4 examines the process of assessing visual evidence. Understanding the visual language, interpreting the visual in search of history, and separating photographic evidence from dramatic license is criterial in today's historical research.

Part II: Eclectic Methods in History suggests the various methods appropriate for electronic-media research based on the nature of the object under study. Chapter 5 looks back at the historical traditions in the legal history of broadcast research and suggests practical approaches for dealing with this rapidly growing discipline. Chapter 6 examines the trends in historical research exploring critical theory appropriate in the analysis of electronic media and looking at the quantitative methods utilized in history. It assesses the movements in historical criticism, social and intellectual history and the application of theory from related disciplines such as the theories of rhetoric, literature, theater, and pop culture applicable to media analysis. Chapter 7 expends beyond the traditional, legal and critical perspectives, looking at the methods of quantitative research appropriate to broadcast history and looks at the abundance historical research utilizing quantitative methods.

Part III: A New Look at Electronic Media suggests some new approaches to popular historical topics. Chapter 8 focuses on cultural studies in radio. Chapter 9 looks at the challenges of research in television. Chapter 10 examines the rapidly changing technology and makes some suggestions for historical analysis as well as providing directives for dealing with the Internet.

Part IV: New Perspectives in Topical Issues provides a broad topical look at history in broadcasting. Chapter 11 examines the specific challenges of history and analysis in race, gender, and media studies. Chapter 12 provides direction in the analysis of local history and the assessment of local history records. Chapter 13 explores the biography looking back at popular and scholarly approaches to the history of people and their lives.

Finally, **Part V: For the Record** concludes with chapter 14 providing an introduction to selected archives across the country and some basic information relative to the specialities of each. Chapter 15 provides a broad overview of what has been accomplished, a historian's challenges, and a look to the future.

—Donald G. Godfrey

Part I

Traditional Historiography

1

Researching Electronic Media History

Donald G. Godfrey
Arizona State University

In the late 1950s, a political science senior visited a broadcast archive for a research paper assignment. His assignment related to World War II and a specific Moscow conference held late in 1943. That conference had been well covered by the CBS Radio Network and the broadcasts had all been preserved, including Secretary of State Cordell Hull's report to the Congress at the meeting's conclusion. The student dutifully scoured the electronic transcriptions of the live radio broadcasts. He reasoned these firsthand accounts of the conference were invaluable pieces of historical evidence. He wrote his paper conforming to the standard, traditional, research style and the assigned length—but received an "F." The professor appended only a brief note of explanation—the broadcast record was, "not a valid research tool."[1]

Decades later we have the opportunity to reverse that young scholar's grade, as we "go beyond the printed descriptions to the primary source material of our age."[2] Broadcasts are now accepted records documenting history. Federal repositories, such as The Library of Congress, the Smithsonian Film Archives, and the National Archives and Records Administration, house our nation's largest collection of electronic media materials. In the 1960s, newsfilm archives grew in both number and quality. The Broadcast Pioneers

---

[1] Milo Ryan, "Here Are the Materials, Where Are the Scholars?" *Journal of the Association for Recorded Sound Collections* 2, no. 2/3 (1970), n.p.

[2] Marvin Bensman, "Foreword," in *ReRuns on File: A Guide to Electronic Media Archives,* ed. Donald G. Godfrey (Hillsdale, NJ: Lawrence Erlbaum Associates, 1992), xvii.

Library (University of Maryland), The Wolfson Media History Collection (Miami-Dade Public Library), the WSB-TV NewFilm Archive (Atlanta), the Peabody Collection (University of Georgia), and the Vanderbilt News Archive (Vanderbilt University) all attest to the growing importance and availability of broadcast records. Similarly, increasing interest in social history and popular culture has led to the growth of television and radio museums across the country—the Museum of Broadcast Communication (Chicago), and the Museums of Television and Radio (New York and Los Angeles) cater to these interests. Just a cursory examination reveals hundreds of nonprofit, private, and commercial collections across the country. Finding one collection often leads to use of another (see chapter 14, "Archive Records").

Among the pioneering scholars recognizing a broadcast as an archival primary resource was Professor Milo Ryan. In February 1956 Ryan stumbled upon a stack of 16-inch electronic transcription radio discs from World War II at KIRO-CBS. There was a total of 52 cases of aluminum and glass disks, what he came to recognize as "a treasure house of broadcast history."[3] They unveiled an eyewitness history of World War II with more than 2,200 CBS network radio newscasts originating daily from March 1938 through April 1945. They included speeches by Winston Churchill, Franklin D. Roosevelt, Adolf Hitler, and hundreds of interviews or talks by reporters and personalities from the war period. Ryan dutifully copied the contents to audio tape, catalogued and created a computerized search mechanism for easy access to the broadcast subjects and personalities, and coined the phrase "phonoarchive" as he organized his find.[4] When it was all set, he wrote, "Here are the materials, where are the scholars?"[5]

In response to Ryan's question, the volume of scholarship has grown substantially over the years (see chapter 15, "Assessing the Record") and there are volumes yet to be written from our broadcast record. Interestingly, those pioneering in historical research were often producers in the commercial media, as they were prompted by the growth of broadcast, film, and video archives/stock shops/libraries. These sources were used creating an explosion of news documentary and information programs on cable, satellite, and broadcast channels. They were researching material to meet a commercial demand of a

---

[3] Milo Ryan, "A Treasure House of Broadcast History," *Journal of Broadcasting* 1, no. 1 (1956–1957): 75–78.

[4] Milo Ryan, *History in Sound* (Seattle: University of Washington Press, 1963).

[5] Ryan, "Here Are the Materials."

program or a network. Similarly, other commercial researchers also produced voluminous pop culture and pictorial histories highlighting the lives and entertainment value of the celebrity people and events. Unfortunately, most of these writings were hardly scholarly—being written from memory, with limited research, produced solely for commercial distribution. Those in the humanities scholarship followed closely where national grants funded noncommercial documentary and research projects. Academic electronic media historians were the first to tackle the media history and the accompanying technical challenges.

Technology aside, electronic media history is exactly like any other historical research—its purpose is the discovery of supportable truths. Broadcast historiography includes description, analysis, interpretation, and evaluation. The researcher's challenge is in amassing a body of organized evidence sufficient to support the reported facts and interpretation. This chapter reviews the basic historical research process and the unique methodological challenges that face scholars who use electronic media records.

WHY STUDY HISTORY?

Most people live for the present. They plan days, weeks, and months ahead, but few give thought to their past. History is about those recorded events of the past. History is the heritage upon which the future is constructed. History is about the preservation, recording, systematic analysis, correlation, and the interpretation of events of the past. Asa Briggs, author of the five-volume *History of Broadcasting in the United Kingdom*,[6] among a host of acclaimed works of English history, says the purpose of history is fourfold: "(1) to obtain a knowledge of English people [and I think he'd include American]; (2) to compare population and social structures; (3) to reconstruct ... family life of our ancestors; and, (4) to provide evidence against which to judge the societal policy of the present day."[7] Briggs adds a personal note describing the research experience, "The historian restores life. He[she] is interested not in dead

---

[6] Asa A. Briggs, *History of Broadcasting in the United Kingdom:* vol. 1, *The Birth of Broadcasting;* vol. 2, *Golden Age of Wireless;* vol. 3, *The War of Words;* vol. 4, *Sound & Vision;* vol. 5, *Competition* (London: Oxford University Press, 1961, 1965, 1970, 1979, and 1995).

[7] Asa A. Briggs, *Social History and Human Experience* (Cedar City, UT: Grace A. Tanner Center for Human Values, 1984), 8.

people but in living people" ... "I have a queer sensation," he says, when, "the dead entries begin to be alive. It is rather like the experience of sitting down in one's chair and finding that one has sat on the cat. These are real people."[8] Christopher H. Sterling, author of several works on electronic media history described history as a single word, "context." History, Sterling continues, is understanding, "the situation [context] at the historical time to really understand what is happening at a given moment."[9] History provides the context for the present day, and the research provides the context for the historical event. Critical historian, Robert W. McChesney, says we study history, "because we are living on the edge of history, and if you want to know where you are going, you have to know where you are coming from. More important, if you want to change this world, to make it better and to preserve what is good, there is an expression for what you are trying to do: make history. And if you want to make history, you had better know what you are doing, or you will do it poorly."[10] Peter N. Stearns, author of numerous mainstream historical works indicates "History should be studied because it is essential to society, and because it harbors beauty."[11] "In the first place," Stearns states, "history offers a storehouse of information about how people and societies behave." Any analysis of the present would be disadvantaged without the analysis of history. "How can we understand genius, the influence of technological innovation ... if we don't use what we know about experience in the past?"[12] It is the past that causes the present and hence the future.

These philosophical scholarly purposes are complemented by pragmatic benefits in historical research. In years past, a person was thought to be more intelligent if he or she could quote the date and the name of a historical event. Unfortunately, mindless memorization accomplishes little and the data is too quickly lost. The study of history can increase communication abilities, facilitate problem-solving skills, and instill the skills of reasoning, deduction, organizing, and analyzing evidence that is prepared in defense of a position. The challenges of historians are like those of good journalists, attorneys, or

---

[8] Briggs, *Social History,* 4.

[9] Christopher H. Sterling, pers. comm. with the author, circa May 2004.

[10] Robert W. McChesney, pers. comm. with the author, circa May 2004.

[11] Peter H. Stearns, "Why Study History?," American Historical Association, http://www.historians.org/pubs/free/WhyStudyHistory.htm.

[12] Ibid.

detectives who after amassing a body of evidence must organize, analyze, present, and defend a case.

Finally, study of electronic media history furthers our knowledge of the role and function of radio and television in society. Writing four decades ago, Barnouw, said, "it is far too early to attempt an assessment of the impact on our civilization of the shift from printed words, as carriers of information, to the ever-present broadcast word, sound and image."[13] Today, that is no longer true, media are widely recognized as vehicles, even drivers, of our current society. They are the focus of popular culture and many other methods of analysis. They are the indexes of the collective thinking of a population as well as important business structures within our environs.

THE HISTORICAL PROCESS

This chapter approaches the examination of the historical method, or historiography, from the widest possible perspective. The term historiography means the study of methods and techniques in historical research as a part of a body of historical writing. In *The Gateway to History,* Nevins indicates that there are few fixed methods in the historical-research process.[14] Briggs suggests that once students have "immersed themselves in the evidence," they will continue, "learning to analyze ... [the evidence] and instead of applying somebody else's framework they will construct their own scaffolding."[15] While true, these statements are overly simplified. Stearns says the process includes, "the ability to assess evidence; the ability to assess conflicting interpretations; and the experience to assess past examples of change"[16] (see chapter 2, "Historical Evidence"). David Sloan and James Startt said journalism history was about "first, gaining an understanding from what others have said about the object of historical study, and from the materials available; second, locating the various sources that are applicable to the inquiry. This includes family sources, archives, museums, data bases, and all other repositories of information; and third, the extrapolation of information from the primary sources and the evaluation of that evidence," they concluded noting, "the historian must place in

---

[13] Erik Barnouw, *A Tower of Babel: A History of Broadcasting in the United States to 1933* (New York: Oxford University Press, 1966), 4–5.

[14] Allan Nevins, *The Gateway to History* (New York: D. C. Heath, 1938), 195–96.

[15] Briggs, *Social History,* 12.

[16] Stearns, "Why Study History?"

context the information they have collected and do this by addressing questions related to causation, generalization, interpretation, and the establishing of significance."[17]

Broadcasting, yet only 84 years old, is still young when compared to other historical subjects and while there are few conventional traditions for dealing with it, we can learn from the traditional approach, and related theoretical constructs, as we work to build the scaffolds for understanding the past.

IDENTIFY THE TOPIC AND REVIEW THE LITERATURE

The first stage in the process of historical research begins with the identification of the topic, meaning the identification of the specific research question. For most, the quest starts as a general interest subject—something that intrigues us. Narrowed, this topic becomes the nucleus of the study. In critical historiography, the topic becomes an *object*. It dictates the research directions undertaken and the evidence gathered. It helps the researcher identify the environment, the era, the interrelationships of people, the politics, and the culture of the period under study. In other words, the topic, question, or object is distinguished by the variables surrounding it and comes into focus as we learn to understand those variables. For example, a journal article, such as Louise Benjamin's "In Search of the Sarnoff 'Music Box' Memo: Separating Myth from Reality," is selectively focused on a single point in history—indeed a specific document.[18] In comparison, Benjamin's *Freedom of the Air and the Public Interest: First Amendment Rights in Broadcasting to 1935* covers a much wider objective: freedom of radio expression into the mid-1930s.[19] In this book-length research, her work helps us understand the development of broadcast specific First Amendment rights. The focus of any study determines depth, breadth, and sometimes the method used.

The inquisitive characteristic that piqued our interest in the topic takes us into the second stage of the process, which is positioning the study within the

---

[17] William David Sloan and James D. Startt, eds., *The Media in America: A History*, 3rd ed. (Northport, AL: Vision Press, 1996), xiii–xiv.

[18] Louise M. Benjamin, "In Search of the Sarnoff 'Radio Music Box' Memo: Separating Myth from Reality," *Journal of Broadcasting & Electronic Media* 37, no. 3 (1993): 325–35.

[19] Louise M. Benjamin. *Freedom of the Air and the Public Interest: First Amendment Rights in Broadcasting to 1935* (Carbondale: Southern Illinois University Press, 2001).

body of existing literature—the literature review. The traditional survey of the literature reviews what is already known and provides the foundation for the collection of new evidence. While the literature review deals primarily with secondary sources, it serves three purposes. First, secondary sources are easily available and provide quick sources of readily available information. Second, these sources provide the researcher with background information. They can help the research focus by directing their attention to what has been written as well as revealing what has not been written. Third, they help the researcher focus and understand the different interpretations that may have already been rendered relative to the topic. In essence, the secondary sources may not only provide information, but a sense of the topic. This literature review involves examination of anything and almost everything written on a given topic— bibliographies, indexes, Ph.D. dissertations, government documents, and the Internet. Internet searches allow a researcher to access heretofore difficult-to-find sources of information—newspaper, journal, and scientific articles. Many journals and periodicals are now found on-line, making the literature review easier by comparison to earlier days. Archives, museums, and special libraries may require travel, but searching on-line for collections in advance can make visits more productive. Reviewing what has already been written refines and defines the topic. This helps position new research within that already existing. In the literature review, the researcher seeks to survey the existing literature and understand the context for the topic. Those footnotes in that literature become trail markers, providing the location for later visiting primary evidence. The basic purpose of the common literature review is to help a researcher position the new research, and point to its contributions to the discipline.

One of the challenges of the literature review is discovering and separating secondary versus primary media evidence then overcoming skepticism of traditional historians. The value of the nation's electronic media archives is increasingly recognized as important, but this record is still questioned by traditional scholars. Why? First, because many programs and media sources contain dubious historical information. Second, producers of media products often have taken dramatic license in creating spectacular stories that are theatrical, but lack a factual base. Third, a traditional historian's deficiency in knowledge of the media process or technology impedes his or her ability to utilize media material as a primary source of evidence. In other words, they lack the knowledge of the process that would allow them to peel back the layers of drama that have distorted the history and reveal any existing truths that might be present.

THE HISTORICAL PROCESS

1. Identify the general topic of interest.
2. Submerge yourself in the literature and the context of the time period.
   - Examine what has been written.
   - Look for possible primary sources.
   - Focus your purpose within the body of literature.
   - Create a purpose that adds to new knowledge.
3. The process of discovery involves uncovering the primary evidence that portrays your story.
4. Analyze the evidence.
   - Weigh the evidence against the tests of authenticity.
   - Examine collaborative, contradictory, and physical evidence.
   - Unravel the layers of that creative process in broadcasting and media to assure the primary evidence is valid.
   - Pay particular attention to visual and aural evidence and need for verification and/or support.
5. Provide supportive evidence wherever the mediated sources may be called into question by the skeptics of media as evidence.
6. Where you work goes beyond traditional chronological patterns of descriptive analysis and into areas such as critical theory. Make sure the theoretical approach is sound.
7. Organize the analyzed evidence around the narrative fact.
8. Write, write, and rewrite.

Ironically, while producers and directors of our media take creative license with works "based-on-a-true-story"—both historians and media practitioners can be considered re-creators of the past. However, their approaches are considerably divergent. Directors create their historical dramas on film, video, or some other electronic media form, while historians create their accounts in prose. Both historians and producer/directors can be considered re-creators of the past, but they diverge on their approaches to their subjects. Historians must remain faithful to the historical records, while directors may take the dramatic license forbidden the historian. For example, the movies and television westerns of the 1950s and 1960s tapped into the myths of the American West of the late 1800s. From settlers bravely crossing the plains to subdue the wilderness and carve out a new life on *Wagon Train* to a frontier marshal, his saloon-keeper girlfriend, and grizzled frontier doctor on *Gunsmoke,* the television personalities embodied high American ideals—independence, honesty, integrity, and fairness—in a setting where equality and liberty were watchwords. As they moved west, settlers from different countries forged a new society, a melting pot, of ideals and customs that personified what it meant to be an American. Historians of 1950s television not only can examine these and other traditional beliefs to understand American culture but also can place the televised stories in the context of the Cold War of the 1950s and 1960s.

Over the last few years, historians have taken "a much more serious view of media, both for historical content and for treatment of historical subjects."[20] *The Journal of American History* regularly reviews commercial films and documentaries, while the History Channel has analyzed the use and abuse of history in its series, *History vs. Hollywood.* Books have also covered the topic of history on film and tape, including O'Connor's *Image as Artifact: The Historical Analysis of Film and Television,* Mark Carnes's *Past Imperfect: History according to the Movies,* Toplin's *History by Hollywood: The Use and Abuse of the American Past,* and Burgoyne's *Film Nation: Hollywood Looks at U.S. History.*[21]

The roots of electronic media's questionable historic value date back to the beginnings of the industry and its purposes. When preeminent historical scholar Allan Nevins described types of primary source materials, broadcasting was not on the list for two reasons: First, Nevins was writing in 1938 and electronic media archives did not exist. Second, he was suspicious of the media as a source too easily manipulated. Nevins's doubts did not disappear with the maturation of radio and television. In 1958, he was still critical, even about a newspaper's record of history. He declared that

---

[20] James West Davidson and Mark Hamilton Lytle, *After the Fact: The Art of Historical Detection,* 4th ed. (Boston, MA: McGraw Hill, 2000), 393.

[21] John O'Connor, ed., *Image as Artifact: The Historical Analysis of Film and Television* (Malibar, FL: Robert E. Krieger Publishing, 1990); Mark Carnes, ed., *Past Imperfect: History According to the Movies* (New York: H. Holt, 1995); Robert Toplin, *History by Hollywood: The Use and Abuse of the American Past* (Urbana: University of Illinois, 1996); Robert Burgoyne, *Film Nation: Hollywood Looks at U.S. History* (Minneapolis: University of Minneapolis Press, 1997).

newspapers were "marred by thinness and spottiness, and overemphasis on editorial personalities and opinions."[22] It is easy to generalize from Nevins's newspaper view to electronic media. The media are commercially driven and have a reputation for the reporting of dramatic sensationalism rather than recording historical fact.

U.S. television newscasts, information programs, and entertainment programs are primarily shelf space upon which the more important products are placed—in television it's the commercial spot; in cable it's the subscription, commercial spot, or pay-per-view; and on the Internet it's a billboard or direct sales. Even the news is indeed *thin,* as Nevins suggests. Television news stories are generally limited to 90 seconds, but radio stories are even shorter. Because of the demands of the time, a 30-minute newscast carries little in-depth information. A televison drama may be founded in history, but dramatization for sensational effect creates distortion at the expense of historical fact. Any good historian rightly questions the source. Criticism of media dramatizations (and increasingly even documentaries) as poor historical-fact conveyors cannot be refuted. The historical record, as seen within television and radio, has indeed been exploited in favor of commercialism. Hollywood films—such as *Pearl Harbor, Titanic, JFK, Nixon,* and *The Passion of Christ*—all have their roots in factual events, and all have been criticized for dramatically distorting those events. It is unfortunate that, when dramatization enters into the creative process, too often the "facts and their probability even plausibility are steadily ignored."[23] The audience, too, is less than discriminative and too often construes dramatization as fact, further challenging today's historians.

Despite traditional and often understandable skepticism, progress has been made in accepting electronic media as a valuable historical resource. Arthur Marwick, writing in *The Nature of History* 30 years after Nevins, did include radio and television in his group of primary source materials, but called for caution.[24] Alice Kessler-Harris noted that the new social historians

---

[22] Allan Nevins, "American Journalism and Its Historical Treatments," *Journalism Quarterly* 36 (Fall 1959): 411–22. See also, Allan Nevins, *The Gateway to History,* rev. ed. (Chicago: Quadrangle Books, 1963), 39–49; Ray A. Billington, ed., *Allan Nevins on History* (New York: Charles Schribner's Sons, 1995), 95.

[23] Jacques Barzun and Henry F. Graff, *The Modern Researcher,* 4th ed. (New York: Harcourt Brace Jovanovich, 1985), 120.

[24] Arthur Marwick, *The Nature of History,* 3rd ed. (London: MacMillan Education, 1989), 325.

had "expanded their search to include new sources,"[25] and Asa Briggs, a British media and social historian, indicated that evidence of every kind, from all kinds of documents "visual and oral" must be examined.[26]

Although broadcast programs, the Internet, and other media sources should not be accepted outright, neither should they be ignored. The historical documentaries, such as *March of Time* (radio 1931–1945 and television 1951–1952), *Hear It Now* (radio 1951), *See It Now* (1951–1957), *CBS Reports* (1961–1962 and 1970–1971), NBC *White Papers* (1960) and ABC *Close-Up* (1960–1963), accurately reflected life at critical times in history. NBC's *The Twisted Cross* (1960) revealing WWII atrocities and Edward R. Murrow's *Harvest of Shame* (1960) reflecting the plight of American migrant farm workers were classics among these series. More recently, PBS film documentaries, such as *Africans in America, The Civil War, One Woman One Vote,* and *Vietnam: A Television History,* have told factual stories of common people and the events of their times.[27] Today's History Channel, Discovery, local and network newscasts and news magazines still suffer from *thinness,* but they are typically based in fact. The challenge is in separating fact from dramatic license, and this is a matter of separating complex secondary information from the creative process to reveal the primary evidence.

Overshadowing criticisms of shallow reporting, commercialism, and dramatic distortion is the fact that electronic media programs do contain factual material. Assessing that material is complex when compared to traditional printed documentation, but this is the challenge for a historian. The researcher must know how to deal with the myriad of differing technological formats that have come and gone over the past eight decades (see chapter 10, "New Media and Technical Records"). Conducting historical research and drawing inferences from the broadcast record necessitates an understanding of the technological capacities of the times. Utilizing technology requires a time commitment, an understanding of media context, and a knowledge of how the technology operated. An archive or museum today will most often have access to the technology to read the broadcast record (as the originals are kept

---

[25] Alice Kessler-Harris, "Social History," in *The New American History,* ed. E. Foner for the American Historical Association (Philadelphia, PA: Temple University Press, 1990), 168.

[26] Briggs, *Social History,* 7.

[27] These are common films and television programs, most of which can be found in a local library or university collection.

for preservation purposes), but the researcher must understand the limits of the technology, within its era, to interpret that record conscientiously. For example in radio, electronic transcriptions [ET] were used in the late 1930s and early 1940s to record live events. These transcriptions resulted in 16-inch aluminum and glass disks, cut with a lathe, and thus allowed limited plays. They were original recordings and each needle drop diminished the quality of the master. The technology prohibited editing—the fact that live events were thus preserved without editing via this technology makes these primary source materials. Perhaps the most notable collections of ETs concern World War II—the Milo Ryan, CBS-KIRO Phonoarchive at the National Archives and the BBC Home-Front Series at the Imperial War Museum, London. These collections preserve newscasts from the war. However, unless these ETs have been duplicated to another format (audio tape or digital formats), they require special technology to list them. The museum/archive normally provides access to the equipment as well as the information source. Discovering the truth, when it is masked in technology, is the challenge of today's electronic media historian, whether the data formats are ET, audio tape, video, photographic, kinescope, film, or the modern digital.

In addition to understanding technology, today's historian must also understand the medium's creative process. Such knowledge helps the researcher separate fact from the layers of the creative production environment to reveal the influence of people, politics, and the decision-making environment. In many cases media records may be compared and substantiated against existing production records, such as scripts, rough drafts, site maps, organizational outlines, production notes, oral histories, and written materials utilized in creating a program or series. This documentation helps the historian identify and evaluate the differing influences within the program. Peeling away the layers of production reveals those illusive historical facts and enhances analytic understanding of the creative process itself.

Citing this evidence hidden within the layers is critical in the specification of primary source material. Nowhere in historiography is documenting the evidence more important than when the researcher uses a media record or an artifact as a primary resource. Researchers must show how facts were revealed and treated within the production process to authenticate and contextualize the program's fidelity to real events. In so doing, the researcher not only informs the reader, but promotes further understanding of the program-creating process. Investigators who are using media information—a program, or any aspect of a program—as a primary source must be able to track, verify, and document the origins of that principal information. If the source is suspect, it is wise to add supporting comparative documentation to the citation. These supportive materials strengthen the validity of the case. Developing these citations is not an easy task because, unlike print media where attribution and referencing are part and parcel of the writer's research process, broadcast producers don't often keep much of a traceable record, or if it is kept, access is limited—but that's what makes the discovery process exciting. In such cases collaborative evidence might be sought from contemporary trade publications. As information passes through the various stages of production, each editorial step in that creative process should be analyzed in terms of the influence of the process on the facts, the information's value as evidence, and the effect of differing individuals within the process. In meeting these challenges, for example, a researcher can take a lesson from oral historians (see chapter 3, "Oral History"). Traditional research places a greater value on contemporary diaries and other personal writings than oral interviews. The oral historian's interview is a questionable source used in isolation, but when the information from the interview can be collaborated through other evidentiary accounts, the oral history interview adds both substance and personal color to the historical record. Note how in Craig Allen's research, *News Is People,* voluminous oral history interviews are given support in quantitative research and primary documents of the time including heretofore untapped news consultants' reports.[28] This comparative procedure is not significantly different from the more traditional historical research—the search for supportable truths is still paramount.

The challenge in media history is discovering these supportable truths within the layers of technology and creative dramatics. In this sense, a trained media historian, who has an understanding of historic technology and production practices, can separate the dramatic chaff from the historic fruits, the secondary from the primary source, thereby, overcoming the blanket skepticism of traditional historians.

DISCOVERY AND ANALYSIS

Historic truths must be derived from *all available evidence.* Evidence—solid evidence—is that which establishes the existence, or nonexistence, of a fact. This is

---

[28] Craig Allen, *News Is People: The Rise of Local TV News and the Fall of News from New York* (Ames: Iowa State University Press, 2001).

the search, the detective work, the discovery process. Put another way, this is the gathering of primary materials, the organization of puzzle pieces, and the building of the case. The first sources apparent from the literature review form the platform and they'll end up in the citations as evidence of your work.

As the researcher explores the evidence, organization begins. Primary materials gathered may be found almost everywhere: the archives, museums, libraries, corporate and individual records. The evidence may first be organized by source—the archive or repository title. Organization would thus be dictated by the repository's organization. The advantage here is in accessing the evidence and providing proper documentation at the time of the analysis and writing. Materials may better be organized following a subject outline or a critical model. This facilitates writing and analysis, but also requires careful documentation for each individual piece of evidence. The advantage of this system of organization is that individual pieces of evidence are more logically arranged as the jigsaw puzzle of discovered facts unfolds.

Detail, detail, details—that's what the discovery process is all about. It is the gathering and the examination of every piece of that puzzle's evidence until the researcher knows how they fit together. It can also lead to that sinking feeling to find a piece of critical evidence that may be missing. "Where did I get this information? Wasn't there more? The citation is incomplete? What happened to the verification for this evidence?" Patterns of careful scholarship in the collection and organization of data are as important as the final results of the research.

In the discovery process the researcher may crisscross the country or be just around the corner in the local library. On the shelves of these repositories are found the personal papers of the pioneers, the corporations, the cultures, the geographic regions of interest. Card catalog, paper registers, and on-line listings often index materials from books, scholarly journals, government documents, and special collections. Archival and manuscript collections are of prime interest to historians as history rests on primary sources. Archive collections are found in numerous locations. One invaluable guide that historians use in finding archives related to their work is the National Union Catalog of Manuscript Collections (NUCMC) maintained by the Library of Congress. In 1993 NUCMC ceased publishing a print version of the catalog, therefore it is best to access the catalog on-line.[29] In the United States two important

---

[29] Library of Congress, *National Union Catalog of Manuscript Collections,* http://www.loc.gov/coll/nucmc/.

repositories are the Manuscript Division of the Library of Congress (www. loc.gov) and the National Archives (www.archives.gov). Papers of individuals active in broadcasting's formation, as well as other materials related to communication topics, can be found in these collections. For instance, the Manuscript Division contains the papers of Josephus Daniels, who, as Secretary of the Navy from 1913 to 1921, was involved in early radio regulation. The National Archives holds the papers of the Federal Communications Commission as well as the papers of its predecessor agencies. State and local government archives house repositories for their respective locales. Special libraries also hold collections of interest to media historians. The Wisconsin State Historical Society Library is one such depository. Its Mass Communication Collection holds the NBC papers among other media materials.

For most media, specialized collection guides exist.[30] Researchers should note that finding programs that aired on radio, broadcast television, or cable television may be difficult. Much of the content of these media was never recorded, while high preservation costs dissuaded others from saving broadcasts. Copyright problems often discourage duplication of tapes and film, but even with these problems, numerous guides supply details of programming.

Computerized searches via the Internet have added speed and additional material a hand search may not reveal. Conversely, a hand search can reveal material not available on the Internet because gaps exist in databases and some data pages only reach so far back into history. For example, unpublished materials such as abstracts of older dissertations are not available. But, as a tool, the Internet adds expediency and convenience to searches. Often, a well-defined search will yield resources for the historian quickly and easily and in a fraction of the time of a traditional search. Historians can determine whether an archive has relevant documents or a library has a pertinent book. The Internet can also aid in bibliographic and secondary source searches. A word of caution for the Internet source: Is an Internet document primary or secondary literature? The rules of evidence are critical in assessing Internet and technological information (see chapter 10). Libraries pay for access to scholarly databases that access citations, abstracts and, sometimes, full texts of scholarly journals, such as Lexis-Nexis and others.

---

[30] For broadcasting, the *Library of Congress Motion Picture, Broadcasting, Recorded Sound: An Illustrated Guide* (Washington, DC: Library of Congress, 2001) is a must. Another comprehensive guide for researchers is Thomas Mann, *The Oxford Guide to Library Research* (New York: Oxford University Press, 1998).

Local historical associations frequently are helpful in locating various collections as are reference librarians and archivists of the library's special collections. A growing number of speech, human communication, journalism, and mass communication departments also house collections of national significance. The University of Utah has recently developed the Public Broadcast Archive, has all the papers of the Philo T. Farnsworth Family, and the Bonneville International CEO Arch L. Madsen; the University of Texas–Austin has the Walter Cronkite Papers, and the Wayne County Indiana Historical Museum houses the Charles Francis Jenkins papers. The Securities and Exchange Commission Reports and the state public utility commissions can be invaluable sources of business records. The more time spent in this detective work the more accurate the historical picture can become and the longer lasting the research contribution (see chapter 14 for a list of the major archives).

Remember—detail, detail, details.

METHODOLOGICAL AND FRAMEWORK PATTERNS

We have focused so far on the importance of defining the topic of our research, conducting the literature review, separating secondary and primary course materials, the special challenges in electronic media primary documentation, and hinted at the development of one's own methodological scaffolding. The traditional method is a narrative re-creation as supported by existing evidence. The organization is typically topical or chronological. However, there are other methodological frameworks and challenges as we will see in successive chapters.

Before a researcher rushes into creating a new method or developing analytic criteria, it is wise to look at the approaches that may have already been proven over the tests of time. In general, research organization can take many forms. As noted, the chronological or topical subject patterns are most common in historical writing—they are descriptive and analytical. The arrangement of the narrative may take the form of a movement study, case history, biography (see chapter 13), institutional concentration, or legal analysis (see chapter 5). The form may follow topical patterns established in the study of biography; studies of race, gender, and ethnicity (see chapter 11, "Understanding the Historical Context of Race and Gender in Media"); or a concentration on local history (see chapter 12). History can readily manifest itself in the application of quantitative theory (see chapter 7). A researcher may even develop a new eclectic approach, as Briggs noted, to create "its own scaffolding" or may borrow from existing patterns within related fields, such as rhetoric, literary, or theatrical criticism (see chapter 6, "Applying Critical Theory to Electronic Media"). The nature of the scaffolding, or methodology, is to support organization, sustain evaluative controls, and confirm the analytic procedures throughout the discovery process.

There is a significant commonality between historiography and critical theory and that is—the critic must also develop her or his own method of analysis. The development of critical theory is not simply the taking of a critical stance—it is theoretical analysis. In developing critical analysis for a historical argument critical methods and patterns do exist, and there is precedent for using them. The review of the literature, in addition to providing information foundations, may provide methodological illustrations, and possible frameworks for theoretical application, which would take the research beyond description and analysis. The challenge for self-constructed analytic criteria is that it must be carefully explained, justified, and able to withstand scrutiny of future researchers who may examine it. The advantage is flexibility, in comparison to the cookie cutter approach where one method is dictated to fit all questions. The challenge in borrowing or adapting a new methodology is to avoid forcing the subject to fit the pattern—rather the pattern of analysis must be appropriate for the object under study. For example, the challenge of *firsts,* or the oldest in history, is always intriguing. The word appears in almost every oral history interview ever conducted, "we were first." But, unfortunately such claims do not make them fact. These firsts fascinate the historian and the professional. For the researcher, the drive is to discover *the first* is a natural curiosity. For the media it is a promotional declaration. For the historian it is a challenge! David Sarnoff claimed the first public demonstration of electronic television as RCA's demonstration at the 1939 New York World's Fair. This was a promotional claim that was hardly contested for decades until those studying Philo T. Farnsworth noted that Farnsworth had performed almost the same theatrical demonstration in Philadelphia at the Benjamin Franklin Institute in 1934, let alone the BBC, 1936.[31] Determining first is not as easy as it sounds: … first at what? … based on what criteria? Define *first.*

Looking at the claim of which station is the first, we see the advantage of utilizing existing and adapted methodology. R. Franklin Smith, examined

---

[31] Donald G. Godfrey, *Philo T. Farnsworth: The Father of Television* (Salt Lake City: University of Utah Press, 2001), 61–68.

"Oldest Station in the Nation," and established the five basic criteria for evaluating competitive claims to that particular title.[32] In this work, Smith provided future researchers with a specific framework. Joseph E. Baudino and John M. Kittross later adapted these criteria and examined four contestants for the title "broadcasting's oldest."[33] They awarded the title to KDKA. Godfrey took issue with KDKA's claim to the title and, utilizing the same criteria directly from Smith and then Baudino and Kittross, he examined Canadian Marconi's CFCF-AM as the claimant to "North America's Oldest."[34] Godfrey and Spencer took their CFCF radio research further, comparing CFCF-TV and the Canadian Television Network with the National Broadcast Corporation.[35] Now, is CFCF-AM really North America's oldest? We have no published literature from our southern neighbor, Mexico, to disprove it at this time. Clearly, the advantage of Smith's framework has been useful in research and analyzing the criteria of these *first* pioneering stations.

Stelzner provides another example of the theoretical application of criteria borrowed from rhetorical critics and linguistics when he analyzed Franklin D. Roosevelt's December 8, 1941, declaration of war.[36] Arguing for the study and analysis of microcosmic topics, he builds his study from the evolution theory of rhetorical critics such as Marie Hochmuth Nichols, Carroll C. Arnold, Douglas Ehninger, and Stanley E. Hyman. Then Stelzner took a very specific historical object for analysis, the radio address of President Roosevelt declaring war on Japan—immediately following the bombing of Pearl Harbor.

Methodological patterns can come from traditional history, it can be adapted or borrowed from complementary methods. As noted earlier, for example, the disciplines of rhetoric, theater, and literary criticism often look at media subjects. In general all historians are critics, and the scholarly criticism

---

[32] R. Franklin Smith, "Oldest Station in the Nation?," *Journal of Broadcasting* 4, no. 1 (1959): 44.

[33] Joseph E. Baudino and John M. Kittross, "Broadcasting's Oldest Station: An Examination of Four Claimants," *Journal of Broadcasting* 21, no. 1 (1977): 61–83.

[34] Donald G. Godfrey, "Canadian Marconi: CFCF The Forgotten First," *Canadian Journal of Communication* 8, no. 4 (1982): 68–69.

[35] Donald G. Godfrey and Davie R. Spencer, "Canadian Marconi: CFCF Television from Signal Hill to the Canadian Television Network," *Journal of Broadcasting & Electronic Media* 44, no. 3 (2000): 437–55.

[36] Hermann G. Stelzner, "War Message, December 8, 1941: An Approach to Language," *Speech Monographs* 33, no. 4 (1966): 419–37.

is known for eclectic design. However, in saying that, caution has to be taken when we apply the term *critic* to media historiography because *criticism* is a term applied to a popular discussion or a review, and it is a term of theory and practice. In the public forum we are all critics. We all indulge in passing judgment on our favorite movies. Criticism is a popular form of discussion and literally everyone has an opinion about the media. Some media feature *professional critics* who provide program reviews, promotion, and comment. Interpersonal discussion and promotion are *not* what a scholarly critical methodologist would consider as criticism. In literary and rhetorical *criticism,* the term denotes theory. For example, *poetics* is the theoretical study of poetry—literary criticism. The practice is in the poetry, literature, or novel. Similarly, rhetoric is the study of persuasion, and the practice is in oratory, speech and writing. The purposes of rhetorical criticism—to describe, analyze, interpret, and evaluate—are similar to the historian. As rhetorical theorist Lloyd F. Bitzer noted, in any research, the justification for the study depends on the historical interrelationships within the "complex of events, persons, [other] objects, and [their] relations."[37] Does that sound familiar? It should. As with a critic, the historian must persuade and provide clear reason, analysis, and fair judgment in rendering a finding. Like the historian the critic must also provide sufficient scaffolding for the argument, analysis, and conclusion.

The purpose of a critical historiography is analysis. The scholar's investigative efforts should reveal what could be a particularly fresh or heretofore discounted point of view. It should reveal that which would not have been readily apparent had the historian followed the traditional patterns of description, chronology, or topical narrative. According to Stevens and Garcia, critical historiography "calls attention to the gaps in history, alternative interpretations and can provide an impetus [for] theory generation."[38] The emphasis here should be placed on "theory generation," because the traditional historian would also argue that revealing those gaps and providing interpretations is their role as well. However, when the methodological approach is criticism, the researcher takes an object of history, and with the application of carefully constructed critical theory, evaluates, interprets, and seeks understanding.

---

[37] Lloyd F. Bitzer, "The Rhetorical Situation," *Philosophy and Rhetoric* 1, no. 1 (1968): 1–14.

[38] John D. Stevens and Hazel Dickens Garcia, *Communication History* (Beverly Hills, CA: Sage, 1980), 31.

Critical historiography is the application of critical methodology upon the object of history. The challenge in critical historiography, in addition to the analysis of history, is being sure that the method of analysis is appropriate to the object of history. It is not always easy to find a clear-cut model that may simply be applied to the historical object. But critical theory does provide research-tested patterns, which may be applied to measure or analyze the historical object. Perhaps the most significant challenge in the application of critical theory to a historical object is the selection of an appropriate model. Meanings change over time and today's model may or may not be appropriate for the analysis of yesterday's event. Great care must be taken in critical history to be sure the analytic theory is appropriate for the context.

We have briefly introduced the idea of criticism, critical methods, and the appropriateness of adapting their criteria in the analysis of a historical object. Are there other criteria in electronic media that might use for critical analysis? What about the visual theories described by Dondis in her *Art of Visual Literacy* or by Zettl in his *Sight, Sound, Motion?*[39] Could theoretical constructs of these theorists be utilized to understand, explain, and evaluate objects of history? These authors break down the elements of visual style focusing on communications. Could these theories help us understand our visual history? Phifer's work in speech and theater suggests that there are seven types of history: biographical, movement studies, regional studies, institutional studies, case histories, selected studies, and editorial studies.[40] Are any of the theatrical methods appropriate to electronic media? Ronald Primeau's *Rhetoric of Television* suggested that even the consumer could become a better viewer through the application of classical theory in their television choices.[41] Several texts offer differing approaches to television, movie, and theatrical criticism. Although most are aimed at a popular culture consumer, they present theatrical constructs that can be applicable in historical research. VandeBerg, Wenner, and Gronbeck, *Critical Approaches to Television,* offer readers techniques for

---

[39] Donis A. Dondis, *A Primer of Visual Literacy* (Cambridge, MA: MIT Press, 1973); Herbert Zettl, *Sight, Sound, Motion: Applied Media Aesthetics,* 4th ed. (Belmont, CA: Wadsworth, 2004).

[40] Gregg Phifer, "The Historical Approach," in *An Introduction to Graduate Study in Speech and Theatre*, ed. Clyde Walton Dow (East Lansing: Michigan State Press, 1961), 52–80.

[41] Ronald Primeau, *The Rhetoric of Television* (New York: Longman, 1979).

analyzing today's television, "systematically and expertly."[42] Their methodologies are as applicable to history as they are to popular culture. Horace Newcomb's *Television: The Critical View,* presents a collection of critical essays from which methodological constructs can be drawn.[43] Truly as the electronic media historian works to construct a scaffolding for organization, a framework for critique, or a theoretical application for the analysis, there are many specialized patterns of theory that can be applied and take the traditional researcher from description, into interpretation, and analysis.

CONCLUSION

The purpose of history is to assess the past that we may more effectively construct the future. Historical research is about restoring life. It is about providing context. It is about our past, which created our present, and hence our future. The study of history also has pragmatic value as it increases a scholar's ability for writing, problem solving, communication, and reasoning. The study of broadcasting and electronic media history is of critical value because these venues are indexes of our global collective thinking.

The historical research process begins with the identification of a topic. These are topics that simply might interest the research. The selection of a topic leads to the review of the literature. This is an emersion in information that has already been written. From this review the research gains an in-depth understanding of the topic and hopefully sees how the proposed new research might enhance understanding. Following a review of the literature the second emersion is in the primary source materials—the discovery of new information. The historical research must derive supportable truth from all of the available evidence. This discovery process will lead to the analysis of the evidence. The historian must weigh different evidence carefully, seeking collaborative and factual information as the evidence is gathered from primary sources. The assessments can be evaluated against traditional rules of evaluation or perhaps put to the test of established critical theory.

The unique challenge in broadcast electronic media history is overcoming the suspicion of the broadcast records or artifacts. Because these sources are so

---

[42] Leah VandeBerg, Larry Wenner, and Bruce Gronbeck, eds., *Critical Approaches to Television* (New York: Houghton Mifflin, 1998), xv.

[43] Horace Newcomb, ed., *Television: The Critical View*, 6th ed. (Oxford: Oxford University Press, 2000).

easily manipulated, because they are so technologically foreign, because there are so many layers of input within the production of a broadcast record—each piece of technology, each player in the record, and each individual participant must be analyzed for the impact on the value of even a single piece of information. Today's historian must have a knowledge of the technology and understand the creative process in order to peel back these layers of information to reveal supportable fact.

The challenge of the historian is very much analogous to the seasoned in-depth reporter, the detective, or the lawyer. The search for the discovery of truth is similar, and the rules of evidence and tests of authenticity are parallel. Researchers in each discipline must understand the topic, immerse themselves in primary factual information, assess that evidence, and recreate a new picture that extends our understanding of the world around us.

2

Historical Evidence: Facts, Proof and Probability

Louise M. Benjamin
University of Georgia

Historical evidence is found in the records that human beings and their activities leave behind—written words, oral traditions, pictorial materials, and physical artifacts, to name a few. Most of the time, these remnants are fragmented and incomplete, but without them history would not exist. For that history to exist, historians must understand how evidence is collected, used, analyzed, and how it can sometimes be abused. Historians must hone their craft carefully as they form explanations of the past to provide understanding of past events, human nature, and their relationship to today. Historians' accounts are rigorously developed through carefully gathering and analyzing evidence and then clearly presenting relationships among those pieces of information in cogent, articulate prose. This chapter covers evidence that historians use in their work as well as the rules used to evaluate those records and artifacts. In general, two basic classes of historical evidence exist: primary and secondary. Within these two classes are subsets of evidence and numerous ways of proving authenticity and credibility of the materials.

PRIMARY AND SECONDARY SOURCES

Primary sources are the building blocks of historical research. They are the contemporaneous records related to the subject under study and they came into being during the time period the historian is studying. They are remnants of the past.

As the historian wants all of the best evidence, he or she must distinguish between first-hand primary material and that which has come from filtered secondary sources. Defining primary and secondary source material is not always simple in media. For example, a reporter is a secondary source when the information reported comes from other sources. On the other hand, a reporter becomes a primary source when she or he directly observes the events of the story. Herb Morrison's recording of the *Hindenburg* disaster, 1937, is a classic primary source. Morley Safer's television reporting on the evacuation airlift from Vietnam, 1975, is a primary source. Bernard Shaw's live accounts of the bombing of Baghdad, 1991, are all examples of reporters directly observing, thus their reports become primary source material. However, even these same people reporting the same facts in retrospect become secondary source figures by citing other participant observers. As news programs begin to intermingle their sources, it is challenging to determine the authenticity and the various participants in the story. Edward R. Murrow's eyewitness radio report from the Buchenwald concentration camp, April 11, 1945, is gripping primary source material. Newspaper reports several days later that quote Murrow and other sources are secondary. David Crockett's infamous video, on the day of Mount St. Helen's volcanic eruption, May 1980, as he is running for his life from the volcano, is a primary photographic source (see chapter 4, "Visual Evidence"). *National Geographic*'s documentary utilizing the footage becomes a secondary source.

Some sources may also be primary or secondary depending upon their use. For instance, a newspaper editorial would be a primary resource if historians were studying the writer and a secondary source if historians were studying events referred to in the editorial.[1] In the same manner, "current affairs literature" can be "used for attitudes and impressions and sometimes as a type of early history of an event."[2] Obviously, journalists' accounts contribute much to this category of history, and often journalists act as "contemporary historians" of the events they cover. Their observations may be considered primary, but their coverage of the event itself supplies only secondary evidence. For example, *The New York Times,* which is considered the U.S. national paper of record, reported the development of the National Broadcasting Company (NBC) in 1926 and, for Erik Barnouw, these reports became crucial primary

---

[1] Arthur Marwick, *The Nature of History,* 3rd ed. (Chicago: Lyceum Books, 1989), 199.

[2] James D. Startt and William David Sloan, *Historical Methods in Mass Communication,* rev. ed. (Northport, AL: Vision Press, 2003), 179.

evidence used in his trilogy of American broadcasting written in the 1960s.[3] Later historians were able to use not only these newspaper accounts, but also the papers of individuals and organizations involved in NBC's formation to weave an even more informative history of the network.[4] Consequently, the newspaper accounts, while important, became secondary evidence to the more revealing primary documents.

To help set out these variations in primary and secondary sources, note the following examples:

Subject	Primary Sources	Secondary Sources
Event	Recording of live event	Edited recordings describing event
Experiment	Personal observations, artifacts	Quoting observations of others
Demonstration	Live recording, planning records	Graphically altered/staged photo
Life story	Diaries, letters, personal papers	Book about the person
Television program	Annotated directors script	Critic's review of the program
Television movie	Production meeting minutes	Public relations release

Traditional primary sources include original unfiltered evidence—written records, printed and other written materials, published and unpublished personal records, official documents, oral sources close to the event, photographic records, radio and television broadcast records, cable television records, new media sources, oral histories, and physical remains.

A scholar's grasp of the subject is reflected in the thoroughness of his or her research and use of primary sources for a direct understanding of the topics under study. As historian Arthur Marwick notes "historical work is generally esteemed serious and scholarly to the extent that it is properly based on the

---

[3] Erik Barnouw, *A Tower in Babel: A History of Broadcasting in the United States to 1933* (New York: Oxford University Press, 1966); Erik Barnouw, *The Golden Web: A History of Broadcasting in the United States, 1933–1953* (New York: Oxford University Press, 1968); and Erik Barnouw, *The Image Empire: A History of Broadcasting in the United States from 1953* (New York: Oxford University Press, 1970).

[4] See, for example, Louise Benjamin, *Freedom of the Air and the Public Interest: First Amendment Rights in Broadcasting to 1935* (Carbondale: Southern Illinois University Press, 2001); Philip T. Rosen, *The Modern Stentors: Radio Broadcasters and the Federal Government, 1920–1934* (Westport, CT: Greenwood, 1980).

primary sources."[5] Without primary sources, history does not exist, but primary sources alone are not "history." Much depends on how those sources are organized, evaluated, and interpreted as evidence.

Secondary sources rely on primary sources, and they are not contemporaneous with the subject era under study. They are interpretations of a primary source—they reflect filtered information that has been passed through one source to another. A book is an example of a secondary source, whereas the collection of original documents used in writing the book is an example of a primary source. Other types of secondary sources include periodical literature, major historical studies, monographs, official histories, biographies, and literature from the time period under study.[6] These sources do have a place in historical research. The good historian uses them for general information, substantiation, description, alternative interpretations, and understanding of the topic. Secondary sources yield ideas and new questions in historical inquiries. But, relying predominantly upon secondary sources denotes faulty, weak historical research. Using primary contemporaneous records, documents, and manuscript collections highlights a historian's research depth.

RULES OF EVIDENCE

Primary sources must be studied critically. That means the analysis of one source or set of sources must be evaluated in light of what is contained in all other relevant sources. Every primary source served a real purpose for those who created it, and their purpose is quite likely different from that of the historian using it later.[7] Take the example of the Declaration of Independence. As a primary document, historians can interpret its historical significance within a larger, complex context of events surrounding its formation by asking a series of questions.[8]

Although the box on the following page by no means contains the only questions historians ask of documents, these questions provide a framework for understanding the process of analyzing primary documents.[9]

---

[5] Marwick, *Nature of History,* 199.

[6] Startt and Sloan, *Historical Methods,* 179.

[7] Marwick, *Nature of History,* 201.

[8] James West Davidson and Mark Hamilton Lytle, *After the Fact: The Art of Historical Detection,* 4th ed. (Boston: McGraw Hill, 2000), 48–70.

[9] Ibid.; Marwick, *Nature of History,* 220–28.

Questioning Historical Documents

- What is the document's surface content?
- How is it arranged?
- What are its major points?
- What might the document have said but did not?
- What intellectual worlds lie behind its words?
- Who were the audiences addressed in the document?
- How does it function within a specific social situation?
- What is its contemporary context?
- Where did the source come from?
- Where was it originally found?
- What type source is it: a private letter, an internal corporate memorandum, minutes of a meeting, published accounts of that same meeting, and so forth?
- Who created it, and for whom was it created?
- What are the author's basic attitudes, prejudices, vested interests?
- How, and for what purposes, did it come into existence?

By answering these questions about the nature of the evidence historians gain a richer understanding of the significance of the facts. For example, these questions were used in research on the famous "Sarnoff Music Box" memo. Beginning with a series of articles published in 1926, David Sarnoff, legendary broadcast leader, claimed that in 1915 he had predicted the advent of broadcasting: "I have in mind a plan of development" declared Sarnoff, "which would make radio a 'household utility' in the same sense as the piano or phonograph. The idea is to bring music into the house by wireless." After he became RCA's president in 1930, Sarnoff's celebrity grew to mythic stature, so that in 1938, Gleason Archer included the story of the "Radio Music Box" memo in his first volume on radio, *A History of Radio to 1926*.[10] Throughout the early 1990s textbooks for both introductory broadcast classes and broadcast history courses cited Archer's work as testament to Sarnoff's prescient genius. Investigation into the evolution of the memo, however, resulted in

---

[10] Gleason L. Archer, *A History of Radio to 1926* (New York: American Historical Society, 1938), 112–13.

the conclusion that the oft-cited memo was not written in 1915, as Sarnoff claimed, but rather as part of a 28-page memo Sarnoff wrote to his superiors at RCA in 1920.[11]

In reaching these conclusions, existing documents were analyzed using the outlined questions. The surface content and arrangement of the 1920 memo showed that it was an internal, lengthy corporate memorandum written by a then-29-year-old Sarnoff solely for his superiors' eyes. Sarnoff's vested interests at the time focused only on career advancement within the ranks of RCA. Sarnoff's attempts to increase his stature in the eyes of the world would come later. In 1920, Sarnoff arranged the memorandum's nine major points in terms of RCA's wireless radio business, and the "memo" portion, item six, did not appear until pages 13 and 14. (Other topics were RCA's general business, patent litigation and related situations, sales and merchandising policies, marine business, sales to the U.S. government, sales to amateurs, sales for other private communication needs, and wired wireless and cab signaling.) The preface to the memo portion of the lengthier memorandum stated that Sarnoff had presented his plan in 1915 to Edward J. Nally, his superior at RCA's predecessor American Marconi, but circumstances at the time prevented implementation. This preamble became important in the final evaluation of the Memo.

In analyzing the document, minor grammatical and punctuation changes made from the 1920 memo to Archer's 1938 rendition were noted. Most notable, however, was a major wording change in the last paragraph of the two versions. The original memo had stated that RCA would greatly benefit from national attention brought it by wireless because "the possibilities for *propaganda and free advertising for the Radio Corporation* (emphasis added) are tremendous." Archer's account changed the wording to "the possibilities for advertising for the Company are tremendous." As research continued, other changes were discovered. In the 1920 memo a distinction had been made between "paid" and "free" advertising earlier in the memo—by 1938, advertising was "paid" while "free advertising" was considered "promotion" or "publicity." More fascinating, however, was the exclusion of the word "propaganda" in Archer's book. The most plausible reason for the removal is the change in the meaning of the word from 1920 to the late 1930s. In 1920 "propaganda" was not a pejorative term as its meaning then was akin to today's concept of

[11] Louise Benjamin, "In Search of the Sarnoff 'Radio Music Box' Memo," *Journal of Broadcasting and Electronic Media* 37, no. 3 (1993): 325–35.

"publicity." Use of the word in the 1920s to describe efforts by both Great Britain and Germany to influence American public opinion about World War I from 1914 to America's entry into the war in 1917 plus the rise of fascism and the Nazis in Europe in the 1930s and their "propaganda" efforts led to the term connoting deception or distortion. Consequently, the term was dropped to avoid misinterpretation or misunderstanding over what it meant in 1938.

The memo was in the papers of Owen D. Young, who initiated the formation of RCA and NBC and who was the chief executive officer of both RCA and its parent company, General Electric, in the 1920s. When researchers first used the collection in the mid-1980s, it was maintained by his family in a private archive, but now the papers have been donated to Young's alma mater, St. Lawrence University in Canton, New York. Thus, the provenance of the memo, or where the memo was originally found, was a credible, trustworthy situation. The Sarnoff Library in Princeton, New Jersey, was another source where the researcher could try to find the original memo or the reply Sarnoff claimed his superior, Edward J. Nally, had written him in 1915. Neither Sarnoff's nor Nally's reply could be found in the collection. So, in 1993, the research concluded that, while Sarnoff likely wrote something to Nally in 1915, that original memorandum had been lost or misplaced. Until it or other evidence was found, no one could assume that Sarnoff had written a memo in 1915 that had the detail of the 1920 memorandum. In addition, by 1920, when the memo cited by Archer was first written, others were also predicting and experimenting with radio broadcasting. "Thus, the 'Radio Music Box' memo and Sarnoff's subsequent claims as a prescient visionary lose their luster because of the five-year discrepancy in the memo's evolution."[12]

However, this early 1990s research did not end the investigation. During the next few years, questions about the memo surfaced and research continued. The search ultimately resulted in a return to the Sarnoff Library in exploration for new research within several scrapbooks kept by David Sarnoff. Two short memoranda in those scrapbooks provided substantive proof. In November 1916 Sarnoff wrote a short memo to E. J. Nally in which he asked for time to discuss his "music box scheme" with Nally as soon as possible. At the bottom in Sarnoff's handwriting was an addendum stating that his proposal could also benefit the American Marconi publication, *Wireless Age*. This memo and Nally's short reply documented that Sarnoff had conceived the idea of a wireless "music box" as early as 1916 and that both he and Nally wanted to

---

[12] Ibid, p. 334.

develop a music service to offer the public. Continuing with the questions posted above, the Sarnoff memo research was amended and, while the original memo was still missing, the short memos analyzed in 2002 revealed that Sarnoff had presented a radio music box plan of some kind to Nally in 1916. Consequently, he should be given credit for the idea of a "radio music box" and for delineating some of its most important points in 1916, including service to the public and for development of a reception device for signals that the public could buy.[13]

Historical research must use primary documents and those documents must be carefully analyzed, if the research is going to contribute to the understanding of early broadcast history. The research must illustrate how primary sources contributed to the historian's work and thus the research contributes to advancing the body of knowledge available on the topic.

Marwick underscores the importance of the primary documentation, "a primary source is most valuable when the purpose for which it was compiled is at the furthest remove from the purpose of the historian."[14] And, with apologies to Orwell, some primary sources are more primary than others. For instance, a handwritten note of which only one copy exists is considered more primary than something which is printed and of which many copies may exist. A personal letter is more primary than a government document printed in the Congressional Record. Consequently it is not just the analysis of the records, but a ranking of primary sources, as a part of the analysis, has evolved with manuscript materials at the top of the hierarchical ladder. Other rungs of the ladder include documents of record such as government sources (e.g., FCC decisions), formal accounts of private organizations (e.g., the National Association of Broadcasters), and private business records (e.g., the NBC papers); polemic documents (e.g., editorial cartoons) from which values and attitudes may be derived. Contemporary pamphlets, periodicals, newspapers, published reports (such as FCC and congressional proceedings) and broadcast programs and technology comprise the bottom rungs on the ladder.[15]

Primary sources offer historians both witting and unwitting testimony. Witting testimony is intentional and deliberate. Unwitting testimony is those meanings and perceptions conveyed inadvertently. Historians find unwitting

---

[13] Louise Benjamin, "In Search of the Sarnoff 'Radio Music Box' Memo: Nally's Reply," *Journal of Radio Studies* 9, no. 1 (2002): 97–106.

[14] Marwick, *Nature of History,* 201–02.

[15] Ibid., 202–05.

> **Ranking Primary Sources**
>
> - Original documents such as: diaries, letters, unedited aural/visuals, and photographs
> - Corporate records, such as: minutes, memos, original scripts, and unedited footage
> - Government records, such as FCC records
> - Oral history interviews
> - Published reports, such as newspaper and magazine articles
> - Edited audio and visual resources, such as radio and TV programs
> - Physical artifacts, such as old radio sets

testimony exceedingly useful, as the participant did not consciously intend to supply any evidence of situations or circumstances he or she often takes for granted.[16] For instance, television news film from the 1963 John Kennedy assassination coverage not only captures the drama of the unfolding news story (witting testimony), but also captures the clothing, attitudes, and social conventions of the times (unwitting testimony).[17] CBS films and videotapes show a respectful press expressing condolences to Senator Ted Kennedy after he gives them a brief statement about the family's plans to travel to Washington, D.C., from Massachusetts. They also show the press and police parading the suspect, Lee Harvey Oswald, before cameras for the public. In a hastily-constructed, televised biography of Kennedy, his surviving brothers, Robert and Ted, are named and their careers mentioned, while his younger sisters are referred to as "the four girls" separating the two men. These three incidents provide valuable insight into the social fabric of the early 1960s. The first illustrates attitudes of the press and paparazzi, who did not hound the deceased's survivors, as they did in the 1990s when Jackie Kennedy Onassis died. The second shows that suspects were not afforded the police protections they are today (in part because of Oswald's later live-on-TV death). The last illuminates women's role in a society that was different from what it is in the twenty-first century. Such unintentional evidence may be extremely helpful, even indispensable, to historians striving to understand the early 1960s.

---

[16] Ibid, 216–20.

[17] CBS News, *Four Days in November*, aired November 17, 1988, Peabody Awards Collection, 88202DCT.

NARRATION, ANALYSIS, AND THEORY

In interpreting and explaining what has happened, historians have not always shared the same views. Startt and Sloan indicate that "in the nearly two centuries that American historians have been writing about the history of communication in this country, they have given accounts that differ widely. One historian might condemn the party press for its partisanship, while another might praise it for its contributions to the American political system. ... Differing perspectives among historians result in pictures and explanations that are multidimensional rather than flat, multicolored rather than monotone."[18] Similarly in broadcast history, authors have both praised and condemned the national networks. *As It Happened* by William S. Paley reflects quite a different picture of the CBS network history, than that of columnist Robert Metz *CBS: Reflections in a Bloodshot Eye.*[19] Similarly, the story of Philo T. Farnsworth in the invention of electronic television differs when told by his wife, Elma G. Farnsworth, in *Distant Vision: Romance & Discovery on an Invisible Frontier;* a popular culture journalist, Daniel Stashower, in *The Boy Genius and the Mogul;* and historian Donald Godfrey's work, *Philo T. Farnsworth: The Father of Television.*[20]

Despite differing points of view, historians realize that their interpretations should not be predetermined. In doing so, they draw from a wide variety of theories and perspectives in crafting their accounts. According to Marwick, historians "employ concepts and generalizations ... that are not the same as having one overarching theory about how societies develop and change."[21]

---

[18] Startt and Sloan, *Historical Methods,* 21.

[19] See William S. Paley, *As it Happened: A Memoir* (Garden City, NY: Doubleday, 1979); Robert Metz, *CBS: Reflections in a Bloodshot Eye* (Chicago: Playboy Press, 1975).

[20] See Elma G. Farnsworth, *Distant Vision: Romance & Discovery on an Invisible Frontier* (Salt Lake City: PemberlyKent Publishers, 1999); Daniel Stashower, *The Boy Genius and the Mogul: The Untold Story of Television* (New York: Broadway Books, 2002); Donald G. Godfrey, *Philo T. Farnsworth: The Father of Television* (Salt Lake City: University of Utah Press, 2001). See also Paul Schatzkin, *The Boy Who Invented Television: A Story of Inspiration, Persistence and Quiet Passion* (Silver Spring, MD: TeamCom Books, 2002); Evan I. Schwartz, *The Last Lone Inventor: A Tale of Genius, Deceit and the Birth of Television* (New York: HarperCollins, 2002).

[21] Marwick, *Nature of History,* 145.

Given the problems facing historians, "and the sorts of answers they can get from primary evidence, there simply is no grand theory which is intellectually fully persuasive. There are theories, but no theory. There are generalizations and conceptual frameworks."[22] Marwick and other historical theorists resist the temptation of a fixed conceptual framework as a cookie cutter approach to history, which works to make the evidence fit within predetermined parameters rather than allowing for independent analysis of the evidence. However, frameworks and historical genre exist.

Among the conceptual frameworks in mass communication, journalism historians Startt and Sloan in their work have employed several broad schools of interpretation: nationalistic, romantic, developmental, progressive, consensus, cultural, and "new left" activist.[23] These approaches offer different lenses through which past events may be perceived, so a brief explanation of each is warranted here.

Nationalistic approaches, used most often in the nineteenth century, advance notions of U.S. leadership in the world's evolution while romanticism, also a nineteenth-century approach, shares this perspective and accentuates the role "great men" played in history's unfolding panorama. Works on the print press illustrate these approaches most clearly. As Startt and Sloan state, Isaiah Thomas's *History of Printing in America,* published in 1810, exemplifies the nationalistic approach, while Eugene Lyons's book, *David Sarnoff, a Biography,* published in 1966, is an example of romanticism in broadcast history.[24] Begun in the early twentieth century, the developmental school emphasizes the continuing evolution of society and attempts to explain and evaluate history through its contributions to the present. Works such as Gleason Archer's books, *History of Radio to 1926* and *Big Business and Radio* (1939), typify this viewpoint.[25] Progressive interpretations, on the other hand, evaluate the past through notions of ideological tensions existing within society's social strata. The past is a struggle for social change, progress, and democracy.

---

[22] Ibid., 150.

[23] Startt and Sloan, *Historical Methods,* 24–45; see also Martha Howell and Walter Prevenier, *From Reliable Sources: An Introduction to Historical Methods* (Ithaca, NY: Cornell University Press, 2001), 88–118.

[24] Isaiah Thomas, *History of Printing in America* (Worcester, MA: Isaiah Thomas, 1810); Eugene Lyon, *David Sarnoff, a Biography* (New York: Harper & Row, 1966).

[25] Archer, *History of Radio*; Gleason L. Archer, *Big Business and Radio* (New York: American Historical Society, 1939).

Charles Siepmann's critique of U.S. broadcasting, *Radio's Second Chance,* published in 1946, uses progressive interpretations.[26] Consensus approaches shun the critical attitude of progressivism and its emphasis on conflict and place emphasis on achievement and unity, not class differences and divisions. Key to the consensus approach is a view of the media's role as useful, stable institutions in American life that perform their duties of informing and entertaining the public responsibly. Works such as William P. Banning's book *Commercial Broadcasting Pioneer: The WEAF Experiment, 1922–1926* exemplify this approach.[27] Cultural history's fundamental premise is that events happen and actors in those events operate in close interrelationships with their environment, or culture. The "new left" activist school, born after World War II, adopted and revised Marxist theory into a new kind of progressive social and cultural history. Robert McChesney's book on the fight over the control of U.S. broadcasting from 1928 to 1935, *Telecommunications, Mass Media, and Democracy,* employs cultural history interpretations.[28] Its many offshoots also include women's history, African American history, and ethnic history.[29]

Historians today often draw from one or more of these various schools as they research explanations of the past. However, according to Marwick, history is not simply the descriptive tale individual historians tell, "history is a systematic subject, which calls for a fully conscious and fully articulated statement of assumptions and methods, which employs generalizations, concepts, and theories (plural), which as and when necessary can be tested by empirical methods, and a subject which has complex, definable, but always expanding ranges of sources and means of exploiting them."[30] Still, history must work, and implied in "working" means "carrying conviction, corresponding with the evidence adduced, fitting in with what we know of the topic and the period."[31] History is a systematic discipline of analysis and presentation of the evidence.

---

[26] Charles A. Siepmann, *Radio's Second Chance* (Boston: Little, Brown, 1946).

[27] William P. Banning, *Commercial Broadcasting Pioneer: The WEAF Experiment, 1922–1926* (Cambridge, MA: Harvard University Press, 1946).

[28] Robert W. McChesney, *Telecommunications, Mass Media, and Democracy: The Battle for Control of U.S. Broadcasting, 1928–1935* (New York: Oxford University Press, 1993).

[29] Banning, *Commercial Broadcasting Pioneer.*

[30] Marwick, *Nature of History,* 151.

[31] Ibid., 154.

In analyzing primary documents, historians ask particular questions as they authenticate the source material. Is this source authentic—is it what it purports to be? To discern the answer to the legitimacy of a source, historians use both internal and external evidence. Internal evidence questions the credibility of the source through technical knowledge of the source: Is this material characteristic of the time, person, or situation under study? For instance, does the style of language, the medium upon which the document exists, the artifact itself conform to what is already known about the time, person, situation? If the answer is "no" to these questions, then the evidence is suspect.

External evidence seeks authenticity through verification. Verification comes through comparison of the object under investigation, with other known evidence from the same author or organization. Such identification establishes the integrity of the material. Sometimes authenticity can be determined with certainty, while other times that is not possible. The process is one of weighing all combinations and possibilities.[32]

The analyses of any primary document can always be called into question: Could the document be a forgery? Has someone tampered with the evidence for selfish purposes? These concerns are not new to electronic media. Some letters attributed to President Abraham Lincoln have been called forgeries.[33] Forgeries and fake records exist. Sham materials, some even excellent counterfeits, have created headaches for those who use or publish them as genuine. Take, for instance, the emergence in 1983 of diaries attributed to Adolf Hitler. When nearly 60 volumes covering the 12 years of the Third Reich emerged from a barn in Eastern Germany, the German magazine *Stern* purchased the work and began publishing it. Eminent British historian Hugh Trevor-Roper heralded the diary as genuine, and the London *Sunday Times* and the U.S. periodical *Newsweek* began publishing English translations. Soon other historians, former Hitler aides, and handwriting experts began questioning the diaries' authenticity, and in May 1983 the West German Federal Archives announced the alleged diaries were crude forgeries made of post-World War II materials. The ink, paper, and binding contained postwar synthetics, and the text itself contained historical inaccuracies and anachronisms.[34] In another

---

[32] Startt and Sloan, *Historical Methods,* 164.

[33] Paul Angle, "The Minor Collection," *Atlantic Monthly,* 143, April 1929, 516–25.

[34] B. Werthmann, W. Schiller, and W. Griebenow, "Naturwissenschaftliche Aspekte der Echtheitspruefung der Songenannten 'Hitler-Tagebuecher,'" *Maltechnik-*

instance, a forensic analyst was called in to examine historic Church of Jesus Christ of Latter Day Saints documents when it was discovered that a private collector was forging materials for commercial exploitation.[35] Although these examples may seem distant, even irrelevant to the electronic media historian, they are not. Remember it is the possible manipulation of the record that makes media suspect as a primary source (see chapter 1). This is not new. In electronic media, reenactments and re-creations of events are categories of fabrication. Despite a producer's good intentions, pictures and sounds may be manipulated to create a desired result. For example, study of British newsreels of the London blitz of 1940 shows they were carefully constructed to show the British resolve. With the blessing of the English government, these films reassured the public as they endured those dark days.[36] Another classic example comes from the 1952 television series *Victory at Sea.* One episode, "The Battle of Leyte Gulf," was entirely constructed of stock footage and scenes shot during other battles, because no cameras were present at that battle. Even though this program was a fabrication, the Naval War College used it for strategic study into the 1970s because of the historical information and interpretation presented in the film. While "there may indeed be very valuable historical observations in the Battle of Leyte Gulf program that have nothing to do with where the pictures of the ships came from," viewers and researchers alike need to watch it critically for what they are seeing is not real evidence of the event.[37] For the historian the tests of authenticity become critical.

The tests of authenticity include comparative witnesses, time and place of the observations, the point of view of the presenter, truthfulness, and the relevant influences of the production process. *Comparative witness* means factually verifying the information from other comparative and perhaps collaborative sources. Complementary, contemporary sources build the stronger case. The

---

Restauro 90, no. 94 (1984): 65–72, cited in Dianne van der Reyden, "Identifying the Real Thing," Smithsonian Center for Materials Research and Education (SCMRE), School for Scanning, sponsored by the National Park Service and managed by the Northeast Document Conservation Center, September 11–13, 1996, New York City, http://www.si.edu/scmre/relact/analysis.htm.

[35] Linda Sillitoe and Alan Roberts, *Salamander: The Story of the Mormon Forgery Murders* (Salt Lake City, UT: Signature Books, 1988).

[36] John E. O'Connor, ed., *Image as Artifact: The Historical Analysis of Film and Television* (Malibar, FL: Robert E. Krieger Publishing, 1990), 313.

[37] Ibid., 314.

Tests of Authenticity

- Can comparative witnesses be found?
- How do the time, place, and proximity of the evidence relate?
- What was the point of view of the source?
- Was the source truthful?
- What was the relative influence of technology?
- Was there any supportive physical evidence, such as artifacts, photographs, and so on?

---

time, place, and proximity requirements of evidence mean that the historian assesses the evidence in relation to its environment. The further away from the event that the record is made, the more likely that external data influenced the record *and* the more complex the evaluation of authenticity. "The closer the time of making a document to the event it records," Gottschalk wrote, "the better it is likely to be for historical purposes."[38] The very nature of broadcast news reporting, where immediacy is so important, infuses great value into a broadcast news resource. The further away from the event the record was made, the more the historical analyst bears the responsibility of summoning additional evidence to determine the value of the record. Extended time between the event and the record of it decreases the primary value of the source. The time reference must also be considered along with other variables surrounding it, the total context and the process. Lengthy periods of time and the extended production process of dramatic television make this a challenging undertaking.

The *point of view* of an evidence source means evaluating the editorial position, the bias, and the experience, and reliability of a source. Even in news programming the challenge is not simple. Does the reporter have a point of view? If the reporter seems to toss editorial intonations into his or her delivery, the analyst must examine the value of the reporter as a source. Are the questions open or leading? Was the reporter biased? Was he or she in a position to observe the facts? Unfortunately today, the researcher also must deal with the ego of the reporter as an eyewitness. Did the reporter recount the facts, or did his or her actions affect the facts as they were presented? Are they reporting

---

[38] Louis R. Gottschalk, *Understanding History: A Primer of Historical Method*, 2nd ed. (New York: Knopf, 1969), 150–55.

the news or are they the object of news? If there appears any distortion of factual information, it must be examined. *Truth* means the researcher has amassed a sufficient body of evidence to establish verifiable fact. If there are contradictions in reported truth, then additional evidence must be acquired and examined.

Finally, if the evidence comes from a media product—film, video, audio, and so forth—then the influences of the production process, the technology, and the people involved in the producing process must be evaluated. For example, in evaluating visual documents, the electronic-media historian can learn from the still-photo historian.[39] The intent of the photographer as creator or author of the information is paramount. Careful investigation is required to:

- recognize the effects of framing within the visual story—the relevant details within the background, middle ground, and foreground of the framing;
- evaluate the effects of any photographic or technological influences, such as lens and computer-graphics effects; and
- consider the technological capacity at the time of the recording.

In addition to these elements of still-photographic analysis, the broadcast historian must assess the elements of sound and motion upon the moving visual record. There are serious ethical, as well as complex historiographical questions.

Authenticating contextual information from the arts and technologies of electronic broadcasting is perhaps nowhere more important than in photography, cinema, photojournalism, graphics, and videography. The photographer or videographer, no matter what his or her genre, is a vital link in gathering information. They represent the pen and paper of the record. In news broadcast situations, the sights and sounds of an event are gathered by the photographer, videographer, or cinematographer—in a movie they frame the story, one film frame at a time. The visuals in media are priceless historical records. Don Brown, for example, gave his life to bring news of the Jonestown massacre (1978). His camera kept rolling, even though he was mortally wounded. David Crockett threw a video camera over his shoulder while running away from Mount St. Helen and captured some of the most dramatic footage ever seen of a mountain's eruption. Unlike these previous events, in 1969, the

---

[39] David E. Kyvig and Myron A. Marty, *Nearby History: Exploring the Past around You* (Nashville, TN: American Association for State and Local History, 1982).

world was an eyewitness to man's planned landing on the moon and broad-casting was there to document this historic event.[40]

Electronic media evidence must pass the same scrutiny as any other source in history. Nevins's analogy between historical research and the courtroom procedure is an accurate one, particularly in relation to the tests of the authenticity of the primary source.[41] The historian must distinguish among resources of documentation as a lawyer in the courtroom distinguishes between original evidence and rumor. The tests of evidence will vary, depending on the topic, circumstances, and time. So it is with the process of historical discovery, the evidence varies with witnesses and circumstances. Bormann indicates much the same in his analogy between historical research and the news reporter. The reporter must "discriminate between statements of fact, statements of opinion, value and ethics ... the grounds upon which the historian makes a judgment ... in the end comes down to the facts that can be observed," and the tests of evidence.[42]

TYPES OF EVIDENCE

As mentioned earlier, sources that historians use fall into several major categories: printed and other written materials, published and unpublished personal records, official documents, oral sources, photographic records, radio and television broadcast records, cable television records, new media sources, physical remains, etc. Oral sources, radio, broadcast television, cable television, and new media are foci of following chapters, so this review will focus on print materials, published and unpublished personal records, official documents, and physical remains.

Printed and written materials comprise much of the primary documents historians use because Western society is a writ-based culture. Official records and documents result from administrative bodies, such as the state and federal governments, church organizations, and educational institutions. All materials record life and operations. These accounts are important to those involved and are passed along to successors. Business enterprises and private

---

[40] National Aeronautics and Space Administration, *Apollo II: Moon Landing, First on the Moon,* documentary (Fresno: California Microfilm, 1969).

[41] Allan Nevins, *The Gateway to History* (New York: D.C. Heath, 1938), 224–25.

[42] Ernest G. Bormann, *Theory and Research in the Communicative Arts* (New York: Holt, 1965), 169–70.

associations, such as nonprofit or charitable organizations, also create documents related to their existence. People keep personal records and some of
these are published as memoirs and autobiographies, while much remains
unpublished and even more is simply lost or discarded. All of the existing written records are invaluable to the historian and form the archival repositories
from which history is written.[43]

Official documents and other formal records chronicle decisions of governing bodies, and administrators present collections of information gathered
by official bodies and otherwise enumerate the actions of these administrators.
The formal records of the FCC and its predecessor agencies, for example, contain its decisions, pronouncements of the commissioners, information gathered in its various investigations of communication industries, memoranda on
a myriad of everyday decisions, and so forth. Information contained in these
documents provides communication scholars with a wealth of detail for their
studies. In the same manner, records of business activities provide historians
with documentation of their actions.

All of these sources provide important evidence historians use, but historians must still analyze the documents in terms of the "how" and "why" of their
creation and dissemination. If published, what were the circumstances of publication? What was the intent of its creators? In other words, *how* and *why* was
this particular document devised and for what purpose? And, why was it disseminated? As Startt and Sloan state, "Many government documents, like
documents pertaining to other organizations, are published with the honest
intent of making information available to the public," but to grasp them completely, scholars still need to question the materials as they would question any
other source.[44] In the Congressional Records for example, were a representative's comments inserted into the records after the fact for election purposes, or
was the representative an active participant in the congressional debate? Often
the actions of businesses and governing bodies are reported in newspapers,
magazines, and the Internet. When used, these stories need to be scrutinized
carefully. Historians need to know about the publication itself. As Startt and
Sloan indicate, "Historians need to know much about a newspaper [or electronic media] to understand it as an historical source. Who produced it, and
how, and why? What type of influence did it have, and why? Was it known
equally for all of its contents? Were there restraints placed upon its opinion,

---

[43] Marwick, *Nature of History,* 208–12.

[44] Startt and Sloan, *Historical Methods,* 178.

and did that opinion conform to some outside interest?"[45] These same questions apply to use of magazine articles, Internet reports, and materials in the nation's growing broadcast archives.

These analytic requirements apply as well to published personal records. Generally, published personal records, including autobiographies, memoirs, speeches, and major addresses, are created with an audience in mind, and historians must understand why and under what circumstances these particular accounts are disseminated. They must ask the traditional analytical questions of the documents in addition to asking: How much, if any, was edited from the original? What was included, and why? What was excluded, and why? These questions help historians assess a published record's value.

Historians prefer the use of original, unpublished materials. Manuscript collections may contain all kinds of personal papers, from personal correspondence, memoranda, and reports to personal diaries, family records, and scrapbooks. These materials are the gold mines of historians' accounts. Libraries, archives, and repositories such as historical societies and private family files house and preserve original source materials. Some archives, such as the U.S. National Archives, maintain millions of records, while others conserve much smaller collections. In using any repository, historians should employ whatever document lists are available to locate materials. Often called "finding guides," these lists or handbooks provide invaluable information on archival holdings and help prepare the historian for a visit.

Historians usually visit manuscript collections personally rather than hire another researcher because historians often carry a lot of their research criteria in their heads and, to modify a phrase of the late Supreme Court Justice Potter Stewart, they know what they are looking for when they see it. Another researcher is hired only if an identifiable item is needed and the historian can specifically tell the researcher what he or she needs. Likewise, requests for documents by mail are usually done only when the material needed can be precisely noted. An example of an item, which could be requested by mail, is a copy of a station's original construction permit. But, if other materials regarding that permit are needed for a history of a station, then the historian should visit the collection.

A visit is especially warranted if the collection holds physical objects, which cannot be duplicated. These objects also comprise primary resources and include "relics, mementos, and an array of things people used in work and

---

[45] Ibid., 19.

leisure as well as in buildings, vehicles of transportation and the instruments of technology."[46] Broadcast and cable technology falls into this category and can be crucial to understanding electronic media's development. Physical objects inform scholars of past ways of doing things. In broadcast, for example, old microphones and receiver sets reveal important aspects of the means of transmission and reception of signals. Such three-dimensional artifacts enrich and enhance understanding of the historical experience.

DOCUMENTS IN BROADCASTING

Broadcast radio, television, cable, and all electronic media have left a number of physical artifacts, audio and video recordings, and numerous other documents in their wake. Historians realize programs often supply evidence not only of their creators, but also of their audiences. From this body of evidence researchers can deduce attitudes, assumptions, and values of both from past programming. In addition, listening to an audiotape or viewing a videotape of a speech, for example, provides a more accurate experience than reading a printed copy. Voice inflection, body posturing, and other nuances add rich texture to the speech. Hearing President Franklin Roosevelt during one of his "Fireside Chats" or Edward R. Murrow's account of the liberation of the concentration camp at Buchenwald gives listeners a far more invaluable account than simply reading the speeches. The Presidential Libraries across the country are full of coverage that would be more appropriately researched using the medium as a source.

To understand audio and video evidence fully the historian must understand how it is, or was, produced. Knowledge of past and present production techniques and values enables the historian to understand choices facing those behind the scenes such as producers, directors, and writers, who constructed the aural and visual materials. For instance, in videotapes of the coverage of John Kennedy's assassination in 1963, the announcements were initially voiced over a still visual image noting the network or station's call letters. These voice-over-slide announcements are understood more fully when historians realize that camera tubes in the 1960s needed at least 20 minutes to warm up to produce an acceptable, steady image. In CBS's coverage, for example, the visual "rolls" and then stabilizes as the director shifts from a slide to Walter Cronkite on the screen. The director had shifted to the moving visual

---

[46] Ibid., 185.

as soon as possible but before the picture was completely "synced" or stable. Today's students, used to instantaneous television pictures, often think the momentary, but noticeable, visual anomaly is their television set or video recorder, not the recording itself.[47]

Historians must take into account the content of audio and video tapes and ask questions of that content. For instance, how might programs have been influenced by their times? Over the years, self-censorship as well as official production codes and regulations affected both radio and television content and production. Sanctioning some content and banning others resulted in practices such as such showing married couples sleeping in twin beds in the 1950s. Those guiding principles affected what audiences received and must be understood by historians studying the time period.

Program audiences also must be considered within the context of their times and expectations. For instance, in December 1937 radio audiences were scandalized when they heard Mae West and Don Ameche as Eve and Adam in an NBC sketch titled "The Garden of Eden" on *The Chase and Sanborn Hour* starring Edgar Bergen and Charlie McCarthy. Quaint and innocuous by today's standards, students often do not understand why audiences were upset by the sexual innuendo in the skit until the context of the late 1930s is explained to them. Nor do they comprehend the full impact of Orson Welles's October 1938 *War of the Worlds* broadcast upon audiences until the fears and tensions surrounding Nazi Germany's actions in 1938 are explained.[48] In March, Hitler annexed Austria (known as the Anschluss), while in September the "Munich crisis" was followed by listeners eager for the latest on Hitler's threat to Czechoslovakia and the eventual agreement that forced that nation to cede the Sudetenland to Germany. Evaluation of how society and its audiences have changed over time adds depth to historical accounts as well as students' understanding of the past.

CONCLUSION

As this chapter has illustrated, the incomplete records that humans leave behind form the foundation for historical work. But, the manner in which

---

[47] CBS News, *Four Days in November.*

[48] See chapter 5 of Christopher H. Sterling and John Michael Kittross, *Stay Tuned: A History of American Broadcasting*, 3rd ed. (Mahwah, NJ: Lawrence Erlbaum Associates, 2002).

historians use and evaluate those fragments provides an understanding of the past. This chapter has presented an overview of the rigor used in carefully gathering and analyzing evidence used in historical studies. In short, historians must be fully aware of the differences between primary and secondary resources. They must carefully use the rules of evidence in their analysis of documents, use of theory in history, and development of their interpretations. As they work, historians must test the authenticity of their evidence against other comparative knowns and vigilantly watch for forgeries and manipulation of materials. A historian is much like the detective or the lawyers, who must examine all the available evidence before presenting a case.

3

Oral History Records

Michael D. Murray
University of Missouri, St. Louis

W^e have all been enchanted by the stories of people's lives. As children we
listened to the stories of our parents and grandparents. As we look back
and remember, we wish we'd had a recorder running. As we grew, teachers and
mentors enriched our lives. In Hollywood and in today's newscasts, audiences
are enthralled with every detail of celebrity lives. Commercial biographies and
autobiographies of a celebrity's life fly off the shelves—some having historical
value, others having little. The oral history tradition is as old as civilization
itself. Before the written and the mediated word—we had the spoken word.
Family histories, genealogy, myth, folklore, stories of moral perpetuity, even
business operations and relationship structures were memorized and passed
from generation to generation—from mind to mind.

Oral history is, first and foremost, all about human memory. It is a historical method used to acquire the details and indelible images retained from life
experiences. Oral histories consist of interviews conducted with people who
have had direct or even indirect knowledge and experience within a specific
topic area. The purpose of this chapter is to provide an overview in the use of
oral history and its challenges in historical research. The objective is to offer
insight, direction, and experience from the field.

Oral history builds on and draws upon traditional forms of evidence.
Virtually anything written down or appearing in print on a particular topic,
if verified for accuracy, could be included in a narrative account. These physical materials exist in the traditional forms of information available as part of
many university, museum, and archive collections: newspaper and magazine
accounts, memoirs, diaries, yearbooks, cartoons, maps, business reports,

recordings, photographs, broadcasts, production and subject files, attendance records, tests, accounts of budgets and budgeting, artifacts, architectural plans, and physical technology. Oral history interviews should be included in any list of archived holdings of a public repository, which allows for follow-up use as well as further analysis and reinterpretation. Oral history adds color and personal context to these traditional forms of evidence and a wide variety of repositories has developed in the field of journalism and media studies.[1]

Oral history has a long and storied past in scholarship traced directly to the introduction of the audio tape recorder at the end of World War II. With the introduction of the tape recorder, oral history was added as a methodology—a means of gathering information heretofore limited by technology. The underlying goal of determining the truth of a situation or event remains the same. Oral history interviews provide a new dimension as part of historical record. They are planned, transcribed for publication, and preserved as a part of historical evidence for historians and scholars of the future. Those who have labored in the most ephemeral medium of broadcasting recognize the value of the printed word and the oral/visual record. Those who labor in history recognize the value of the repository of those records.

THE ORAL HISTORY ASSOCIATION

Over the past few decades, the use of oral history has grown considerably in popularity among scholars, particularly as a result of smaller and more easily accessible videotape equipment and the growth of special collections and the number of projects emphasizing their unique benefits. Founded in 1966, the Oral History Association (OHA) offers a wide range of suggested methods

---

[1] See, for example: Maurine Hoffman Beasley, "Oral History," in *Guide to Sources in American Journalism History,* ed. Lucy Shelton Caswell (Westport, CT: Greenwood, 1989), 91–98. For additional background on direction in the field, see Maurine Hoffman Beasley and Richard R. Harlow, "Oral History: Additional Tool for Journalism Historians," *Journalism History* 6 (Fall 1979): 98–102; Douglas Gomery, "Methods for the Study of the History of Broadcasting and Mass Communication," *Film & History* 21, no. 2–3 (1991): 55–63; Allen Smith, ed., *Directory of Oral History Collections* (Phoenix, AZ: Oryz Press, 1987); Frederick J. Stielow, *The Management of Oral History Sound Archives* (Westport, CT: Greenwood, 1986); Donald Godfrey, comp., *Reruns on File: A Guide to Electronic Media Archives* (Hillsdale, NJ: Lawrence Erlbaum Associates, 1992).

and standards to help guide the development of the profession and the use of oral history. Some of their initiatives have resulted in very tangible and positive results for use by those who conduct oral history interviews.[2]

The OHA guidelines were developed in the early stages of the organization to help insure that all parties in the process, including potential sponsoring collections and organizations, had a basic understanding of the advantages and potential drawbacks of oral interviewing. They have recently addressed concerns for the independent, unaffiliated researchers, as well as developed approaches to complex issues related to the use of videotape and new technology, including the Internet. The OHA offers "Principles and Standards" providing an informed basis for peer review and independent judgment with respect to oral history research. It provides informed opinion regarding the status of the need for institutional approval in obtaining oral history interviews with an extensive background that the tradition upheld some standards and protocols in approaches unique to oral history. The result was the distinction of not having to seek institutional (IRB) approval for the use of oral history, in most cases an issue that had been debated for some time.[3]

---

[2] Donald A. Ritchie, *Doing Oral History* (New York: Twayne Publishers, 1995). Ritchie has been at the forefront of these efforts. See also Donald A. Ritchie, "Oral History Evaluation Guidelines," Oral History Association, Pamphlet Number 3, Adopted 1989 [also under the Chairmanship of Donald A. Ritchie] (Washington, DC: U.S. Senate Historical Office, revised Sept. 2000). See also Donald A. Ritchie and Linda Shopes, "Application of the Department of Health and Human Services Regulations for the Protection of Human Subjects at 45 CFR Part 46, Subpart A to Oral History Interviewing" (Washington, DC: Oral History Association and American Historical Association, 2003). This clarifies that Oral History is excluded from IRB review. The U.S. Office for Human Research Protection (OHRP), part of the Department of Health and Human Services, determined that Oral History interviews do not involve research defined by HHS and are excluded from Institutional Review Boards.

[3] George Pospisil, "Common Rule," 45 CFR part 46 (Bethesda, MD: Oral History Association, October 2003). Pospisil explains the OHRP decision regarding application of the "Common Rule," which sets regulation governing research involving human subjects, defining research as "systematic investigation, including research development, testing and evaluation, designed to develop or contribute to generalized knowledge." The type of research encompassed by these regulations involves standard questionnaires with large anonymous samples, not open-ended interviews with

The Oral History Association's "Oral History Evaluation Guidelines," suggests the most important aspects of the experience including considerations regarding choice of subjects; the relationship between the interviewer and her or his sources; the need for adequate disclosure of goals and representation regarding eventual use of material for repository. They also address the need for understanding in dealing with contracts and other binding legal agreements, and the proper use of equipment. As an important addition today, the guidelines discuss the role and performance of the video crew involved in recording the interview. They provide a list of basic questions, which is sometimes useful although they may be shopworn and overgeneralized, thus requiring preparation beyond someone's mere list.[4]

In many ways, the OHA serves in an advocacy role in insuring that interviewees are informed of all their rights in the many aspects of the interview process, some of which they might not otherwise consider. Issues regarding control and access of the record, disposition and dissemination of material, ownership rights, copyrights, royalties, and the various formats of the oral record are extremely important today. In addition, the process of editing with the current potential for electronic editing and on-line distribution must be considered as well. All options for potential use should be discussed with oral history sources, and the most simple and obvious rule is that the research should make no promises unless they can be fulfilled. Exploitation of interviewees and sensitivity to the discussion of certain topics must be considered. Restricted access and even source anonymity may frequently be offered as a means of insuring that the rights of the interviewee are taken fully into account and that they and their words are treated fairly. The OHA is a reservoir of information for anyone new to the oral history process.

Oral records are, of course, by no means limited to oral history interviews. They also include kinescopes, programs, recorded speeches, stories, tales, songs, or other forms of oral expression. These must also be factored when conducting primary research. We most often regard oral history as a critical form of primary source information, because the individuals were close to an

---

identifiable individuals who give interviews with "informed consent" characterizing oral history. Only oral history projects that conform to a regulatory definition need to submit research protocols for IRB review.

[4] Elliot G. Mishler, *Research Interviewing: Context and Narrative* (Cambridge, MA: Harvard University Press, 1986); Trevor Lummis, *Listening to History: The Authenticity of Oral Evidence* (Totowa, NJ: Barnes & Noble Books, 1988).

event or person. As such, it is no wonder that the most intense, most nerve-wracking, often even life-threatening assignments tend to be the ones that resonate in the memory bank and are frequently called upon to be resurrected in an oral history interview. Comparisons to traditional newsgathering and reporting are inevitable, but there are also differences between news and oral history interviews, beginning with the purpose, nature, and scope of the interaction.[5]

ORAL HISTORY VERSUS NEWS GATHERING

The oral history researcher and the reporter have many things in common. For many media scholars, their extended journalistic-style interviews began as a result of their undergraduate education, which exposed them to interviewing, reporting, and writing skills. Students are often enamored with special stories of famous national figures and value interviewing as their most critical and important assignments.

Basic interviewing skills do translate from the news gathering profession to scholarship. In-class interviewing assignments enhance projects in communication and journalism as a reporter learns the importance of the open-ended, closed, and leading question formats. Used by both, these three techniques also basically differentiate the oral historian from the reporter. Although the oral historian benefits from the skills learned in reporting, there are challenges as well. *Open-ended* questions, those that allow the interviewee to reflect upon a response, are the stock-in-trade of the oral historian. A skilled oral history interviewer waits for the interviewee to fully respond to the question. Such a response may cover extended periods of time, often 20 to 30 minutes in length. While the oral historian is under no time constraints, the reporters, in contrast, are under severe time deadlines. They need a story by a deadline. So, the reporter often asks the closed questions. *Closed questions* produce short answers, a phrase or even just a word, yes or no. Such a technique often produces dialogues and wonderful sound bites, but limited historical information. In oral history closed questions provide specific information (e.g., birth dates, addresses, relationships, etc.). However, open-ended questions are the ones that supply the truly in-depth substance. The reporter who wants a

---

[5] See David Henige, *Oral Historiography* (New York: Longman, 1982); Valerie Raleigh Yow, *Recording Oral History: A Practical Guide for Social Scientists* (Thousand Oaks, CA: Sage, 1994).

particular response asks a *leading question,* which directs the interviewee toward a particular response.

Both oral historians and reporters, like so many people in the field of broadcasting, must become seasoned interviewers and be prepared for the interviews to facilitate the interviewees' recalling of complex stories—as opposed to simple personality profiles or celebrity-style interviews.[6] Oral history is a historical research tool. It is supplemented by good reporting skills, but not limited by them.

It is often suggested that researchers with backgrounds in reporting, who engage in oral history projects, think initially in terms of the logical comparisons between those jobs and the people who hold them—and there are some. But at the same time, obvious differences exist:

1. As noted, deadlines make a difference. The time line for the gathering and reporting of information is dramatically different, as are expectations on how the information will fit together in an established format.

2. The tendency might be to think in terms of the inverted pyramid style of presentation for news, but in oral history the story is a narrative reflection of the mind of the interviewee.

3. A reporter's unrecorded phone calls, or even notes from such calls, do not constitute oral history. This is reporting. Oral history requires different procedures, transcripts, documentation, and archiving.

Another obvious difference or dimension between news interviews and an oral history account is the nature of the source. In both news and history, there seems to be a preoccupation with individuals and unnamed sources being the target of oral history and reportage. In recent years, some prominent journalists have employed oral history approaches and it occasionally backfires with the lack of ability to corroborate information and quotes and the perspective of time. Such was the case with Bob Woodward, of Watergate reporting and Woodward and Bernstein fame with a book about decision making at the highest government levels. Woodward's new book, *Plan of Attack,* was second-guessed in some quarters for his use of 75 unnamed sources, including both military and administration officials, and two interviews with the president.

---

[6]J. Herbert Altschull, "The Journalist and Instant History: An Example of the Jackal Syndrome," *Journalism Quarterly* 50 (Fall 1973): 389–96; Allan Nevins, "American Journalism and Its Historical Treatments," *Journalism Quarterly* 36 (Fall 1959): 411–22.

Mr. Bush spoke on the record, but others talked only on the condition that their identities not be revealed. *60 Minutes* read transcripts of the interviews and listened to the tapes to verify the accounts told by people who took part at those meetings, including one on March 19, when the President gave the order to go to war. Prior to publication of *Plan of Attack,* the contents were guarded closely. In one exchange on December 11, Woodward asked the president, "'Well, how is history likely to judge your Iraq war?' And he said, 'History,' and then he took his hands out of his pocket and kind of shrugged and extended his hands as if this is a way off. And then he said, 'History, we don't know. We'll all be dead.'"[7] This interview exchange reflects a unique dimension in discussing the dynamics of oral history, because it is the total trust of Bob Woodward that creates a willingness to accept so many unnamed sources. Such techniques and controversies sell news and books, but it does not always produce accurate history.

Credited for the development of oral history collections as a means of providing an integrated narrative, Allan Nevins's beginnings in the arena of oral history have provided a better appreciation of the value of extending the scope of their inquiry to those beyond officeholders or those holding high-level administrative positions.[8] He suggests oral history projects differ from the journalistic interview with respect to access and additional means of gathering information. Broadcast and print journalists are usually unwilling to share information with their sources, once the information is gathered. Whereas oral historians tend to want information verified by alternate sources for the record and checked for historical accuracy, the reporter merely juxtaposes an opposing point of view with a story.

In terms of source-checking and verification, the oral historian needs to provide support for the accuracy of the thoughts and words expressed in the interview when constructing his or her case. Verifications can come from other sources as well as traditional sources of evidence.

Most researchers in communication, mass communication, journalism, or telecommunication would maintain that reporters who come up with rapid-fire questions on the way to filing a story would not qualify for research excellence. Although many of the basic interviewing skills translate from news

---

[7] From "Woodward Shares War Secrets," *60 Minutes,* CBS News, aired April 18, 2004.

[8] See Allan Nevins, *The Gateway to History,* rev. ed. (Chicago: Quadrangle Books, 1963).

gathering professionals to scholars, the style and preparation for interviewing are considerably different. One would hope that the oral historian would have spent months rather than days (or just hours) preparing to construct a story based on the evidence.

One of the most consistent themes in the history of broadcast research is the failure of broadcasts and documentary records to adequately do justice to the themes they frequently explore. Those who have studied the history of broadcast news are well aware of the fact that questions regarding coverage of armed conflict have, for example, been repeated since the introduction of television news. Similarly, issues regarding the camera's ability to capture the "truth" of any social setting or situation, beginning in extended series format with the William C. Louds, "An American Family" on PBS, revealed a large number of cinema-verité questions. These included manipulation of content, portrayal of subjects as one dimensional, and the role of promotion in presenting the information. Too little attention has been paid to the repeated stories and the nature of sources of information.

Reporters are often just as impressed by the need to spend time in writing an account true to the experience, and this is especially true in some visual stories. Although a picture is worth a thousand words, video shot in a heated political context is notoriously untrustworthy going back to the earliest, most cursory studies, such as those of Kurt and Gladys Engel Lang. Their account of "MacArthur Day in Chicago," and other early televised events are often cited as the most outrageous examples of how pictures can be very deceptive.[9]

Some of the most highly valued journalistic interviews and broadcast interviewing have included moments of confrontation in which an attempt is made to elicit hidden or false information. The broadcast historian cannot accept this edited style or technique of ambush-style questioning as history and normally rejects information obtained under stress or duress. In some journalistic interviews there have been well-known incidents in which interviewers have injected statements meant to challenge, to clarify, and thus direct. The oral historian must attempt to contextualize these responses using additional evidence or, if available, the unedited outtakes of the interview.

Some of broadcasting's most celebrated on-camera interviewers, including Mike Wallace and Ted Koppel, have used confrontational techniques to elicit

---

[9] Kurt Lang and Gladys Engel Lang, *Television and Politics* (Chicago: Quadrangle Books, 1970); Erik Barnouw, *Tube of Plenty: The Evolution of American Television*, 2nd rev. ed. (New York: Oxford University Press, 1990).

information from sources. Most of the available videotape compilations from *60 Minutes,* usually anniversary programs from the program's storied past, include a segment from a Barbra Streisand interview in which Wallace confronts the Hollywood celebrity regarding what are characterized as her dealings, or lack of interaction with her mother. An interesting and ironic aspect for the viewer is that the interviewee turns the tables on the interviewer and says: "You enjoy this don't you?" The implication is that conflict is the source of motivation for the reporter and thus distorts history. This is true even though the growth of what has become popularly known as "psychohistory" has resulted in efforts to uncover the deep thoughts of many political and business figures with Richard Nixon being one of the most often dissected in this particular genre. Behavior and both public and private statements have been analyzed in the same way that psychiatry uses nonverbal cues to evaluate beliefs, attitudes, and values.

The issue of editing often arises and the rule of thumb is that an unedited interview is a much more valuable source. On some occasions, especially when multiple interviews are available, sources will repeat themselves and, on occasion, in some detail.

When it comes to following up with additional interviews or permission to publish, the historian has a different obligation to the source than does the journalist. A general rule has been that the higher the status of individuals, the less likely they will be concerned about inaccuracies. Nevertheless, errors can be avoided and contexts preserved with proper protocol and permission.

APPROACHING ORAL HISTORY

The best oral historians, whether reporters or academic researchers with a topical interest, tend to be scholars who have carefully prepared, researched a particular subject area, and have specific outlined questions for their interview subject. They come to the interview familiar with the relevant and available evidence on a topic and with the responsibilities and OHA standards, as mentioned—all providing the general framework for guiding subjective interviewers' conduct, such as the applications of the source material.[10]

---

[10] See James Hoopes, *Oral History: An Introduction for Students* (Chapel Hill: University of North Carolina Press, 1979); Michael Frisch, *A Shared Authority: Essays on the Craft and Meaning of Oral and Public History* (Albany: State University of New York Press, 1990).

The process of seeking an oral history interview begins with an explanation to the interviewee of how the information will be used (e.g., in scholarly articles, books, press reviews, films,). In the interest of self-disclosure and to avoid future problems, the scholar is wise to indicate a broad use of the information from the interview and have the interviewee sign a release form agreeing to the most probable uses. Information originally intended for a book or another scholarly project may, for example, provide substance for a documentary. Disclosure sets the stage and avoids confusion or any potential bad feelings. Of course, ends vary considerably for different researchers, but OHA standards make it crystal clear for those involved that, while motivations and goals differ, the explanation of objectives to those potential subjects remains of constant importance. They reinforce a level of social responsibility on the part of the researcher that must pervade the entire enterprise even though the spirit of the various inquiries may vary considerably. As researchers start their approach to an interview subject, disclosure is not only important for organizational and legal purposes, but in developing compatibility and trust with the subject.

The long-term aspirations of the oral historian guide performance when it comes to organizing research projects. In preparing for the oral history interview, the researcher investigates secondary sources and primary evidence. For example, in *Television in America* and *Indelible Images,* contributing authors focused first on pioneering stations, documents, and individuals contributing to their success.[11] They examined preliminary internal documents such as station files, program schedules, films, tapes, photos, promotional brochures, print advertising, rate cards, and sales letters, as well as feature stories, biographical profiles, and FCC documents—all before the interviews began. Researchers also investigated the background and experience of the people who played important roles in key areas such as personnel, programming, production, promotion, management, and overall station development. The research of these documents prepared the authors so that they were then informed enough in reaching out for the interviewees' personal recollections. This is the basis for the oral history interview.

---

[11] Michael D. Murray and Donald G. Godfrey, eds., *Television in America: Local Station History from across the Nation* (Ames: Iowa State University Press, 1997); Mary E. Beadle and Michael D. Murray, eds., *Indelible Images: Women of Local Television* (Ames: Iowa State University Press, 2001).

PREPARING FOR THE ORAL HISTORY INTERVIEW

In the opening phases of preparation prior to the interview, you should correspond with the interviewee and explain your key interests. Speak to friends who have worked with and for your subject and alert them of your interest in an oral history interview. These will lead to other sources. For example, if Tom Brokaw is your subject, you will find that Jim Upshaw, a professor at the University of Utah, contributed a profile about his former employer for the topic "NBC News" in the *Encyclopedia of TV News.*[12] These discoveries lead to additional interviews as well as preparation and verification opportunities.[13]

Interviewers must establish a rapport with the subject and, at times, must convince the subject that the project would benefit from their perceptions, judgments, and interpretations. Assure them that they can provide further understanding as they fit into a broader historical picture. Let your interviewee feel they have control, even in some aspects of disclosure. If this is to become part of an archive, tell them where and how access will be provided. Most major archives and sources try to make material available without restriction, but controls can be put in place, if the interviewee desires. Most interviewees will be flattered at the prospect of preserving their life story.[14]

---

[12] James Upshaw, "Tom Brokaw," in *Encyclopedia of Television News,* ed. Michael D. Murray (Phoenix, AZ: Oryx Press, 1999).

[13] See additional examples in Michael D. Murray, "And That's the Way He Is: Interview with Walter Cronkite," in *The Political Performers* (New York: Praeger, 1994), 230. See also David Schoenbrun's comments about "Murrow's Boys," in University of Maryland Broadcast Pioneers Oral History Project, May 30, 1974; Stanley Cloud and Lynne Olson, *The Murrow Boys* (Boston, MA: Houghton Mifflin, 1996), 410; Joel Connelly, "Walter Cronkite Pontificates on Trends in TV News Today," *St. Louis Post-Dispatch,* May 15, 1998, Editorial sec., 8; Joe Wershba, "The Broadcaster and the Senator," undated manuscript, later portion published as "Murrow vs. McCarthy: 'See It Now,'" *New York Times Magazine,* March 4, 1979.

[14] For other oral history interviews by the author, see Michael D. Murray, "End of an Era at CBS: A Conversation with Bill Leonard," *American Journalism* 8, no. 1 (1991): 46–62; "Creating a Tradition in TV News: A Conversation with David Brinkley," *Journalism History* 21, no. 4 (1995): 164–69; "The World of Change in TV News: A Conversation with Garrick Utley," *American Journalism* 14, no. 2 (1997): 223–30; and "Reporting Histories' First Draft: A Conversation with Byron Pitts," *Television Quarterly* 33, no. 4 (2003): 26–33.

Experienced interviewers suggest that preparation for an oral history interview begins with the collection of potential questions as one of the first and most logical steps in the information-gathering process. But they also acknowledge that the process actually starts much earlier. At the very least, an adept interviewer will attempt to locate and read all available biographical material on their source. They will also attempt to read all relevant material under their source's authorship or, in the case of a broadcast, under their supervision. Nothing is more embarrassing to an interviewer than to have a source say they have covered similar territory in a book or article they may have published years before. If the interviewee has held an important position for any length of time, it is likely they have addressed important issues before. The more important the position, the more likely that material has been covered again and again. It is also critical to review news clips from key periodicals, especially those relating to the subject matter as well as any prior interviews.

In some cases, when the source has not shared information previously, it is worth asking whether there are any special areas or questions the source might consider out-of-bounds or off-limits. In many instances when dealing with national and even local broadcasters, family-related and other personal issues are left alone due to privacy concerns. The oral historian is wise to approach questions of privacy with delicate preparation and presentation. It is important to develop a trusting relationship before approaching issues that may be difficult to discuss. The oral history interview is not the time for an ambush. Offer to secure the information once the interview is transcribed with "permission only access," to be directed by the interviewee. This is a common procedure in many archives.

Preparation means that an interviewer is more likely to be familiar with the things their source enjoys talking about. This leads to opportunities that may otherwise be missed and it adds an important dimension to the results of the interview itself. For example, a reference to a previous interview can be a stepping-off point, even when conducted for a national publication or broadcast as opposed to an oral history interview.

As a prelude to any oral history interview with someone of stature, Tom Brokaw, for example, one must gather and read all of the books, newspaper clippings, and magazine articles about NBC News including Brokaw's own widely accepted books.[15] Rereviewing questions set out by the Oral History

---

[15] Michael D. Murray, "A Passion for Politics: A Conversation with Tom Brokaw," *American Journalism* 17, no. 3 (2000): 109–17. Brokaw quotes are from this source.

Association is a good starting point, but the questions may be shopworn, so the researcher must be prepared for the specific subject material interview and develop independent as well as OHA questions.

The objective of preparation is to fill gaps as opposed to duplicating what is already known and ultimately to provide a complement to material available elsewhere, including previous oral history interviews. For interviewing people who have no celebrity status, the researcher may review family histories, local histories, scrapbooks, photo collections, and visit with others who knew or worked with the interview subject. During any preliminary interview, discussions should be kept on the broader scope of the subject, and targeted toward developing a relationship with the interviewer. The researcher has to be careful that the preliminary interview doesn't turn into the interview.

Another related strategy found very helpful in preparing for interviews, especially while working on local history projects, is to use photo albums as a source of ideas in helping to jog memories related to particular events. A word of caution—it is not a good idea to review the family photo album with the interviewee before the interview, because you're likely to be asking the same questions and the second response is going to be limited by that preparatory interview, which likely was not recorded. While working on a station history for Metromedia in 1987, a series of oral history interviews was conducted with station pioneers, most of whom had remained long-term employees from days of previous ownership by the Pulitzer Publishing Company. Upon conducting preliminary and phone interviews, it was discovered that most of the sources had retained photos of themselves from important station "firsts." These were covered for posterity and broadcast at a time when independent photographers often documented important big-city events for the multitude of newspapers for instances in which staff photographers may have missed a big story. In some instances, the station employees had also been functioning in another role. In the early era of this particular station, it was usual for a reporter to have been covering a big story for both radio and television, or, in some cases of very wide-ranging or national importance, for both the local affiliate station and the parent network. In some of those instances, national figures appear to reinforce the importance of the event and anecdotes regarding their behavior were among some of the most vivid memories. In a number of instances, oral history has been effectively employed to supplement the record remaining from the beginnings of the visual medium. As this book is being prepared, the ranks of the pioneers of television are starting to thin considerably. Few remaining pioneers are still active in the field.

There is some controversy about the value of conducting preinterviews in preparation for the interview. Preinterviews, even by telephone, can form the basis for a more in-depth interaction and also provide something of an index or outline for what may follow. This approach may well determine the extent of future access and the level of candor an interviewer may win from an important source. The best approach to the actual preinterview focuses on your intentions—disclosure. Additional questions may include the closed, short, pointed queries to elicit specific answers. It is sometimes true, however, that if a source is short on answers at the outset of an interview, the prospects for a more extended interview may increase more so a level of flexibility allowing for elaboration may sometimes help to further the cause. The preinterview can also detract from the more substantive interview if the same questions are posed.

On some occasions a source will express an unwillingness to go forward with publication of an interview. Once an interview transcription is complete, sources sometimes express unhappiness or reluctance with the outcome, saying they did not express themselves adequately. When that happens, it is best to provide the subject with the opportunity to make a second interview, clarifying any parts desired. These can easily be inserted into the transcript or transcribed as a second interview. In the case of some interview sources and correspondence, an unhappy beginning can actually lead to treasure later on. The bad experience simply serves as what might be called "the shake-down" cruise to test the honesty of the process and a willingness to take the time to get things right.

If there are rough spots or tough questions that one expects may elicit a delicate response it is obviously better to hold those questions until other important material is gathered. If a single oral history interview relies heavily on the recollections of experienced individuals with considerable tenure in a leadership position, it would also be worth preparing some questions to elicit aspects of the "big picture" to demonstrate your acknowledgment of the difficulty of the task at hand. Keep a file and copious notes on the interview, including the setting—if conducted at a workplace location, office, or residence. These can be helpful, just as it would in preparing a feature story, biographical sketch, or work-related profile. Office photos, evidence of organizational awards and recognition and, of course, diplomas, tell an important story about a person and can be used as a jumping-off point for additional questions or a rallying point about particular historical issues or events. Frequently, an editorial cartoon or a framed letter from an important source will jog memories or generate details useful to an interviewer. Preparation puts the interviewer on a par with the interviewee.

CONDUCTING THE INTERVIEW

Preparation accomplished—you are now ready for the day of the interview. First, take polite control of the physical environment. The researcher should place him or herself in a position where two people can converse easily, eye-to-eye. It is most certainly advantageous to have a quiet space where telephones, fans, air conditioners and, in general, the ambient noise is minimal. Celebrity interviewees are used to this controlled situation, but those who've not been under the lights or the physical presence of recording equipment may find it intimidating, and they have to be comfortable before they'll be open to your questions.

Second, put your interviewee at ease. Help her or him remain calm and comfortable. You'll likely be conducting the interview in their home or office, so make only those physical arrangements that facilitate the interviewee and be sure your subject is as comfortable as your equipment—remember your priorities at this stage of the arrangement.

Third, conduct the interview with no one else in the room. Again in celebrity interviews it is easy to maintain a focus, but in the most common situations there may be loved ones nearby and it is easy for the interview to become a dialogue, as that extra person begins to correct the memory of the interviewee. Do another interview with that third person, if it is desired, but keep oral histories one-on-one.

Finally, be casual about the equipment. Explain how you'll be using it and as you place the microphone on your subject start with some of the trivial questions that will assist in warming up and comforting the interviewee. On the practical side, it is important to check all video and audio equipment to insure that it is in proper working order. This is an opportunity to acquire specific information regarding things like birth dates, hometowns, and so forth, while you are getting microphone checkups and noting the time codes or counter on the recording machine. Of course, while you start with the equipment, you also make preparations for taking copious notes during the interview as a means of keeping on top of key points or contradictions.

Jotting down ideas during the interview—taking those copious notes, can be very helpful as a means of keeping track of important details you want to ask about later. This is a critical concept—listen, ask follow-up questions later, do not interrupt your interviewee's response. You can get the interviewee to repeat or spell out names, or clarify a location *after* you've covered the main points. The interviewer must also be flexible in the presentation of the question organization and approach, following the mind of the interviewee. Although you may have your questions nicely developed in chronological order, the interviewee will establish the order from his or her mind. And remember, it is their mind you are trying to access. So, jot down those notes, ask those follow-up questions later, listen, and let the interview flow.

Nothing is more important in conducting the interview than the self-discipline. It requires you to honestly *listen* to your interviewee. As you asked those open-ended questions, consider what happens in the mind of your subject. The question is posed, he or she thinks about the appropriate response, this pause between your question and the response may be minimal or a few seconds. But what happens is that your subject immediately formulates an intrapersonal response. Think of it as a circle, the question is posed at the apex of the circle, the mind goes completely around the circle, to the point of where the question began. Then the interviewee begins to verbalize this completed thought, and it is not complete until the interviewee has returned to the apex of the question. Now, if the interviewer interrupts before the respondent has completed the full-circle thought, then only a portion of the mind has been recorded.

Best advise for conducting an interview, "shut-up and listen."

PROCESSING THE INTERVIEW

The challenge of processing the interview begins in preparation, in the preinterview disclosure discussions where releases were signed and vital information—names (with correct spelling), contact information (for follow-up), and permissions for use. The process continues during the interview as you prepare and label tapes for transcription. Careful labeling with names, dates, time, tape numbers, and so forth are essential elements for preparation and transcribing.

An oral history interview is a written transcript—transcribed verbatim. The transcript is edited with a great deal of care to conform to the written word—generally meaning the insertion of periods, paragraph indentations, and so on—denoting conversational structure. It does not include any cutting or pasting of these same words, sentences, and paragraphs. A heavily edited transcript becomes only a secondary source.

The OHA recommends preservation of both the recording and the transcript. Many historians have found local universities, libraries, archives, and so forth, more than anxious to accept the recordings as a part of their archives. Such placement enhances the value of the interview as it can be cited as in a repository and available for future research.

CRITICISM OF ORAL HISTORY'S EVIDENCE

The most critical concerns about the evidence value of an oral history interview relate to failed memory, closeness to the subject, attempts to distort the historic record to inflate one's own reputation, and time/space influence on the memory. First is dealing with failed memory. In preliminary preparation as you establish a rapport with the subject, you're going to make a critical judgment: Is the mind of the interviewee clear and crisp, will it elicit an accurate memory? If the subject is experiencing an illness or has been drinking, postponing the interview may be advisable. If "grandma" is forgetful, but "sometimes she still remembers," this too, may be a flag of concern. Some oral history subjects are considerably better at relating detailed stories than are others. This is a judgment call.

The second concern is the interviewee's closeness to the subject. The memory provided by interviewees will naturally carry a personal bias. Perception is their reality—not necessarily historical truth. You are interviewing them because they were close to an event, because they experienced something unique, made specific contributions, and so forth. Because they were close to the subject, so they will have distinct points of view, which must be later verified by additional research. If their story is proven to be true, the oral history provides color in manuscript narrative, as well as primary documentation. If the story is opposed, the researcher must examine all the evidence, and differing points of view have to be described and authenticated.

Another concern is a purposeful or boastful distortion of history. Persons closest to an event often have the greatest stake in the interpretation of its significance and their role in it. Those closest to the scene or situation are viewed as most likely to convey an accurate rendering of the event. They also are most likely to have a particular point of view that may or may not be accurate. A celebrity's ego may significantly distort influential statements and judgment—for purposes of promotion, not history.

Finally, the time and place criticism is perhaps most significant. Distance a memory from the event, by time and place, and other influences will affect recall. In other words, an interview conducted immediately after the event is likely to produce more accurate information. Insert *time* between the event and the interview and a different story may be recalled, because between the time of the event and the interview, there are many influences that may have crept into the experiences of the interviewee and thus influence the response. For example, differing cultures have broad, common-based experiences that often permeate the oral histories of the culture—someone of Jewish heritage has an exodus story; someone of Mormon heritage has a westward movement story that includes an encounter with Native Americans; similarly African Americans and Hispanics have unique and common experiences that all find their way into personal history—these constitute wonderful folklore, but not necessarily historical fact. Nowhere are the rules of evidence and verification more important than in cross-checking the oral history record.[16]

Finally, in terms of evidentiary requirements there are attempts to take credit where credit may not be due. For example, a "first" or an "exclusive" can become especially troublesome in a field of broadcasting where large egos and bragging rights interfere with historical accuracy. It can become confusing when differing sources make the same claim. At the national level a good number of broadcast journalists have made a name for themselves by claiming "exclusive" interviews, sometimes in the hope of gaining added exposure by virtue of ties to a hot news story. Such claims in history have to be supported by the evidence, not just the memory.

CONCLUSION

The oral history method has grown in popularity over the years since World War II and the inception of portable audio and video recorder. It has grown from a news reporting technique, to a method for recording individual family history, and central to the historiographical methods for obtaining heretofore unavailable evidence. It is all about capturing the images of the mind.

The Oral History Association is the professional organization providing an overall direction and orientation for the discipline. Their guidelines direct the differing stages of the interview process and the considerations regarding

---

[16] See Paul Thompson, *The Voice of the Past: Oral History,* 2nd. ed. (New York: Oxford University Press, 1988); Ronald J. Grele, ed., *Envelopes of Sound: The Art of Oral History,* rev. ed. (Westport, CT: Meckler, 1990).

disclosure, and they even provide suggested questions for the interview itself. These directives are a starting point.

The parallels between news reporting and oral history interviewing are significant. Both utilize similar questioning techniques. The key difference in the interview itself being that the oral historian has time to listen to the complete response, which will generally last much longer in an oral history setting than under the glaring lights of the news camera. It is important to note that perhaps a key difference between a news and an oral history interview is the handling of the sources. A news reporter's notes or editing recordings do not constitute the best oral history. Oral history interviews are transcribed verbatim and placed in a repository for future research.

Establishing a relationship with a desired interviewee is essential to the success of any interview. The interviewee must feel comfortable and at ease in your approach and in relation to your questions. Preparation is the key to the relationship and the interview itself. Preparation for the interview begins with a review of the literature, the creation of an outline list of questions. Preparation puts the interviewer on a common ground with the interviewee. Conducting the actual interview is really about one word—listening. The historian who interrupts the interviewee loses a portion of thought, and thus a portion of history. Finally, the oral history interview produces a verbatim transcript. Heavily edited, partial notes are only secondary sources of evidence.

The critics of the oral history method point to failed memories, distortions, and time and space considerations to suggest that oral history is not the best evidence. This criticism requires the researcher to verify the oral history facts through collaborative interviews and with additional evidence.

Oral history at its best provides synergistic evidence that can add color and demonstration to the collection of facts within any given historical account.

4

Visual Evidence

Mary E. Beadle
John Carol University

"The camera doesn't lie," is an old saying that seemed to have considerable truth for many years. Many people consider still that "Seeing is believing," another popular maxim—whether in motion or in still photography, people believe what they see.[1] Certainly for the historian, the knowledge of the past 150 years has been enriched greatly by the collection of visual records that have survived. These collections provide life, color, and awe to our understanding of the past. Are these perceptions accurate?

Still pictures have been used to document life since the middle of the nineteenth century. Fortunately, many of these photographs are still available to the historian. One example is the Civil War photographs of Matthew Brady, which are viewed as so significant that a print made directly from one of his negatives is considered to be quite valuable. The development of the motion picture, at the end of the nineteenth century, increased our ability to understand and interpret events. This was enhanced further by the invention of videotape in the 1950s. Now, in the early portion of the twenty-first century, we are experiencing the rapid shift to digital media, including the transfer of many historical pictures to that form.

The historian must be able to interpret visual evidence based on only a small slice of reality—a single photograph, a piece of film, or a program. To analyze visual evidence effectively, the researcher needs to understand the technology of still photography, film, and video and how an image can be

---

[1] Alex Jones, exec. dir., *Seeing Is Believing: How Can You Tell What's Real?* (Washington, DC: Newseum, 1997), videocassette. 17 min.

modified (as well as being able to consider the other influences that impact the interpretation of the image). What influenced the photographer to take the picture? What limitations were there? What choices were there in capturing reality? What images were not taken? Were the images modified? How and why?

The purpose of this chapter is to address these questions and aid the historical scholar in interpreting the growing collections of visual evidence. First, a brief history and technology of still photography, motion-picture film, and videotape will place the different technologies in context. Second, a discussion follows on the considerations of the language used in the visual media, with examples drawn from film and television. That section includes a discussion on how the directors' and producers' choices influence the audience's perception. Third, a discussion of editing introduces the historical scholar to the various treatments in visual storytelling. Understanding these processes is critical when assessing the visual evidence and interpreting the meaning conveyed by any series of visual images. Finally, the chapter concludes with an exploration of the various forms of visual modifications that occur and discusses interpreting the visual in history, within the context of ethical concerns as they apply to nonfiction photographs.

THE HISTORY AND TECHNOLOGY OF PHOTOGRAPHY

Elements of photography can be traced back to the ancient Greeks. The precursor device, the camera obscura or dark room, was described by Leonardo Da Vinci and detailed by Giambattista della Porta by 1550. Light passing through a small opening creates an image on the surface on which it falls. This became known as the pinhole effect. Rooms converted to be used as a camera obscura ranged in size from 8 or 10 feet or more on a side. The small rooms were first used for the novelty of the image alone. Later, performances were held outside for the enjoyment of those inside. At the other extreme, were tabletop devices where one surface was replaced by glass or tissue paper and the image viewed from under a dark cover. These were used by artists to get the perspective of a scene correct. It has been suggested that some of the old masters may have used them.

The concept of recording an image permanently on some solid material did not develop rapidly and experimenters labored for many years before a workable system of photography was developed. They struggled with such problems as insensitive material that required much longer exposures than they perceived, images that came out negative (which were considered use-less), and the problem of making the medium insensitive to light after the exposure, thus making the picture permanent.

Officially, credit for photography goes to Louis Daguerre (recognized by the French Academy), but he drew heavily from others including his deceased partner Joseph Niepce. In 1839, in Paris, Daguerre galvanized silver onto a copper plate and then exposed it to iodine vapors in a closed box, creating light-sensitive silver-iodide. Early exposures took as much as 30 minutes. The exposed plate was developed with mercury vapor and sealed behind glass to protect the fragile image. Some artists tinted the pictures before they were sealed. The daguerreotype, as they were known, yielded only a single image, but was a success, as many people wanted to have and leave behind a true image of themselves. Only the rich had been able to afford paintings and the photograph was much more realistic. Large numbers of people in Europe and America rushed to have their pictures taken and many businesses sprang up. Today, daguerreotypes are quite valuable.[2]

At the same time in England, William Fox Talbot also was working on photographic processes. On hearing of Daguerre's success, he rushed his own efforts, which produced a second approach: first, providing a simple way to make pictures permanent and, second, inventing a way to make more than one copy. Rather than copper, Talbot used paper as the medium for his chemi-cals. His process yielded a negative, but he remedied this by projecting light through the first image onto a second piece of paper, resulting in a positive pic-ture. This printing process is the basis of most of the duplicate photographs that have existed since that time.

Wet-Plate Process

The next significant development in photography came in 1851 after Da-guerre's discovery. Frederick Archer produced a new process that yielded high-quality pictures. The material was known as collodion and caused the chemi-cals to stick firmly to glass. (The term is derived from the Greek word "kolla" which means glue.) With glass as the film carrier there was no "texture" prob-lem created as there was with paper, so the pictures were excellent and could be printed endlessly. However, the chemistry was such that the "film" had to be made just before it was used and be quickly processed thereafter. This was

---

[2] Beaumont Newhall, *The Daguerreotype in America*, 3rd ed. (New York: Dover, 1976).

known as the "wet-plate process" because the film lost sensitivity when it dried. It resulted in photographers in the field traveling with wagons on which they had built a darkroom, so that the film could be made, the picture exposed, and then it was developed very quickly. They traveled, not only with their darkrooms, but also with all the chemicals and boxes of sheets of glass. It was cumbersome, but the results were excellent, so it was widely used. It is quite amazing to consider that photographers, using this process, climbed mountains, traveled to the polar regions, and went just about any other place imaginable, taking all their materials with them.[3]

Whole books of photographs from this era are available which highlight the quality work that was done 150 years ago. The wet-plate process was used for the next 30 years and is responsible for the many pictures we have from the Civil War. The wet-plate process remained as the primary system until 1878 when chemistry advanced, so that the plates could be made in advance and didn't need to be processed immediately. This was known as the dry-plate process and, for the first time, a photographer could buy a box of plates that were ready to shoot and could be processed when it was convenient.[4]

Other Methods of Printing

Daguerreotypes and wet plates were relatively expensive and the market for them was somewhat limited. A second approach, also invented by Archer, was the ambrotype, which was based on the discovery that if a wet plate was slightly underexposed, bleached with acid, and then placed against black velvet, the negative image would appear to change to positive. These images were mounted in small cases and were quite popular. Like the daguerreotype, each image was unique. The tintype, which was similar to the ambrotype process, consisted of a sheet of metal painted black with collodion that was poured on it. The resulting pictures were fairly good, although no copies could be made. The major factor was they were cheap and easy to produce and ordinary people rushed to have their pictures taken. Many tintypes have survived and collections of them are common.[5]

---

[3] Michel Frizot, ed., *The New History of Photography* (Köln, Germany: Könemann, 1998).

[4] Ibid.; O. Henry Mace, *Collector's Guide to Early Photographs* (Radnor, PA: Wallace-Homestead, 1990).

[5] Newhall, *Daguerreotype in America;* Mace, *Collector's Guide.*

The third development was the sudden popularity of photographs used for what we might think of as business cards. With the proper manners of the era, it was common to call on someone's home and then leave a business card instead of speaking with the homeowner. The result was the carte de visite, French for "visit card" which was essentially a photograph of the visitor. These, and a slightly larger version called cabinet cards, remained popular through much of the later 1800s. These too were based on collodion. Their popularity began in France where Napoleon is supposed to have sent photographs of himself to the Austrians he was about to meet in battle.[6]

The Halftone Process

After 40 years of photography, no simple process for including them on the printed page existed. The most common approach was the wood cut which was really quite remarkable. Skilled artisans would create mirror images of a scene by carving them into the surface of a wooden block. The block would then be loaded into the press along with the type and the drawing would be printed on the page. These carvers had great talent for many of the reproductions were outstanding. It was common for them to work from a photograph, particularly when preparing pictures of some person. They also worked from drawings made by sketch artists who often covered events. These artists could be considered the earliest photojournalists.

Finally, in 1880 the halftone process was developed. In this process, pictures were rephotographed through a screen that broke the picture up into thousands of tiny dots. In a part of the picture that was dark, the dots would be closer together and sometime start to merge. In lighter areas, the dots would be smaller and further apart and, in white areas, they were nonexistent. Newspapers did not rush to use this process, and it was not until 1900, when the *Illustrated American* began publication, that emphasis was put on pictures for the first time.

Flash: A Need for Light

For many years photographers used flash powder to provide light in dimly lit areas. It might best be described as low-grade dynamite. A handful of the powder was placed on a T-shaped platform and held in the air. The shutter was

---

[6] Mace, *Collector's Guide.*

opened and the powder ignited. It went off with a flash of light and a significant bang. Eventually the powder came packaged in premeasured sizes, but it still resulted in some injuries and blackened faces. It remained the primary source of photographic light for about 40 years.

After the first World War, the flashbulb was developed. This was a glass bulb containing some flammable magnesium. Each bulb was good for one flash and varied in size from little bigger than a pencil eraser to monsters nearly 6 inches across. The bigger the bulb the more light it emitted and the larger the area which could be photographed. Photographers went into the field with as many as they could stuff in their pockets. For most news work, the bulb was about the size of a plum. Flashbulbs were the primary source of portable, photographic light until the 1960s. At first they were fired separately from the camera, as was flash powder, but gradually a means of synchronizing the flash with the opening of the shutter was developed and the bulbs became part of the camera.

The third step in the evolution of flash was the electronic system invented by Harold Edgarton in the 1930s. Edgarton was a scientist who needed a means of taking high speed pictures in scientific experiments with rapidly moving objects. He developed a flash tube that could be repeatedly fired. The flash was very bright and extremely brief, at least 1/1000 of a second and in some cases as fast as 1/40,000 of a second. He produced unheard of pictures such as a bullet piercing a playing card. He modified the system so it could flash repeatedly in rapid succession to show various stages of the same brief event. He did not originally see the potential, but as photographers saw examples of his work they began clamoring for some of the equipment. As technology progressed, the rather cumbersome system got smaller and smaller until the tiny units we see built into cameras today were developed.

Cameras and Equipment

During the first hundred years of photography, enlarging was essentially nonexistent. To obtain large pictures, the principle explained by Della Porta's finding that the distance from the pinhole to the back wall determined the size of the picture was used. The need for large pictures resulted in large cameras to hold large sheets of glass. Some were more than 18 inches on a side. Small cameras, such as the Kodak Brownies, resulted in pictures that were only 1½ to 2 inches on a side. Even the box cameras came in sizes, some nearly 10 inches across. By 1920 enlarging was becoming established and cameras began to shrink, although the standard newspaper photographer's camera (usually a Speed Graphic) remained large until about 1960. These used film that was 4 x 5 inches. This size could be printed directly into the paper, without enlarging, saving time.

One of the major factors in both smaller cameras and enlarging was the improvement of the lenses. The clarity of the glass improved, which gave greater resolution. Resolution is the ability to make detail appear sharp and clear. With good resolution in the negatives and in the glass of the enlarger, pictures can be made larger from small negatives.

In the first two-thirds of the twentieth century, cameras came in many sizes with varying lens qualities. Toward the end of the century, most of these disappeared with the primary survivor being the 35 millimeter (mm) camera. The 35mm refers to the width of the film it uses. The first 35mm cameras were developed in Germany by the Leitz Optical Company, famous for their Leica cameras ever since. As the lenses improved, they also became more versatile. This included developing the wide-angle lens, which could incorporate more into a picture, and the telephoto lens, which could take pictures from a great distance.

Another area of development was the film itself. The first film, the daguerreotype, demanded long exposures and could not be reproduced. The wet plate still needed long exposures to the light but, though cumbersome, could produce copies. The dry plate was a bit more sensitive to light and much easier to use. George Eastman's roll film (1886) was still easier to use and was sensitive enough that shutters were needed to control the amount of light reaching the film. Previously, lenses used caps that were removed when an exposure was to be made. By today's standards, film remained relatively insensitive until after World War II, when new technology resulted in film that needed much less light to take good pictures. Additionally, during this whole period, the resolution of the film improved so that enlargements could be made that retained their clear images. Work on film with greater sensitivity and higher resolution continues today.

Digital Photography

The most important advance in photography in the 1990s was the development of digital photography. Digital photography combines elements of film photography and computer imaging. Most digital cameras use a charged-coupled device (CCD) that is sensitive to light. The chip reacts to the strength of light and translates that into a numeric equivalent. The light also is passed through red, green, and blue filters (RGB) to determine the color. When the various numbers are combined, software determines a specific color for each segment (numeral) of the picture. After a CCD chip creates an image, the data is sent to another chip in the camera that converts the data into the format for compressing graphics like JPEG (named for the Joint Photographic Experts Group, the organization that developed this format). The camera stores this data in its internal memory. In most cameras, this takes a few seconds so you can't keep clicking like you can with a film camera. These images can be downloaded into a computer and then, using additional software programs such as Photoshop (see following section), the images can be manipulated. Although many people consider the digital photograph superior to film, in digital photography (except in very expensive cameras) the light still has to be strong. In traditional photography, film can have higher sensitivity, so the use of various types of film means these operate in a greater range of light levels.

SOCIAL IMPACT OF PHOTOGRAPHY

Since the beginning of photography, visual evidence was used to record history and effect social change in America. Although some pictures were made of the Crimean War in the 1850s, photojournalism probably started with Matthew Brady and the Civil War. Brady was a portrait photographer in Washington. Abraham Lincoln went to Brady for a campaign photo, which turned out well and Lincoln credited it with being one of the things which got him elected. He and Brady became friends and when the Civil War started, Brady asked President Lincoln's permission to photograph the war. The President gave him a pass which got him onto the various battlefields.

Using the wet-plate process, Brady began covering what activities he could. Because of the film's low sensitivity, action shots were not possible, so they took many posed pictures of the soldiers and the dead on the fields after the battles. Though this seems limited, it provides us with a record of the war. Brady invested his own money into the pictures, but the destruction and loss of life were so great that, after the war, no one was interested in his pictures until many years later.

William H. Jackson traveled West and took many landscape pictures of the mountains and other sights that were totally unknown to Easterners. His work included photographs of Yellowstone National Park. When Congress was considering establishing a National Park to protect this unique environment, an exhibit of Jackson's photographs was set up in a nearby room. Land speculators were already lobbying to defeat the park concept, but the bill passed. Many gave Jackson's exhibit credit for the success—which led to our national park system.

Francis Benjamin Johnson, one of the first woman photographers, did the first picture story, on Hampton Institute, a school for Blacks. Not only was it a unique way to tell a story, but it was the first time Blacks had been pictured as well dressed and studying science and the arts. Additionally, Johnson discovered the concept called the *third effect.* This is when two pictures are put side by side. Each picture has its own "meaning" or subject, but the two together can produce a joint meaning as well (also see section on juxtaposition).

In the 1880s Jacob Riis was an immigrant journalist who came to America in the flood of immigrants of the late 1800s. When he found work as a journalist, he set about trying to do something about the terrible conditions in which the immigrants were living. About this time photographic flash powder was developed. Riis combined his desire to tell the story of the suffering of the immigrants with the invention of the photographic flash and began photographing the conditions, such as the "flop houses," where men paid 5 cents per night for a little space in a cellar or unheated building so they would not have to sleep on the streets. Riis published a book, *How the Other Half Lives,* which combined narrative and pictures about the subject.[7] The book had considerable impact and it did lead to the development of some assistance and effort to improve conditions.

Another social problem that photography influenced was child labor. In 1909, Lewis Hine, a schoolteacher and photographer, was employed by a group trying to establish better laws regarding child labor. Gradually he gathered shots of all sorts of situations, including boys, covered with coal dust, who spent their days picking pieces of rock from the coal that was coming up out of the mine. When the *National Child Labor Laws* were passed, Hine's photographs were credited as one of the major factors in convincing Congress to take action. Hine also became interested in the plight of the immigrants that still were coming to the United States by the thousands. He continued Riis's work by photographing these people and the conditions in which they lived.

---

[7] Jacob Riis, *How the Other Half Lives: Studies among the Tenements of New York* (New York: Charles Scribner's Sons, 1890); online ed., http://www.yale.edu/amstud/ inforev/riis/title.html; paperback ed., Sam Warner, ed. (London: Penguin Books, 1997).

During the 1930s the Farm Security Administration (FSA) was interested in recording the effects of the drought and depression in the west central part of the United States. The head of the FSA, Roy Stryker, felt that the disaster should be recorded and pictures used to convince Congress to provide more help. He hired a group of young photojournalists to travel the country and record what was happening. Unknown at the time, many of them became famous. Perhaps the best know was Dorothea Lange. Other leading photographers were Arthur Rothstein, Walker Evans, and Ben Shahn. All produced outstanding works that are highly regarded today. These photographers took hundreds of powerful pictures which recorded the era and did contribute to Congress passing aid bills. To some extent, today's welfare system can be traced to the work of these photojournalists.

The FSA also made motion pictures to demonstrate the power of the dust storms on people and the land. *The Plow That Broke the Plains* is one of the more famous films that resulted from this decision. Produced and edited by Pare Lorentz, the power in this film is due, in part, to Lorentz's editing technique—he edited with the music, not separate from the music. The music, which was composed by Virgil Thomson, used simple folk melodies and religious anthems and themes to reflect both good and bad times on the plains. "This approach to editing would account for the expressive power and unity that are held responsible for much of the artistic sense of Lorentz's films."[8] Noted historian Erik Barnouw explained that in this film "editing and composing became a unified process."[9] This film is a good example of the power that music has in shaping perceptions of the visual images.

More recently, the course of history probably was influenced by the powerful pictures, both still and motion, that came from the Vietnam War. Huynh Cong Ut's picture of a naked young girl screaming as she flees a napalm attack and the summary execution of a spy, photographed by Eddie Adams, are probably foremost among them.

Such pictures provide powerful reminders of social problems and must be considered in the context of the previous discussion. Did Dorothea Lange pose the people? Was this evidence of the problems or did the photographers manipulate the scene prior to taking the shot? Did they manipulate the

---

[8] Robert Snyder, *Pare Lorentz and the Documentary Film* (Reno: University of Nevada Press, 1994), 35.

[9] Erik Barnouw, *Documentary: A History of the Non-fiction Film,* 2nd ed. (New York: Oxford University Press, 1993), 117.

pictures after taking the photo? These questions must concern the historian when looking at visual evidence for proof/understanding of past events, because visual evidence does have the power to change the perceptions of people about events.

THE HISTORY AND TECHNOLOGY OF CINEMA

The development of moving images (cinema) parallels the development of still images (photography). Both trace their history back to the camera obscura and the magic lantern. The idea of projecting a series of individual images so they would appear to be moving was first proposed by Peter Mark Roget in 1824. Roget's idea, known as the Law of Persistence of Vision, stated that the human eye retains an image for a fraction of a second so it is possible to pass individual images rapidly before the eye so they overlap, which gives the impression of movement. Simple animation devices quickly were invented to prove this idea. Eventually the animation devices and the magic lantern machines were combined to project animated sequences on a wall. The work of Niepce, Daguerre, and Fox Talbot laid the groundwork for moving pictures as well as still photography. What was needed was a camera that would produce a series of photographs and a means of rapidly projecting the series of photographs.

Technology Provides a Moving Image

In 1873, Eadweard Muybridge set up a series of 12 cameras to photograph a running horse thereby creating in a film of the racing horse. In 1884, Etienne-Jules Marey invented a photographic gun that exposed 12 pictures on a revolving circular glass plate. In 1887, he was using Kodak film in his photographic gun and by 1888 he was using an electric motor to advance the film. In 1893, C. Francis Jenkins claimed to have invented the first motion-picture projector and took out a patent in the United States in January of 1894. Jenkins is also a pioneer in mechanical televison and the first American to produce a television picture.

Although Marey had shown the possibility of moving pictures and Jenkins had obtained a patent, it was Thomas Edison who produced the first workable motion-picture camera, the *kinetograph* and an individual viewing device called the *kinetoscope*. Edison also developed the use of perforated film with sprocket holes to pull the film through the camera. The machine was not easy to move since it was quite heavy. As a result, Edison filmed in a studio referred to as the Black Mariah, as some felt it looked like a hearse. Rather than project the film to a group, Edison used the kinetoscope to set up parlors, called peep-show parlors, where people could pay a penny to see about 1 minute of film.

While Edison was still working on his film system, in France, the Lumiere brothers developed a smaller camera that they could take outside. They had also developed a means of projecting film, holding the first public showing in 1895. Because of the camera's portability, the Lumieres began shooting events on location and may be considered as one of the founders of news and documentary film. However, early in film's history it also was recognized that the camera could be used for storytelling. Georges Melies in France and Edison in the United States developed the film narrative by connecting various scenes together. Melies produced the impressive *A Trip to the Moon* and an employee of Edison, Edwin Porter is credited with the first modern film with his *Great Train Robbery* in 1904. A decade later, D. W. Griffith advanced techniques using angles, camera movement, closeups, juxtaposition, and editing in his controversial *Birth of a Nation* (see section on visual language).

As film developed two uses evolved: the extension of film as photography and the use of film in theaters. Some films were used like early photographs to document real life. But, early in the development of film it was clear that the camera could be used for storytelling in a new way. First Edison, and then others, turned film storytelling into an entertainment business that led to the silent era and later to the film industry of today.

HISTORY AND TECHNOLOGY OF VIDEOGRAPHY

A third type of visual evidence used by a broadcast historian is videotape or videodisc. Saving moving images to tape was developed after World War II. In the 1950s Ampex developed a reel-to-reel, two-inch tape recorder that recorded sound and pictures. Like the early film cameras developed by Edison, these machines were quite large and could not be moved out of the studio environment. Prior to that, television programs that were saved using kine-scopes (film made directly from the camera tube) were shot on film or done live.

Magnetic-tape recording uses a plastic tape coated with particles of metal-lic oxide. Video and audio signals cause an electromagnet to pulse and this magnetizes the particles of oxide in a pattern related to the picture and sound. On playback, the tape passes a coil and the patterns are transformed into electrical signals that are then translated back to picture and sound. This is known as analog recording because the patterns on the tape are similar to the electrical patterns caused by the audio and video signals. In addition to the video and audio information, video recording also uses a series of synchronizing pulses. The purpose is to coordinate the operation of the sweep signal so that all receivers viewing a particular picture are coordinated. If sync pulses are missing, rolls, noise, and distorted pictures result.

The Ampex recording system magnetized the particles directly across the tape. Although it seems very different, television is actually a series of still pictures called frames, much the same as motion-picture film. Four magnetic heads were needed, each recording part of the video information for one frame. Thirty frames were needed for each one second of program. This resulted in long, heavy rolls of tape for each hour of program. Initially, prices for tape were in excess of 300 dollars per hour. This format was referred to as *quad scanning* (quadraplex or four-head) and is no longer in use.

In the 1970s, smaller portable cameras and recorders were developed making it possible to move outside of the television studio. To use a smaller roll of tape, a *helical scan* was developed. Although this system continued to use analog recording, the scanning system laid information down in a diagonal pattern. Since this took up less width, the size of tape was reduced to three-quarters of an inch and was put into a cassette. The helical scan is still used today on all analog tape. Various formats were developed for this new scanning system that used tape sizes from three-quarters of an inch to one-quarter of an inch.

In the 1980s, two methods of recording onto a videodisc were developed using analog technology. RCA developed a system that was similar to a phonograph record with a stylus that moved over grooves. Each disc was about 12 inches across. However, it failed to develop enough popularity to survive. The other system used a laser disc with a laser beam that read the information embedded in a plastic disc. Originally developed by MCA and Philips, Pioneer bought the system in 1982 and renamed it LaserDisc. Both systems originally were playback only. Today, videodiscs, or DVDs, use digital technology to record sound and moving pictures. Moving digital images record like digital photography, and each part of the image is scanned and encoded with a 0 or 1, similar to computers. The information is read by a laser. Digital video was first developed in 1986 by Panasonic, in a format known as Beta SP. Sony developed other digital formats including D-1 (1987), D-2 (1986), and D-3 (1991). Additionally, Sony developed digital Betacam in 1983. However, to prevent the proliferation of formats to interfere with commercial development, in 1995, manufacturers agreed on one standard format.[10]

UNDERSTANDING AND INTERPRETING THE MOVING IMAGE THAT HAS BEEN EDITED

In utilizing film and videotape, the researcher is confronted by the fact that these media are edited easily and, in many instances, it is difficult to perceive the point or nature of the changes. It is therefore valuable to have some understanding of the editing process.

In the case of film, the original may be either positive or negative. To ascertain if the film went through the camera, the film should be examined to determine if there are any points where a splice exists—where the film has been glued back together. If there are no splices, it is reasonably certain that it is as photographed. Film, however, is readily copied, so reproductions of the original can show no splices. In the most common editing system, known as the double system, sound and pictures are manipulated separately so that one can be altered without affecting the other. A common technique is to remove a portion of a presentation, such as a speech, and then cover the spot with another picture. Frequently, when one of these cutaways is seen, close attention to the sound will reveal that the tone and inflection of the end of a sentence do not match the beginning of the next sentence. The new sentence may start just a fraction of a second too early for normal speaking. Reversing the process, a visual segment can be eliminated and replaced with something else, without having any effect on the audio portion. While the edits are very visible on the initial piece of film, making a copy thoroughly masks the changes. A famous case where this was done occurred in 1971 when CBS aired a program called *The Selling of the Pentagon*. Shortly after the broadcast, it was discovered the producers had reconstructed a speech by lifting sentences from various locations in the text and covering the moves with shots of the audience. In the process, statements that the speaker had not made, were created.

---

[10] Albert H. Abramson, *The History of Television: 1942–2000* (Jefferson, NC: McFarland, 2003); Lynn Gross, *Telecommunications: An Introduction to Electronic Media,* 6th ed. (Madison, WI: Brown and Benchmark, 1997); Sydney Head, Christopher Sterling, and Lemuel Schofield, *Broadcasting in America,* 7th ed. (Boston, MA: Houghton Mifflin, 1994).

Videotape is edited by two methods. The first is known as linear editing, which is a copying process where all the changes are made in this transition. Again, the surest way of evaluating a tape is to find an original tape with no picture changes, suggesting that tape went through the camera. Segments can be edited out in the copying process, but, for example, in a speech, it is very unusual for the image in the very end of the first segment to match perfectly the positioning of the image at the start of the second segment. This results in an image twitch known as a jump cut, revealing that something has been removed. With audio, a portion can be removed and the edit covered with a different picture. Listening for small anomalies in the pacing and delivery is one way to determine if the tape has been edited.

The nonlinear video system is computer-based and popular because of its flexibility. The computer programs have been refined and simplified to the point that virtually anyone can use them at home. Although the linear process degrades the copy slightly and sometimes is a clue to the identification of an altered copy, the nonlinear approach, once mastered, enables making many changes that are virtually undetectable. However, since the nonlinear process is relatively new, an older tape is more likely to have a linear edit, and the audio break clues will still exist—except in very sophisticated situations.

OTHER CHANGES TO FILM AND VIDEO TAPE

Two other alterations are possible, although neither may have much meaning to the researcher. Around 1990, a means of colorizing black and white videotape was developed, and utilized particularly for making old Hollywood movies more attractive. An experienced video technician can usually spot the difference from original color. The length of a program is not a reliable element either, as a device has been developed that speeds up the film or tape in a copying process, but then corrects the sound so that the anticipated "chipmunk sound" associated with speeded tape does not occur. This practice is used to create more time for commercials.

Another alteration can have some significance for the historian. An aspect ratio is the relationship of screen width to screen height. Traditional television and classic film use a 4:3 ratio, which means the screen is three units high and four units wide. A wide-screen motion picture uses a 1.85:1 ratio; Panavision uses a 2.35:1 ratio, and HDTV uses a 16:9 ratio. The variety of film formats used in Hollywood films results in image shapes that do not fit neatly onto the 4:3 ratio of the standard television screen, although the newer HDTV screen can fit the wide screen film without much picture loss from the sides. However, during a transfer from one medium to another, portions of the image may be omitted and relationships altered. Many times it is done so cleverly that the average viewer is unaware of the changes. This means the historian must examine a video carefully when it is not an exact replication of the original film. Not only may significant elements on the edges have been removed, but the presentation can be altered electronically. For example, two people standing some distance apart in the original could be seen as two adjacent closeups. This suggests that in important situations, the historian needs to seek the original or at least determine if there is any record of alterations in the transfer process.

THE EDITING PROCESS FOR FILM AND VIDEOTAPE

The footage from the camera is the starting point for the finished film or video. Many effects, moods, and combinations are available while constructing the final product in the editing room. For the historian to interpret film and videotape, an understanding of the choices made in the editing room and the impact those choices have on meaning is very important.

Transitions

One of the first considerations in editing is how one picture changes into another. The historian should be aware that transitions can affect the way viewers react to the film or tape. Transitions can influence the mood and the atmosphere of the viewing environment. The most frequently used transition is the cut, so named for the fact that a scene in the exposed film stock is cut with a scissors and glued to the previously selected scene. This yields an instantaneous change. In general, cuts suggest that the two attached shots take place at the same time, in the same location, the second shot being just another view, perhaps closer or from another angle. This is not always done and directors jump from location to location using cuts. Unless the intent is to confuse the viewer (which happens), the second shot will differ sufficiently from the first so that the location change is clear. Rapid cuts are used to convey intensity to the viewer. Television commercials use this technique to create excitement about their product. Any analysis of film or videotape should include an awareness of this technique.

The second common transition is the dissolve, so named because the arriving shot seems to blend into the previous shot. The process involves fading out one shot while fading in the other. Dissolves are used to signify changes in time or location and are still common, though they have fallen into disfavor with some directors. The change is less abrupt than the cut and so is more appropriate in slower-paced situations, such as coverage of a funeral, in some musically based scenes, and in some romantic situations. The dissolve can influence perception of time and influence the perceived relationship between two unrelated events. For example, a scene of a crowded subway may dissolve into a scene of cattle. Careful analysis of this type of device indicates to the historian the director's perception about a particular event.

The third basic transition is the fade, which usually means the shot slowly disappears or appears. The color black is most commonly used in a fade, but red and white are also used on occasion. The fade usually signifies a beginning or ending, though television has led us to view the fade as the precursor of a commercial. It signifies to the audience a complete break with the previous segment and creates a sense of loss of energy.

Digital video effects (DVE) provide alternative transitions for video tape. These video effects include freeze frame, stretching, tumbling, or morphing from one image to the next. These types of effects often are used in popular entertainment material such as music videos. Michael Jackson's video, *Black and White,* is a good example of the use of morphing as a transitional device, used to convey a message of the unity of the human race.

Timing Elements

A variable on the transition is the rate at which it occurs. It is important for the historian analyzing film or videotape to be aware of how rapidly the picture is changed. This is called a cutting rate. A slow cutting rate communicates low tension and a relaxed situation. As tension and action rise, so does the cutting rate until the scenes are just flashing by. Actually, tests show that the rates of heart beat and breathing rise in the observer as the cutting rate increases on the screen.

Another area for analysis is the pacing of the film. In the earlier days of film, many editors felt that a shot couldn't be much shorter than 3 seconds or the audience wouldn't understand it. MTV and many experiments have shown we can read pictures much more rapidly. However, the editor and filmmaker consider the readability of any shot when determining how long it should be on the screen.

Screen Direction

Another aspect of editing is screen direction. If an actor starts left to right across the screen on his way to his car, the audience subconsciously assumes that the car is somewhere off to the right. If, in the next shot, the actor is now moving right to left, the audience assumes that he has changed his mind and is returning. Shots have to be planned to account for where the audience will assume things are. If two people are conversing in head shots, the audience expects them to be facing so that a face-to-face illusion is created. If both are facing in the same direction, the assumption is that they must be talking to some silent third party or at least looking at something in that direction. If the shots are reversed, we get a back-to-back situation which might suggest some sort of argument or disagreement.

Since the audience will try to relate each new picture to the former, a soldier looking off into space followed by a shot of a woman and child will be interpreted to mean the soldier is dreaming of his family (see section on juxtaposition or third effect). The researcher needs to be cautious when analyzing a sequence to ensure that adjacent pictures actually have a relationship and to determine why the two were put together. The second shot could actually be related to the following sequence. Unrelated, somewhat neutral shots have been used simply as a break in a sequence or at its end and have no purpose in the storytelling or reporting.

EDITING PATTERNS

Many movies and television programs begin at the beginning and tell the stories to the end, often called the narrative technique. However, many variations exist. Understanding the various editing techniques and their impact on the message will help the historian identify situations where added skepticism is needed. Knowing what can be done will help identify what could have been done to create a different impression.

Narrative Style

A common narrative technique is to begin at the end to show the outcome and then go back to the beginning and show the audience how the story got to that situation. A good example is the classic, *Citizen Kane,* which begins with the character's death and then spends the rest of the film exploring what led up to it. A lesser version is the flashback wherein the story jumps backward for a while to clarify or expand on a situation or, perhaps, function as the memory of some daydreaming by the actor. Another technique is called foreshadowing. In this instance, the audience is let in on some element the cast doesn't know about, so that an event can be anticipated. This could range from a washed-out bridge ahead of a speeding car, to a service man coming home on leave unexpectedly.

When telling the story, the editor has several other techniques available. Their use is dependent on the situation. In the popular chase scenes, dynamic editing is common. In this case we get the perspective of the pursued, looking backward at the pursuers, then the view of those in pursuit. It can be thought of as two views of the same activity. Another approach is parallel cutting. This is the story of two events that probably are related, but each group has little or no knowledge of the other. They may not even be happening at exactly the same time. This enables the director to tell two or more stories simultaneously, usually with some coming-together at the end. The film, *American Graffiti,* had four stories running in parallel.

Montage

A montage is a series of scenes related to a single topic, without continuity, but with greater emotional impact. The events pictured may even have happened at different times, such as a sequence of a man's life from childhood to old age. Montages generally compress considerable time into a shorter period. However, in the "Odessa Steps" sequence from the film *Potemkin,* the montage is actually used to expand time.

Crosscutting

When two related events are happening simultaneously, the director may utilize crosscutting. In this case the editor may jump back and forth between stories, which are almost certainly related, showing what is going on with each, preliminary to the two stories coming together. This can build considerable tension. Consider the simultaneous events of a mother preparing to take her baby for a walk in a stroller as, in another part of town, a bank robbery is about to occur. The robbers, in a high-speed exit, head down a street that will take them across the path of the mother and the stroller. The question, will they all arrive at the intersection at that same moment? is on everyone's mind. Cutting back and forth, at a gradually increasing rate, creates the suspense.

Cutaways

Just what to show the audience is often a question for the director. Frequently it is more effective to show someone's reaction to the event, rather than the event itself. A fight, with sound effects, while we see the anguished face of someone observing the blows, is often more potent than the fight itself. This technique uses cutaways. The cutaway helps to tell the audience how to react and also is called a reaction shot. Consider the difference between that unseen fight with a cutaway, if the observer is giggling instead of looking on in horror. Animals also are popular subjects for cutaways, particularly in comedies. The 11 o'clock evening news show is a good place to see cutaways in action. When, during a speech by the mayor, you suddenly see a shot of a reporter taking notes or even another video camera operator, you can be sure that a piece of the speech has been cut out. The cutaway has been used to conceal the jump cut that would result if we could see the point where the cut in the speech was made.

Jump Cut

A jump cut happens when a person or an object seems to jerk or jump from one screen position to another. This occurs due to editing. For example, during a newscast, only a few seconds would be permitted for the coverage of the mayor's speech. The editor might choose two short comments made by the mayor that occurred at different times during the speech. If the camera remained in the same position but the mayor moved, the mayor would appear to jump from one position to another. This can be distracting to the viewer so a cutaway is used to cover the jump. However, jump cuts also may be used to convey a quick change in time or other audience reactions the director may want.

The researcher needs to understand editing patterns to appreciate the methods used to present the story or influence the audience. The cutting rate, the frequency of switching between segments of the story, and the use of chase-type sequences are tools the researcher needs to understand in appreciating how a story was told and when, where, and how the director and the editor sought to influence the viewer.

Juxtaposition

Juxtaposition is a very effective storytelling device. Two conflicting situations are crosscut together, usually for the contrast between them. A sequence on starving children might be intercut with well-fed and well-housed race horses. A sequence like this was used by Edward R. Murrow in the television documentary, *Harvest of Shame.* To underscore the terrible conditions of migrant workers, Murrow intercut between the beautiful stables of horses and the workers crammed into a truck. This can be carried further. In the controversial documentary, *Roger and Me,* filmmaker Michael Moore intercuts an elaborate General Motors Christmas party with sequences of out-of-work families being evicted from their homes on Christmas Eve. Then, the audio is reversed so that we hear the choir singing, while watching the eviction. This is an example of ironic juxtaposition.

Here again, the researcher is faced with the fact that editing can create impressions that are not reality. It can suggest where one thing or person is in relationship to another, when this is inaccurate. It can suggest actions that did not occur. For example, if someone is walking toward some goal and moves first one way and then another across the screen, it can seem that there is searching going on or that the person is lost or confused. The historian must consider how the movement or confrontation is presented to get a clearer understanding of the real or intended circumstance and relationships.

VISUAL LANGUAGE AND LITERACY

Although the photographer or director of film and video has many tools available, the best visual representations are usually those where the audience is quite unaware of the techniques that are being used. Everything fits together so well that it seems more a matter of logic than techniques. To understand the image making process more fully, however, it is necessary to have an understanding of the tools, how they work, and what they accomplish. Dondis refers to this as visual literacy.[11] Just as a historian needs to be literate to use written sources, the use of visual evidence requires the historian to be literate

---

[11] Donis A. Dondis, *A Primer of Visual Literacy* (Cambridge, MA: MIT Press, 1973).

visually. Examples to illustrate literacy will be taken from well-known films, since these are available readily through video rental and can be used by the historian to study this language. However, since these films were transferred to videotape, some of the information is lost and, therefore, the full impact of the visual is not contained. The techniques described here are used every day in the films, video and photographs that we see. These comprise the aesthetics of the visual and have an impact on the audience's perception of the image.[12]

The section presents an overview of the most frequently used devices and their meaning in historical interpretation. The techniques discussed are used by photographers, directors, filmmakers, and videographers. Therefore, these terms are used interchangeably throughout this section. Careful analysis is required to recognize the effects of this technology as well as the intended and unintended records preserved in visual evidence.

The Lens

The lens is a collection of pieces of glass that is designed to gather and focus the light on the film in the camera. However, all lenses are not alike. Many people are aware of the collection of lenses we call a telescope. This combination brings distant objects closer. There is also a second combination of glass that takes a very wide shot and is known as a *wide-angle lens.* In between the extremes of each are other lenses which have the same characteristics, but to lessor degrees.

Lenses are defined in terms of their focal length usually measured in millimeters. A telephoto lens will have larger numbers and wide angles will be small. For many years the normal lens on the popular 35mm cameras was the 50 millimeter. Today, many of the "point and shoot" cameras use a shorter lens. Although they vary with the type of camera, on the 35mm camera, telephoto begins at about 70mm and extends to extremes of at least 1,000mm. This latter lens will give you a close shot from a considerable distance. Wide angles begin at about 35mm and drop down to as low as 9mm (known as a fisheye lens) where the images are circular and very distorted.

The significance of these different lenses is the way they affect the shot. The amount the lens shows side to side is one factor. A wide-angle lens expands space so that the environment of the shot seems more expansive than

---

[12] For a comprehensive discussion, see Herbet Zettl, *Sight, Sound, Motion: Applied Media Aesthetics,* 3rd ed. (Belmont, CA: Wadsworth, 1999).

it really is. The wide angle, by getting more into the shot, also gives the audience a better perspective of relationships within the scene. Wide-angle lenses also distort things that are close to it. Many commercials and even some comedy films have used this distorting quality by having the talent practically push their face into the camera for the comic effect. The popular *Ernest* films commonly use this technique.

As one might expect, telephoto lenses compress space so that things are caused to appear closer together than they really are. Newspaper photographers often use a telephoto lens to emphasize the amount of traffic on local streets. The result is that the cars seem to be bumper to bumper, even when they're not.

Another variable that affects the picture is the simple process of how the photographer took the picture. Any image eliminates part, often most, of a total scene. Even the photographer's decision to shoot or not to shoot influences the result, as does the lens that is utilized. As discussed previously, there is a difference between the picture from a wide-angle lens versus a telephoto lens even though the subject is identical. The circumstance of the picture may also affect the result. In a fast-moving situation, some things will be missed or there could be a significant occurrence at the moment the photographer is busy recording another aspect. Therefore, any photograph, video, or film will only give part of the message about a particular circumstance or event. The more pictures that are taken, the more we approach reality, but we never fully attain it.

For the historian, lens tricks can be one of the most critical elements to evaluate. In a picture of several famous individuals, perhaps political leaders, where they are standing in relation to each other can be significant. However, even the environment in which they are standing can be influenced by the lens. How big was the room? A short, wide-angle lens can double the size of the environment. How close were they standing? Again the wide angle will give the appearance that they were further apart than they may have been. Conversely, in considering a picture of a major leader and his or her key advisors, the closeness of other individuals to the leader is often used to rank their status. A telephoto lens-compressing characteristic can advance someone standing several feet behind to make it appear that the individual is virtually whispering in the leader's ear.

The wide-angle and telephoto lenses do give clues to their presence. As a lens gets "wider" it tends to cause straight, vertical lines near the center of the picture to bow outward slightly. Vertical lines along the edges will begin to appear that they are toppling toward the center.

The long telephoto compresses front to back, and the clue is to study all the elements in the picture to determine if the spacing seems appropriate. Telephone poles that begin to look like a picket fence are good indicators of compression. Signs that appear too close together are another. If a picture has been tightly cropped, many of these clues may be removed, but a certain skepticism must be retained. Perhaps there is another picture from a different angle that will aid in determining actual relationships.

Focus

The purpose of focus is to make it possible to see the picture. Out-of-focus shots are rarely popular. However, a photographer or director can use selective focus to make just the part of the scene that he or she wants you to see stand out. This can give a foreground–background relationship, where something near the camera is somewhat out of focus while action in the background is clear. Of course, the reverse can be true. Furthermore, a film or television camera, changing the focus during the shot can direct the viewer's attention. An example might be a shot of a man sleeping in a chair with something in the foreground that's out of focus. A change of focus reveals an empty whiskey bottle, which is intended to explain why the man is asleep … or is he passed out?

Wide-angle lenses have considerable depth of field, which is the amount of the picture that is in focus, beginning at the lens and moving toward the background in the picture. These lenses make it possible to see most of the scene clearly. The more telephoto a lens becomes, the less depth it has, so a director may choose a lens on the basis of how much is to be revealed. Lighting adds another variable because a high light level will increase depth, while less light will make the area in focus decrease. The classic film, *Citizen Kane,* is famous for its extensive and effective use of shots with extreme depth of field.

For the researcher, the environment of a picture can be very important. Shallow focus, which degrades the background to the point that it is not distinguishable, can eliminate key clues as to the circumstance. Faces of individuals present can be blurred beyond recognition. In examining such a picture, it is easy to forget that significant elements may have been hidden. Likewise, foreground elements can be reduced to a mere fuzzy area which would eliminate its value. There is no ready solution except searching for other pictures with a different perspective, however, awareness that things can be hidden by focus is vital in drawing information from photographs.

Point of View

Camera placement is known as point of view. From whose (or even what) point of view are we seeing the shot? Are we a fly on the wall, a participant, or an observer? Are we seeing it from above, below, or through a window? Why did the director choose to shoot from this particular location?

Most people taking snapshots hold the camera at eye level while standing. Most filmmakers vary the camera height extensively for several effects. From our childhood of looking up at adults who were taller (and more powerful), we associate looking upward with prestige and power, so a director will place the camera low for a shot when the talent is to be conveyed as dynamic, in control, or threatening. Likewise, a downward shot tends to belittle a character and make them less significant. Watching camera placement in a scene can tell you about the relationship of the characters and the message intended by the photographer. Shots downward, from above, also have the advantage of showing a scene in more depth. Imagine trying to get the sense of the number of marching soldiers in a parade while standing at ground level.

The elevated camera is used in the classic film *High Noon*. The embattled sheriff, deserted by the townspeople, stands, a tiny figure, alone in an empty town, awaiting a gun battle with a gang of outlaws. In the documentary *Triumph of the Will*, director Leni Riefenstahl made most of her shots of Hitler in an upward direction, giving him a godlike or superior characteristic. For historians, camera angles can provide perspectives on environment that might not otherwise be available and helps them to analyze the attitude the filmmaker wishes to convey to the audience about the status of an individual or situation.

Camera Movement

Though one of the common ills of amateur films and tapes is too much camera movement, a professional director often has the camera moving constantly. The secret, of course, is knowing why and how the camera should move. One approach is to start a shot close and then pull back further and further, revealing more and more of the environment. This can be carried to extremes, with a crane shot, often utilizing a construction crane or the extreme, a helicopter. This can be a very powerful effect. In *Gone with the Wind*, Scarlett walks among the wounded southerners of the Civil War. A slow crane shot upward reveals the incredible extent of the dead and dying in the scene. In the classic western *High Noon,* the shot pulls upward, away from sheriff Gary Cooper, to reveal everyone in town is hiding, leaving him to face the outlaws alone.

Cameras move to give the audience a different perspective, to provide a greater sense of the three-dimensional nature of the scene or to reveal more about it. An effective variation is to have the moving camera pass behind objects or people, momentarily hiding the action, just as if the viewer were walking around. Another common camera move is the traveling shot where the camera is mounted on a vehicle and moves with the action. Sometimes the camera is on a small wheeled platform on miniature railroad tracks so it can move smoothly in a desired direction. Sometimes traveling shots are created through special effects.

The historian needs to consider the purpose of any camera movement and what it is intended to convey. In professionally made material, movement is not accidental. Again, the movement can provide different views that can help in the analysis of other aspects of the picture. This can be particularly valuable with documentary and news footage where events are being recorded, rather than a story being told. The moving camera was first used in some of the Lumiere Brothers' footage from the late nineteenth century. Archival material like this provides an excellent opportunity for historians to view cities, dress, and environments that were not specifically the subject of the film.

Shots

One of the key tools of the photographer or director is the actual picture put on the screen. These would range from extremely wide (EW) to extremely close (ECU). A simple way of approaching this variety is to think of the element of dramatic impact. In most situations, the closer the shot is to the subject, the more dramatic or intense the situation. Wide shots (WS) establish the environment and show the physical relationships between the actors, but they are at the low end of the dramatic scale. As we move toward the actors, we become more conscious of them as individuals and of the scene. Medium shots (MS) show us the players, but much less environment. Continuing inward we reach waist shots (medium closeups [MCU]) and then chest shots (or closeups [CU]), where many scenes are played. Moving forward we reach the head shot and then the face shot, which is basically from chin to eyebrows. Now we get a good view of anguish, perspiration, and intensity. The extreme is the eye shot where drama is highest and the audience's involvement with the talent is greatest. While longer shots can have drama in certain situations, closer in is usually stronger.

Another popular shot is the over the shoulder. As its name implies, the camera placed behind one actor, including his or her shoulder and the side of the head in the picture. The remainder of the frame is devoted to the face of the other talent. This gives the advantage of both showing the relationship and giving a face shot at the same time. Commonly, you will see a conversation photographed, in part, as a series of over-the-shoulder shots, first from one side and then the other.

A shooting variation that has its applications, but which can be overdone, is the subjective camera. In this case, the lens becomes the eyes of one of the participants, so that everything is seen from that perspective. This can be very effective, particularly in suspenseful situations, as the talent walks down a darkened hall or through a threatening neighborhood. At least one complete film (*Lady in the Lake*) has been shot totally with a subjective camera, but it was not well received.

An analysis of the shots can help the historian understand the intention of the photographer. Television soap operas are notorious for their use of close ups and the emotional impact conveyed. Directors like John Ford are well known for their use of long shots to express the wide-open spaces of the American West (*She Wore a Yellow Ribbon*). Orson Wells chopped holes in the floor to achieve the extreme up angles in *Citizen Kane*. Careful analysis may indicate the personal style of a director, which may help the historian understand the person behind the camera.

Composition

Composition is the arrangement of all the elements in the shot. The word frame is used to describe the edges of the picture. Within the frame, the director plans the shot for maximum impact or to convey a feeling. Several tools are available. First is the word frame, but this time it can refer to an arch, a window or some tree branches among hundreds of other things used to make someone or something stand out. Our eye is drawn to objects in frames.

Another device is the use of lines. This could be a road, railroad track, path, or stream. The diagonal line is particularly popular, as it tends to catch our eye and lead it to the desired point. Think of a shot with a sidewalk coming out of the lower, left-hand corner of the frame and extending diagonally across the picture. In the distance, walking toward us we see a young woman. The line draws our attention to her so that we know she is important. Other lines may be vertical to suggest majesty (columns outside a government building). Horizontal lines (girders) suggest strength. Curved lines are considered beautiful or artistic. The S-shaped curve is particularly effective to achieve this impression. Lines running in all directions (as one might see in the debris of an area hit by a flood) give a feeling of chaos.

Shots and composition are basic tools of the painter, photographer, filmmaker, and videographer. They contribute to the film's effectiveness and the impact on the viewer. The historian needs to become sensitive to these devices, so that when someone is framed by an arch or the jagged glass of a broken window, the researcher recognizes that these were done for a purpose and were not accidental.

Light

Photography, film, and television depend on light to create the picture. They make extensive use of light to create moods and emphasis. Many directors try to light so that it seems the light is coming from some obvious source such as a window. This is realistic lighting. Shafts of light can act as spotlights, highlighting particular locations or people. Two lighting techniques are high-key and low-key lighting.

High key is bright and essentially shadowless. It usually is associated with happy times. Any game show, such as *Wheel of Fortune,* uses high-key lighting. Low key is a bit more complex, because it isn't the direct opposite of high key. Low key is very contrasty lighting with areas of dark shadows and areas of sometimes quite harsh, bright light. Low key is associated with mystery or drama. Of course, totally dim light is used as well, usually with a dramatic purpose. Director Ingmar Bergman lights the old man in *Wild Strawberries* in dark and light shadows. In *Wild Child,* director Francois Truffaut lights the water, which the boy associates with happiness and freedom

The direction of the light also is a factor. Lighting an actor from the front hides lines and wrinkles, and is very popular with older actors trying to play younger roles. As the light moves around to the side, it becomes more dramatic. A purely side-lit scene gives an actor's face half in shadow and half in light. Moving the light still further around ultimately back lights the subject and creates a silhouette, if no other light is on the scene. The side-lit face is very dramatic and will reveal every pore and scar if the shot is close enough.

Occasionally a director will narrow a beam of light so that only part of the face, usually the eyes, is revealed.

The historian must recognize the role lighting plays in any situation. It can influence the appearance of news footage as readily as dramatic video. A scene lit by a raging fire is different from one lit with professional equipment. If taken outdoors, the direction of light and the analysis of shadows can indicate the time of day. Lighting can make a studio scene look realistic or can be used to emphasize a theme or mood. How a scene was lit, the angle from which the light comes, and the lighting source are all factors that need to be considered when drawing information from visual evidence.

Time

When viewing film or video footage, an important consideration for the historian is the perception of time. Many film and television scenes seem to be linear; that is, they seem to take as long as the activity should take. In reality, most things take too long, so the editors resort to telescoping. Assume you are to go to the store. It may take a minute or more—very boring if on film. However, if we see you start, pass through a door, see your feet on some steps and then the sign indicating WalMart as you enter, the same movement was accomplished in, perhaps, 10 seconds. Studies show that the audience will accept considerable telescoping.

Time expansion is the opposite of telescoping. In this case the editor wishes to make things last longer. This may be to emphasize the event or just to get more screen time out of an expensive stunt. Shooting in slow motion is one obvious solution, but the editor can accomplish the same thing by giving you a variety of views of the same action. Each may be of the same instant, but when shown in sequence, the time is extended. One of the more famous slow-motion sequences is the final death scene in *Bonnie and Clyde*. Trapped by the police, they are riddled with dozens of bullets. Viewed in slow motion, the result has been called a "Dance of Death." Actually the scene was shortened before the film was released, as the producers felt there was too much impact on the audience.

Through the use of editing, time is manipulated by the film or video director. The historian should be aware of this manipulation and the possible effect it has on the interpretation of an event. By telescoping time, an event can seem more intense or shorter than when it occurred. For example, a riot in the streets with college students after a football game, may have occurred over a few hours. The news footage may take those events and present them in 30 seconds.

Symbolism

Symbolism is a technique of showing something that suggests something else. Two lines on the chalk board have little meaning, but, cross them in the form of a crucifix and suddenly you have the symbol of Christ and the whole Christian religion. Symbols come in many forms. In the "Odessa Steps" sequence from *Potemkin,* there are three shots of stone lions, first in repose, then awakening, and finally alert. Would this not suggest the reaction of the population to the attack? In the documentary *Best Boy,* the subject, a retarded man, is being trained to live on his own. After a sequence where the camera follows him closely, the camera suddenly pauses and lets the man walk ahead on his own, the shot widening symbolizing the man's growing independence and expanding world.

Many films, videos, and photographs have objects in them that may be considered symbolic. This may even include the colors used for dress or decoration. The historian must spend some time looking for the meaning that may be revealed in the details of a scene.

Special Effects

Special effects supposedly were discovered by the Frenchman, Georges Melies. It seems he was out filming one day when his camera jammed. He fixed it and resumed shooting. When the film was developed, he discovered that, by coincidence, a wagon was in front of the camera when it stopped and a hearse was there when it resumed. Melies had found a way to turn a wagon into a hearse. Double printing uses two negatives printed onto one piece of photographic paper or film. Pioneer filmmakers learned that you could run two films through the printer and add an effect on the master film. In the very early *Dreams of a Rarebit Fiend,* a double printing places an area about the sleeper where we can see his nightmares, the result of overeating.

King Kong is noted for another special effect, single-frame animation. The gorilla was actually a flexible doll only 18 inches tall. The action was created by taking a single shot or frame of film, then moving the model slightly and then taking another picture. Using this slow, painstaking process, any action could be created. Incidentally, all the camera angles were shot upward to give the model a greater sense of size and power. Another common technique was rear projection. Photographs and motion pictures were projected onto the back of a translucent screen. The actors performed in front of the screen with the visual image as a backdrop. Double printing and painted backdrops added to the effect. In many early films, backdrops provided scenery that would otherwise be expensive or impossible to obtain.

Miniatures have long been used to create effects and events that would be difficult to create full size. *King Kong* made numerous uses of miniatures as did *2001: A Space Odyssey* and all the *Star Wars* films. Today, most of these effects are created using computer programs.

Nearly everyone has seen the TV weatherperson pointing out the cold front on colorful maps. If you have been in the studio, you know that actually there are no maps and the talent is pointing into thin air, standing in front of a blue curtain. The maps are generated by a computer. The computer can be instructed to insert the map anywhere blue is present. (Obviously, blue shirts and suits are out.) The talent watches a TV receiver to know where to point. Filmmakers use a similar process known as the blue screen (sometimes green) method. When you see traffic out a car window, you may actually be seeing a blue-screen image in the window of a car sitting in the studio. A prop person may be bouncing the car slightly to add realism.

Many people feel that videotape ultimately will replace film because the special effects are so much easier to do electronically. Two techniques which can be done in either medium are variations of the freeze frame. The first is done by pausing the video recording or holding the negative of the film and printing that one frame over and over as long as desired. The impact can be considerable. The second variation is the strobe effect where the printer holds a frame in a freeze for a moment, then skips ahead and holds another frame. This too can go on as long as desired. The result is the jerky movement associated with dancing under strobe lights.

Once understood, the techniques and tools used by photographers, filmmakers, and video editors help the historian interpret the image's meaning. Without this knowledge, a critical evaluation and analysis of visual evidence would be difficult.

CHALLENGES OF HISTORICAL RESEARCH
USING VISUAL EVIDENCE

Format

One of the problems facing researchers is the transition to digital formats. Visual documents needed by broadcast historians—such as photographs, video, and film—are being produced electronically and saved on floppy discs and hard drives. As digital formats continue to evolve, current software may not be able to read the older forms. There is already a generation of early material "that can't be played any more because the equipment on which they play is obsolete."[13] Archives and museums have attempted to preserve this equipment, but access is not always readily available. Even the networks have been driven to tracking down and recalling old technicians to reactivate discarded machines so that early tapes could be played—as in the case of an early video recording of a Fred Astaire dance special. For the material that is available, the historian will need to be familiar with a variety of software programs and equipment, even those that may be outdated.

Although the process of exposing and processing motion-picture film is similar to still photography, there are differences that can complicate the researcher's work. One is film size. In the late 1800s, several widths were used and George Eastman supplied widths more or less to order. Film could be anywhere from three-quarters to three and three-quarters inches wide. By 1892, Edison was primarily using 35mm and this format rapidly evolved to be a standard that continues today. In pursuit of the home-movie market, manufacturers were soon splitting the film into 17.5mm to make it cheaper. Competitors produced other widths that further complicated the matter. In 1923, Kodak offered 16mm film which became a popular form for documentaries and industrial producers. Later, it became the standard for television news. The home market evolved further in 1932, when Kodak offered a still narrower version, 8mm that brought the costs down to a range that many families could afford and became the basis for most home movies. These diverse film sizes also varied in the spacing between the sprocket holes and damage can occur to old film if not played on the correct equipment. The crux of the problem is that it is difficult to find projectors that will show many of these

---

[13] Scott Carlson, "The Uncertain Fate of Scholarly Artifacts in a Digital Age," *The Chronicle of Higher Education* 50, no. 21 (2004): A25.

varieties. This is particularly true when seeking to examine amateur footage; it may be difficult to find the appropriate projector so that the film can be viewed at all.

Television news film is a considerable resource for historical evidence. Researchers may discover that film shot in the 1960s by television news departments was a negative, rather than the usual positive. To be able to play this film, equipment that will reverse polarity is needed. Not all archives may have this equipment.

Another aspect of film, with which the researcher should be acquainted, is the manner in which sound was recorded. Initially it was an optical process, with the information recorded along one edge of the film. The optical system was utilized in the thousands of projectors that were found before the advent of videotape. The optical sound system did not yield high-quality sound and was cumbersome to edit and reproduce. However, by the 1960s a new method was utilized, particularly by television stations' news departments. This process replaced the optical track with a strip of audio tape about 2mm wide. This increased the quality and eased sound transfers, but the researcher should be aware that, today, projectors that can play "mag track film" are relatively rare. Only those locations that have invested in this more expensive type of projector will be able to serve your needs. Many locations will be unwilling to project mag track film on a traditional projector, even for just the picture portion, as the sprocket teeth of the projector could damage the audio track.

Tape formats also have changed many times since the 1950s and none of them are compatible. Tape size can vary from the original 2 inches to a ½ inch. They can be on reel-to-reel or cassette and may not be compatible with all brands of machines even though the tape size is the same. Formats include Sony Betamax, VHS, SVHS, and Hi-8. Sixty different formats were on the market at one time or another (see chapter 10, "New Media").

Digital video uses hard drives and flash cards for storage and this may present a problem for future archival work. The variety of available formats and software to run the programs that recorded the original material may no longer exist.

Storage

Finding original footage from the early days of filmmaking is very unusual, because the film, which carried the emulsion, was made of an unstable, highly flammable material. It was a serious fire hazard and eventually was replaced.

Explorer and documentary filmmaker, Robert Flaherty, lost all his film while editing the 1920 *Nanook of the North,* in a fiery moment caused by a spark from a cigarette, forcing him to return to the Arctic and completely reshoot. Additionally, the film base's instability causes it to disintegrate totally over time so that opening a newly discovered can of film could reveal nothing but dust. The only way to preserve the early works has been to rephotograph the original film, which became a major, though expensive, project in the latter years of the twentieth century and continues today.

Intense cold is one of the few ways to save this type of film. One of the great discoveries in recent years has been finding many cans of early film in a landfill behind a defunct Alaskan movie theater. The fragile early film stock was replaced by an inflammable type, logically called safety film, after numerous theater projection booth fires. An enemy of all film is a deterioration process that results in the production of ascetic acid and is referred to as the vinegar syndrome because of the obvious odor. Storing film in metal cans, which often was the case with television news departments, accelerates the process. The defense here is archival plastic cans, preferably with a design that permits air to circulate through the cans so that the acid does not build up in them. High humidity also can damage film.

For photographs preserved on film, the negative becomes grainier in storage. The quality of the image degrades over time and the usefulness of the image may be diminished. For video tape, the tape can become brittle and tear. Another problem is that tape adhesive breaks down and oxide comes off. This results in clogged recording heads and possible loss of the sync pulse that makes the picture not viewable.

Another potential issue for historians is the sheer amount of material that is preserved. Although historians believe that all material available should be looked at before writing, there may be so much material in digital storage, that historians will have to become more selective in what they read. This brings into question the traditional methods that are used in historiography.

Since digital images are easy to capture, they are also easy to delete. So, although there may be a massive amount of material in digital storage, there also may be much that is eliminated by the photographer or editor just because the cost of storing vast amounts of material is not feasible or the value of the image is not appreciated at the moment. This was made evident during the Clinton-Lewinsky scandal. The photographer, Dirck Halstead (who took the picture of the President hugging Ms. Lewinsky), saved the image on his hard drive. Other photographers apparently had erased the image. "We still don't know the long-term implications of what that moment captured in time will have in years to come. As photojournalists we have not only the privilege of witnessing history, but we also have the responsibility of saving it."[14] As Halstead reminds us "The most banal of photographs when looked at 100 years later have lives of their own."[15]

Concerns over storing digital information have led the Library of Congress to investigate this issue. The National Digital Information Infrastructure Preservation Program (NDIIPP) will study the issues involved in digital storage of all forms of documentation. System migration (i.e., copying digital information from one system to the next as they change over time) and the related issue of authenticity make the use of visual evidence more difficult. "With electronic systems, the presumption of authenticity must be supported by evidence."[16] This evidence should include written material further increasing the research demands on the historian.

Modification

Since the beginning of photography, the visual record has been manipulated. Manipulation can occur before the shot is taken by changing or staging the elements of the picture. The famous Civil War picture of a dead sniper behind a stone wall has tremendous impact on the viewer even today. However, the photographers responsible for that shot, moved a corpse into position to take that photo.

Other changes occur in the darkroom. Photographers scrape emulsion off of the glass plates to remove elements they do not want. Others expose two or more glass negatives to the same piece of paper to create pictures that are not true representations. Some changes are considered acceptable, even though they do affect the final picture. The first of these is cropping. This process involves removing portions of the picture that misfocus attention or are distracting. Contrast is another acceptable modification. The photographer, through the choice of paper and chemicals, can create an increase or decrease in contrast. Dodging and burning are other processes whereby a picture may

---

[14] Dirck Halstead, "The Importance of Saving Your Photography," *The Digital Journalist,* http://www.digitaljournalsit.org/issue0312/halsteadcommentary.html.

[15] Ibid.

[16] Yvette Hackett, "The Search for Authenticity in Electronic Records," *The Moving Image* 3 (Fall 2003): 100–107.

be lightened or darkened so it is more easily seen. Burning can be carried to the edge of manipulation by darkening areas to the point where things are obscured. Sometimes the outer part of the picture is darkened all the way around, creating a spotlight effect called vignetting. Though long accepted, dodging and burning more recently have come under attack. In 2003, a photographer lost a North Carolina Press Photographers Association Award when he admitted to dodging and burning.[17] One of the new high-end professional cameras has dodging and burning capabilities in the camera. Today, these processes are all available through the use of computer software.

It should be noted that the previously described cropping process changes many of the pictures that are available. Because cropping changes what the audience sees, it has an effect on the perception of the event. For example, a story about President Clinton showed him with his head bowed and his advisor George Stephanopoulos looking concerned beside him. The photo was used for a story about the Whitewater controversy. However, the photograph was taken weeks before during a scheduling meeting and originally included Clinton, Stephanopoulos, and press secretary Dee Dee Meyers. In looking at the originally uncropped version of the photo a different impression is given to the audience.[18] For news and other nonfiction businesses, the historian must consider all of these influences on their interpretation of visual records to maintain their credibility.

With the arrival of the halftone process, pictures in newspapers were not far behind. By the early part of the twentieth century, tabloids were common, each looking for a bigger scandal and more revealing pictures. As is true today, if they didn't have the picture they created it. A common device was to have actors pose in some compromising scene and then paste shots of the faces of the famous parties over those of the actors. Constructed pictures became known as composographs. Sometimes three or more pictures would be combined to get the desired results.[19] The result was rephotographed to give the appearance of an original picture. The success of the tabloid papers made other newspapers much more conscious of the importance of pictures in

---

[17] Kenny Irby, "A Photojournalistic Confession," *The Digital Journalist,* http://www.digitaljournalsit.org/issue0309/kirby.html.

[18] Thomas Wheeler, *Phototruth or Photofiction? Ethics and Media Imagery in the Digital Age* (Mahwah, NJ: Lawrence Erlbaum Associates, 2002), 124.

[19] Ken Kobre, "The Long Tradition of Doctoring Photos," *Visual Communication Quarterly* 2 (Spring 1995): 14–15.

attracting readers. Today, that same technique is used. One infamous example is where *Texas Monthly* published on their cover a composite photograph of the former Texas governor, Anne Richards, and political rival Clayton Williams. Their heads had been transplanted on two figures who were dancing together.[20] It gave the impression that at one time the two were friends.

Another form of modification was trick photography that used a variety of devices, particularly mirrors, to create unreal images. Some of these were quite ingenious but usually can be identified by the unlikely nature of the finished product. Retouching is another form of modification that was common through the twentieth century. Using small brushes and a variety of inks or paints, portrait photographers routinely enhanced the looks of people, removing moles and scars, and improved complexions to the point that the subjects barely recognized themselves. Other alterations may be done for taste or political correctness. Some alterations are obvious and instantly recognized as such or could be minor and technically insignificant changes. Some changes enhance what's there. This might include fixing a scratch, cleaning and repairing negatives, cropping, shading or increasing exposure (dodging and burning), color correction, or airbrushing (cosmetic retouching). These types of changes usually are not considered important to the veracity of the photo.

With patience and skill, it was possible to accomplish many changes in pictures from the twentieth century. During the Cold War, Western leaders devoted considerable time to studying pictures of Soviet leaders. It was a common practice in the USSR for individuals that had fallen out of favor to be removed from previously taken pictures. The photographs were reissued, neatly retouched, so the offender had disappeared. It gave a hint as to the machinations inside the Kremlin.[21]

Any image that may have had an electronic phase in its past is a potential victim of modification, and judgments about visual evidence must include this possibility. Awareness of any manufacturer's name on the back of the picture may offer guidance, since the name may be associated more with electronics than photography. While chemically made photographs can be altered, it is not as easy and may become evident upon critical examination. The ease with which alterations can be made through electronic image processing and the speed in which changes can be made, removed, and redone invite alterations.

---

[20] Wheeler, *Phototruth or Photofiction?,* 150.

[21] Dino Brugioni, *Photo Fakery: The History and Techniques of Photographic Deception and Manipulation* (Dulles, VA: Brassey's, 1999), 149–51.

This creates a problem for the historian as to what are original, unmanipulated images and sounds and which are not. As noted, it is possible to eliminate people and objects from the frame, or in video, to make human lips move and add conversation.

Just as it is important for the historian to be knowledgeable about visual aesthetics, because its implications are considerable in evaluating visual material, the researcher needs to be familiar with the software's capabilities. One of the most used computer-based programs to manipulate digital images is Photoshop, the image processing system from Adobe.

Photoshop

Photoshop has three versions: PhotoDeluxe for beginners; Photoshop Elements, which offers most of the image processing techniques of the more advanced version; and the full Photoshop, which is upgraded regularly and offers more capabilities than most individuals will ever learn. Additionally, there are other image processing systems on the market, including several that are included in new computers as one of the incentives for purchase.

The advantages of Photoshop and other similar programs are extensive. They have improved, repaired, and literally saved thousands of pictures that were poorly made or had suffered from damage or age. Among the changes these systems can make are brightening an image, modifying the contrast, improving focus, and cropping. Each change can be tested and changed again. Color can be adjusted over a wide range of hues and saturations, or a color picture can be converted instantly to black and white. An additional asset is that any change can be reversed, usually even after several additional changes have been made.

Some of the other capabilities are the source of potential problems for researchers. It is not a particularly difficult challenge to remove objects and people from the background or eliminate the entire background completely, destroying a researcher's reference point. Furthermore, using a system called layering, it is possible to take an individual or object and present it in an entirely different location. A young couple standing in front of their home could be transposed, with little difficulty, to posing in front of Niagara Falls. Objects within a picture can be relocated, central parts of a picture can be eliminated to move two elements closer together, and multiple pictures can be blended into one seamless image.

The capabilities of Photoshop are not limited exclusively to photographs, as the same process can be used with anything that can be scanned. Therefore, drawing and sketches can be modified. In some graphic work this is a boon, as stray pen marks, dirt, and evidence of erasures are eliminated easily. However, parts of the image could be totally removed or elements added with a little deft electronic penmanship. For the historian, there is no easy way to detect these changes. The challenge is to find original footage or a photograph or a written document that indicates the types of changes that were made to the original.

Uses of Manipulation Software

One of the primary places where manipulation is likely to occur is on magazine covers. Even on *news* magazines, the covers are viewed more as advertising devices than as news related. In 1994, *Time* and *Newsweek* ran the same photo of O. J. Simpson on their covers after he had been accused of murdering his ex-wife. On the cover of *Time,* the photograph had been made to appear darker and Simpson more sinister. The manipulation was obvious to the public since the magazine cover on *Newsweek* had not been altered. Even the respected *National Geographic* was caught rearranging the location of the Pyramids to improve the composition of a picture. A problem can arise when a cover shot loses its connection to the cover and starts to exist as a separate entity. It easily can be perceived as an authentic photograph.

In the video world, computer-generated changes to the picture are becoming routine and capable of being done in real time. Anyone who has watched a professional football game has probably observed the yellow line that appears to indicate the distance the offensive team must make. It seems very real, for, if a player runs across the line, it disappears behind him and reappears as he passes. This is a computer insertion to the picture and not something on the field. Likewise, virtual advertising is occurring, as a computer adds billboards that appear to be along the walls of the stadium, although they only exist in the video signal and are not visible to those in attendance. Additional software is used in many programs to enhance the looks of the participants. This is done in real time and removes wrinkles and other evidence of age so that a 65-year-old newscaster may suddenly appear to pass for his late forties. These technologies would be available in any video-produced movie as well.

UNDERSTANDING CONTEXT

In the movie *Wag the Dog,* the creation of reality plays an important part in the plot. A Hollywood producer is hired to create the illusion that we are at war to deflect the focus on a troubled President. It is clear from this scene that the possibility of creating reality is easily done and the movie makes the audience wonder if this has actually happened. It is a powerful statement to historians on the issues that confront interpretation of the past in a digital media age.

As noted throughout this chapter, the historian that is using photography, film, or video to study the past, is faced with a number of challenges. First is the necessity to understand the technology and tools used by the various media. The message of the visual image can be interpreted in various ways and understanding visual language is critical. Knowledge about the possible changes that could occur to the image, especially by computer software, also is necessary. Shafer reminds historians they "must not isolate individual words."[22]

Changes to images have been done for a variety of reasons and purposes and the historian needs to consider the context in which the picture was taken. "Contextual information about the art of broadcasting is perhaps nowhere more important than in photography, cinema, photojournalism, and videography.... The intent of the photographer as creator or author of the information is paramount."[23] In critical analysis of visual evidence, the historian must not isolate a picture, but strive to understand the reason the visual image was made. To help in this analysis, the intent of the author may be considered in three ways: art, entertainment, and documentation.

Art

Some images are created purely for artistic reasons. This may include exploring new tools, such as computer graphics. In the past, this included using techniques to change the image to convey a particular meaning by the artist. These images may be used for illustration only and often are obvious in their manipulation. One example is computer-generated collages where fractal images are

---

[22] Robert J. Shafer, "Using Evidence: Internal Criticism," in *A Guide to the Historical Method,* 3rd ed., ed. Robert J. Shafer (Homewood, IL: Dorsey Press, 1980), 151.

[23] Donald G. Godfrey, "Broadcast Archives for Historical Research: Revisiting the Historical Method," *Journal of Broadcasting & Electronic Media* 46, no. 3 (2002): 499.

repeated over and over.[24] The creator of an image is exploring the aesthetics of the medium to communicate to an audience.

Entertainment

Some images are created for entertainment, promotion, or advertising. Here the purpose is to capture the audience so that they may be persuaded to buy a product or participate in an entertainment event. This includes modifying images so people look perfect, such as the cover girl and Hollywood star that have their bodies digitally slimmed down or lines removed from their faces. The infamous cover on *New York Newsday* was a composite of Olympic skaters Nancy Kerrigan and Tonya Harding and was used to capture attention to sell the magazine.[25] *Spy* magazine did a parody of a *Vanity Fair* cover of a pregnant Demi Moore when they featured a pregnant Bruce Willis (her husband at that time) on their cover.[26] Most people recognize that entertainment and advertising use images to excite or draw in an audience. However, Wheeler believes that "nonfiction photography's presumed relationship to reality was disrupted" when these images began to appear.[27]

News, Documentary, and Documentation

Some images are created as a representation of reality. Photojournalism and documentaries are examples of this area. Photojournalists have opposed misleading or altered pictures always, especially in hard news. Digital and commercial concerns make this rule bendable. For the historian, whose job it is to understand and interpret the past, this is a dilemma. Abrams pointed out that, "We're in a photo-illustration age. We're not in an age of reportage."[28] For example, the use of the altered O. J. Simpson magazine cover is claimed by the artist to be within the bounds of practice since he was tying to convey a

---

[24] William Mitchell, *The Reconfigured Eye: Visual Truth in the Post-photographic Era* (Cambridge, MA: MIT Press, 2001), 170–72.

[25] Janet H. Abrams, "Little Photoshop of Horrors: The Ethics of Manipulating Journalistic Imagery," *Print* (November/December 1995): 28.

[26] Wheeler, *Phototruth or Photofiction?*, 154.

[27] Ibid., 51.

[28] Abrams, "Little Photoshop of Horrors," 6.

mood.[29] In the field of nature photography, it has been assumed that the photos are authentic, capturing reality as it occurs in nature. However, that is not always the case. For example, noted nature photographer Art Wolfe's 1994 book, *Migrations,* was about one-third digitally enhanced.[30] In a story about zebras, it was revealed that a famous image of zebras that appeared in that book was digitally cloned and multiplied. There is concern that this use of photography can damage the documentary and journalistic aspect of the visual professions.

Documentation of events also may be available through personal or corporate archives. Often photographs or videotapes are taken of family, or other events, and provide a record of time and place. Many of these works were done without professional training and, therefore, include technical problems that may contribute to difficulty in analyzing the material.

A photo illustration is a common device used in newspapers and magazines in which the image of the photograph is created separate from the story. As its name implies, it is used to illustrate a story for which it is difficult to produce an actual photograph. For example, a feature story about drugs could include a photograph of a table of drug paraphernalia that had been assembled solely for the purpose of the story. These photos are placed in the story as any photograph would be. A notation that it is an illustration should be in the lower, right-hand corner. However, it isn't uncommon to find this has been omitted. Pictures that start out as photo illustrations can lose that identity when they are reused and, therefore, may contribute to an inaccurate historical record.

Today, entertainment and news can easily be confused. Current television programs that have the format of news, such as *Entertainment Tonight,* but only contain entertainment content help contribute to this confusion. Docudrama is another area that sends a mixed message. How much is reality and how much is created by the writer? Examples, such as Oliver Stone's *JFK,* demonstrate the impact a fictional account may have on the perception of a real event. This makes it very important for the historian to check a variety of alternative sources that may include visual and written evidence. However, this also has been compounded by the digital age. Written material that once was

[29] Wheeler, *Phototruth or Photofiction?,* 44.

[30] Art Wolfe, *Migrations: Wildlife in Motion,* text by Barbara Sleeper (Hillsboro, OR: Beyond Words Publishing, 1994); Kenneth Brower, "Photography in the Age of Falsification," *The Atlantic Monthly,* May 1998, 95.

in the form of hard copy, memos, or letters now takes the form of emails that are easily lost. Tape recordings may help but may not be available and also are open to manipulation. Additionally, interviews with people that were present during an event isn't always practical.

Legalities

Additional concerns for the historian are legality and copyright. Traditional infringement or forgery protections do not seem adequate in the digital age. For example, in 1980 a poster company created a photo montage of President Reagan's face imposed on the body of Ronald McDonald and electronically placed in front of a McDonald's restaurant. McDonald's sued the poster company and a judge agreed and granted a restraining order against the poster company. They also filed a copyright infringement suit against the poster firm.[31] Documentary evidence, such as photos and videotapes of crimes, has become commonplace and the public and courts need to trust that the evidence has not been altered. Alterations of videotape can be detected, but digital alteration leaves few or no traces.[32] If the experts cannot detect alterations, it is doubtful that historians would be able to detect alterations.

How to Identify Altered Images

Many in the media field believe we are entering into a new age of visual representation, where illustrations and documentary evidence merge and the audience cannot differentiate one from the other. Yet, to the historian, one is primary evidence and the other, secondary altered evidence at best. For the historian, it is absolutely essential to tell one from the other. There has been some effort to help do this. The use of a symbol to indicate that a photo has been manipulated has had widespread discussion, but has not been adopted as the standard for the profession. Guidelines employed by the professionals in the field may help the historian to ask the right questions about an image. The American Society of Media Photographers' "Code of Ethics" indicates that altering the content of a news photograph is prohibited and alteration should

---

[31] Brugioni, *Photo Fakery.*
[32] Ibid., 196.

be disclosed both for editorial feature and illustrative photographs.[33] The National Press Photographers Association's "Code of Ethics" states, "In documentary photojournalism, it is wrong to alter the content of a photograph in any way (electronically or in the darkroom) that deceives the public."[34] If a symbol is not used, it is very difficult to determine manipulation. However, the researcher is still obliged to ask appropriate questions about the visual documents. Wheeler suggests a Qualified Expectation of Reality (QER) standard adopted from Mitchell.[35] The criteria include the viewfinder test (no use of digital processing to remove, add, or rearrange objects in a photo), the nonfiction photography's process test (shoddy execution makes manipulation obvious), the technical credibility test (the use of standard darkroom procedures such as correcting technical defects) and the test of obvious implausibility (no expectation of reality in an obviously unreal photo). If these standards cannot be met, then Wheeler advocates for disclosure of alterations with a symbol.

ANALYSIS OF VISUAL EVIDENCE

This chapter has presented a lot of information needed by the broadcast historian to understand, interpret, and analyze visual evidence. It is a complex process. The amount of information may seem overwhelming so a rubric or scheme of analysis that facilitates a more ordered examination of the material may be helpful. Two sources give the broadcast historian guidance; one a more general approach to the document; the other a more specific approach to the details of the evidence. A summary of each is presented.

In *The New Nature of History,* Arthur Marwick suggests questions that the historian should ask regarding sources.[36] These questions easily can be applied to visual media by substituting the word "image" for "source." The questions would then include, Is the image authentic? (Authenticity is established through the provenance of the image.) When was the image produced? How does this particular image relate chronologically to other images? How did the

---

[33] American Society of Media Photographers, "Code of Ethics," http://www.asmp .org/culture/code.php.

[34] National Press Photographers Association, "Code of Ethics," http://www.nppa .org/professional_development/business_practices/ethics.html.

[35] Wheeler, *Phototruth or Photofiction?.*

[36] Arthur Marwick, "The Historian at Work: Forget 'Facts,' Foreground Sources," in *The New Nature of History* (Chicago: Lyceum Books, 2001), 152–94.

image come into existence and what was its purpose? How was the document understood by contemporaries? How does the image relate to knowledge obtained from other sources? Of course, asking the questions is not the same as finding the answers. However, providing context and analysis to visual evidence is a critical role for the broadcast historian.

In *Nearby History,* Kyvig and Marty suggest that visual documents are mediated documents and, therefore, require a "reading."[37] This calls for putting words with the picture that give meaning to the reader. For the historian to "read" an image, moving or still, it requires a systematic analysis of the image. Since this is a mediated artifact, the historian can begin to form "a consciousness of the photographer."[38] As stated previously, the historian needs to understand the purposes, biases, and circumstances in which the photographer worked. Who was the person behind the lens?

From the analysis of the person behind the camera, the historian can begin to analyze the content of the image. What is in the frame? What is omitted from the frame? How might your perceptions change if you saw more or less than is included? The place the image was taken also should be considered. Was it taken indoors? … outdoors? … in an artificial or natural setting? What might the sounds and odors be like? What would be enhanced if you knew the answers to the context of the event?[39]

Time is another important consideration, which includes the time of day, the year, and the era. The details of the picture and the artifacts in it may add to historical understanding. The historian might ask: How does the picture enable interpretation of the details and how do the details help draw conclusions about the time and place of the event?[40]

Technical and artistic aspects, previously discussed, can also help the historian. Lighting, focus, positioning, and framing also could be looked at in determining the importance of individuals in the picture such as, Are people touching? What is their arrangement? Is one person dominant? Are any particular emotions projected?[41]

---

[37] David Kyvig and Myron Marty, *Nearby History: Exploring the Past Around You* (Nashville, TN: American Association for State and Local History, 1982).

[38] Ibid., 125.

[39] Ibid., 127.

[40] Ibid.

[41] Ibid., 128.

Overall, the historian should ask questions to decide if the image is appropriate for historical purposes. Does it present an accurate record? Does it say something significant about the subject or photographer? Does it provide insight into the culture? Are time and place clear? Most important, Kyvig and Marty remind us that the use of visual images in historical research should follow these principles: accuracy, use of outside data to substantiate the record, a clear relationship to the story, a caption to help the reader interpret the meaning, and good technical reproduction.[42]

CONCLUSION

Visual evidence for the broadcast historian is immensely important. However, the increased likelihood of some type of electronic manipulation makes it important for the historian to understand the technology and tools of the various visual media. The credibility of the historian and their work may be at risk. In the past, the negatives or first-generation videos frequently were kept. Today, with the glut of electronic images that are possible, storage is a concern and photographers may delete digital images. Historians need to understand the reasons the creator made the image and the context in which the image was made. Documenting the authenticity of the image will be a challenge as formats change and digital information is transferred from one system to another.

Susan Sontag in her critique of photography reminds us of the purpose of an image and the role the historian plays in understanding the past because of that image. "Photographs are not windows which supply a transparent view of the world as it is, or more exactly as it was. Photographs give evidence often spurious, always incomplete—in support of the dominant ideologies and existing social arrangements. They fabricate and confirm these myths and arrangements."[43] She further states that the images tell us what we should look at about what is in the world. The historian's job is to help make sense of this world through critical analysis—an analysis that has become more important and more complicated in the digital age of the visual.

---

[42] Ibid., 132.

[43] Susan Sontag, *On Photography* (New York: Farrar, Straus, and Giroux, 1977), 13.

Part II

Eclectic Methods in History

5

Legal Methods in the History of Electronic Media

Kyu Ho Youm
University of Oregon

L aw plays a pervasive role in American society. This should come as little surprise, given that the United States was founded upon the rule of law. Law's defining role is all the more true in the case of the American press because the First Amendment to the U.S. Constitution "reaffirms the structural role of free speech and a free press in a working democracy."[1] Undoubtedly, the evolutionary process of press freedom has shaped the history of American mass media, especially since the early nineteenth century. Thus, as Timothy Gleason noted, "The history of freedom of the press *is* legal history, which is to say that the history of freedom of the press cannot be studied without paying attention to the law of freedom of the press."[2] Additionally, he characterized the meaning of press freedom as "one of the most important questions" for historians in making sense of journalism and communication history.[3]

The nexus between press freedom and mass communication history becomes more clear-cut when it is placed in a sociocultural, political, and economic context. In his 1947 article on communication law research, Fred S. Siebert observed: "Almost every research project in the broad area of communications involves economic, political, or social as well as legal problems, and

---

[1] Akhil Reed Amar, *The Bill of Rights: Creation and Reconstruction* (New Haven, CT: Yale University Press, 1998), 21.

[2] Timothy W. Gleason, "Historians and Freedom of the Press Since 1800," *American Journalism* 5, no. 4 (1988), 230, 233.

[3] Ibid., 247.

in many cases it is impossible to separate the strictly legal from the other aspects."[4]

The never-ending debate about indecency in broadcasting is a good illustration. Congress and the Federal Communications Commission are now all out to "clean up the airwaves." Whether politically motivated or not in an election year, their sweeping legislative and administrative actions showcase how various social, political, cultural, and economic forces can galvanize Congress and the FCC into action on indecent broadcasting.

The House of Representatives in March 2004 passed a bill that would increase the maximum penalty for an indecency violation from $27,500 to $500,000 and authorize the FCC to bring license-revocation proceedings against broadcasters with three or more indecency fines. A broadcast indecency bill pending before the Senate would authorize the FCC to consider extending its indecency rules to include violent programming on TV. It would further expand the FCC's enforcement authority by empowering the Commission to fine individual speakers as well as broadcast licensees.[5]

In many ways, the indecency rule on broadcasting, as it first evolved into part of the Radio Act of 1927 and was then incorporated into the Communications Act of 1934 (and now Section 1464 of the federal Criminal Code) exemplifies how the history of a law in its origin, interpretation, and enforcement can offer a telling story of the broadcasting media. Why is broadcasting still denied the full range of First Amendment privileges enjoyed by the print media? Equally important, is it appropriate for the FCC to act as the censorial guardian of cultural morality with a mixed-bag record? Likewise, the history of the now-abolished Fairness Doctrine highlights the inherent tension between the First Amendment rights of broadcasters and the "public interest, convenience, and necessity" justification of the Communications Act for broadcast regulation.

Legal research on the broadcasting media's history should be contextual, not only for its target audience but also for researchers themselves. For "it is imperative that substantive legal issues and problems of interest to mass

---

[4] Fred S. Siebert, "Research in Legal Problems of Communications," in *An Introduction to Journalism Research,* ed. Ralph O. Nafziger and Marcus M. Wilkerson (Baton Rouge: Louisiana State University Press, 1949), 26.

[5] See Katherine A. Fallow, "The Big Chill? Congress and the FCC Crack Down on Indecency," *Communications Lawyer* 22, no. 1 (Spring 2004): 1.

communication researchers be put in the context of the law generally."[6] The research methods in the broadcasting media's history, as in other mass communication areas, may vary with the purposes of the legal research involved. However, they are likely to overlap when the research aims to provide "a means for *understanding* and for *explaining* communication and law."[7] Furthermore, the interdisciplinary approach to communication law encourages more eclecticism in research methods.

Regardless of whether one single method or a multitude of methods are used for legal research on the broadcasting media's history, the key question is: Why do legal research from a historical perspective? The answer to this threshold question is that legal research on the broadcasting media's history provides a historical overview of the institutional and noninstitutional confrontations—between the government and the media and between the media and the nongovernment elements. The benefits of such research as the one under discussion are immediate (e.g., class reports, conference papers, journal articles, or thesis/dissertation projects) or long-term (e.g., book projects, policy reports, or litigational preparations). Nonetheless, if the research deserves to be called "good legal scholarship," it should contain a claim that is novel, nonobvious, useful, sound, and seen by the reader to be novel, nonobvious, useful, and sound.[8]

LITERATURE ON LEGAL METHODS IN BROADCASTING MEDIA

There are few journal articles or book-length monographs that focus on legal research methods in mass media, much less of the broadcasting media's history. More often than not, some essays deal with legal research in mass media generally. For example, Donald M. Gillmor and Everette E. Dennis's work explains legal research in media law.[9] Among the topics covered in their book

---

[6] Donald M. Gillmor and Everette E. Dennis, "Legal Research in Mass Communication," in *Research Methods in Mass Communication,* 2nd ed., ed. Guido H. Stempel III and Bruce H. Westley (Englewood Cliffs, NJ: Prentice-Hall, 1989), 331.

[7] Jeremy Cohen and Timothy Gleason, *Social Research in Communication and Law* (Newbury Park, CA: Sage, 1990), 12.

[8] Eugene Volokh, *Academic Legal Writing: Law Review Articles, Student Notes, and Seminar Papers* (New York: Foundation Press, 2003), 9.

[9] See Gillmor and Dennis, "Legal Research."

chapter are legal research tools, various types of mass communication legal research, and publication outlets for research in mass communication law.

Fred Siebert's chapter is valuable to those interested in the early phase of legal research on communication law. It is descriptive and prescriptive in addressing the status of research on communication legal problems and the methods of communication law research and in critiquing and proposing legal problems for future research. In identifying legal problems in radio broadcasting, he writes:

> Should defamation over the radio be considered a slander or libel? Should radio because of its mechanical peculiarities be granted special immunities for liability, for instance for "ad lib" programs? Does the station management have power to censor or should he have this power? What changes are needed in the regulations of the Federal Communications Commission?[10]

In his *American Journalism* article, Gleason analyzes the historiography of freedom of the press between the nineteenth century and the mid-1980s. He is critical of the "law office history," characteristic of many studies of press freedom since 1800. "The historiography of freedom of the press is riddled with works in which historical fact is used selectively to buttress free-press theories in present battles," Gleason argues. "Such work may have a place in courtrooms and campaign speeches, but it adds little to better understanding about the history of freedom of the press."[11] He proposes an "integrated approach" to the study of freedom of the press because press freedom in any historical period is not limited to a question of legal doctrine and theory, press practices, or public tolerance of dissident speech.[12]

In a similar but broad vein, Cohen and Gleason suggested in their book that media law scholars should transcend their traditional focus on case law and constitutional analyses. Instead of arguing that communication researchers forgo legal method altogether, however, they urge communication scholars to use *both* legal and social research methods as tools in building theories of communication and law.[13] They want communication law scholars to avoid falling into the trap of "First Amendment reductionism which takes the

---

[10] Siebert, "Research in Legal Problems," 40.

[11] Gleason, "Historians and Freedom," 231.

[12] Ibid., 234.

[13] Cohen and Gleason, *Social Research,* 133.

researcher[s] on a too easy path toward simple advocacy."[14] The Cohen and Gleason book is a refreshing challenge to communication law scholars who tend to emulate much of the noncommunication legal scholarship with a narrow, advocacy-oriented vision.

The *Journal of Broadcasting & Electronic Media* (note: title updated) and *Public Telecommunications Review* published articles about research resources relating to broadcasting and about access to FCC documents. They're dated and in need of revision, yet they are still useful in providing directional points. Don R. Le Duc's article suggests that broadcasting law researchers should go beyond legal index systems because "they have been designed primarily for practicing attorneys and therefore offer only a narrow flow of relevant past decisions providing precedents for current legal questions." Directly relevant to broadcasting law and regulation research is his four-step approach: (1) how to locate all relevant documentation; (2) how to conduct parallel searches to extend access points; (3) how to narrow the focus of the documentation search; and (4) how to assess the validity of collected documentation.[15]

Joseph M. Foley's article supplements Le Duc's by providing guidelines for locating various printed broadcast legal documents. It discusses unofficial commercial publications distinct from official governmental publications, and all the major publications are given detailed attention. Its appendix includes the forms of citation and the list of abbreviations used in legal citations. The Foley article is about what documents are available rather than about how to locate them.[16]

Two years after Le Duc's and Foley's articles, Erwin G. Krasnow and G. Gail Crotts published a guide on how to obtain information and documents from the FCC. Its key information is still relevant, although its currency is diminished considerably, because it is nearly 30 years old. Nonetheless, the authors' discussion of the Freedom of Information Act (FOIA) is detailed and thorough, and its appendixes list FCC addresses and telephone numbers as well as reprint a sample of a FOIA request letter.[17]

---

[14] Everette E. Dennis, "Foreword," in Cohen and Gleason, *Social Research,* 7.

[15] Don R. Le Duc, "Broadcast Legal Documentation: A Four-dimensional Guide," *Journal of Broadcasting* 17, no. 2 (1973): 131.

[16] Joseph M. Foley, "Broadcast Regulation Research: A Primer for Non-Lawyers," *Journal of Broadcasting* 17, no. 2 (1973): 147.

[17] Erwin G. Krasnow and G. Gail Crotts, "Inside the FCC: A Guide for Information Seekers," *Public Telecommunications Review* 3 (July–August 1975): 49.

Several works provide examples of historical context in the evolution of law. Louise Benjamin traces broadcasting's early First Amendment rights.[18] Marvin Bensman looks at the very beginnings of broadcast regulation.[19] Donald Godfrey, Godfrey and Benjamin, and Godfrey and Val Limburg take a closer look at the evolution of policy within the context of people, policy, and congressional maneuvering.[20]

SELECTING RESEARCH TOPICS IN BROADCASTING MEDIA LAW

As in research on other subjects, legal research will likely become a futile exercise unless you have a problem worthy of a systematic investigation. To some of you, identification of a research problem might be a matter of inspiration. Nonetheless, few media law scholars and historians wait for their moment of revelation in their search for a topic. Instead, they make directed efforts to look for what they consider a problem "big enough to be important and interesting but small enough to be manageable."[21]

Once you decide on a worthy topic for your term paper, discuss it with your professor and others.[22] In all probability, they can help you determine whether too much already exists on the topic or whether there's less substance

---

[18] Louise M. Benjamin, *Freedom of the Air and the Public Interest: First Amendment Rights in Broadcasting to 1935* (Cardondale: Southern Illinois University Press, 2001).

[19] Marvin R. Bensman, *The Beginning of Broadcast Regulation in the Twentieth Century* (Jefferson, NC: McFarland, 2000).

[20] Donald G. Godfrey, "Senator Dill and the 1927 Radio Act," *Journal of Broadcasting* 23, no. 4 (1979): 477–89; Donald G. Godfrey and Louise Benjamin, "Radio Legislation's Quiet Backstage Negotiator: Wallace H. White, Jr.," *Journal of Radio Studies* 10, no. 1 (2003): 93–103; Donald G. Godfrey and Val Limburg, "The Rogue Elephant of Radio Legislation: Senator William E. Borah," *Journalism Quarterly* 67, no. 1 (1990): 214–24.

[21] Volokh, *Academic Legal Writing*, 11.

[22] The term paper that the hypothetical "you" prepared was revised substantially for presentation at the 1999 Association for Education in Journalism and Mass Communication (AEJMC) convention and for publication in the *Federal Communications Law Journal* in May 2000; see Kyu Ho Youm, "Editorial Rights of Public Broadcasting Stations vs. Access for Minor Political Candidates to Television Debates," *Federal Communications Law Journal* 52, no. 3 (2000): 687.

IDENTIFYING LEGAL PROBLEMS

University of California, Los Angeles, law professor Eugene Volokh has a list of tips on how to identify law research problems. Although primarily for law students, the tips are equally relevant to those interested in broadcasting media legal research:

1. Think back on *cases you've read for class* that led you to think "this leaves an important question unresolved" or "the reasoning here is unpersuasive."

2. Try to recall *class discussions* that intrigued you but didn't yield a well-settled answer.

3. Read the *questions that many casebooks include* after each case ....

4. Read *recent Supreme Court cases* in fields that interest you, and see whether they leave open major issues or create new ambiguity or uncertainties.

5. Ask *faculty members* which areas of the law they think have been unduly neglected by scholars ....

6. Ask *practicing lawyers* which important unsettled questions they find themselves facing.

7. Check the *Westlaw Bulletin* (WLB), *Westlaw State Bulletin* ... and *Westlaw Topical Highlights* ... databases ....

8. Check *http://www.lawtopic.org,* a law review topics clearing house ....

9. Read Heather Meeker's *Stalking the Golden Topic: A Guide to Locating and Selecting Topics for Legal Research Papers,* 1996 *Utah L. Rev.* 917.*

*Volokh, *Academic Legal Writing,* 11.

---

to the research problem than you think. In selecting and refining the topic for legal research, it is worth paying attention to the caveats for *beginning* history researchers.[23]

---

[23] Robert Jones Shafer, ed., *A Guide to Historical Method,* 3rd ed. (Homewood, IL: Dorsey Press, 1980), 43–45.

First, make sure that sufficient source material will be available for your topic's study. This should be a nonissue. Most university and law libraries have substantial collections of the primary and secondary source materials. Further, the interlibrary loan service and free, or fee-based, electronic sources can be used efficiently to supplement the existing library materials. If access to relevant materials is a challenge or there is a dearth of library resources, however, you should devise an alternative search strategy. As media law scholar Louise W. Hermanson (University of South Alabama) stated: "Doing quality legal research at a small university with limited resources requires creativity, planning, and perseverance."[24]

Second, choose a topic that is interesting *and* important, not only to you as a researcher but also to your audience on and off campus. Choosing "interesting and important" research topics has a great deal to do with your own familiarity with the broader fields—such as mass communication, law, and international journalism.

Third, make the subject narrow enough to permit an in-depth examination. Your paper on televised political debates could be expanded beyond broadcasting law issues to various political, economic, and social pressures that public television and the FCC have to address. Additionally, you could examine the government's right to free expression, or lack thereof, under the First Amendment. Your refinement of the subject enables you to cover a better defined segment of it.

Fourth, is the subject chosen within your research skills in mass communication? Did you take any general research methods or legal and historical research methods in mass media as an undergraduate or as a graduate student? Also, are there any language or related barriers in handling research material on your topics?

Fifth, to make your research have impact (beyond receiving good grades for your coursework), it must be more than descriptive (i.e., just explaining the law as is). It must contribute knowledge to the field by "say[ing] something that hasn't been said before by others."[25]

Sixth, your subject must have *unity* insofar as it can be discussed separately from the other subjects surrounding it. Your paper on access to television

---

[24] Louise W. Hermanson, "Quality Legal Research Possible Even with Limited Resources," *Media Law Notes* 20 (Fall 1993): 14. See also Jeanne Swann Scafella, "Legal Research in the Hinterland," *Media Law Notes* 18 (Spring 1991): 3.

[25] Volokh, *Academic Legal Writing*, 13.

debates for minority candidates would revolve around access to broadcasting media for political candidates and the public's right to know under the First Amendment.

Finally, the topic for your research should not be the kind of subject inherently difficult to investigate. It should not raise problems relating to any legal and social constraints, such as reputational injury, privacy invasion, or ethical dilemmas.[26]

DISTINGUISHING PRIMARY FROM
SECONDARY SOURCES IN LEGAL RESEARCH

Before discussing various methods of legal research on broadcasting history, be sure that the distinctions between primary and secondary sources (i.e., legal and historical research) are in order. In historical research, it is crucial to determine whether certain records on the past event are primary or secondary (see chapter 2).[27]

In legal research the authoritativeness of the materials is decisive in differentiating primary from secondary sources. Hence, "primary authority" and "secondary authority" are interchangeably used with primary and secondary sources, respectively.[28] Thus, "primary sources are authoritative statements of legal rules by governmental bodies," while secondary sources are "materials about the law that are used to explain, interpret, develop, locate, or update primary sources."[29] For example, statutes, court decisions, and the rules and

---

[26] For a useful discussion of various legal and social constraints on information gathering, see Jean Ward and Kathleen A. Hansen, *Search Strategies in Mass Communication,* 3rd ed. (New York: Longman, 1997), 28–29.

[27] Maryann Yodelis Smith, "The Method of History," in *Research Methods in Mass Communication,* 2nd ed., ed. Guido H. Stempel III and Bruce H. Westley (Englewood Cliffs, NJ: Prentice-Hall, 1989), 323.

[28] Suzanne E. Rowe, *Oregon Legal Research* (Durham, NC: Carolina Academic Press, 2003): 4–5.

[29] Roy M. Mersky and Donald J. Dunn, *Fundamentals of Legal Research,* 8th ed. (New York: Foundation Press, 2002), 10.

regulations of administrative agencies are primary source materials.[30] In legal research, newspapers, magazines, and broadcast tapes are not primary sources.

Primary authority in legal research is further divided into mandatory and persuasive authority. Whereas "mandatory authority is binding on the court that would decide a conflict if the situation were litigated," persuasive authority is "not binding, but may be followed if relevant and well reasoned" because it is from a different jurisdiction or it is not produced by a governing body with lawmaking power.[31] As U.S. Circuit Judge Richard Posner noted recently, the essential distinction between primary, mandatory authority and persuasive authority is whether the authority is "informational" (persuasive) and "precedential" (mandatory).[32]

Research on access rights of political candidates to television debates can be started by asking what primary sources and secondary sources to check. Among the primary sources to be identified are the court decisions, federal and state, the Communications Act and other related statutes, and FCC rules and regulations. Congressional records (e.g., committee hearings on the Presidential Debates Act of 1992 and the Democracy in Presidential Debates of 1991) need to be searched. All the state and federal court decisions should be searched because of their crucial value to the research.

The secondary sources to be checked include books, law reviews, nonacademic publications, popular and trade press reports, and Association for Education in Journalism and Mass Communication or Broadcasting Education Association conference papers. Why is it necessary to look through these and other secondary sources? More than anything else, scholarly sources are

---

[30] For example, primary sources in law would include *United States Code, Statutes at Large, United States Code Annotated, United States Code Service, Congressional and Administrative News, Congressional Index,* or the *United States Congressional Record.* The federal court decisions are published in *United States Reports, Supreme Court Reporter, United States Supreme Court Reports—Lawyer's Edition, Federal Reporter, Federal Supplement, Media Law Reporter,* or the *United States Law Week.* The Federal Communications Commission rules and decisions are found in *Federal Communications Commission Reports, Federal Communications Commission Record,* Pike & Fischer's *Radio Regulation,* Pike & Fischer's *Communications Regulation, Federal Register,* and the *Code of Federal Regulations.*

[31] Rowe, *Oregon Legal Research,* 5.

[32] Richard Posner, "No Thanks, We Already Have Our Own Laws," *Legal Affairs* (July–August 2004): 40.

especially helpful to the legal researcher. First, they help the researcher to develop a better understanding of "the sometimes bewildering array of statutes and court decisions" and to keep up with the current development in the legal doctrine about the topic.[33] Second, their usually detailed documentation provides the researcher with extensive references to both primary and secondary source materials.[34]

FINDING SOURCE INFORMATION: A LEGAL RESEARCH STRATEGY

Legal research is the process of locating the law that governs an individual or institutional activity and materials that explain or analyze that law.[35] As indicated earlier, there are a number of primary and secondary sources for

---

[33] Morris L. Cohen and Kent C. Olson, *Legal Research in a Nutshell,* 7th ed. (St. Paul, MN: West Group, 2000), 7.

[34] Secondary sources in legal research would include any of the professional publications or the academic journals such as *Advertising Age, Broadcasting & Cable, Editor & Publisher, Quill, American Journalism, Gazette, Journal of Broadcasting & Electronic Media, Journal of Media Economics, Journal of Radio Studies, Journalism & Communication Monographs, Journalism & Mass Communication Quarterly, Journalism History, Mass Communication & Society, Newspaper Research Journal, Public Relations Review,* and *Telecommunications Policy.* The specific communication law journals include *Columbia-VLA Journal of Law & the Arts, CommLaw Conspectus: Journal of Communications Law & Policy, Harvard Journal of Law & Technology, Journal of Art & Entertainment, Loyola of Los Angeles Entertainment Law Journal, Rutgers Computer & Technology Law Journal, Berkeley Technology Law Journal, Cardozo Arts & Entertainment Law Journal, Communications & the Law, Federal Communications Law Journal, Free Speech Yearbook, Hastings Communications & Entertainment Law Journal, Media Law & Policy,* and the *Michigan Telecommunications & Technology Law Review;* legal trade publications such as *American Journalism Review, Columbia Journalism Review, Communications Lawyer, Free Speech, Legal Affairs, Media Law Notes, Media Law Reporter Newsnotes, News Media & the Law, News Media Update, Newsletter on Intellectual Freedom,* and the *Student Press Law Center Report;* and finally, legally oriented newspapers and magazines such as *Legal Newspapers & Magazines, American Lawyer, Legal Affairs, Legal Times, Los Angeles Daily Journal, National Law Journal,* and the *New York Law Journal.*

[35] Cohen and Olson, *Legal Research,* 1.

legal research on the electronic media. They range from a whole gamut of print to computer databases of government to commercial sources. Identifying those sources is essential to successful research. More important, as John R. Bittner notes, "choosing the proper strategy at the outset will save valuable time and will make more effective use of the materials available."[36] Nonetheless, where and how to start legal research vary from individual to individual. To some extent, this depends on an individual's preference and familiarity with particular research tools: "Start with materials which you can use most effectively."[37]

Yet the preresearch step is whether or not you have a clear idea of what you want to know (i.e., what is the research problem you're working on?). Defining the problem can be done by consulting an array of secondary sources instead of primary. The advantages of secondary sources over those of primary sources at the beginning of research are considerable:

> The mass of primary sources can seem forbidding and using a subject index or digest to find cases or statutes on point is often frustrating. Primary sources by themselves often are not very straightforward. Secondary materials, on the other hand, try to *explain* and *analyze* the law. They offer easier access, while providing food for thought. They summarize the basic rules and the leading primary sources and place them in context, allowing the researcher to select the most promising primary sources to pursue.[38]

At the outset of your research, secondary sources will be helpful. The *American Law Reports* (*ALR*), for example, selects leading cases and analyzes the subject of the court decision. The *ALR* annotation is comprehensive and contextual in that it "brings into perspective the current standing of case law in other jurisdictions."[39] As a result, you can find background information and refine your focus further. General-interest law journals, which are not solely interested in mass communication law, contain significant articles analyzing the current developments in the field. The "high-impact" law journals such as the *Yale Law Journal* and *Harvard Law Review* are particularly important because they publish articles by some of the finest legal scholars in the nation.

---

[36] John R. Bittner, *Law and Regulation of Electronic Media,* 2nd ed. (Englewood Cliffs, NJ: Prentice-Hall, 1994), 456.

[37] Cohen and Olson, *Legal Research,* 13.

[38] Ibid., 15.

[39] Bittner, *Law and Regulation,* 456.

These journals provide more thorough analyses of court cases and major topics than books do. The titles of those general law journals are found in *Index to Legal Periodicals and Books* and *Current Law Index*. A considerable number of communication law journals started publishing in the 1980s, focusing on communication and related topics. This apparently resulted from the Bureau of National Affairs' publication of *Media Law Reporter*, the weekly loose-leaf service that carries the full text of most precedent-setting federal and state court decisions on media law. These communication law–related journals publish research on First Amendment law on freedom of expression.

Trade journals and newsletters of academic and professional organizations can be excellent sources of information about current developments in broadcasting law and regulations. For example, the spring 2004 issue of *Communications Lawyer* carries an informative analysis of the ongoing congressional and FCC moves to reform various indecency measures. News on various legal issues is available from daily and weekly newspapers, both legal and nonlegal. Some major general newspapers such as *The New York Times, The Washington Post,* and *The Wall Street Journal* are extensive in their coverage of development in the law. To legal researchers, they provide information about new court decisions and articles on developing legal topics. A good illustration is *The New York Times* story on Clear Channel Communications' agreement with the FCC to pay $1.7 million in indecency fines.[40] Legal newspapers and magazines are also published, although their coverage of news and topics in law is uneven. *Legal Times, National Law Journal, American Lawyer, New York Law Journal,* and the *Los Angeles Daily Journal* publish articles of national, regional, and local interest. James C. Goodale's "Did Janet Jackson Have a Right to Do It?" exemplifies the relevancy of the legal newspaper to communication researchers on indecency in television.[41]

Communication law is more popular than ever as a subject for authors. More than 20 general-interest communication law books and treatises have been published by journalism and law scholars and practitioners. Some of them are updated annually. Communication law books and treatises are crucial to legal research as secondary sources. Also, a number of special-topic law books have examined broadcasting law and regulations. By synthesizing

---

[40] Jacques Steinberg, "Clear Channel Is Said to Settle Accusations of Indecency," *The New York Times,* June 6, 2004, C1.

[41] James C. Goodale, "Did Janet Jackson Have a Right to Do It?," *New York Law Journal,* April 2, 2004, 3.

decisions and statutes, they provide a sense of order for their readers on those often confusing individual cases.

In connection with the growing need to update their books, some communication law authors maintain their companion Websites. For example, Paul Siegel's Website "features updates to the text to keep the book [*Communication Law in America*] as current as possible, given the rapidly changing nature of this course content."[42] Thus, some of the books and treatises on communication law are no longer as dated as they were in the past, when their Websites are maintained by the authors. Probably the lengthy list of various communication law–related books, prepared by Thomas L. Tedford and Dale A. Herbeck, is particularly relevant to researchers who want to peruse the index on books on freedom of speech and the press.[43]

In starting legal research, the language of the law can be a challenge to those who are new to the law. As a noted lexicographer Bryan A. Garner stated, "Anglo-American law has a language of its own, consisting in a vocabulary with an unusually large number of foreign phrases, archaic words and expressions, terms of art, and argot words."[44] Hence, the need for a good law dictionary is required in understanding various terms of art, which are different from their ordinary meanings in nonlaw settings.

The law dictionary par excellence is the newly revised *Black's Law Dictionary.*[45] Its definitions are much clearer than its previous editions and offer, where necessary, contextual backgrounds. The now-abolished "fairness doctrine" of the FCC, for instance, is defined as "a former FCC rule that required the broadcast media to furnish a reasonable opportunity for discussion of

---

[42] From Paul Siegel's Website, http://www.ablongman.com/Siegel, as a companion to his book, *Communication Law in America,* 2nd ed. (Boston, MA: Allyn & Bacon, 2002). Also see Wayne Overbeck's Website, http://www.overbeck.com, as a companion for his book, *Major Principles of Media Law* (Belmont, CA: Wadsworth, 2004); and the companion Website at http://www.bc.edu/free_speech/ for Thomas L. Tedford and Dale A. Herbeck's book, *Freedom of Speech in the United States,* 5th ed. (State College, PA: Strata, 2005) that contains annual updates of notable decisions.

[43] Thomas L. Tedford and Dale A. Herbeck, *Resources for Teaching Freedom of Speech* (State College, PA: Strata, 2005).

[44] Bryan A. Garner, "Preface to the First Edition," in *A Dictionary of Modern Legal Usage,* 2nd ed. (New York: Oxford University Press, 1995), xiii.

[45] Bryan A. Garner, ed., *Black's Law Dictionary,* 8th ed. (Eagan, MN: West Publishing, 2004).

conflicting views on issues of public importance." The "fairness doctrine" entry of *Black's Law Dictionary* notes "The FCC abandoned the fairness doctrine in 1987."[46]

Legal scholar Eugene Volokh, cautioning against relying on an intermediate secondary source that cites the original, wrote:

> If you're discussing a case or a statute, read, quote, and cite the case or statute itself. Do not rely on other cases, articles, treatises, or encyclopedias that mention the source. Check the original .... Intermediate sources may seem authoritative, but they're often unreliable, whether because of bias or honest mistake. You can't let their mistakes become your mistakes.[47]

CONSTITUTIONAL AND STATUTORY LAW MATERIAL

A constitution is the supreme law of the jurisdiction. The First Amendment to the U.S. Constitution, which guarantees freedom of speech and the press, is directly more pertinent to print and broadcast media than any other provision of the Constitution. Given that the preeminent source of law in American society is legal text, it is important to find the relevant text of the Constitution. No less significant is locating the court decisions that interpret this text. The Constitution cannot be understood for its practical meaning unless relevant decisions of the U.S. Supreme Court and of the lower federal courts are examined.

The text of the Constitution appears in numerous publications including *Black's Law Dictionary.* It is also printed in the *United States Code,* the official publication of federal statutes. More valuable in legal research are *United States Code Annotated* and *United States Code Service.* These annotated statutory publications are far more than the text of the Constitution. They provide abstracts of the cases interpreting each clause of the Constitution or its amendments. The annotations are updated annually throughout the year. Also, various digests of federal court cases and *ALR* annotations provide additional court interpretations of the Constitution.

The Constitution of the United States of America: Analysis and Interpretation (Library of Congress and latest supplement) should be a more useful starting point for research on the First Amendment questions such as: What is freedom of broadcasting media distinguished from freedom of print media? It

---

[46] Bryan A. Garner, "Fairness Doctrine," in *Black's Law Dictionary,* 634.

[47] Volokh, *Academic Legal Writing,* 95–96.

offers a thorough analysis of Supreme Court decisions on each provision of the Constitution.[48]

The "original intent" of the framers of the Constitution is used by the courts in interpreting the meaning of a provision or clause of the Constitution. *The Federalist* by Madison, Jay, and Hamilton and the *Documentary History of the Ratification of the Constitution* are indispensable as historical sources on the development of the Constitution.[49]

Statutes passed by Congress are published as "session laws." The official session laws are arranged by date of passage and published in separate volumes as the official *Statutes at Large* for each session of Congress. Because the *Statutes at Large* is a chronological arrangement of statutes, its utility as a research tool is limited. But for a legal historian, it is still important as a source on law. Historical researchers use the *Statutes at Large* to determine what specific language was enacted into law and also to determine the date of effect (or repeal) of a particular provision of a federal law such as the Communications Act.

Otherwise, researchers will turn to "codes," which compile statutes and arrange them by subject. The statutes are grouped into broad subject topics, called "titles." The topics are subdivided into sections. The laws governing the broadcast media are in Title 47 of the official *United States Code (U.S. Code)*. The "equal time" provision of the Communications Act is in Title 47 of the *U.S. Code* Section 315, hence cited as 47 *U.S. Code* § 315.

The *U.S. Code* has historical notes, cross references, and other research aids, as well as the actual text of federal statutes. But its value to legal researchers is hampered by two major shortcomings: no timely updates and no information about court interpretations of code sections. Researchers most often use one of the two annotated codes mentioned earlier: *United States Code Annotated (USCA),* published by West Group, and *United States Code Service (USCS),* published by Lexis Publishing. In addition to the text of the law and notes of court decisions, they include references to legislative

---

[48] United States, *The Constitution of the United States of America: Analysis and Interpretation* (Washington, DC: Government Printing Office, 1996).

[49] For background sources on the Constitution, see Leonard W. Levy, Kenneth L. Karst, and Dennis J. Mahoney, eds., *Encyclopedia of the American Constitution,* 4 vols. (New York: Macmillan, 1986 and supp. 1992); Kermit L. Hall, ed., *The Oxford Companion to the Supreme Court* (New York: Oxford University Press, 1992); Kermit L. Hall, ed., *The Oxford Guide to United States Supreme Court Decisions* (New York: Oxford University Press, 1999).

history, administrative regulations, and various secondary sources. They are updated by supplements, pocket parts, advance service pamphlets, and recompiled volumes as necessary. *USCA* and *USCS* are selective in their annotations of court decisions. Probably because of its more extensive case annotations, *USCA* is regarded as "perhaps the *best* place" to research federal laws.[50]

The *United States Code Congressional and Administrative News (USCCAN)* of West Group and the *USCS Advance* of Lexis Publishing provide the texts of federal enactments much faster than *Statutes at Large.* To legal research on broadcasting history, however, *USCCAN* is particularly valuable because of its reprints of selected congressional committee reports, which are the most important sources of legislative history.

Research on legislative history, which refers to the documented information considered by the legislature prior to enacting a law, requires a working knowledge of the legislative process.[51] Congressional Information Service's *CIS/Index* indexes reports, hearings, prints, and documents by subject, title, and bill number. The *CIS/Annual* includes *Legislative Histories* volumes, which provide references for each public law to bills, hearings, reports, debates, presidential documents, and any other legislative actions.

The *Congressional Index* of the Commerce Clearing House (CCH) is another excellent source of the status of current legislation. It includes information about legislative history of statutes and the names of congressional committee members. While they are not as important as committee reports in researching legislative history, floor debates can be "the best available legislative history source" when bills are amended on the floor. The *Congressional Record* is the key source of edited transcripts of congressional deliberations.

Under the doctrine of precedent in U.S. law, courts are expected to follow their precedents, and lower courts must follow decisions of higher courts in the same jurisdiction. This requires finding cases on point and determination of whether those cases are still valid law and have not been reversed, overruled, or otherwise discredited. "Access to 'case law' ... is, therefore, often crucial

---

[50] F. Leslie Smith, Milan Meeske, and John W. Wright II, *Electronic Media and Government* (White Plains, NY: Longman, 1995), 13.

[51] Congressional Quarterly's *Guide to Congress,* 5th ed. (Washington, DC: CQ Press, 2000), is a useful source.

when one is asked to research a legal issue," write legal research specialists Roy M. Mersky and Donald J. Dunn.[52]

U.S. Supreme Court decisions are published officially in the *United States Reports*. They are also published in two commercial court reports, West's *Supreme Court Reporter* and Lexis-Nexis's *United States Supreme Court Reports, Lawyers' Edition*. Researchers prefer the commercial versions of the *United States Reports* because of their prompt publication schedule and various editorial features such as syllabi and "headnotes."[53] The *United States Law Week* is a fourth source of the U.S. Supreme Court decisions. It is published by the Bureau of National Affairs and reproduces Supreme Court opinions with few editorial features. It aims to quickly disseminate the Supreme Court cases during the current term.

Lower federal court decisions are published by West Group in the *Federal Supplement* for the federal district courts and in the *Federal Reporter* for the federal appellate courts. There are no official reports exclusively for cases of the federal district courts and the U.S. courts of appeals. Only a small fraction of the federal district court cases is reported in the *Federal Supplement*. The decision on whether to publish in the *Federal Supplement* is entirely up to the judge writing the opinion. Only those cases ordered by the federal appellate courts to be published appear in the *Federal Reporter* if they are deemed to be of precedential value. The *Federal Appendix,* which started in 2001, includes all the *unreported* cases of the U.S. courts of appeals. Those cases have no precedential value, but they contain facts and application of settled law relevant to a research question under investigation.

The most powerful search method in case law research is through digests, which reprint in a subject arrangement the headnotes from court reports. Undoubtedly digests are valuable as case finders, but they have inherent shortcomings:

> They consist simply of case abstracts, with no explanatory text, and the researcher must often wade through many irrelevant entries to find citations to significant authorities. Digest entries may reflect dicta and may even misstate points of law in the cases they abstract. Unless a case has been

---

[52] Roy M. Mersky and Donald J. Dunn, *Legal Research Illustrated,* 8th ed. (Eagan, MN: Thomson West, 2002), 21.

[53] "Headnote" refers to a brief summary of a legal rule or significant facts in a case that precedes the printed opinion in court reports.

directly reversed or modified, the digests don't indicate that it may no longer be a good law. It is essential to locate and read the cases themselves in order to find those which are actually pertinent, and then to verify their status through other means.[54]

The West Group's key number system is considered the most comprehensive digest system.[55] The researcher can find the topics and key numbers to use West's digest system by using a descriptive-word index (e.g., political debates on TV) after analyzing the factual and legal issues involved in a research subject, by surveying a relevant legal topic (e.g., public television broadcasting), or from the headnotes of a case known to be on point (e.g., *Arkansas Educational Television Commission v. Forbes,* 523 U.S. 666 [1998]).

One of the most valuable loose-leaf services on court cases on mass communication is *Media Law Reporter* (1978–present). It publishes all U.S. Supreme Court decisions and significant federal and state court decisions in media law.[56] The user's aids for *Media Law Reporter* include the topical index, tables of cases, and index digests. On the topical index of *Media Law Reporter* are "broadcast media," "cable television," "Communications Act," "electronic media," "Federal Communications Commission," and "television and radio."

Administrative agencies characterize American government. This explains in part why "it is probably *government agencies* that have the most profound effect on daily life."[57] As Thomas A. Schwartz noted, "Administrative law has a prominent place in the study of communication law.... Virtually every communication business must attend at least some administrative law."

---

[54] Cohen and Olson, *Legal Research,* 92–93.

[55] "Key number" in West's digest system refers to a permanent number given to a specific point of American case law.

[56] *Media Law Reporter* is probably the most comprehensive court reporter on mass communication law in that (quoting Cynthia Bolbach, managing editor of the *Media Law Reporter*) "at least 95 percent of cases that get even to the earliest stages of a court proceeding are picked up by the *Reporter's* far-flung cadre of correspondents, and appear in the publication, if not in official and other unofficial case reports." Donald M. Gillmor, *Power, Publicity, and the Abuse of Libel Law* (New York: Oxford University Press, 1992), 129.

[57] Steven L. Emanuel, *Lexis-Nexis for Law Students,* 3rd ed. (Larchmont, NY: Emanuel, 1997), 6-1.

The FCC is the most important federal administrative agency on communication law to implement the "public convenience, interest, or necessity" mandate of broadcasting under the Communications Act. This independent agency is empowered to promulgate regulations—detailed rules aimed to enforce the Communications Act.

Administrative law comprises the regulations, rulings, and decisions made by government agencies through their rule-making, rule-interpretation, and rule-enforcement authority. All federal agency rules and regulations, including those of the FCC, are first published in the *Federal Register (Fed. Reg.)* chronologically. The daily *Fed. Reg.*, which is analogous to a session law in text, is crucial to researching FCC law. For no FCC order or regulation has general legal effect unless it is first published in the *Fed. Reg.* Most important, the FCC is required to publish any possible changes in its rules and regulations in the *Fed. Reg.* through published Notices of Proposed Rulemaking in order to allow public comment.

The *Fed. Reg.* is not access-friendly to researchers because of its chronological publication. The *Code of Federal Regulations* (*CFR*) provides subject access to federal regulations including those of the FCC in force. The regulations in the *CFR* are collected from the *Fed. Reg.* and organized by subject matter in a similar way as the *U.S. Code.* The *CFR* contains 50 titles, and Title 47 is for FCC rulings and policies. While *CFR* volumes are updated and replaced throughout the year, the *CFR Index and Finding Aids* volume is revised annually. Official FCC decisions were published in *FCC Reports* until 1986, when the *Reports* was replaced by *FCC Record.*

Important alternatives to *Fed. Reg.* and the *CFR* are the commercially published loose-leaf services for FCC and other administrative regulations. They are thoroughly indexed and frequently supplemented. Also, they integrate rules and regulations with related primary source material; hence, they provide convenience and current access to administrative law. Pike and Fischer's *Communications Regulation,* previous edition published as *Radio Regulation* (1948–1995), is a case in point.[58] Pike and Fischer is the best source for researching FCC rules and decisions and relevant court cases and statutes. Its comprehensive coverage, indexing, weekly updating, and cross-referencing

---

[58] Pike and Fischer, *Communications Regulation: Current Service* (Bethesda, MD: Pike and Fischer, 1995–). For the most up-to-date information on Pike and Fischer's *Communications Regulation,* see "Communications Regulation," http://www.pf.com/commreg.asp.

with *FCC Reports* and the *CFR* are incomparable. Broadcast law specialist Don Le Duc noted the unsurpassed value of Pike and Fischer in research on broadcasting law and regulation:

> [T]he availability of the Pike and Fischer service [is] a risky supposition perhaps, but … as essential a prerequisite to effective legal research as a computer terminal is to empirical research. In each case substitute techniques are possible, but the extra burdens imposed by the lack of proper facilities may demand more time than any results could justify. Purchase and maintenance costs of this service can be argued on a broader basis than research, however, for teaching "broadcast regulation" without *Radio Regulation* [now *Communications Regulation*], the primary source reference, is about as effective as teaching television production without a camera, with a ½-inch system comparable to Pike and Fischer in both areas of expense.[59]

Pike and Fischer "can be intimidating and frustrating for the novice to use without guidance and patience."[60] Pike and Fischer's *Desk Guide to Communication Law Research* (1993) is useful because it discusses how to conduct research using the *Radio Regulation* series (1948–1995). The major change, when switching to the newer *Communications Regulation* series (1995 to the present), is that Pike and Fischer adopted a new headnote classification system based on FCC rule numbers.

Pike and Fischer's service has three basic parts:

1. The "Current Service" contains all current laws, regulations (including proposed rules) and treaties relevant to communications regulation.

2. The "Digests" contain summaries of Notices of Proposed Rulemaking (NPRMs), Report and Orders, other agency decisions, and state and

---

[59] Le Duc, "Broadcast Legal Documentation," 144, n. 9. The annual subscription to the full-service loose-leaf print version of *Pike & Fischer* is substantial, costing more than $4,495 per year. See "Communications Regulation," http://www.pf.com/commreg.asp.

[60] F. Leslie Smith, "How to Use Pike & Fischer," in *Electronic Media and Government: The Regulation of Wireless and Wired Mass Communication in the United States* by F. Leslie Smith, Milan Meeske, and John W. Wright II (White Plains, NY: Longman Publishers, 1995) 17, is a concise guide on using Pike and Fischer and recommended, although it does not directly bear on Pike and Fischer's *Communications Regulation*.

federal court cases relevant to FCC regulations. The Digests are organized by subject matter based on the FCC rules codified in the Code of
Federal Regulations.

3. The "Cases" contain the full text of all items summarized in the Digests.

To an extent, telecommunication law scholar Matthew Jackson said, Pike and
Fischer's *Communications Regulation* provides "one-stop shopping."[61]

ELECTRONIC SOURCES IN LEGAL RESEARCH

A comprehensive legal research mandates asking when and how to best
use electronic resources. Given that "just about anything is available on the
Net,"[62] online legal research appears to replace traditional legal research.
Nonetheless, it is too presumptuous to conclude that doing online research
is already making print-based research obsolete. Undoubtedly, electronic
research through computer databases such as Lexis-Nexis and Westlaw is
unbeatable in updating and checking the currency of law on broadcasting and
other areas. But its informational online coverage is still limited. "There's lots
of great stuff that isn't available and likely never will be," said Joseph Janes,
chairman of library and information science at the University of Washington
in June 2004.[63]

Online research on the Web tends to be elemental in locating a statute,
agency regulation, or court case, in checking case citations, and also in checking the history of court cases. No case digests or annotations to statutes or
agency rules are available in online resources. Thus, they're not good enough
as a tool for more sophisticated research. And yet free online resources maintained by government agencies, universities, law schools, law firms, special
interest groups, etc., provide an increasing number of primary and secondary
materials.

---

[61] E-mail from Matt Jackson, professor of telecommunication, Pennsylvania State
University, to the author (July 1, 2004) (on file with author). My discussion of the
Pike and Fischer search in this chapter is drawn from Professor Jackson's previous
panel presentation on legal research.

[62] Kathy Biehl and Tara Calishain, *The Lawyer's Guide to Internet Research* (Lanham, MD: Scarecrow Press, 2000), 2.

[63] Katie Hafner, "In a Wired Age, Library Stacks Get Dustier," *Register-Guard,* June
21, 2004, A1.

ONLINE SOURCES VERSUS PRINT

Suzanne E. Rowe, director of the Legal Research and Writing Program at the University of Oregon Law School, suggests asking six "fundamental" questions in deciding whether to use online sources rather than print material:

1. "*What* is the document?" [Distinguish among documents on line more carefully.]

2. "*Who* wrote the document?" [Check and double-check the sources of the documents on their authoritative nature and accuracy.]

3. "*When* was the material published?" [Determine the date of its publication and also the scope of its coverage.]

4. "*How much* context is provided?" [Know whether the user's tools include a table of contents, topic outlines, or a list of statutes.]

5. "*How much* does it cost, and who is paying?" [Use cost-free print and/or online sources first if they're an option in legal research.]

6. "*How fast and how efficient* will research be?" [Depending on your experience and the stage of your research, research in print can be quicker and more efficient than online research—or vice versa.]*

*Rowe, *Oregon Legal Research*, 156–60.

LEXIS, Westlaw, and other commercial databases offer far more than free online resources. In this light, the principle, "you get what you pay for," is more of a reality in using fee-based services for legal research.[64] The main reason for using LEXIS, Westlaw and other pay services is "gaining access to the pagination of the *official* text, headnotes, and Key Numbers of opinions, and the absolute latest versions of statutes and codes. If you need to locate a volume and page citation and Shepardize [i.e., update] the case, you will have to pay to do that online."[65]

---

[64] Biehl and Calishain, *Lawyer's Guide*, 42–43.

[65] Ibid., 43 (emphasis added).

INTERNET RESOURCES

- **Code of Federal Regulations.**
  http://www.access.gp.gov/nara/cfr/cfr-table-search.html
- **Constitution of the United States of America.**
  http://www.access.gpo.gov/congress/senate/constitution/toc.html
- **Federal Communications Commission.**
  http://www.fcc.gov/
- **Federal Courts Finder.**
  http://www.law.emory.edu/FEDCTS/
- **Federal Register.**
  http://www.access.gpo.gov.80/su_docs/aces/aces140.html
- **Find Law.**
  http://www.findlaw.com/
- **Government Printing Office.**
  http://www.gpoaccess.gov/index.html
- **Harvard Law Review Association.** *The Bluebook: A Uniform System of Citation*, 17th ed. http://www.legalbluebook.com/changes.html
- **Hieros Gamos: Law and Legal Research Center.**
  http://www.hg.org/index.html
- **Lexis-Nexis.**
  http://www.lexis.com/
- **Library of Congress.** *National Union Catalog of Manuscript Collections* (*NUCMC*).
  http://lcweb.loc.gov/coll/nucmc/nucmc.html
- **Loislaw.**
  http://loislaw.com/
- **Meta-Index for U.S. Legal Research.** Georgia State University College of Law. http://gsulaw.gsu.edu/metaindex/
- **Pike & Fischer's Communications Regulation.**
  http://www.pf.com/commreg.asp
- **THOMAS: Legislative Information for the Public.**
  http://thomas.loc.gov
- **VersusLaw: Online Legal Research Tools.**
  http://www.versuslaw.com
- **Westlaw: Online Legal Research Service.**
  http://www.westlaw.com

VALIDATING AND UPDATING THE
SOURCE MATERIALS—"SHEPARDIZING"

In analyzing a broadcasting law topic, locating legal authority on point is the sine qua non of legal research. Equally important is determination of how that authority has been treated later—by federal and state courts, Congress, or FCC or other government agencies. Accordingly, researchers in broadcasting law must ensure that the cases, statutes, and other primary source materials they use continue to represent "good" law. This is more compelling than ever because law is constantly changing at an accelerated pace. No legal research is complete until each and every legal authority is updated in one way or another.

Updating the law in legal research is often called "Shepardizing," because the first major updating tool was *Shepard's Citations.*[66] *Shepard's Citations* of Lexis-Nexis covers constitutions, statutes, administrative rules and regulations, court rules, law review articles, and *ALR Restatements,* among others. Westlaw's equivalent of *Shepard's Citations* online is *KeyCite.* Nonetheless, it is not identical to *Shepard's* in its content and service features. Thus, it is suggested that "to ensure absolute thoroughness in any research it is really necessary to access both *Shepard's* on Lexis-Nexis and Westlaw's *KeyCite.*"[67] Online updating through Lexis's *Shepard's* or Westlaw's *KeyCite* is more effective than working with citation information in print sources. The online sources are much easier to use and quicker in updating than the print ones.

When should Shepardizing start in the legal research process—early or late? Early Shepardizing will obviate the kind of additional research or conceptual rethinking that might entail later updating. This is because late Shepardizing in legal research comes after a line of analysis that is no longer the current law. Needless to say, the most important part of Shepardizing law on broadcasting or other subjects is to analyze the impact of the citing authorities. For example, if your research is on the raging controversy on indecency on radio and television, you might ask, in the course of Shepardizing the leading U.S. Supreme Court's case, *FCC v. Pacifica Foundation:* Has the U.S. Supreme Court modified or overruled the 1978 case? Has the Communications Act on

---

[66] George S. Grossman, *Legal Research: Historical Foundations of the Electronic Age* (New York: Oxford University Press, 1994), 66–69.

[67] Mersky and Dunn, *Legal Research Illustrated,* 310.

indecency statute you examined been revised, or is it in the process of being revised? Has the FCC changed its indecency rules and regulations?

STOPPING RESEARCH AND STARTING WRITING

When will research stop and writing start? Or will research and writing be done simultaneously? Determining when to stop legal research is inextricably interrelated with the question whether enough research has been done to make the researcher feel confident that research has been based on complete and accurate information. Overresearching or underresearching a legal topic involves many variables such as physical constraints (e.g., time and money), nature of the research project (simple or complex), and accessibility of information. Cohen and Olson offer a practical answer:

> [T]ry several approaches to the research problem and compare results. If a review of the secondary literature, a digest search, and online queries produce different conclusions, more research is necessary. When these various approaches lead to the same primary sources and single conclusion, chances are better that a key piece of information has not eluded you.[68]

Insofar as Shepardizing is a crucial part of legal research, however, there is no such thing as complete termination of the research process for writing. Shepardizing broadcasting law cases and other authorities should continue until the moment the results of your legal research are submitted for conference presentation or journal publication.

Shifting from research to writing is not a discrete process at all; it is more of a changing emphasis in legal research. For starting writing "just means shifting your primary energies to writing" while supplementing your initial research which did not touch upon some of your research focuses.[69] In legal writing as

---

[68] Cohen and Olson, *Legal Research,* 18–19. See also Rowe, *Oregon Legal Research,* 185 ("If you have worked through the research process and found nothing, it may be that nothing exists"); Merksy and Dunn, *Fundamentals,* 20 ("In many instances, an obvious repetition of citations or absence of new information suggests that enough research has been done"). For a historical ten-question approach to "how much research is 'enough,'" see James D. Startt and William David Sloan, *Historical Methods in Mass Communication* (Hillsdale, NJ: Lawrence Erlbaum Associates, 1989), 154–55.

[69] Volokh, *Academic Legal Writing,* 67.

in other academic writing, all the usual writing tips apply with equal force: "Write well by being clear, direct, precise, and accurate."[70] And some of UCLA law professor Volokh's excellent suggestions for legal writing are profoundly instructive.[71]

It is almost axiomatic that there is no writing—only rewriting. Thus, going through many drafts is required. This is derived from the premise that the first draft should be finished well before the deadline. When is rewriting warranted? "If you need to reread something to understand it."

In reading the draft, your imagined reader's perspective should be the guiding light because it may be sharply different from yours. One feasible way to do this is to have the draft read by a discerning classmate who is willing to read carefully and to practice "tough love" as a critique. How can you take full advantage of your professor's (and other equally discerning readers') comments on your draft? Treat them as a "global" suggestion to challenge you to do better in writing and substance as well. That is, use their informed comments to ask yourself whether the unmarked part of your paper has the same kinds of problems noted by your professor and others.

Is your paper beset with or free from logical flaws in writing? Reexamine all the categorical assertions apiece, your overly sweeping insistence on perfectionism, your possibly false either-or dichotomies, your universal (read: overbroad) criticisms, and your erroneous metaphors or undefined or ill-defined terms.

And finally, proofread the draft with utmost care. Peruse it for possible errors in grammar, spelling, word usage, or punctuation. For the credibility of the researcher/writer is on the line, regardless of the substance of the writing.

WHERE TO PUBLISH LEGAL RESEARCH

Where to publish legal research will be determined by two factors: "(1) form and style of the research paper, and (2) the audience one desires to reach."[72] *Journalism and Mass Communication Quarterly* (*JMCQ*) and similar mass communication journals do not accept the kinds of law review manuscripts

---

[70] Beth Luey, *Handbook for Academic Authors,* 4th ed. (New York: Cambridge University Press, 2002), 13.

[71] See Volokh, *Academic Legal Writing,* 69–94.

[72] Gillmor and Dennis, "Legal Research," 350.

PROOFREADING

Here's Volokh's seven-question formula for proofreading:

1. (For each sentence) What information does this sentence communicate to readers that they *don't already know?*

2. (For each sentence) Has this information—or even part of it—*already been communicated by a previous sentence?*

3. (For each sentence) Are this sentence and the previous sentence *so closely related* that part of the first sentence is repeated in this one?

4. (For each word, phrase, or sentence) Can I *eliminate this without changing the meaning?*

5. (For each phrase in a sentence) Is this how *normal people talk?*

6. (For each word) Does this word communicate *exactly what I want it to?*

7. (For each noun) *Should this noun be a verb, adjective, or adverb* instead?*

*Volokh, *Academic Legal Writing,* 93.

---

that tend to be voluminous, extensively documented, and advocacy-oriented. *Communication Law and Policy,* the refereed journal of the Association for Education in Journalism and Mass Communication (AEJMC) Law Division, resulted from media law scholars' efforts to address the strictures of *JMCQ* and other nonlaw journals on manuscript submissions.

The target audience of legal research in journalism and mass communication is considerably different from that of law reviews. The practical impact of *Journalism and Mass Communication Quarterly* (*JMCQ*), *Journal of Broadcasting & Electronic Media* (*JOBEM*), and other similar journals on the legal community is negligible when compared with law journals. Media law professor Clay Calvert of Penn State, who has published extensively in law journals, argues: "Lawyers use them [law journal articles] to form legal arguments and often cite them in briefs to supplement case law and statutory authority. They also are constantly cited by courts and have greatly influenced the shape of the law."[73]

---

[73] Clay Calvert, "Should You Publish in a Law Review?," *Media Law Notes* 30 (Spring 2002): 1.

What's the best way to get legal research published in journalism and mass communication journals or law reviews—or both? Does finding good ideas and doing sound research guarantee publication? Knapp and Daly say No, adding: "Whereas rigorous thinking and methodological precision increase your chances for publication, you must also understand and follow certain rules associated with the publication process. In other words, success in publishing is a result not only of *what* one produces, but *how, when, where,* and *to whom* it is presented."[74]

Prior to submission of manuscripts to refereed communication journals, four factors should be considered: the prestige of the journal; the suitability of the paper to the journal; the needs of the journal; and the journal editor's image.[75] Similar to conference papers, journal manuscripts should target the "right" audience, be free from writing errors, contain a good introduction, resist overwriting, and get the references right.[76]

Unlike *student-edited* law reviews, refereed journalism and mass communication journals and faculty-edited law journals such as *Communication Law and Policy* prohibit simultaneous submissions. Also, blind reviews are typical of academic nonlaw journals in determining acceptance or rejection of manuscripts for publication.

SUMMARY AND CONCLUSIONS

The basic modus operandi of scholarly research, whether it relates to law or not, requires you to find and use the only information that is "relevant, reliable, *and* current." To attain this fundamental goal of your information search in law, you must follow the absolute rule: "Be thorough."[77] Any research you're engaged in is designed to make sure that thoroughness is the touchstone against which your work is tested.

In checking various primary and secondary sources, your first order of business is to know who have been and will be the key players (administrative

---

[74] Mark L. Knapp and John A. Daly, *A Guide to Publishing in Scholarly Communication Journals* (Mahwah, NJ: Lawrence Erlbaum Associates, 2004), 5.

[75] Ibid., 9–10.

[76] Ibid., 14–17.

[77] Elizabeth Fajans and Mary R. Falk, *Scholarly Writing for Law Students: Seminar Papers, Law Review Notes, and Law Review Competition Papers,* 2nd ed. (St. Paul, MN: West Group, 2000), 52.

agencies, lawmakers, courts, or private interest groups—or all of them) in framing the legal issues you're researching. The source material relevant to your research is closely intertwined with what kind of actions these players have taken or will take.

As Don Le Duc aptly described in the early 1970s, locating and at the same time expanding the informational access point(s) in primary and secondary sources will offer you a holistic perspective. This will surely lead to your narrowing of the search more relevant to your research focus. Actual information gathering should be preceded by a careful documentation and critical evaluation of the processes (administrative, adjudicatory, or congressional) and their participants. For the relevance, currency, and reliability of the located sources is most likely to be affected by the proceedings producing the information you'll use for your research. The authoritativeness of the information gathered should be calibrated into broadcast legal research because the validity of the information is often contingent upon how the proceedings have been conducted.

Your legal research on broadcasting media cannot and should not be limited to documented sources, while ignoring human sources such as experts, government officials, or lawmakers who are related to your topic. Librarians are often underused as sources of information on your topic. Also, if you are doing a case analysis, your contact with the attorneys involved in the case can be a treasure trove for you. Furthermore, your participation in an electronic discussion group in your area of interest will help you network with other people and stay current.

6

Applying Critical Theory to Electronic Media History

John Armstrong
Furman University

A t the end of World War I, radio was not yet a part of most Americans' everyday lives. The wireless was still the province of military signal units, ships at sea, and civilian hobbyists. Two decades later, on the eve of World War II, U.S. radio had become a mass medium that brought entertainment, news, culture, and ideology into millions of homes. In 1926, NBC was founded as the first radio network. In 1927, Congress passed the Radio Act, creating the Federal Radio Commission (FRC) to regulate broadcasters. In 1933, President Franklin D. Roosevelt broadcast his first "fireside chat" to the nation. In 1934, Congress passed the Communications Act and replaced the FRC with the Federal Communications Commission (FCC). In 1938, Orson Welles broadcast his "War of the Worlds" radio play, which thousands of panicky listeners mistook for news reports of a real invasion from Mars.

No serious historian questions the reality of these events, or denies the general contours of radio's development in the United States. More than six decades later, however, historians are still interpreting the "how" and the "why" of broadcast radio's emergence in the United States. They continue to theorize about the significance of the foundation of NBC or the Radio Act. And they examine previously ignored events, people, and programs in radio history to understand their significance. This dynamic process of interpretation and reinterpretation, this relentless application of theory to generate new understanding of old events, is characteristic of critical theory and its use in the history of electronic media.

One of the most satisfying aspects of reading history is that it is often a good story, well told. Because narrative flow is so valued in historical writing, historians often leave explicit discussions of theory out of their prose, or at least confine it to an introductory section. But make no mistake: Theory can play a crucial role in historiography. By now, readers of this book will appreciate how scholars have enriched the history of electronic media by uncovering new documents, artifacts, or other qualitative and quantitative evidence. This chapter demonstrates how, in much the same way, the historian's critical stance toward his or her topic can contribute to the rigor and depth of electronic media history.

In this chapter, a *critical* approach, as noted in chapter 1, is understood as the practice of description, interpretation, and evaluation in electronic media history.[1] Toward this end, the historian becomes a "critic," but not in the sense of a reviewer who comments on the quality of, for example, a movie—generally on the basis of personal taste. Instead, the historian/critic of electronic media employs theory to interpret the "how" and "why" of historical events and to evaluate their significance. And the historian/critic must do so with the same rigor that he or she uses in locating historical evidence and testing its authenticity.

In the physical sciences, a theory is a systematic explanation of phenomena that can be verified by repeatable results in an experiment. Since historians study past human behavior and thought, they are unable to conduct experiments. But they can use theory to help them understand the past as more than a series of random events. For our purposes, *critical theories* can be understood as systematic concepts of human action and consciousness that historians use to test, augment, or replace previous understandings about events, people, and power in electronic media history. Once again, early radio offers an example of how critical historiography has challenged reigning notions of meaning and significance.

In her history of radio's development in the first decades of the twentieth century, Susan Douglas examines the role of radio amateurs—ancestors of today's ham radio operators—who thrust the wireless into the popular imagination and pioneered the practice of transmitting radio signals to distant,

---

[1] Malcolm O. Sillars and Bruce Gronbeck, *Communication Criticism: Rhetoric, Social Codes, Cultural Studies* (Prospect Heights, IL: Waveland Press, 2001), 7.

random listeners.[2] As Douglas demonstrates, a form of broadcasting emerged from the practices of radio hobbyists. In Douglas's view, the activities of these radio tinkerers were more than just a colorful footnote to the serious business of mass broadcasting that soon followed. Rather, the amateurs developed a social practice—broadcasting—that radio stations, networks, and mass audiences would emulate. This is a fresh interpretation of the origins of broadcasting, which has tended to emphasize major institutions, such as the Radio Corporation of America, and major figures, such as RCA Chairman David Sarnoff who claimed some credit for "inventing" the idea of radio broadcasting.[3] The historian E. P. Thompson argues that: "As some of the leading actors of history recede from our attention—the politicians, the thinkers, the entrepreneurs, the generals—so an immense supporting cast, whom we had supposed to be mere attendants upon this process, press themselves forward."[4]

Douglas's reinterpretation of radio history is informed by a rigorous examination of evidence that other historians often overlooked: contemporary newspapers and radio magazines that glamorized the amateurs and popularized wireless communication. Just as important, Douglas's new account of radio history is driven by a critical-theoretical approach, cultural studies, that stresses the formation of beliefs and values—and even social practices like broadcasting—through a process of cultural interpretation and negotiation. This process has implications for societal power, because it takes place in everyday life as well as in the circles of political and economic elites. The origins and intellectual underpinnings of cultural studies are examined later in this chapter. But by applying a theory of how humans make sense of their world to a convincing body of empirical evidence, Douglas challenges previous assumptions about the meaning and significance of amateur radio. For Douglas, the meaning of the amateur's use of radio is that it was an embryonic form of broadcasting. Its significance is that it helped establish the conditions for mass radio and, later, mass television broadcasting, the quintessential electronic media of the twentieth century.

---

[2] Susan J. Douglas, *Inventing American Broadcasting, 1899–1922* (Baltimore, MD: Johns Hopkins University Press, 1987), 292–314.

[3] See Louise Benjamin, "In Search of the Sarnoff 'Radio Music Box' Memo," *Journal of Broadcasting & Electronic Media* 37, no. 3 (1993): 325–35.

[4] Edward P. Thompson, "History and Anthropology," in *Making History: Writings on History and Culture* (New York: New Press, 1994), 205.

Susan Douglas's interpretation of radio history is an example of the role critical theory can play in the historiography of electronic media. The remainder of this chapter examines the theoretical origins, the methodological practices, and the practical challenges of critical research as it is now practiced by electronic media historians. It also evaluates some attempts to expand the theoretical and methodological reach of critical media history.

REVIEW OF LITERATURE:
CRITICAL RESEARCH AND MASS MEDIA

We can trace this chapter's theme—the scholar acting as a critical analyst of electronic media—to the late 1930s and 1940s and the work of Max Horkheimer and Theodor Adorno. Although Horkeimer and Adorno concentrated on contemporary rather than historical mass media, they anticipated subsequent critical research by developing an interpretive, theoretically grounded methodology. Horkeimer and Adorno also foreshadowed two important threads of electronic media history when they explored both the cultural and industrial aspects of mass media.

Horkheimer and Adorno were members of the Institute of Social Research in Frankfurt, Germany. The researchers of the Frankfurt School sought to explain the role of culture in perpetuating social and political inequality. Although they started from a Marxian perspective, Institute researchers drew on sources as diverse as Sigmund Freud and his theories about subconscious human drives, and Max Weber and his notions of rational administration in modern institutions.

After the Nazis came to power in Germany, many members of the Institute fled to the United States and American society became an important object of inquiry.[5] Horkeimer and Adorno would spend much of their exile in Los Angeles, center of the movie industry, and they became particularly interested in entertainment media and the ideology it conveyed to mass audiences. Horkheimer and Adorno's media studies were part of an even more ambitious analysis. Their famous essay "The Culture Industry: Enlightenment as Mass Deception" appeared as a single chapter in a more general indictment of

---

[5] Martin Jay, *The Dialectical Imagination: A History of the Frankfurt School and the Institute of Social Research, 1923–1950* (Berkeley: University of California Press, 1973), 212.

western culture and the philosophical traditions of the Enlightenment.[6] Enlightenment ideals of logic and science, they argued, had created a mass society in which people had little autonomy or individuality.[7] Based on their analysis of popular films and radio programs, Horkheimer and Adorno concluded that mass media had an important role in this process. They theorized that the rational, industrial basis of modern mass media led them to shape monolithic messages that had a psychologically deadening effect and deprived audience members of social agency.[8]

The term that Horkeimer and Adorno coined for the modern entertainment media was the *Culture Industry*. By fusing two concepts that were not typically associated—culture and industry—Horkheimer and Adorno offered new ways to think about mass media. They emphasized the importance of the corporate control and economic mission of media. Horkheimer and Adorno also suggested means by which political and social control could be exerted through popular culture.[9] And finally, they demonstrated that to study mass media was to study power in a modern, industrial society. For these reasons, some scholars believe that Horkheimer and Adorno's comprehensive and theoretically driven media research marks the beginning of critical communication studies.[10]

Communication scholars now generally appreciate that mass media have both cultural and industrial components. This complexity has inspired electronic media historians to employ a variety of research methods; these methods often have little to do with the original, Marxian orientation of the Frankfurt School. Moreover, critical histories of electronic media are built on the investigation of historical evidence, a method that was largely absent from Horkeimer and Adorno's work. Nonetheless, by stressing both the cultural and industrial aspects of media, Horkheimer and Adorno anticipated two threads of scholarship that have diverged into distinct forms of research

---

[6] Max Horkheimer and Theodor W. Adorno, "The Culture Industry: Enlightenment as Mass Deception," in *Dialectic of Enlightenment* (New York: Continuum, 1944), 120–67.

[7] Ibid., 42.

[8] Jay, *Dialectical Imagination,* 216–17.

[9] Barry Brummett, *Rhetoric in Popular Culture* (New York: St. Martin's Press, 1994), 76.

[10] Douglas Kellner, *Media Culture: Cultural Studies, Identity and Politics between the Modern and the Postmodern* (New York: Routledge, 1995), 28–29.

known as "cultural studies" and "political economy." The next sections examine influential literature in each area.

Investigating Culture

In our everyday conversations, we often associate "culture" with the fine arts. In the academic discipline of communication, however, a "culture" is often understood to be a group of people who share meanings about the world. Within critical media scholarship, this understanding of "culture" helps shape basic research questions: What does electronic media content—TV programs, radio shows and Web pages—reveal about a culture at a particular moment in its history, and what role do electronic media play as people make sense of their world? This is the "cultural" approach that is associated with the cross-disciplinary movement known as cultural studies. The cultural approach is also driven by theories about the importance of culture in shaping societies and history.

An early theorist of cultural studies was the British scholar Raymond Williams, who believed that culture should be at the forefront of social and historical analysis. Williams had a sweeping concept of culture that extended beyond works of art or expression, and included the activities of everyday life. Although traditional histories tend to emphasize the role of great individuals, or of impersonal economic and social forces, Williams thought that culture—the way that people communicate and make sense of their world—was an overlooked factor in history. Williams also believed that scholars could conduct "historical criticism" of intellectual and imaginative works and other evidence that would help them understand the influential meanings and values within a particular culture.[11]

A historical study that explores this notion of culture is E. P. Thompson's *The Making of the English Working Class,* published in 1963. His work is far more than a chronology of industrial milestones, food riots and Parliamentary Acts. Thompson interpreted letters, pamphlets, newspapers, ballads, and church sermons to learn how the consciousness of the emerging class of English workers was shaped through the conflict of the Industrial Revolution.[12]

---

[11] Raymond Williams, *The Long Revolution* (New York: Columbia University Press, 1961), 41–42.

[12] Edward P. Thompson, *The Making of the English Working Class* (New York: Pantheon, 1963), 444.

The approach of Williams and Thompson to cultural research influenced a generation of British scholars who examined late twentieth-century media and popular culture. This line of media research became known as British Cultural Studies. British Cultural Studies has a Marxian orientation and examines how dominant and subordinate social groups struggle over the meanings of cultural products; these meanings have important implications as people become conscious of their positions in social and political hierarchies.[13] An influential theorist of British Cultural Studies is Stuart Hall, who asserts that although media messages are "encoded" (produced) with dominant ideologies, they may also be "decoded" (negotiated) with oppositional meanings by members of socially marginal groups.[14] In this respect, British Cultural Studies is a sharp departure from Horkheimer and Adorno, who viewed popular culture as monolithic in both its ideology and its impact upon audiences.[15]

In the United States, critical, cultural research has been shaped by a confluence of British Cultural Studies, critical theories of the Frankfurt School,[16] rhetorical criticism, and pragmatist philosophy. Contemporary rhetorical criticism is a descendant of the studies of rhetoric by classical thinkers such as Aristotle and Cicero; their ideas were primarily devoted to evaluating and improving the persuasive abilities of public speakers. However, by the late twentieth century, a branch of rhetorical studies was concentrating on the persuasive messages carried in popular culture. This shift of attention to popular culture was driven by the recognition that much of the power in society was defined and negotiated in people's everyday encounters with the messages of popular culture.[17]

Pragmatist philosophy emerged in America in the late nineteenth century. A key figure was John Dewey (1859–1951), who emphasized the role of community and communication in forming our understanding of the world. Whereas British Cultural Studies investigates communication as resistance to the top-down imposition of dominant ideology, Dewey theorized about the

---

[13] John Storey, "Introduction: The Study of Popular Culture and Cultural Studies," in *Cultural Theory and Popular Culture: A Reader,* 2nd ed., ed. John Storey (Athens: University of Georgia Press, 1998), xiii.

[14] Stuart Hall, "Encoding, Decoding," in *The Cultural Studies Reader,* ed. Simon During (New York: Routledge, 1993), 98–102.

[15] Horkheimer and Adorno, "Culture Industry," 120.

[16] Jay, *Dialectical Imagination,* 298.

[17] Brummett, *Rhetoric in Popular Culture,* 52–66.

formation of communities—through communication— that enabled people to cope with the material, social, and ethical challenges of life. For Dewey, this idea of communication and culture was synonymous with democracy.[18] Communication historian and theorist James Carey has been an important expositor of Dewey's ideas in contemporary media studies. Carey captures Dewey's sense of culture when he argues that: "To study communication is to examine the actual social process wherein significant symbolic forms are created, apprehended, and used."[19]

Contemporary cultural studies have been influenced by other social and intellectual theories, but their general orientation still stresses critical examination of media products and their interpretation by audiences. Because of their emphasis on messages and audiences, cultural studies tend to pay less attention to the media institutions that create messages; the investigation of this realm is the second, distinct thread of critical media research.

Political Economy

As generally understood by media scholars, "political economy" denotes the structure, control, economics, and regulation of media industries; it encompasses the "industrial" aspect of Horkheimer and Adorno's research. Because contemporary economics tends to focus on questions of market efficiency, another approach that explores the broader social implications of economic policy has come to be called *political economy*. This term hearkens back to a period from the mid-1700s to the mid-1800s, when "political economists" such as Adam Smith, David Ricardo, and John Stuart Mill not only produced mechanistic theories of efficient markets driven by human self-interest, but also merged political science, economics, and policy studies to consider the broader implications of economic and social policies.[20] In this spirit, political economy in contemporary media studies extends beyond narrow issues of economic efficiency for media companies and consumers, and explores how

---

[18] John Dewey, *The Public and Its Problems* (New York: H. Holt and Company, 1927; reprint Athens, OH: Swallow Press, 1954), 148–49.

[19] James W. Carey, "A Cultural Approach to Communication," *Communication* 2 (December 1975): 17.

[20] Milton Mueller, "Why Communications Policy Is Passing 'Mass Communication' by: Political Economy as the Missing Link," *Critical Studies in Mass Communication* 12, no. 4 (1995): 460–68.

economic and other forces influence media's impact on society.[21] Unlike cultural studies, which search for evidence of power relations in media texts and audience reception, power is more overt in political economy, which emphasizes ownership, control, and government regulation of media institutions.

An early political economist of the mass media was Dallas Smythe. Like many subsequent political economists, he examined a basic characteristic of many U.S. media: their support by advertisers. Smythe drew on Marxist economic theory to produce a novel concept of advertiser-supported media. According to Smythe, their essential economic function was to manufacture and sell the "commodity" of audiences to advertisers, rather than programs to audiences.[22] His notion calls into question the assumption that commercial media operate in a competitive market in which audiences have the autonomy and power that market theory accords to buyers. It has also inspired other analyses of the role of the audience in the political economy of broadcasting.[23]

Another influential political economist was Herbert Schiller. In his best-known book, *Mass Communications and American Empire,* Schiller argues that media are integral to a post-World War II system in which U.S.-based companies dominate the economies and cultures of nations around the world. For Schiller, media-driven "cultural imperialism" paves the way for U.S. economic dominance.[24] He argues that a reform of U.S.—and thus world—media can only come through broader structural changes in U.S. society.[25]

Ben Bagdikian is also an influential, critical writer on the political economy of media industries. In four editions of *The Media Monopoly,* first published in 1983, he examines the steady consolidation of mass media. He argues that media have grown into monopolies or near-monopolies with an

---

[21] Vincent Mosco, *The Political Economy of Communication: Rethinking and Renewal* (Thousand Oaks, CA: Sage, 1996), 41.

[22] Dallas W. Smythe, "Communications: Blind Spot of Western Marxism," *Canadian Journal of Political and Social Theory* 1, no. 3 (1977): 3–7.

[23] See Eileen Meehan, "Heads of Household and Ladies of the House: Gender, Genre, and Broadcast Ratings, 1929–1990," in *Ruthless Criticism: New Perspectives in U.S. Communication History,* eds. William S. Solomon and Robert W. McChesney (Minneapolis: University of Minnesota Press, 1993), 204–21; Ien Ang, *Desperately Seeking the Audience* (New York: Routledge, 1991).

[24] Herbert I. Schiller, *Mass Communications and American Empire* (New York: Augustus M. Kelley, 1970), 16.

[25] Ibid., 163–64.

all-encompassing interest in profits. The drive for profits saps resources that should be devoted to journalism and, in turn, detracts from media's role as watchdogs in a democratic society.[26] Unlike Smythe and Schiller, Bagdikian has a pluralist perspective that views American society as a collection of competing economic and political forces. For Bagdikian, the balance has swung too far toward major media companies, but a healthy correction is possible through existing democratic institutions.[27]

Another scholar, David Demers, questions the pervasive assumption within political economy that the expansion of corporate media is unhealthy for democracy.[28] His argument is structural and institutional, although he provides some evidence of media content that supports his claim, particularly for the newspaper industry. Demers draws on managerial theory to argue that the increasingly corporate nature of media has created a class of autonomous, professional managers that places greater, not less, emphasis on information diversity, product quality, and other nonprofit goals.[29]

Although these scholars approach political economy from diverse perspectives, they all hold out examples of what political economy can mean in communication research. We next consider examples of political economy and cultural studies in the historiography of electronic media.

CRITICAL RESEARCH: METHODS, CHALLENGES, AND ISSUES

The challenges, methods, and issues of critical research can be illustrated by examples of historical research on electronic media. After examining cultural studies and political economy, we consider some other, innovative approaches to electronic media history and, finally, explore ways to think about the role of technology in electronic media history.

Cultural History

As we have seen, an important object of cultural analysis is media content such as television and radio programs; these and other objects of interpretation are

---

[26] Ben H. Bagdikian, *The Media Monopoly*, 4th ed. (Boston, MA: Beacon Press, 1992), 151.

[27] Ibid., 236.

[28] David Demers, *Global Media: Menace or Messiah?* (Cresskill, NJ: Hampton Press, 1999).

[29] Ibid., 153.

often referred to as "texts." Scholars who conduct textual analysis of media content are confident that it will yield evidence about a culture in a particular time and place. As one scholar puts it, a text is the "mouthpiece" for a culture.[30]

An example of historical, textual analysis is media scholar Herman Gray's study of *Frank's Place,* a program with African-American themes and characters that aired on the CBS network during the 1987 television season. Gray was curious about how the practices and sensibilities of people on the fringes of dominant culture are expressed in mass media.[31] He examined the narratives and characters for the season's series and found what he calls an "African-American sensibility" that was typical of the time as the program represented the habits, practices, manners, and nuances of Black Americans.[32] But Gray also found that, although many of the show's characters also expressed this sensibility through discourse about racism, social inequality, and cultural difference, those ideas were simplified and contained so as not to challenge a mass audience that included White Americans. For Gray, this containment of African-American sensibilities and aspirations was indicative of the larger American culture of the late 1980s.[33]

Gray's findings, that a mass-audience television program reflected and negotiated tensions within the larger culture of the late 1980s, demonstrate the kind of social knowledge that the methods of cultural studies can yield when applied to historical inquiry.[34] What Gray's study does not address, however, is how the messages of *Frank's Place* were received or interpreted by audience members in the late 1980s. As we have seen, this too is a concern of cultural studies, particularly as conceptualized by Stuart Hall.

Although textual analysis can yield messages about a specific culture, it offers no direct evidence of how they are understood by an audience. Yet audience reception remains an important object of cultural analysis. As media theorist Thomas Streeter points out, "The goal of the interpretive tradition ... is

---

[30] Brummett, *Rhetoric in Popular Culture,* 29.

[31] Herman Gray, "Recodings: Possibilities and Limitations in Commercial Television Representations of African-American Culture," in *Connections: A Broadcast History Reader,* ed. Michele Hilmes (Belmont, CA: Wadsworth, 2003), 278.

[32] Ibid.

[33] Ibid., 283–84.

[34] Douglas Kellner, *Critical Theory, Marxism and Modernity* (Baltimore, MD: Johns Hopkins University Press, 1989), 141–42.

not simply finding social life in symbolic works, but finding the work of symbols in social life."[35] However, the question of audience reception of media messages can also present a daunting evidentiary challenge for historical researchers. Scholars of contemporary media can obtain empirical evidence about audiences through interviews, or through direct participation and observation as audiences receive and discuss media messages.[36] But historians of electronic media are constricted in their access to such evidence. It may be possible to locate audience members for some historical media, but the older the media program, the less likely a researcher is to find surviving listeners or viewers. Another way to retrieve historical evidence of audience reception is through printed material: articles, letters, diaries, and other documents.

Media scholar Julie D'Acci illustrates one approach to critical audience analysis in her study of the 1980s television series *Cagney & Lacey.* D'Acci examined various aspects of the show, including the way it was interpreted by individual audience members. For evidence of audience reception, she analyzed fan letters written to the program's producers.[37] *Cagney & Lacey* was the first prime-time, network detective series that featured two females in the starring roles. The fan letters allowed D'Acci to explore how viewers—especially females—interpreted the series's sometimes complex messages about feminism and applied them to the circumstances of their own lives.

Oftentimes, however, critical historians simply lack empirical evidence through which to analyze audience response to media texts. Elizabeth Mechling and Jay Mechling faced this obstacle in their study of Walt Disney's messages about atomic energy in the 1950s. Through children's books, exhibits at the Disneyland amusement park, and a television program, Disney constructed a narrative that helped "naturalize" and "domesticate" the atom at a time when the Cold War gave ominous hints of its danger.[38] Although they discuss Disney's access to multiple mass media, their study is primarily a textual analysis of Disney messages about the atom. But they also recognize that

[35] Thomas Streeter, *Selling the Air: A Critique of the Policy of Commercial Broadcasting in the United States* (Chicago: University of Chicago Press, 1996), 17.

[36] James A. Anderson, *Communication Research: Issues and Methods* (New York: McGraw-Hill, 1987), 295–96.

[37] Julie D'Acci, *Defining Women: Television and the Case of* Cagney & Lacey (Chapel Hill: University of North Carolina Press, 1994), 177.

[38] Elizabeth Walker Mechling and Jay Mechling, "The Atom According to Disney," *Quarterly Journal of Speech* 81, no. 4 (1995): 450.

audience members play a crucial role in the cultural process. Since their study has no empirical evidence of audience response, their strategy is to read the texts for "spaces" that might permit "reading against the grain" of Disney's pronuclear narrative.[39] In effect, they attempt to identify the interpretive options available to the 1950s audience members, while acknowledging that, under the circumstances, it was impossible to analyze the reactions of real audience members. Because their study came four decades after the actual events, Mechling and Mechling lacked Julie D'Acci's proximity not just to historical media, but also to the historical audience. While their strategy of analyzing the audience's interpretive options makes no unwarranted assumptions, it also illustrates the challenge inherent in identifying audience responses to decades-old media texts.

With their emphasis on media texts, Herman Gray's study of *Frank's Place* and Elizabeth Mechling and Jay Mechling's analysis of Walt Disney's nuclear discourse are typical of historical cultural research. Although both studies discuss the historical media institutions that transmitted the messages, their emphasis is on interpretation of messages. Media institutions themselves take center stage in the second thread of media history, political economy.

Political Economy

Until three decades ago, historians generally portrayed the political economy of U.S. broadcasting as a natural expression of American cultural values, economic practices, and political attitudes. Two fresh interpretations of the radio industry's emergence illustrate critical approaches to media historiography. In his 1980 book, *The Modern Stentors,* Philip Rosen explicitly argues that the form in which American radio emerged between 1920 and 1934 was far from inevitable. Rather, the structure of the nascent U.S. radio industry was shaped by the political and economic climate of the 1920s and 1930s, and by the interplay of businessmen, the prospective market, politics, and bureaucrats. Within a slightly different context, with a small variation of events, a much different system might have emerged.[40] This question of historical interpretation is a crucial one for political economists, because the economic regulatory system that emerged by the mid-1930s was the blueprint not only for radio

---

[39] Ibid., 442.

[40] Philip T. Rosen, *The Modern Stentors: Radio Broadcasters and the Federal Government, 1920–1934* (Westport, CT: Greenwood, 1980), 3–4.

broadcasting but, later, for broadcast television.[41] Although Rosen portrays American broadcasting's historical fusion of private enterprise and government oversight as a robust, pragmatic system, he dismisses the notion that the American public had any substantive role in its formation as a "myth."[42]

An even more pointed challenge to the traditional view of U.S. broadcast history came with Robert McChesney's book. Like Rosen, McChesney examines the crucial period when the FRC pushed many noncommercial broadcasters off the air and established radio as a for-profit medium.[43] Also like Rosen, McChesney identifies an active but unsuccessful opposition movement that tried to prevent the commercialization of broadcasting. But unlike Rosen, who dismisses the reform movement as a narrow interest group,[44] McChesney introduces evidence that the radio reformers represented the only serious attempt to engage the public in a democratic debate over the structure and mission of U.S. broadcasting. His depiction of the behind-the-scenes politicking to install commercial broadcasting not only challenges the old, consensus view of that process, but also the claim of the broadcast industry that it embodies the inevitable "American System" of broadcasting.[45]

Although its emphasis is that of traditional political economy, McChesney's study also ventures into an area that is more typically a concern of cultural studies—the audience. An important contention of his book is that a large segment of the listening audience was hostile to the commercialism that came to dominate U.S. broadcasting by the mid-1930s.[46] Although this historical interpretation lacks the detailed documentation of other aspects of McChesney's book, it hints at the utility of uniting a traditional concern of cultural studies—the audience—with political economy.

As the examples of McChesney, Gray, Mechling and Mechling, and Rosen suggest, there is rarely a neat divide between political economy and cultural studies in electronic media research. However, a recent trend is consciously to join the two approaches for a comprehensive form of electronic media history.

---

[41] Ibid., 182–83.

[42] Ibid., 181–82.

[43] Robert W. McChesney, *Telecommunications, Mass Media, and Democracy: The Battle for the Control of U.S. Broadcasting, 1928–1935* (New York: Oxford University Press, 1993), 25–37.

[44] Rosen, *Modern Stentors*, 161.

[45] McChesney, *Telecommunications*, 256–59.

[46] Ibid., 94–103.

A Unified, Critical Approach

Media research, like many human activities, tends to move along well-worn paths. For decades, cultural studies and political economy have tested fundamentally different explanations for historical phenomena. Cultural studies emphasize that media messages convey ideas from the broader culture, and that they are interpreted by audiences. Political economy stresses that media industries are shaped by economics and policy and generally assumes that the industry plays the crucial role in determining media content. But it is often practical and even desirable for electronic media historians to combine the traditional methods of cultural studies and political economy. What theorist Douglas Kellner terms a "unified, critical approach" to research can sometimes provide a broader and more nuanced understanding of electronic media history.[47] Ironically, this approach is also reminiscent of Max Horkheimer and Theodor Adorno's "unified" analysis of the culture industry.

Julie D'Acci's study of *Cagney & Lacey*, already discussed, is an example of a unified, critical approach to media research. D'Acci's intent was to conduct a case study of how femininity is defined in prime-time television.[48] She examined *Cagney & Lacey*'s original conception in 1974, the CBS network's economic calculus in finally deciding to air the series seven years later, the writing and production of individual episodes, the complex messages conveyed in series narratives, and the program's reception by audiences. As D'Acci states, her research explores the specific conjunctions of industry, reception, text, and context.[49] D'Acci had some advantages that are rarely available to historical researchers. Although her book was published six years after CBS cancelled *Cagney & Lacey*, her research began while the show was still in production and she was able to observe the cast, crew, and writers at work.[50] As noted earlier, she also had access to thousands of fan letters, as well as correspondence from network executives and publicity firms.[51] Nonetheless, her study serves as a model for researchers who wish to integrate institutional and production analysis with textual and audience analysis. The result is a comprehensive investigation of the process by which complex cultural messages about

---

[47] Kellner, *Critical Theory*, 141.
[48] D'Acci, *Defining Women*, 4.
[49] Ibid., 7.
[50] Ibid., xi.
[51] Ibid. (statement on back book cover).

women's power in society are shaped, transmitted, and then received by audiences.

Another example of historical scholarship that merges political economy and cultural studies is Michele Hilmes's analysis of the "Lux Radio Theatre," a popular radio series of the 1930s and 1940s. Hilmes's intent was to examine the ways in which the influence of cultural institutions could interact with broader cultural values to shape a media text. In a chapter in her book *Hollywood and Broadcasting: From Radio to Cable,* Hilmes offers a sophisticated analysis of the Lux Theatre's radio version of the Hollywood film *Dark Victory.* Through a synthesis of cultural and institutional analysis, Hilmes demonstrates how the "broadcast" influence of the CBS radio network, the "advertising" influence of the Lever Brothers soap company, and the J. Walter Thompson advertising agency, and the "Hollywood" influence of producer Cecil B. DeMille shaped specific production and narrative features of the broadcast.[52] Hilmes was fortunate that an audio recording of the broadcast had survived, but she also merged textual analysis with a critical analysis of the three dominant institutions in the program's production. As a result, she was able to analyze the *Dark Victory* broadcast as a detailed example of the encoding/decoding process theorized by Stuart Hall and to identify ways that institutional imperatives influenced the encoding process.[53]

A third example of the possibilities in unifying political economy and cultural studies is Thomas Streeter's study of a crucial historical episode in communication policy. Drawing on the philosopher Michel Foucault's notion of discourse, Streeter examines the "discourse of new technologies" that helped alter the balance of power between broadcast television and cable in the late 1960s and early 1970s.[54] Streeter asserts that discourse was a factor in the FCC's shift from a policy that protected local broadcasters from cable competition to one that permitted incursions by the cable industry. He argues that the features of discourse, as theorized by Foucault to include themes, blind spots, and gaps, helped forge an unlikely alliance among the cable industry, professional groups, and some media reform organizations. The discourse

---

[52] Michele Hilmes, *Hollywood and Broadcasting: From Radio to Cable* (Urbana: University of Illinois Press, 1990), 96–110.

[53] Ibid., 97–98.

[54] Thomas Streeter, "The Cable Fable Revisited: Discourse, Policy, Politics and the Making of Cable Television," *Critical Studies in Mass Communication* 4, no. 2 (1987): 174–200.

created "a terrain that helped make possible some major actions in the policy arena, actions that simple self-interest—of either a pluralist or Marxist class variety—would not warrant."[55]

Streeter's historical analysis is an innovative application of theories associated with cultural studies—and normally applied to texts and audiences—to historical media policy. This short essay cannot do justice to all theories that are relevant to critical media research. However, it will examine one notion of media that has been particularly associated with electronic media.

Medium Theory

While sometimes called "medium theory," medium theory is actually a diverse family of theories that share a common premise: The means through which people communicate has an impact beyond the content of their messages. Medium theorists sometimes assert that the special characteristics of a communication medium can shape cultures and societies.[56] Harold Adams Innis is an influential medium theorist who theorized that the crucial historical role of communication systems in the organization and administration of great empires.[57]

By far the best-known medium theorist, Marshall McLuhan famously argued that "the medium is the message" and emphasized the role of television viewing in shaping modern consciousness.[58] Another more recent medium theorist, Joshua Meyrowitz, theorizes that modern mass media merge the distinctions between public and private spheres, blur the borders between public and private behaviors, and sever the traditional distinction between physical place and social "place."[59]

---

[55] Ibid., 175.

[56] Joshua Meyrowitz, *No Sense of Place: The Impact of Electronic Media on Social Behavior* (New York: Oxford University Press, 1985), 19.

[57] Harold A. Innis, *Empire & Communications* (Toronto: University of Toronto Press, 1972), 7.

[58] Marshall McLuhan, *Understanding Media: The Extensions of Man* (New York: Signet, 1966), 28.

[59] Meyrowitz, *No Sense of Place,* 8.

As a historian of electronic media, Susan Douglas has shown a willingness to experiment with diverse theories and genres.[60] In her book *Listening In,* she examines the distinctive, intrinsic qualities of the radio medium. She offers empirical evidence, including contemporary audience research, to support her assertion that, as radio evolved in the 1920s and 1930s, radio listening "reactivated, extended, and intensified particular cognitive modes that encouraged, simultaneously, a sense of belonging to a community, an audience, and a confidence that your imaginings, your radio visions, were the best and truest ones of all."[61] Her assessment of the radio medium's unique cultural and emotional impact is far less sweeping than the medium theories of Innis, McLuhan, or Meyrowitz. Yet, in a more modest way, *Listening In* reminds historians to consider the unique, intrinsic qualities of each electronic medium as it was experienced by audience members in a specific historical context. It also suggests a perennial question for historians: Should media technology be considered an autonomous historical force, or as another artifact of the cultural process?

The Challenge of Technology

The historian of technology Merritt Roe Smith wrote: "Who among us would deny that it is easy to be drawn into technology-driven explanations of cultural and historical processes?"[62] The theory that technology is the driving force in history is called "technological determinism"; applied to communication, technological determinism holds that technology is the dominant, determining factor when there are changes in mass media.[63] The electronic mass media with the longest history in the twentieth century, radio and television, are strongly associated with new technologies, as is their younger cousin,

---

[60] See Susan J. Douglas, *Where the Girls Are: Growing Up Female with the Mass Media* (New York: Times Books, 1994); here Douglas uses the memoir genre to analyze the typical media experiences of a female member of the baby-boomer generation.

[61] Susan J. Douglas, *Listening In: Radio and the American Imagination from Amos 'n' Andy and Edward R. Murrow to Wolfman Jack and Howard Stern* (New York: Times Books, 1999), 39, 124–60.

[62] Merritt Roe Smith, "Technological Determinism in American Culture," in *Does Technology Drive History? The Dilemma of Technological Determinism,* eds. Merritt Roe Smith and Leo Marx (Cambridge, MA: MIT Press, 1994), 35.

[63] Brian Winston, "How Are Media Born?" in *Connections: A Broadcast History Reader,* ed. Michele Hilmes (Belmont, CA: Wadsworth, 2003), 4.

the Internet. Raymond Williams pointed to a tendency to think of technology as developing in isolation, abstracted from the larger culture.[64] This view of technology has had several important implications for historical inquiry. It can foreclose the possibility that the technology was a product of human intentionality whereby people decide to develop a technology for particular purposes at an opportune moment in the history of a society. It also forecloses the possibility that the technology was shaped by the values, assumptions and social relations of the time and place in which it emerged.

Another of Susan Douglas's studies, *Inventing American Broadcasting*, was the first example of critical historiography in this essay; we now return to it as an example of how the insights and methods of cultural studies can be specifically applied to technology, a topic that is sometimes exempted from critical analysis. Douglas's demonstration of the role of radio amateurs in broadcast radio's emergence is a striking contradiction to the notion that the broadcasting system that emerged was dictated by the internal logic of radio technology. It represents a form of historical interpretation in which media are freed from the presumption of technologically driven inevitability. This, in turn, opens their trajectory of historical development to critical, historical inquiry.

CONCLUSION

Critical, historical, research cannot be defined by one theory, nor can it be defined by one research method. But it can still be defined in useful ways. As the introduction to this chapter suggests, it is characterized by the interpretation of historical evidence and by the application of theory to explain and evaluate historical events. The examples of critical research offered in this essay suggest another characteristic: concern with power in society and a willingness to investigate its sources and manifestations in electronic media. Social and political power has consequences for people's lives in all societies, including democracies. This commitment to explore an issue of consequence suggests another, even more basic aspect of critical research: engagement. Following a tradition that dates back to the research of Max Horkheimer and Theodor Adorno, critical scholars have analyzed media with an eye to their fundamental implications for gender, racial, political, or economic relations in society. This does not mean that every study of media economics constitutes critical

---

[64] Raymond Williams, *Television: Technology and Cultural Form* (Hanover, NH: Wesleyan University Press, 1992), 7.

political economy, nor does it suggest that every study of media texts or audiences amounts to critical cultural studies. James Carey, an influential theorist of culture and communication, points out that an uncritical approach to cultural studies celebrates popular culture, yet fails to consider power, dominance, subordination, and ideology as central issues.[65] The researchers of the Frankfurt School had a term for research that addressed narrow questions of, for example, how many households tuned into a particular radio program: "administrative research."[66] Critical research and administrative research ask different questions, have different purposes, and are addressed to different audiences. Media scholar Oscar Gandy captures the orientation of critical research when he describes a work of political economy: "It is not critical because it questions received notions or calls to task prominent figures or comes, on occasion, to negative conclusions. Rather, it is critical because it examines and asks readers to examine, fundamental questions regarding its subject."[67]

The examples offered in this chapter suggest that critical research is not, nor should it be, the property of a particular intellectual tradition. As media scholar Milton Mueller points out, "Defining terms in a way that permits only one school or one angle of 'criticism' creates an intellectual ghetto."[68] At the same time, regardless of the methods inquiry, or the theories being tested, the best kind of critical research will be driven by the rigorous collection and examination of historical evidence. As the historians Joyce Appleby, Lynn Hunt, and Margaret Jacob note, "History is never independent of the potsherds and written edicts that remain from a past reality, for their very existence demands explanation."[69]

In the twentieth century, media entered people's lives as never before in human history.[70] There is little reason to believe that this phenomenon will be

---

[65] James W. Carey, "The Origins of the Radical Discourse on Cultural Studies in the United States," *Journal of Communication* 33, no. 3 (1983): 313.

[66] Theodor W. Adorno, "Sociology and Empirical Research," in *The Adorno Reader,* ed. Brian O'Conner (Malden, MA: Blackwell Publishers, 2000), 178.

[67] Oscar Gandy, "Foreword," in *The Politics of TV Violence: Policy Uses of Communication Research,* ed. Willard D. Rowland Jr. (Beverly Hills: Sage, 1983), 9.

[68] Mueller, "Why Communications Policy," 468.

[69] Joyce Appleby, Lynn Hunt, and Margaret Jacob, *Telling the Truth About History* (New York: W.W. Norton, 1994), 255.

[70] Brummett, *Rhetoric in Popular Culture,* 54–56.

reversed in the twenty-first century. As electronic media expand and evolve, so too will the body of historical evidence they leave for scholarly examination. The methods and theories of historical media research are likely to evolve as well. What will remain constant is the opportunity to investigate profound questions about a pervasive force in modern life.

7

Quantitative Methods in Broadcast History

Robert K. Avery
University of Utah

It may seem strange to readers of a book devoted to historical and critical research methods in electronic media to find a chapter focusing on quantitative methodology. Indeed, some contemporary historical scholars hold the basic assumptions of social scientific research in such contempt that young readers of this book may have been influenced already, and hence developed either a well-acknowledged bias or unintentional skepticism toward the principles of so-called empiricism or logical positivism as many social scientists have developed toward historiography. Recognizing that this might well be the case, we would ask the reader to suspend immediate judgment on any particular methodology and consider the contributions of this chapter with an open mind.

We should remember that the basic methods of quantitative scientific inquiry actually predate the entire history of broadcasting and other electronic media. Long before the operations of the broadcast media had accumulated a history of their own, scholars from the fields of anthropology, sociology, psychology, political science, and the emerging discipline of communication, were asking questions about the possible impact of the media of mass communication. Concerns about the direct and indirect effects of various print and film media, either to society in general or to specific individuals in particular, were already setting the research agendas of social scientists. Their scholarly perspective and the strategies of their investigations were drawn from classical physical science that employed a model of empirical analysis based on objective observation and theories of probability. With benefit of hindsight, we can now view these pioneering efforts as having emerged within their own idiosyncratic historical contexts that suggest as much about the political and social influences of the time as their own well-intentioned "objective" scientific contributions. In recent years there have been gallons of ink and reams of paper devoted to arguing the application of the scientific method to explaining the conditions, circumstances, and influences of the media of communication. In fact, one alarming consequence of the growing popularity of critical and cultural studies in the field of media studies is the absence of serious scientific methodological preparation in some communication Ph.D. programs of study. This absence or lessened emphasis does an enormous disservice to critical and historical scholars who must make frequent judgments about the appropriateness of empirical research data uncovered in their research, or the recognition of when quantitative data may contribute to a critical or historical investigation.

ASSUMPTIONS AND FUNCTIONS OF QUANTITATIVE RESEARCH

For those of us who entered the academy during the 1970s and 1980s, the seminal work of Fred N. Kerlinger, *Foundations of Behavioral Research,* was viewed as essential reading. Without exception, every communication research methods book written since the mid 1960s owes a considerable debt to this important volume, and this brief chapter is no exception. Kerlinger states that the great American philosopher, Charles Peirce, observed that there are four fundamental ways of knowing.[1] First, is the method of tenacity, where we hold dearly to what we believe as an undisputable truth. We do not necessarily have any evidence to defend the truthfulness of our claim, we simply know that it is so. Such tenaciousness is grounded in a powerful conviction that can just as easily cloud our capacity for objective observation than lead us to report verifiable evidence. Sometimes the method of tenacity leads us to uphold a position that is in fact true, and sometimes it does not. The problem is that if beliefs that are held to tenaciously are not called into question, they can lead to incorrect conclusions. A second method of knowing is the method of authority. Here the truthfulness of a claim is buttressed by a source external to us, that is, what we believe to be a reputable source. This is a fairly common and frequently acceptable method for acquiring knowledge. Our physics professor

---

[1] Fred N. Kerlinger, *Foundations of Behavioral Research: Educational and Psychological Inquiry* (New York: Holt, Rinehart and Winston, 1964).

is an expert on how to compute velocity under varying conditions, and our family physician is a reputable source regarding treatment for an identified illness. The potential problem here is that everyone is capable of making errors even within their own area of expertise. And even more important, we risk increasing the possibility of error when we extend their authority beyond their specific knowledge area. Some authoritative sources will dispense correct and incorrect information with comparable passion and apparent expertise.

A third method of knowing is called the intuitive method or the *a priori* method. Those arguing for the superiority of this approach suggest that *a priori* evidence agrees with a position of accepted reason, that is, it simply "stands to reason." This is the philosophical perspective that purports that free and reasonable citizens when allowed to debate openly will naturally gravitate to a truthful and self-evident conclusion. The frequently voiced virtues of a participatory democracy and the notion of a "marketplace of ideas" are consistent with this point of view. Finally, the fourth method of knowing is the method of science. Here Kerlinger states, "The scientific approach has one characteristic that no other method of attaining knowledge has: self-correction. There are built-in checks all along the way to scientific knowledge. These checks are so conceived and used that they control and verify the scientist's activities and conclusions to the end of attaining dependable knowledge outside of himself [or herself]."[2] From Kerlinger's vantage point, the scientific method is to be most respected when it comes to factual knowledge because the findings of empirical research are capable of independent verification by other scientists.

Since most humanistic study deals with questions of value or policy, some humanistic scholars, including historians, believe that quantitative methodologies are for others and not themselves. But increasingly, questions of public policy are requiring that the data from quantitative research be brought to the table to advance a position that has been traditionally value-driven. For example, in the area of broadcast regulation the fundamental principle of diversity of ownership has been widely accepted for being in the public interest. Yet, when the Federal Communications Commission (FCC) began reconsideration of its cross ownership rules in 2003, the FCC made it clear that either changes in policy or maintenance of the status quo would be determined by arguments supported by factual evidence drawn from empirical research. For future historians writing about the early 2000s in the evolution of U.S. broadcast regulation, a knowledge of the research evidence on which policy

---

[2] Kerlinger, *Foundations of Behavioral Research*, 7.

decisions were made will be critical to providing an evaluative account of how well these policymakers fulfilled their responsibility to the American citizenry. This is not to suggest that future historians will need to have a knowledge of social science that will enable them to actually conduct the same quantitative research themselves, but rather that they will have adequate knowledge of, and appreciation for, this research genre to make informed judgments about what they are reading.

In his revisionist essay that sets forth the position that public broadcasting in the United States has been systematically disenfranchised by policymakers, Willard D. Rowland takes the position that American broadcast history has been largely atheoretical.[3] That is to say, that unlike more contemporary accounts that are guided by critical theories, early historical scholars were focused on attempting to provide an accurate, factual, and highly objective account of the past, totally free of a political point of view. Today, most historians are guided by a theoretical perspective and believe that their scholarship is contributing to the advancement of that perspective. Such well-respected contemporary broadcast historians as Susan J. Douglas, Robert McChesney, Susan Smulyan, and Thomas Streeter are representative of this relatively new tradition.[4] In contrast to the earlier atheoretical work in broadcast history, the basic aim of science, and hence all quantitative methodologies, is theory. It is theory that permits the scientist to provide explanations, create understanding, offer predictions, and specify the conditions for control. Again, according to Kerlinger, "A theory is a set of interrelated constructs (concepts), definitions, and propositions that present a systematic view of phenomena by specifying relations among variables, with the purpose of explaining and predicting

---

[3] Willard D. Rowland, "Continuing Crisis in Public Television: A History of Disenfranchisement," *Journal of Broadcasting & Electronic Media* 30, no. 3 (1986): 251–74.

[4] Susan J. Douglas, *Inventing American Broadcasting, 1899–1922* (Baltimore, MD: Johns Hopkins University Press, 1987); Robert McChesney, *Telecommunications, Mass Media, and Democracy: The Battle for the Control of U.S. Broadcasting, 1928–1935* (New York: Oxford University Press, 1993); Susan Smulyan, *Selling Radio: The Commercialization of American Broadcasting, 1920–1934* (Washington, DC: Smithsonian Institution Press, 1994); Thomas Streeter, *Selling the Air: A Critique of the Policy of Commercial Broadcasting in the United States* (Chicago: University of Chicago Press, 1996).

the phenomena."[5] In an experimental design, the researcher manipulates an *independent* variable in order to measure its effect on a *dependent* variable. By controlling the conditions under which the predicted outcome will occur, the researcher is able to provide an explanation of the observed phenomena. The researcher sets forth a hypothesis about the relationship between the independent and dependent variables, which is then tested under specified circumstances, thus allowing for the researcher to make judgments about the soundness of the theory. By definition, then, this is a deductive method of inquiry, where theory precedes the advancement of specific hypotheses. It also assumes causation, in that the independent variable is the cause of the effect on the dependent variable. Both deductive thinking (as opposed to inductive or individualistic) and notions of causation are the subjects of frequent academic debate, and hence sometimes spark the unfortunate drawing of lines in the sand between social science and humanistic approaches to acquiring knowledge. Such distinctions of purported superiority for either viewpoint serve no useful function and often contribute to a narrowness of research perspective. It is of far greater importance to remember that no one has a corner on truth, and that different methodologies are necessitated by different research questions. Multiple world views contribute to our understanding of the human condition and the challenges faced by societies at various moments in their development.

While the world of the physical sciences allows for formal theory testing as outlined earlier, the realities of human life and behavior do not always permit even a quasi-scientific approach to inquiry. Consequently, the quantitative methodologies on which historians can draw take on many different forms and derivations. Some of these employ inferential statistics that permit predictions and generalizations, while others use descriptive methods that are case sensitive and situation bound. Whereas a controlled experiment might exhibit considerable scientific rigor, it can sacrifice realistic real-world conditions. Historians must be mindful that when utilizing the quantitative results of other researchers that different quantitative methods employ different kinds of data that carry corresponding levels of precision and confidence. Survey data derived from a "uses and gratifications" written questionnaire is not the same as the probability statistics generated from the laboratory studies of televised depictions of violence. Although any media historian who makes use of the empirical data drawn from quantitative methodologies needs to have far

---

[5] Kerlinger, *Foundations of Behavioral Research,* 11.

more exposure to the protocols of the approaches than can be offered here, some rudimentary background should prove helpful.

TYPES OF DATA AND MEASUREMENT INSTRUMENTS

You have been reminded elsewhere in this volume about primary versus secondary sources of data, the rules of evidence gathering, and the importance of making sure that documents uncovered in your research are authentic. The same expectation of careful scrutiny also should be brought to the analysis of quantitative data that are used by the historian to form judgments of fact and interpretation. Within the realm of scientific measurement there are four types of data: nominal, ordinal, interval, and ratio. *Nominal* data refer to the assignment of numbers on the basis of "qualitative" rather than "quantitative" designations. Such demographic information as gender, age, ethnicity, education, and income level might fall into this category. Here, arbitrary numbers (1 = female and 2 = male) are assigned to enable the researcher to place people into groupings.

Ordinal data are frequently found along with nominal information and express a relationship between two or more values. For example, when survey respondents are asked to identify their frequency of television viewing and the instrument states: "How many hours do you watch TV each day: _____ Less than 1 hour, _____ 1 to 3 hours, _____ 3 to 5 hours, _____ More than 5 hours," the respondents are being asked to provide ordinal data. In other words, ordinal data allow us to use such qualifiers as "more than" or "less than" between observations because they designate a relationship between the groupings. Similarly, mass communication researchers frequently design questionnaires that ask respondents to rank order their preferences between various media of communication (i.e., newspapers, magazines, radio, television, Internet). Ranking one medium first, another second, and so on, provides the researcher with the relative relationship between the preferences, but says nothing of the magnitude between the choices.

Interval data allow for the researcher to not only express relationships between data points, but also indicate that the distances between the points are equal in magnitude.

Broadcasting researchers have long sought out the opinions of radio and television audience members by asking respondents questions by way of telephone or mail questionnaires. For example, an interviewer who states: "Please give me your impression of the following television personalities by reacting to my statements by using 1 of 5 responses—(1) Strongly Agree, (2) Agree, (3) Undecided or Not Sure, (4) Disagree, or (5) Strongly Disagree—'Peter Jennings is the best news anchor on TV'" is collecting interval data. In other words, the numerical values associated with each response (i.e., 1 through 5) are spaced equally. Hence, for statistical purposes, the interval between 1 and 2 or 2 and 3 is the same distance as between 4 and 5. This form of scaling instrument has been used extensively in mass communication research and is called a "Likert-type" scale, after its creator, Rensis Likert. Another popular interval scaling instrument found in the broadcasting research literature is the "Semantic Differential" scale that purports to locate people, objects, or concepts in "semantic space." Here a researcher might be trying to see how television audience members locate the top-five news anchors across a series of bipolar, 7-point scales with such descriptors as Trustworthy-Untrustworthy, Honest-Dishonest, Informed-Uninformed, Prepared-Unprepared, and so forth.

Finally, the fourth type of measurement or data type is called *ratio*. Here the researcher has data that meet all the tests of interval data but also has an absolute zero point. For purposes of our discussion, it is enough to remember that meeting the tests of ratio data open a larger range of statistical analyses, hence enabling the researcher to engage in more powerful and sophistical quantitative testing.

It is important for the broadcast historian to have at least an awareness of the different kinds of data generated by quantitative (and some qualitative) methodologies for a number of reasons. First, of course, the historian needs to know enough to either evaluate or seek out help in evaluating the kinds of methods and data used in statistical reports at different points in time. For as long as the medium of radio has existed as a commercial enterprise, the advertising and broadcasting industries have been generating statistical reports. Similarly, since the early 1920s social scientists have been trying to assess the effects of the mass media on readers, listeners, and viewers. Nominal and ordinal data from such studies meet the conditions for the use of nonparametric statistics, whereas interval and ratio data can be subjected to the more powerful parametric statistical tests.

Second, throughout the twentieth century we witnessed ever-increasing levels of quantitative research sophistication that brought us new findings that redirected the theoretical contours of our discipline. Questions about direct media effects gave way to questions about more indirect influences, and rather simple univariate models have given way to multidimensional research designs. The arrival of new data collection methods, new analytic procedures, and the accumulation of research findings have impacted the evolution of the media industries themselves. Just as social scientists have found a symbiotic relationship between the media and their audiences, the compilations of economic statistics have contributed to decision making that has reshaped industry structures and content. Tracing the evolution of broadcasting and other electronic media cannot escape a consideration of the quantitative information that led to sustained performance or major shifts and redirections within the industries themselves.

SELECTED RESEARCH METHODS

Perhaps no other quantitative methodology within the field of broadcasting has been used more often or has generated more information than the audience *survey*. According to Lowery and DeFleur, it was in the 1920s that "the basic techniques were finally put together. Sampling theory and applied procedures had been developed by statisticians and had come into use by scientists in many fields. The idea of sampling was combined with systematic interviewing procedures and adapted for use in many kinds of sociological studies. This new approach to social research was so effective that it was quickly adopted by opinion pollsters, market researchers, and many other professionals."[6]

As should be obvious, then, survey methods come in many different types and serve many different functions. Broadcast ratings, political and opinion polling, and uses and gratifications studies all use some form of survey methodology. Surveys are administered through telephone or face-to-face interviews, through the mail using paper and pencil instruments, and increasingly via the Internet and the World Wide Web. Some surveys are designed to collect specific information from a cross section of a given population at a particular moment in time in order to gain an understanding of viewers or listeners reactions to a particular program or coverage of an event. Countless surveys of all types were conducted immediately after the terrorist attacks on the World Trade Center and the Pentagon on September 11, 2001. A wide range of academic scholars, professional research organizations, and government agencies quickly moved into the field to glean a profile of how people experienced, interpreted, and reacted to the events of that day.

---

[6] Shearon A. Lowery and Melvin L. DeFleur, *Milestones in Mass Communication Research: Media Effects,* 3rd ed. (White Plains, NY: Longman, 1995), 72–73.

From a longer historical vantage point, the famous broadcast of the *War of the Worlds* on the CBS radio network's *Mercury Theatre on the Air,* October 30, 1938, provides a classic example of how survey research has been central to the historical study of that important event. This dramatic broadcast offered listeners a fictional account of a Marian invasion that used on-the-scene reporting techniques that were popular at the time. To the amazement of CBS executives, more than a million listeners believed the fictional account to be true and were frightened by what they heard, leading to a panic of unprecedented portions. While depth interviews and newspaper clippings helped provide researchers with anecdotal information, the Office of Radio Research at Princeton University made use of several essential surveys to compile the findings reported in Hadley Cantril's classic work, *The Invasion from Mars: A Study in the Psychology of Panic.*[7] Generations of broadcast historians have mined these data to gain a fuller understanding of the scope and complexity of the event.

Whereas the surveys that immediately followed the *War of the Worlds* broadcast and the live television coverage of the September 11th terrorist attacks more than 60 years later were designed to gather information from a cross section of the public at a specific moment in time, numerous surveys are conducted each year that are intended to provide *longitudinal* data. Longitudinal designs provide for the systematic sampling of a specific population at regular intervals using the same survey procedures. The matching of research methods over time allows researchers to make critical comparisons of their data sets across extended periods, even though they are sampling different people. Such surveys allow for the tracking of audience perceptions, viewing preferences, number of receivers, listener education levels, or any one of countless other variables over time. Here the broadcast historian is supported by a wealth of statistical information generated by numerous reputable firms with state of the art sampling procedures and data collection methods. Such agencies as the U.S. Census Bureau, U.S. Bureau of Labor Statistics, Department of Commerce, Federal Communications Commission, Corporation for Public Broadcasting, Radio Advertising Bureau, Electronic Industries Association, A.C. Nielsen Company, and the National Association of Broadcasters, issue regular statistical reports at least annually that enable the historian to follow various industry, consumer, and audience trends. Such statistical

---

[7] Hadley Cantril, *The Invasion from Mars: A Study in the Psychology of Panic* (Princeton, NJ: Princeton University Press, 1940).

publications as *Broadcasting Yearbook, Television Factbook, Statistical Abstract of the United States, Radio Marketing Guide and Fact Book for Advertisers, Consumer Electronics Annual Review,* and *Television Digest* provide information that is both reputable and easily accessible.

Highly respected American broadcasting historians, Christopher H. Sterling and John Michael Kittross have provided fellow historians with a most valuable collection of "Historical Statistics on Electronic Media" in the 2002 edition of their seminal study, *Stay Tuned: A History of American Broadcasting.*[8] This volume serves as a model for how historical research benefits from the skillful inclusion of quantitative data throughout the narrative. The collection of statistics compiled for fellow scholars includes such useful data for historical comparisons as number of stations on the air, network affiliations, annual revenue figures, radio and television programs by day-part and genre, and audience reach and market penetration. Sadly, these authors report that they have experienced increasing difficulty gaining access to some statistical data that in recent years has become proprietary or simply unavailable due to deregulation.

Although much of the quantitative *trends* data representing large populations reported by various governmental and statistical measurement firms utilize sampling procedures that generate different samples at different moments in time, this is not the only longitudinal design available to the researcher. In addition to the trends data that are compiled from different samples, *panel* studies enable the researcher to track the same respondents across time. Using this longitudinal approach, researchers can follow shifts in media preferences, attitudes, uses, or other respondent variables using data drawn for the same collective of individuals at specified time intervals. This is a very powerful design as it limits the amount of potential error introduced by the sampling of different respondents, but its greatest challenge to the researcher is keeping the panel intact over time. Panel designs are successful in accurately reporting changes in the dependent variable to the extent that respondents agree to continue their participation in the research project. As the mortality rate of participants increases, the strength of the summary data decreases. Some critics of panel designs point to the error introduced by respondents' repeated exposure to the same set of questions, thus making the

---

[8]Christopher H. Sterling, and John Michael Kittross, *Stay Tuned: A History of American Broadcasting,* 3rd ed. (Mahwah, NJ: Lawrence Erlbaum Associates, 2002), 823–75.

panel sensitized to the measurement instrument itself, and hence affecting the respondents' listening or viewing behaviors or the behaviors or perceptions they report.

Despite the potential shortcomings of panel designs, major studies using this approach have been an important mainstay of the mass communication research literature for decades. Being able to identify changes in voter preferences or attitudes has made panel studies especially appealing to political communication scholars since the 1940s. The pioneering work of Lazarsfeld, Berelson, and Gaudet on how voters make up their minds during a presidential election has served as a classic model for generations of researchers who have attempted to achieve their level of success using panel designs.[9] Both the size of this exemplary panel and the controls employed by the researchers to assure the accuracy of their findings have been frequently difficult to match by more recent studies because of increased research costs and growing reluctance on the part of survey participants. For example, a much more modest panel study by Anderson and Avery that was designed to track the changes in voters' perceptions of the presidential candidates' positions on various issues throughout the campaign revealed the difficulty of sustaining respondent involvement over time.[10] Of course, the most well-known panels used for generating audience research data are those assembled by the A.C. Nielsen Company for the purpose of collecting television program ratings. While these quantitative measurement techniques have been the subject of constant debate since their inception decades ago, they continue to be the basis on which millions of dollars are spent each year by advertisers. As noted earlier, the data reported by Nielsen has been an important asset to some our discipline's most respected broadcast historians.

Although controversial in the minds of some contemporary critics, it should be noted that panel studies also have been employed frequently within the literature on media effects. The importance of panel studies has grown in favor among social scientists as more narrowly conceived laboratory experiments came under attack for being too simplistic and artificial. While

---

[9] Paul F. Lazarsfeld, Bernard Berelson, and Hazel Gaudet, *The People's Choice: How the Voter Makes Up His Mind in a Presidential Election* (New York: Columbia University Press, 1944).

[10] James A. Anderson and Robert K. Avery, "An Analysis of Changes in Voter Perception of Candidate Positions," *Communication Monographs* 45, no. 4 (1978): 354–61.

subject to all the criticisms of panel studies found within the field of political communication, those reputable studies of television influences in everyday life provide important historical benchmarks. For example, the shift in focus from the direct effects of exposure to portrayals of televised violence among children to a more functional perspective involving how children make use of television content is well-illustrated by Schramm, Lyle, and Parker's comprehensive treatment, *Television in the Lives of Our Children.*[11] Similarly, the massive two-volume collection issued by the U.S. Government Printing Office in 1982, *Television and Behavior: Ten Years of Scientific Progress and Implications for the Eighties,* affords important historical evidence regarding the status of scientific inquiry and the communication policy issues of the time.[12] One might argue that important works such as these failed to change the contours of broadcast industry performance in any lasting way, but there can be no question that the serious study of television's impact on human behavior and the hearings that grew out of these investigations represented an important historical marker in the development of public interest and concern about media influence.

Interestingly, these investigations and numerous others that were to follow also illustrate a growing reliance within the research community on another important quantitative method—*content analysis.* Human communication messages, in all their rich variety, lend themselves to systematic, rigorous analysis, whether verbal, nonverbal, audio, video, or photographic. In other words, the various messages can be subjected to specific rule-governed evaluation that meets the requirements of quantitative analytic methodologies. At the most basic level, content analysis allows for the systematic description of the message, including the presence or absence of certain defining characteristics, the frequency of specified elements, and the establishment of a baseline for other kinds of measurement. The descriptive data generated by content analysis allow for the researcher to set forth hypotheses about the relationship between independent and dependent variables. For example, to return to the discussion of FCC cross-ownership policies mentioned earlier in this chapter, a researcher could use content analysis to test the relationship

---

[11] Wilbur Schramm, Jack Lyle, and Edwin Parker, *Television in the Lives of Our Children* (Palo Alto, CA: Stanford University Press, 1961).

[12] David Pearl, Lorraine Bouthilet, and Joyce Lazar, eds., *Television and Behavior: Ten Years of Scientific Progress and Implications for the Eighties* (Washington, DC: U.S. Government Printing Office, 1982).

between broadcast station group ownership (independent variable) and local news coverage (dependent variable) to test the hypothesis that the growth of large corporate owners of broadcast stations has had a negative impact on local news coverage. To adequately conduct such a study, the researcher would need to define the appropriate universe of news broadcasts and select samples of newscasts from the same broadcast outlets during periods of local and group ownership. If the researcher has hypothesized that group ownership results in a decrease of comprehensive local coverage and the data from systemic content analysis provides evidence consistent with this position, the researcher has grounds for providing an interpretation of the observations reported. This is not to suggest that the researcher can lay claim to a direct causal link, but rather it is evidence that can be used in advancing an argument for either the maintenance of existing rules or a change in communication policy. An advocate for a competing point of view must either counter with a competing interpretation of the findings or provide equally credible evidence that support a competing viewpoint. As noted earlier, the use of quantitative data in policy formation has become increasingly popular as courtroom litigation is requiring greater levels of factual information in defense of policy decision making.

It is impossible to imagine contemporary broadcast and electronic media historians to succeed in their scholarship without a firm understanding of the important role content analytic research has played, and continues to play, in the evolution and regulation of these industries. Indeed, the original findings of careful content analysis can be used by the historians themselves in helping to understand and interpret the past. Such influential scholars as Bernard Berelson, Ithiel de Sola Pool, and George Gerbner, among others, have written extensively on the protocols and practices of content analytic work and the value of this quantitative approach for communication research.[13] This research tradition has contributed countless studies to both sides of the debate regarding the possible negative effects of televised violence, and

---

[13] Bernard Berelson, *Content Analysis in Communication Research* (New York: Free Press, 1952); Ithiel de Sola Pool, ed., *Trends in Content Analysis* (Urbana: University of Illinois Press, 1959); George Gerbner, Ole Holsti, Klaus Krippendorff, William Paisley, and Philip Stone, *The Analysis of Communication Content: Developments in Scientific Theories and Computer Techniques* (New York: Wiley, 1969).

it has helped spawn a number of theories regarding media use and the roles media play.[14]

Increasingly, content analysis, along with other quantitative methods, is being used in combination with various qualitative methods to create a broader understanding of various happenings and events. Such methods as in-depth interviews, focus groups, and participant observation are frequently employed to complement or extend the findings gleaned from content analysis. Dominick and Wimmer argue that the next generation of media researchers should be trained more as data analysts than statisticians and that they will need to have an understanding of both quantitative and qualitative approaches.[15] Similarly, in Pardun's analysis of 159 qualitative studies published in the *Journal of Broadcasting & Electronic Media* between 1978 and 1998, she found that the majority of the authors contributing these articles conduct both qualitative and quantitative research.[16] Clearly, the broadcast historian cannot escape grappling with this ever-growing literature.

Two examples drawn from the constantly expanding research literature are presented here to support this conviction. Napoli has published findings generated by a quantitative analysis of policy decisions of the Federal Communications Commission between 1966 and 1995.[17] His purpose was to content analyze the decisions rendered by the FCC over the 30-year period in order to describe the actions and then test for stakeholder influence using a logistic regression analysis. The author explains that the literature on American broadcast regulation identifies four principal stakeholders with the active potential to influence FCC decision making: Congress, the President, the electronic media industry, and U.S. citizens. The dependent variable for this study was the individual broadcast policy decision that was coded as either

---

[14] Glenn G. Sparks, *Media Effects Research: A Basic Overview* (Belmont, CA: Wadsworth, 2002); Jennings Bryant and Dolf Zillmann, eds., *Media Effects: Advances in Theory and Research* (Mahwah, NJ: Lawrence Erlbaum Associates, 2002).

[15] Joseph Dominick and Roger Wimmer, "Training the Next Generation of Media Researchers," *Communication and Society* 6, no. 1 (2003): 3–9.

[16] Carol J. Pardun, "An Analysis of Qualitative Research in the *Journal of Broadcasting & Electronic Media,* 1978–1998," *Journal of Broadcasting & Electronic Media* 44, no. 3 (2000): 529–35.

[17] Philip M. Napoli, "The Federal Communications Commission and Broadcast Policy-making—1966–95: A Logistic Regression Analysis of Interest Group Influence," *Communication Law & Policy* 5, no. 2 (2000): 203–33.

"deregulatory" or "pro-regulatory." Napoli utilized a multipart search strategy to scan the FCC's electronic database and subjected the decisions identified to an elaborate coding scheme that included issue type and potential stakeholder influence. He then generated data (independent variables) about the make-up and composition of each stakeholder group to assess their influence potential. The highly sophisticated regression analysis and the detailed discussion of the involvement of each group are too extensive to be summarized here, but from a historian's perspective, the findings speak not only to the portion of the FCC workload that never receives any public scrutiny, but also the workings of the backstage players who direct much of the policy decision-making process, as opposed to the Commissioners themselves. The author concludes that the findings of the study did not account for the potential influence of all potential stakeholders, but within its limitations, the study affords clear evidence of repeated White House and Congressional influence during the three-decade period. Furthermore, he argues, any regulatory reform movement must situate the decision-making role of the FCC within a more definitive political context of the actual influences if genuine reform is to be possible.

Chesebro conducted a longitudinal quantitative and qualitative analysis of primetime network television series from the 1974–1975 through the 1998–1999 season.[18] Using an analysis system based on the critical writings of Kenneth Burke and Northrop Frye, the author categorized each program as representing ironic, mimetic, leader-centered, romantic, or mythical communication systems. He then evaluated each program for the value orientation exhibited by converting the five communication systems to corresponding value systems—existentialism, individualism, authority, idealism, and theology. Chesebro's findings indicate that during the second half of the 1970s American prime-time television programming emphasized the value of "individualism" as a principal approach to resolving symbolic conflicts. Primetime shows aired between 1980 and 1985 tended to promote idealism and authority, and in the second half of the 1980s and early 1990s authority was the primary value for conflict resolution. Primetime series in the mid and late 1990s featured alternating values of individuality and authority to solve conflict. His analysis and interpretations move well beyond the categories and quantitative results that he reports, as he contextualizes the findings of

---

[18] James W. Chesebro, "Communication, Values, and Popular Television Series: A Twenty-five Year Assessment and Final Conclusions," *Communication Quarterly* 51, no. 4 (2003): 367–418.

his longitudinal content analysis within the major historical events of each period.

The studies by Napoli and Chesebro serve as examples of current research where the boundaries between distinctly different longitudinal quantitative and qualitative methods have become blurred. If the recent forecasts of mass communication research methodologists are accurate, we can expect to see this trend not only continue but to accelerate in the years ahead.

SUMMARY AND CONCLUSIONS

The purpose of this chapter was to introduce the historiographer to the world of quantitative methods and to suggest how the data derived from these scientific approaches could contribute to the research pursuits of the critical and historical scholar. It was noted at the outset that quantitative approaches to the study of human communication have fallen out of favor in recent years at some academic departments, but those of us who have been working in the academy for the past three or four decades have observed the cyclical nature of most theoretical and methodological approaches. The academic pendulum continues to reverse its course periodically, and the scholar who fails to recognize the value of multiple historical methodologies risks losing the potential understanding that might be gained and the breadth of preparation that could prove central to one's career.

There are numerous approaches to acquiring historical knowledge, and the demands of the "real world" remind us that the need to support positions of value with scientifically derived quantitative findings is becoming increasingly necessary in the formation of public policy. As early as the 1950s historians in such disciplines as political science and sociology were becoming aware of the need for quantitative methods to provide acceptable historical accounts that did not rely on such imprecise descriptors as "typical," "significant," "widespread," and "growing" without the substantiation of numerical data.[19] Business history fell victim to similar criticisms as readers external to the field expected more from historians than fascinating and inspirational narratives about notable merchants, gifted

---

[19] Lee Benson, "Research Problems in American Political Historiography," in *Common Frontiers of the Social Sciences,* ed. Mirra Komarovsky (Glencoe, IL: Free Press, 1957).

entrepreneurs, and successful companies.[20] The history of broadcasting and electronic media is equally enhanced by quantitative data that enable the historian to not only tell a more complete and compelling story, but to defend historical claims with evidence that withstands public scrutiny.

It is impossible within the space of a single chapter to offer the reader more than a very brief snapshot of how selected quantitative methods are conducted and how they might contribute to one's own program of critical or historical scholarship. Many well-written and carefully developed introductions to the rich array of methodologies available to the reader can be found in such frequently consulted volumes as Wimmer and Dominick, Adams, Smith, and Hocking, Stacks, and McDermott, among many others.[21] Entire volumes on how to conduct and report specific quantitative studies using any one of a number of research approaches are readily available. But it is important to remember, however, that media critics and historians should not expect to find a "cookbook" for using quantitative methods in their work, as the potential uses of the data derived from such studies will be determined by the research questions advanced. Quantification adds a new dimension of understanding that can broaden and deepen the critical scholar's familiarity with the subject. Exactly how such approaches might be utilized, however, may require a renewed commitment to acquiring a greater appreciation of the functions and benefits of quantitative research. As explained by Rowney and Graham, "Depending on one's perspective, the quantitative mood in history can be seen either as the advance guard of a movement toward greater methodological sophistication or as an attempt to transform history into a social science. In either case, it behooves historians to find out more about it."[22]

---

[20] Kenneth A. Tucker, ed., *Business History: Selected Readings* (London: Frank Cass & Company Limited, 1977).

[21] Roger D. Wimmer and Joseph R. Dominick, *Mass Media Research: An Introduction* (Belmont, CA: Wadsworth, 2003); Robert C. Adams, *Social Survey Methods for Mass Media Research* (Hillsdale, NJ: Lawrence Erlbaum Associates, 1989); Mary John Smith, *Contemporary Communication Research Methods* (Belmont, CA: Wadsworth, 1988); John E. Hocking, Don W. Stacks, and Steven T. McDermott, *Communication Research,* 3rd ed. (Boston, MA: Allyn & Bacon, 2003).

[22] Don K. Rowney and James Q. Graham, *Quantitative History: Selected Readings in the Quantitative Analysis of Historical Data* (Homewood, IL: Dorsey Press, 1969), x.

Part III

A New Look at Electronic Media

8

A Survey of Cultural Studies in Radio

Michael C. Keith
Boston College

How can a social institution, like radio, be truly evaluated as to its present performance?—Paul Lazarsfeld[1]

Radio functions as more than just a technology or a method of communication, but as a node of cultural exchange.—Susan Merrill Squier[2]

From the inception of radio broadcasting, the medium has inspired an interesting (and recently a growing, though still limited) range of studies by both scholars and journalists. Continued attention from such government agencies as the Federal Radio Commission and Federal Communication Commission make it abundantly clear that the medium has been viewed as a significant cultural part of the nation. From the earliest broadcasts, radio was expected by many to serve an egalitarian function in the world. To that end the medium was intended (by regulators if not broadcasters) to operate as a public trustee with an obligation to address the needs of its growing audience.

As might be expected research examining radio's cultural role during its formative years was scant due to the evolving nature of its programming as well as the lack of interest on the part of critics and academicians who viewed radio as little more than a frivolous popular experiment. Only as President Franklin Roosevelt took to the airwaves in the early 1930s to rally the nation

---

[1] From Paul F. Lazarsfeld and Patricia L. Kendall, *Radio Listening in America: The People Look at Radio—Again* (New York: Prentice-Hall, 1948).

[2] From Susan Merrill Squier, ed., *Communities of the Air: Radio Century, Radio Culture* (Durham, NC: Duke University Press, 2003).

behind his administration's plan for economic recovery from the Depression did scholars begin to take serious notice of the medium's role as a cultural force and instrument for change.

Both domestic and foreign events in the late 1930s increased researchers' awareness of radio's impact in the lives of Americans. As the specter of world war grew in Europe, network correspondents conveyed the alarming details to listeners. Meanwhile a Halloween eve broadcast in 1938 graphically and imaginatively depicting an invasion of aliens from Mars caused widespread panic and clearly demonstrated the puissant hold radio had developed on the country's citizenry. Just 3 years after this fictional attack from outer space, the Pearl Harbor raid thrust the nation into a war in which radio would prove instrumental in galvanizing efforts to defeat the enemy.

Among the earliest work on the social and psychological relationship of listening audiences with radio broadcasting are those forged by Cantril and Beville.[3] Censorship and freedom of speech were on the minds of broadcasters from the medium's launch and was adequately addressed in a study by Summers.[4] In the 1940s Paul Lazarsfeld, Hadley Cantril, and Matthew Chappell with Claude Hooper offered benchmark studies, mostly centered on audience listening patterns and preferences.[5] Certainly Lazarsfeld's book is a touchstone in audience use of the medium. Meanwhile, Siepmann provided valuable insight on the audio medium within a sociocultural context as the first full postwar decade got underway.[6]

While the years following the country's victory in WWII brought with them a great sense of promise and prosperity, they were a turning point in radio's fate. The introduction of television would mark the end of the medium's short-lived golden age and all but remove it from the radar of scholars. For the next several decades radio would become a forgotten medium to

---

[3] Hadley Cantril, *The Invasion from Mars: A Study in the Psychology of Panic,* with the complete script of the famous Orson Welles broadcast (Princeton, NJ: Princeton University Press, 1940); Hugh Malcolm Beville Jr., *Social Stratification of the Radio Audience* (Princeton, NJ: Princeton Office of Radio Research, 1939).

[4] Harrison B. Summers, ed., *Radio Censorship* (New York: H.W. Wilson, 1939).

[5] Paul F. Lazarsfeld, *Radio and the Printed Page* (New York: Duell, Sloan and Pearce, 1940); Cantril, *Invasion from Mars*; Matthew N. Chappell and Claude E. Hooper, *Radio Audience Measurement* (New York: Stephen Daye, 1944).

[6] Charles A. Siepmann, *Radio, Television, and Society* (New York: Oxford University Press, 1950).

communication researchers, who would turn their attention to television disregarding radio and its new emphasis on popular music and youth.

Although not abundant, articles on radio appeared in various communication and mass media journals during this period. However, their focus was seldom on radio's cultural role but were principally industry-centric, dealing with the business, performance, and production aspects of the medium. Barnouw's landmark three-volume broadcasting retrospective, while making no claims to being a cultural appraisal of radio, does discuss topics such as gender, race, and religion in that context.[7]

In the early 1990s revived interest in broader radio studies became apparent with several publications examining aspects of the medium's place in society—Vargas's book is one such example.[8] At the forefront of this belated movement was the creation of the first academic publication devoted to the study of the medium—the *Journal of Radio Studies*. Throughout the last decade an increasing number of radio histories possessing an interest in radio's cultural ramifications were published—Hilmes's is a standout among them—along with several monographs (many by this chapter's author) examining specific instances of radio's role in various segments or subgroupings of the country's population.[9]

In the new millennium, radio studies has at long last established itself as a viable field of scholarly inquiry. Coinciding with this has been the addition of radio in culture and society courses at a handful of colleges and universities, among them Boston College, Michigan State University, and the University of Kansas. Douglas's estimable book, the first of the new century, offers extensive commentary on the cultural influence of radio.[10] That same year a propitious title from U.K. radio scholar David Hendy assessed the cultural impact of the

---

[7] Erik Barnouw, *A Tower in Babel: A History of Broadcasting in the United States to 1933* (New York: Oxford University Press, 1966); Erik Barnouw, *The Golden Web: A History of Broadcasting in the United States, 1933–1953* (New York: Oxford University Press, 1968); Erik Barnouw, *The Image Empire: A History of Broadcasting in the United States, from 1953* (New York: Oxford University Press, 1970).

[8] Lucila Vargas, *Social Uses and Radio Practices: The Use of Participatory Radio by Ethnic Minorities in Mexico* (Boulder, CO: Westview Press, 1995).

[9] Michele Hilmes, *Radio Voices: American Broadcasting, 1922–1952* (Minneapolis: University of Minnesota Press, 1997).

[10] Susan J. Douglas, *Listening In: Radio and the American Imagination* (New York: Times Books, 2000).

medium within a global context.[11] In 2002 a breakthrough collection of laudable essays pertaining to the manifold and diverse aspects of the medium's cultural history appeared in Hilmes and Loviglio's integral book and, in 2003, Squier's lucent and innovative anthology that devoted itself to an analysis of radio's consequential cultural presence was published.[12] The same year, *The Radio Journal* debuted in Britain offering further testimony to the growing global interest by scholars in the medium.[13]

This chapter pursues the line of inquiry Michele Hilmes sets forth in her cultural history of U.S. broadcasting, as she asks about the context of radio's development vis à vis social, cultural, and technological forces.[14] These and more questions are still in need of answers. What follows is a selective overview of publications that assume a cultural approach in their examination and assessment of the medium. It is not intended to be comprehensive or fully inclusive but does strive to traverse a good part of its terrain. Due to space limitations, the primary emphasis here is on American studies of this topic. Rather than a chronological breakdown of the canon, cultural studies of radio are presented in topical categories—politics, gender, race, religion, family, and so on.

POLITICS

Many feel that the 1990's explosion in talk radio was responsible for changing the landscape of American politics in the early part of that decade, so it is not surprising that there is a plethora of books dealing with this subject. Among those offering worthwhile assessments of the way in which the medium and its talk-meisters influenced voters is Levin's, whose telling assertions are drawn from interviews with hundreds of listeners in the Boston area.[15] Scott also employs an extensive audience survey to determine the influence of chat hosts

---

[11] David Hendy, *Radio in the Global Age* (London: Polity Press, 2000).

[12] Michele Hilmes and Jason Loviglio, eds., *Radio Reader: Essays in the Cultural History of Radio* (New York: Routledge, 2002); Squier, *Communities of the Air*.

[13] Ken Garner, ed., *The Radio Journal* (Glasgow: Glasgow Caledonian University, 2003–2004).

[14] Michele Hilmes, *Only Connect: A Cultural History of Broadcasting* (Thousand Oaks, CA: Wadsworth, 2002).

[15] Murray B. Levin, *Talk Radio and the American Dream* (Lexington, MA: Lexington Books, 1987).

on public opinion.[16] She harks back to the benign talk shows of the 1960s to underscore her claim that, three decades later, conversation radio has morphed into something that is far more scabrous and doctrinaire. Kurtz provides a candid, no-holds-barred evaluation of political talk radio's influence as does Hutchby's monograph.[17]

Assessments of talk radio's cultural influence and political power are readily available in academic journals. For example, Hofstetter and Gianos examine the social hierarchy of talk radio listeners, while Hollander analyzes national survey findings that cite talk listeners as more politically active and engaged.[18] Armstrong and Rubin contend that talk radio promotes interpersonal communication, while Rubin and Step examine the affect of attraction, motivation, and interaction on talk radio listening.[19] Then, Hall and Cappella evaluate the influence of talk programming on the outcome of the 1996 presidential election, while Page and Tannenbaum assess the nature of the public's role in this genre.[20] Rehm cites the value of talk radio in expanding public discourse.[21] Finally, Chinn's book provides an incisive programming profile of a

---

[17] Gini Graham Scott, *Can We Talk? The Power and Influence of Talk Shows* (New York: Perseus, 1996).

[17] Howard Kurtz, *Hot Air: All Talk, All the Time* (New York: Crown, 1996); Ian Hutchby, *Confrontation Talk: Arguments, Asymmetries, and Power on Talk Radio* (Mahwah, NJ: Lawrence Erlbaum Associates, 1996).

[18] C. Richard Hofstetter and Christopher Gianos, "Political Talk Radio: Actions Speak Louder than Words," *Journal of Broadcasting & Electronic Media* 41, no. 4 (1997): 501–15; Barry A. Hollander, "Talk Radio: Predictors of Use and Effects of Attitudes about Government," *Journalism and Mass Communication Quarterly* 73, no. 1 (1996): 102–13.

[19] Cameron B. Armstrong and Alan M. Rubin, "Talk Radio as Interpersonal Communication," *Journal of Communication* 39, no. 2 (1989): 84–94; Alan M. Rubin and Mary M. Step, "Impact of Motivation, Attraction, and Parasocial Interaction on Talk Radio Listening," *Journal of Broadcasting & Electronic Media* 44, no. 4 (2000): 635–54.

[20] Alice Hall and Joseph N. Cappella, "The Impact of Political Talk Radio Exposure," *Journal of Communication* 52 (2002): 332–50; Benjamin I. Page and Jason Tannenbaum, "Populist Deliberation in Talk Radio," *Journal of Communication* 46, no. 2 (1996): 33–54.

[21] Diane Rehm, "Talking over America's Electronic Backyard Fence," *Media Studies Journal* 7, no. 3 (1993): 63–69.

popular chat station, and Barker's gives a thorough evaluation of the politics of persuasion at play on the nation's airwaves.[22]

Several noteworthy articles focus on the influence of political talk show hosts. As might be expected given his prominence, those dealing with Rush Limbaugh far out number the rest. Among studies providing particular insights and evaluations into the cultural phenomenon of this staunchly conservative talker are those by Lewis; Harris, Mayer, Saulino, and Schiller; Kay, Ziegelmueller, and Minch; Swain; and Larson.[23] In their own way, each of these articles contributes further understanding as to why this particular radio talker has come to dominate the field.

Several books and articles probe the role of radio in American politics beyond the talk show venue. *Is American Radio Democratic?*, an early book by Frost, considers whether the medium is a democratic enterprise and expresses some doubts.[24] A recent book by Roscigno and Danaher delves into radio's participation in the U.S. labor movement of the early 1930s.[25] Brown, Craig, and Clark document the early participation of radio in political culture.[26]

---

[22] Sandra Hardy Chinn, *At Your Service—KMOX and Bob Hardy: Pioneers of Talk Radio* (St. Louis, MO: Virginia Publishing, 1997); David C. Barker, *Rushed to Judgment?* (New York: Columbia University Press, 2002).

[23] Tom Lewis, "Triumph of the Idol: Rush Limbaugh and a Hot Medium," *Media Studies Journal* 7, no. 3 (1993): 51–61; Chad Harris, Vicki Mayer, Catherine Saulino, and Dan Schiller, "The Class Politics of Rush Limbaugh," *The Communication Review* 1, no. 4 (1996): 545–64; Jack Kay, George Ziegelmueller, and Kevin Minch, "From Coughlin to Limbaugh: Fallacies and Techniques of Propaganda in American Populist Talk Radio," *Journal of Radio Studies* 5, no. 1 (1998): 9–21; William N. Swain, "Propaganda and Rush Limbaugh: Is the Label the Last Word?," *Journal of Radio Studies* 6, no. 1 (1999): 27–40; Charles U. Larson, "Radio, Secondary Orality, and the Search for Community: A Case Study of 'A Prairie Home Companion,'" *Journal of Radio Studies* 3 (1995–1996): 89–105.

[24] S. E. Frost, Jr., *Is American Radio Democratic?* (Chicago: University of Chicago Press, 1937).

[25] Vincent J. Roscigno and William F. Danaher, *The Voice of Southern Labor: Radio, Music, and Textile Strikes, 1929–1934* (Minneapolis: University of Minnesota Press, 2004).

[26] Robert J. Brown, *Manipulating the Ether: The Power of Broadcast Radio in Thirties America* (Jefferson, NC: McFarland, 1998); Douglas B. Craig, *Fireside Politics: Radio and Political Culture in the United States, 1920–1940* (Baltimore, MD: Johns

Powell's and Delli Carpini's articles deal with the more recent role that radio has played in politics.[27]

RACE AND ETHNICITY

African American presence in early radio was scant but did exist, mostly in the form of minstrelsy and ventriloquy. Several recent books examine the involvement of Blacks in the medium (as well as their portrayal by it) from the 1920s through present day. Sampson surveys the historical contribution of Blacks in radio prior to the arrival of television.[28] George offers a detailed account of the rise of the first Black deejays.[29] Ely focuses on the social implications on racial attitudes engendered by *Amos 'n' Andy*.[30] Barlow provides a solid history of Black radio, emphasizing the challenges it faced in an inequitable media culture.[31] Savage examines radio in the context of racial politics.[32] Williams evaluates the role of African American radio personalities in the assimilation of Blacks migrating north following World War II.[33] Cantor provides a detailed profile of the nation's first all-Black station.[34] MacDonald considers Richard

---

Hopkins University Press, 2000); David Clark, "Radio in Presidential Elections," *Journal of Broadcasting* 6, no. 3 (1962): 229–38.

[27] Adam Clayton Powell III, "You Are What You Hear," *Media Studies Journal* 7, no. 3 (1993): 71–76; Michael X. Delli Carpini, "Radio's Political Past," *Media Studies Journal* 7, no. 3 (1993): 23–35.

[28] Henry T. Sampson, *Swingin' on the Ether Waves* (Lanham, MD: Scarecrow Press, 2005).

[29] Martha Washington George, *Black Radio … Winner Takes All: America's 1st Black Deejays* (Philadelphia, PA: Xlibris Corporation, 2003).

[30] Melvin Patrick Ely, *The Adventures of Amos 'n' Andy: A Social History of an American Phenomenon* (New York: Free Press, 1991).

[31] William Barlow, *Voice Over: The Making of Black Radio* (Philadelphia, PA: Temple University Press, 1999).

[32] Barbara Dianne Savage, *Broadcasting Freedom: Radio, War, and the Politics of Race, 1938–1948* (Chapel Hill: University of North Carolina Press, 1999).

[33] Gilbert A. Williams, *Legendary Pioneers of Black Radio* (Westport, CT: Praeger, 1998).

[34] Louis Cantor, *Wheelin' on Beale: How WDIA–Memphis Became the Nation's First All-Black Radio Station and Created the Sound that Changed America* (New York: Pharos Books, 1992).

Durham's "Destination Freedom" radio scripts in the context of the Black protest movement.[35] Ward assesses the medium's involvement in the southern civil rights struggle.[36] Hilmes and Barnouw devote portions of their consequential narratives to the implications of racial stereotyping.[37]

Several articles and book chapters also devote themselves to the question of race in the audio medium. Carcasson and Aune evaluate the national radio broadcast of Justice Hugo Black, who employed the medium in the 1930s to respond to accusations concerning his alleged ties to the Ku Klux Klan.[38] Hattaway and Brinson report on the Alabama Negro Extension Service Broadcasts.[39] Keith interviews several prominent figures on the question of racial bias in American radio.[40] Meckiff and Murray consider the image of the Black soldier.[41] Shields and Ogles look at Black liberation radio through the microstation movement.[42] Soley and Hough investigate levels of Black ownership.[43]

Publications focusing on other ethnic minority groups are not in as great abundance as those devoted to African Americans. Keith offers the first

---

[35] J. Fred MacDonald, ed., *Richard Durham's Destination Freedom: Scripts from Radio's Black Legacy, 1948–50* (New York: Praeger, 1989).

[36] Brian Ward, *Radio and the Struggle for Civil Rights in the South* (Gainesville: University of Florida Press, 2004).

[37] Hilmes, *Radio Voices*; Barnouw, *A Tower in Babel, The Golden Web,* and *The Image Empire*.

[38] Martin Carcasson and James Aune. "Klansman on the Court: Justice Hugo Black's Radio Address to the Nation," *Quarterly Journal of Speech* 89, no. 2 (2003): 154–70.

[39] Allison M. Hattaway and Susan L. Brinson, "Race & Radio: The Alabama Negro Extension Service Broadcasts," *Journal of Radio Studies* 8, no. 2 (2001): 372–87.

[40] Michael C. Keith, *Talking Radio: An Oral History of American Radio in the Television Age* (Armonk, NY: M. E. Sharpe, 2000).

[41] Donald Meckiff and Matthew Murray, "Radio and the Black Soldier during World War II," *Critical Studies in Mass Communication* 15, no. 4 (1998): 337–56.

[42] Steven O. Shields and Robert Ogles, "Black Liberation Radio: A Case Study of Free Radio Micro-broadcasting," *Howard Journal of Communication* 5, no. 3 (1995): 173–83.

[43] Lawrence Soley and George Hough III, "Black Ownership of Community Radio Stations: An Economic Evaluation," *Journal of Broadcasting* 22, no. 4 (1982): 455–67.

detailed study of the use and application of radio by Native Americans.[44] Theodore Grame's book provides worthwhile statistical data and information regarding indigenous and other ethnic broadcasting.[45] Murphy reviews the nature of indigenous radio in Alaska.[46] Smith and Brigham discuss the evolution of Indian language programming.[47] Eiselein produces a native radio listening report for CPB.[48] Coleman examines the effects of indigenous radio in rural Alaska.[49] Smith and Cornette offer a study of Indian radio in the Dakotas.[50]

There are also a few publications on less publicized ethnicities. Joseph Migala provides a monograph on the cultural significance of Polish-American radio.[51] Downing's article assesses the state of ethnic minority radio in the United States.[52] Casey Lum provides a retrospective of New York Chinese language wireless radio.[53] Paredes discusses the surge in popularity of Spanish language radio.[54]

---

[44] Michael C. Keith, *Signals in the Air: Native Broadcasting in America* (Westport, CT: Praeger, 1995).

[45] Theodore Grame, *Ethnic Broadcasting in the United States* (Washington, DC: American Folklife Center, 1980).

[46] James E. Murphy, "Alaska Native Communication Media: An Overview," *Gazette* (Fairbanks, AK), 1982.

[47] Bruce L. Smith and Jerry C. Brigham, "Native Radio Broadcasting in North America: An Overview of Systems in the United States and Canada," *Journal of Broadcasting & Electronic Media* 36, no. 2 (1992): 183–94.

[48] Eddie Bill Eiselein, *Indian Issues* (Browning, MT: Spirit Talk Press, 1993).

[49] Alice White Coleman, "Radio in the Alaska Bush: Native Responses to Cultural Diffusion," *Journal of Radio Studies* 6, no. 2 (1997): 7–14.

[50] Bruce L. Smith and M. L. Cornette, "Eypapaha for Today: American Indian Radio in the Dakotas," *Journal of Radio Studies* 5, no. 2 (1999): 19–30.

[51] Joseph Migala, *Polish Radio Broadcasting in the United States* (Boulder, CO: East European Monographs, 1987).

[52] John D. Downing, "Ethnic Minority Radio in the United States," *Howard Journal of Communication* 2, no. 2 (1990): 135–48.

[53] Casey Lum, "An Alternative Voice from Afar: A Brief History of New York's Chinese Language Wireless Radio," *Journal of Radio Studies* 2 (2000): 355–72.

[54] Mari Castanede Paredes, "The Transformation of Spanish-Language Radio in the U.S.," *Journal of Radio Studies* 10, no. 1 (2003): 5–16.

GENDER AND SEX

Women were for many years ghettoized by radio writes Hilmes.[55] The role of females was restricted in early radio as it was in most professions in the first half of the twentieth century. Radio reflected the prevailing attitude about women's subordinate place in the workforce through programs that invariably depicted women as domestic caregivers rarely to be found in careers beyond those related to home and hearth. Despite the formidable barriers against women's participation in the new medium, recent studies argue that the so-called "weaker" sex made important contributions to radio and in doing so helped their cause in the quest for equality. In 2001 two books provided the first thorough examination of the experience and activities of women in radio broadcasting. Donna Halper's pioneering monograph sheds substantial first light on the contributions of women to radio within the context of culture's attitudes and expectations of the gender.[56] Perhaps most importantly, Halper has rescued the record of some formerly forgotten pioneers. The second of these full length studies was published in the U.K. and edited by Caroline Mitchell. This initial anthology offers a range of essays on the feminist view of the medium as a tool for economic and social empowerment.[57]

Nancy Signorielli's collection of profiles on women in mass communication, provides discourse on gender discrimination and stereotyping.[58] In two monographs, Michael Keith interviews prominent women broadcasters regarding the challenges and bias they encountered in a male dominated profession. In the latter study, Keith details the experiences of female deejays and engineers in commercial underground radio as well as their contributions to this unique and culturally sentient programming genre.[59] Marita Mata

---

[55] Hilmes, *Radio Voices*.

[56] Donna L. Halper, *Invisible Stars: A Social History of Women in American Broadcasting* (Armonk, NY: M. E. Sharpe, 2001).

[57] Caroline Mitchell, *Woman and Radio: Airing Differences* (London: Routledge, 2001).

[58] Nancy Signorielli, ed., *Women in Communication: A Biographical Sourcebook* (Westport, CT: Greenwood, 1996).

[59] Michael C. Keith, *Voices in the Purple Haze: Underground Radio and the Sixties* (Westport, CT: Praeger, 1997); Keith, *Talking Radio*.

discusses the social influence of women in popular radio.[60] Marguerita Ruffner probes women's attitudes as reflected by the medium.[61] Lauren Goodlad offers a thoughtful exegesis of gendering in alternative radio.[62]

Disquisition on gay and lesbian presence in radio is scarce. This may well be a reflection of society's long-standing reluctance to address homosexual issues. Phylis Johnson and Michael Keith offer the first book-length study of alternative lifestyle groups determined to enhance awareness of their tenuous social footing through radio broadcasts, while Edward Alwood focuses part of his examination of gays and lesbians on their portrayal by radio news media.[63] Articles on the subject appear in a handful of journals, among them John Tulloch and Simon Chapman review broadcast debates about AIDs, and Kevin Barnhurst documents election year coverage of the gay and lesbian question on National Public Radio.[64]

COMMUNITY AND FAMILY

One of the areas of interest to media scholars has been the effect of radio on community and family. That is to say, how has the medium played a part in the evolution and configuration of these core institutions? Given radio's mandated responsibility as public trustee, it has attempted (not always willingly or successfully) to provide programming that reflects public issues, needs, and interests.

---

[62] Marita Mata, "Being Women in the Popular Radio," in *Women in Grassroots Communication*, ed. Pilar Riano (Thousand Oaks, CA: Sage, 1994).

[61] Marguerita Anne Ruffner, "Women's Attitudes Towards Radio." *Journal of Broadcasting & Electronic Media* 17, no. 1 (1972–1973): 85–94.

[62] Lauren M. E. Goodlad, "Packaged Alternatives: The Incorporation and Gendering of 'Alternative' Radio," in *Communities of the Air: Radio Century, Radio Culture*, ed. Susan Merrill Squier (Durham, NC: Duke University Press, 2003).

[63] Phylis Johnson and Michael C. Keith, *Queer Airwaves: The Story of Gay and Lesbian Broadcasting* (Armonk, NY: M. E. Sharpe, 2001); Edward Alwood, *Straight News* (New York: Columbia University Press, 1998).

[64] John Tulloch and Simon Chapman, "Experts in Crisis: The Framing of Radio Debate about the Risk of AIDS to Heterosexuals," *Discourse and Society* 3, no. 4 (1992): 437–67; Kevin G. Barnhurst, "Queer Political News: Election Year Coverage of the Lesbian and Gay Communities on National Public Radio, 1992–2000," *Journalism* 4, no. 1 (2003): 5–28.

Several books concentrate on the nature of the interface between the medium and the communities to which stations are licensed. Fairchild assesses the levels of access and equity in community radio.[65] Keith chronicles the deeds and altruistic agenda of counterculture outlets, Milam espouses the virtues of service and activism.[66] Lewis and Booth stress the potential of the medium for constructive public communication, and in a very early study, Atkinson examines network contributions to the community through educational programming.[67]

The microradio movement with its passion for neighborhood service has inspired a handful of full-length works and book chapters. Soley discusses so-called "free" radio from a civil disobedience perspective, and Dicks and McDowell attempt to shed light on the rise in unlicensed audio broadcasting.[68] Ruggiero analyzes the efforts of media giants in banning low-power, community-oriented stations.[69] Bensman uses the movement as a contemporary backdrop to his history of broadcast regulation, Walker devotes chapters of his alternative retrospective of radio to the rise and agenda of low-power FM, and Huntemann evaluates the politics of the micromedium.[70] Carpenter

---

[65] Charles Fairchild, *Community Radio and Public Culture: Being an Examination of Media Access and Equity in the Nations of North America* (Cresskill, NJ: Hampton Press, 2001).

[66] Keith, *Voices in the Purple Haze*; Lorenzo Wilson Milam, *Original Sex and Broadcasting: A Handbook for Starting a Radio Station for the Community* (San Francisco, CA: Mho & Mho Works, 1988).

[67] Peter M. Lewis and Jerry Booth, *Invisible Medium: Public, Commercial, and Community Radio* (Washington, DC: Howard University Press, 1990); Carroll Atkinson, *American Universities and Colleges That Have Held Broadcast License* (Boston, MA: Meador, 1941).

[68] Lawrence C. Soley, *Free Radio: Electronic Civil Disobedience* (Boulder, CO: Westview Press, 1999); Steven J. Dicks and Walter McDowell, "Pirates, Pranksters, & Prophets: Understanding America's Unlicensed 'Free' Radio Movement," *Journal of Radio Studies* 8, no 2 (2000): 329–41.

[69] Greg Ruggiero, *Microradio & Democracy: (Low) Power to the People* (New York: Seven Stories Press, 1999).

[70] Marvin R. Bensman, *The Beginning of Broadcast Regulation in the Twentieth Century* (Jefferson, NC: McFarland, 2000); Jesse Walker, *Rebels of the Air: An Alternative History of Radio in America* (New York: New York University Press, 2001); Nina Huntemann, "A Promise Diminished: The Politics of Low-Power Radio," in

chronicles her experiences operating low-power illegal outlets in two California cities, and Hillard and Keith probe the impact of media concentration on
local radio programming and community service.[71]

A number of journal articles have explored radio's community service
involvement. Rowland discusses the meaning of the public interest standard,
while Ehrlich and Contractor probe the place of shock programming in the
context of "community service."[72] Smith looks back at the FCC's first public
interest campaign designed to eliminate fraudulent medical ads, and Surlin
expounds on the approach to community ascertainment legislation by a
minority station.[73]

The medium's contribution to life in rural America has inspired recent
journal studies. Riney-Kehrberg examines the listening habits of Kansas farm
women—taking a lead from much earlier works on the subject appearing in
the 1940s and 1950s.[74] Likewise echoing earlier studies, Craig looks at the
medium's companion role to farmers, and Podber investigates early radio in
rural Appalachia.[75]

Communities of the Air: Radio Century, Radio Culture, ed. Susan Merrill Squier
(Durham, NC: Duke University Press, 2003).

[71] Sue Carpenter, *40 Watts from Nowhere* (New York: Scribner, 2004); Robert L.
Hilliard and Michael C. Keith, *The Quieted Voice: Rise and Demise of Localism in
American Radio* (Carbondale: Southern Illinois Press, 2005).

[72] Willard D. Rowland Jr., "The Meaning of 'the Public Interest' in Communica-
tions Policy, Part II: Its Implementation in Early Broadcast Law and Regulation,"
Communication Law and Policy 2, no. 4 (1997): 363–96; Matthew C. Ehrlich and
Noshir S. Contractor, "'Shock' Meets 'Community Service': J. C. Corcoran at
MOX," *Journal of Radio Studies* 5, no. 1 (1998): 22–35.

[73] F. Leslie Smith, "Quelling Radio's Quacks: The FCC's First Public Interest Pro-
gramming Campaign," *Journalism Quarterly* 71, no. 3 (1994): 594–608; Stuart H.
Surlin, "Ascertainment of Community Needs by a Black-oriented Radio Station,"
Journal of Broadcasting 16, no. 4 (1972): 421–29.

[74] Pamela Riney-Kehrberg, "The Radio Diary of Mary Dyck, 1936–1955: The
Listening Habits of a Kansas Farm Woman," *Journal of Radio Studies* 5, No. 2 (1998),
66–79.

[75] Steve Craig, "The Farmer's Friend: Radio Comes to Rural America, 1920–
1927," *Journal of Radio Studies* 8, no. 2 (2001): 330–46; Jacob J. Podber, "Early
Radio in Rural Appalachia: An Oral History," *Journal of Radio Studies* 8, no. 2
(2001): 388–410.

Radio's place in family life has generated a modicum of interest among scholars. Harry Leon Levin produced an astute monograph on applying the medium in family planning.[76] Sidonie Matsner Gruenberg, W. R. Clark, Herta Herzog, and Paul Lyness offer early studies in the relationship of children with radio, focusing on the way particular broadcasts modify the behavior and habits of young listeners.[77] Mark Runco and Kathy Pezdek examine the medium's impact on children's creativity and thought processes.[78] Paul Dennis investigates the effects of golden age radio programs on children and comes up with some compelling conclusions, while Patricia Greenfield and Jessica Beagles-Roos argue radio's greater cognitive impact on children.[79] Anthony Roberto, Gary Myers, Amy J. Johnson, Charles K. Atkin, and Patricia K. Smith offer insights and implications from a radio-based health communication query.[80] Sharon Lee Hammond, Vicki Freimuth, and William Morrison also examine health messages but rather as they pertain to teens.[81]

---

[76] Harry Leon Levin, *The Use of Radio in Family Planning* (Oklahoma City, OK: World Neighbors, 1974).

[77] Sidonie Matsner Gruenberg, "Radio and the Child," *Annals of the American Academy of Political Science* 177 (January 1935): 123; W. R. Clark, "Radio Listening Habits of Children." *Journal of Social Psychology* 12 (1940); Herta Herzog, *Children and Their Leisure Time Listening to the Radio: A Survey of the Literature in the Field* (New York: Office of Radio Research, Columbia University, 1941); Paul I. Lyness, "Radio's Young Audience Habits," *Broadcasting* 25 (September 1950).

[78] Mark A. Runco and Kathy Pezdek, "The Effect of Television and Radio on Children's Creativity," *Human Communication Research* 11, no. 1 (1984): 109–20.

[79] Paul M. Dennis, "Chills and Thrills: Does Radio Harm Our Children?," *Journal of the History of the Behavioral Sciences* 34, no. 1 (1998): 33–50; Patricia Greenfield and Jessica Beagles-Roos, "Radio vs. Television: Their Cognitive Impact on Children of Different Socioeconomic and Ethnic Groups," *Journal of Communications* 38, no. 2 (Spring 1988): 71–92.

[80] Anthony J. Roberto, Gary Myers, Amy J. Johnson, Charles K. Atkin, and Patricia K. Smith, "Promoting Gun Trigger-lock Use: Insights and Implications From a Radio-based Health Communication Intervention," *Journal of Applied Communication* 30, no. 3 (2002): 210–30.

[81] Sharon Lee Hammond, Vicki S. Freimuth, and William Morrison, "Radio and Teens: Convincing Gatekeepers to Air Health Messages," *Health Communication* 2, no. 2 (1990): 59–67.

Peter Christenson and Peter DeBeneditis add further discourse on children's use of radio.[82]

WAR

A number of strong volumes offer insight into radio's role and participation during wartime, most focusing on World War II. Howard Blue uses radio drama to reveal the presence of censorship during and after the global conflict, Michael Sweeney likewise provides a study on wartime censorship.[83] Gerd Horten concentrates on the cultural politics of propaganda.[84] Horst Bergmeier and Rainer Lotz tell the story of how the Nazis used American music for propaganda purposes.[85] Mark Berstein and Alex Lubertozzi focus on the war work of Edward R. Murrow and his "boys," and Patrick Morley explores the acrimonious squabble between Armed Forces Radio and the BBC.[86] Chapters in tomes by Fred MacDonald, Michele Hilmes, and Erik Barnouw also devote considerable print to wartime radio.[87] Charles Rolo and Sherman Dryer were the first to inquire into the relationship between the medium and World War II, although both offer their own

---

[82] Peter G. Christenson and Peter DeBeneditis, "Eavesdropping on the FM Band: Children's Use of Radio," *Journal of Communication* 36, no. 2 (1986): 27–38.

[83] Howard Blue, *Words at War: World War II Era Radio Drama and the Postwar Broadcasting Industry Blacklist* (Lanham, MD: Scarecrow Press, 2002); Michael S. Sweeney, *Secrets of Victory: The Office of Censorship and American Press and Radio in World War II* (Chapel Hill: University of North Carolina Press, 2001).

[84] Gerd Horten, *Radio Goes to War: The Cultural Politics of Propaganda during World War II* (Berkeley: University of California Press, 2002).

[85] Horst J. P. Bergmeier and Rainer E. Lotz, *Hitler's Airwaves: The Inside Story of Nazi Radio Broadcasting and Propaganda Swing* (New Haven, CT: Yale University Press, 1997).

[86] Mark Berstein and Alex Lubertozzi, *World War II on the Air: Edward R. Murrow and the Broadcasts that Riveted a Nation* (Naperville, IL: Sourcebooks, 2003); Patrick Morley, *"This Is the American Forces Network": The Anglo-American Battle of the Air Waves in World War II* (Westport, CT: Praeger, 2001).

[87] J. Fred. MacDonald, *Don't Touch That Dial: Radio Programming in American Life, 1920–1960* (Chicago: Nelson-Hall, 1979); Hilmes, *Radio Voices*; Barnouw, *The Golden Web*.

unique take on the subject.[88] A number of news and war correspondents (Shirer, Severied, Cronkite) disseminated printed accounts regarding their days covering the war for the networks and these can be useful in gaining a further appreciation and awareness of the medium's valuable function during wartime.

There are fewer articles than might be expected on this broad subject in communication journals. Jennifer Fay notes the decline of foreign language broadcasting during World War II; Ronald Garay looks at government regulation during this period.[89] Paul Heyer, Gary Morson, and Hoard Koch analyze the war themes in Orson Welles's 1938 alien invasion broadcast.[90] Two books provide good coverage of the U.S. external services during the cold war: Geroge Urban produces a memoir of his time as director of Radio Free Europe, while James Critchlow gives a telling insider's account of cold war broadcasting at Radio Liberty.[91] Indeed, there is plenty of literature on radio as a propaganda instrument, and much of it is historical.

RELIGION

The topic of religion has long been of curiosity to radio studies scholars—many inquiries date back to the late 1940s. Its presence on the dial and its impact on audiences has been the subject of several recent monographs. Tona Hangen presents a concise depiction of the development of evangelical religion coinciding with radio's own rise, and Paul Apostolidis offers a careful

---

[88] Charles Rolo, *Radio Goes to War: The "Fourth Front"* (New York: Putnam, 1942); Sherman Harvard Dryer, *Radio in Wartime* (New York: Greenberg, 1942).

[89] Jennifer Fay, "Casualties of War: The Decline of Foreign Language Broadcasting during World War II," *Journal of Radio Studies* 6, no. 1 (1999): 62–80; Ronald Garay, "Guarding the Airwaves: Government Regulation of World War II American Radio," *Journal of Radio Studies* 3 (1995): 130–48.

[90] Paul Heyer, "A Reassessment of Orson Welles' 1938 War of the Worlds Broadcast," *Journal of Communication* 28, no. 2 (2003): 149–65; Gary Saul Morson, "The War of the Well(e)s," *Journal of Communication* 29, no. 3 (1979): 10–20; Hoard Koch, *The Panic Broadcast: Portrait of an Event* (Boston, MA: Little, Brown, 1970).

[91] George R. Urban, *Radio Free Europe and the Pursuit of Democracy* (New Haven, CT: Yale University Press, 1998); James Critchlow, *Radio Hole-in-the-Head: Radio Liberty, An Insider's Story of Cold War Broadcasting* (Washington, DC: American University Press, 1995).

portrait of conservative evangelical talk radio.[92] Three books by Donald Warren, Ronald Carpenter, and Sheldon Marcus provide well-informed studies of the infamous radio priest Charles Coughlin.[93] Howard Dorgan offers an account of grassroots radio religion in Appalachia.[94] Hal Erickson has assembled a directory of the programs and personalities of inspirational radio.[95] Marilyn Matelski renders a critical history of Vatican radio.[96] Catholic priests Fr. Leslie Rumble and Fr. Charles M. Carty present a 3-volume collection of the best questions and answers from their radio call-in show broadcast in the late 1930s from both Sydney, Australia, and St. Paul, Minnesota.[97] These prove to be propitious, if not curious, records of the religious and moral concerns and fixations of the listening audience.

There have been a number of salient essays devoted to the topic. A sampling would include Ronald Johnstone's inclusive survey of the audience for religious radio, Quentin Schultz's probe into evangelical broadcasting, and Michael Casey and Aimee Rowe's examination of Father Coughlin's rhetorical themes.[98]

---

[92] Tona J. Hangen, *Redeeming the Dial: Radio, Religion, and Popular Culture in America* (Chapel Hill: University of North Carolina Press, 2002); Paul Apostolidis, *Stations of the Cross: Adorno and Christian Right Radio* (Durham, NC: Duke University Press, 2000).

[93] Donald Warren, *Radio Priest: Charles Coughlin, the Father of Hate Radio* (New York: Free Press, 1996); Ronald H. Carpenter, *Father Charles E. Coughlin: Surrogate Spokesman for the Disaffected* (Westport, CT: Praeger, 1998); Sheldon Marcus, *Father Coughlin: The Tumultuous Life of the Priest of the Little Flower* (Boston, MA: Little, Brown, 1986).

[94] Howard Dorgan, *The Airwaves of Zion: Radio and Religion in Appalachia* (Knoxville: University of Tennessee Press, 1993).

[95] Hal Erickson, *Religious Radio and Television in the United States, 1921–1991: The Programs and Personalities* (Jefferson, NC: McFarland, 1992).

[96] Marilyn Matelski, *Vatican Radio: Propagation by the Airwaves* (Westport, CT: Praeger, 1995).

[97] Fr. Leslie Rumble and Fr. Charles M. Carty, *Radio Replies in Defence of Religion Given from the Catholic Broadcasting Station 2Sm Sydney, Australia,* 3 vols. (St. Paul, MN: Radio Replies Press Society, 1938; repr., San Francisco: Tan Books, 1979).

[98] Ronald L. Johnstone, "Who Listens to Religious Radio?," *Journal of Broadcasting and Electronic Media* 16, no. 1 (1972): 91–102; Quentin J. Schultze, "Evangelical Radio and the Rise of the Electronic Church, 1921–1948," *Journal of*

FURTHER RESEARCH

Other astute inquiries into radio's cultural role include Gary Coville and Patrick Lucanio's discourse on the romance and impact of technology.[99] Michael Brian Schiffer provides a thought-provoking and paradigmatic case study on the impact of radio's portability, and Gerald Nachman writes about golden age programs as a cultural force.[100] Andrew Crisell appraises the medium's role in popular-culture development, and Peter Fornatale and Joshua Mills critique posttelevision radio's reinvention.[101] Gene Fowler and Bill Crawford examine border radio, and Robert Hilliard and Michael Keith's monograph is on obscene and indecent broadcast discourse.[102] Emily Edwards and Michael Singletary review radio music subcultures, while Steven Smethers and Lee Jolliffee survey the live music era on rural Midwestern radio stations.[103] Michael Keith audits nocturnal programming, and Eric Rothenbuhler analyzes commercial

---

Broadcasting and Electronic Media 32, no. 3 (1988): 289–306; Michael Casey and Aimee Rowe, "Driving Out the Money Changers: Radio Priest Charles E. Coughlin's Rhetorical Vision," *Journal of Communication and Religion* 19, no. 1 (1996): 37–47.

[99] Gary Coville and Patrick Lucanio, *Smokin' Rockets: The Romance of Technology in American Film, Radio, and Television, 1945–1962* (Jefferson, NC: McFarland, 2002).

[100] Michael Brian Schiffer, *The Portable Radio in American Life*, repr. ed. (Tucson: University of Arizona Press, 1992); Gerald Nachman, *Raised on Radio* (New York: Pantheon, 1998).

[101] Andrew Crisell, *Understanding Radio*, 2nd ed. (London: Routledge, 1994); Peter Fornatale and Joshua E. Mills, *Radio in the Television Age* (Woodstock, NY: Overlook Press, 1980).

[102] Gene Fowler and Bill Crawford, *Border Radio: Quacks, Yodelers, Pitchmen, Psychics, and Other Amazing Broadcasters of the American Airwaves* (Austin: University of Texas Press, 2002); Robert L. Hilliard and Michael C. Keith, *Dirty Discourse: Sex and Indecency in American Radio* (Ames: Iowa State University Press, 2003).

[103] Emily D. Edwards and Michael W. Singletary, "Life's Soundtracks: Relationships Between Radio Music Subcultures and Listeners' Belief Systems," *Southern Communication Journal* 54, no. 2 (1989): 144–58; J. Steven Smethers and Lee B. Jolliffee, "Singing and Selling Seeds: The Live Music Era on Rural Midwestern Radio Stations," *Journalism History* 26, no. 2 (2000): 61–70.

radio as communication.[104] Elmer Smead and Louise Benjamin study the relationship between freedom of speech rights and public interest responsibilities and obligations.[105]

IN THE AIR AHEAD?

Despite the recent promising rise in the output of studies dealing with radio's place in American culture, it remains an underreported area in media research. The overall neglect of radio by scholars until recently has resulted in a gap in the appreciation and understanding of the significant way the medium has contributed to the lives of its listeners and the world it serves. Particularly lacking are studies that go beyond the recent crop of archetypal monographs focusing on the use of the medium by specific disenfranchised segments of society. Certainly further research might be undertaken in counterculture, indigenous, gay and lesbian, extremist, and minority radio, as well as in a host of other elided areas. Today the likelihood that this will happen is better than it has been due to the existence of a first-rate journal and the widening awareness among communication scholars and the academic community as a whole of the significant place of radio in American culture.

---

[104] Michael C. Keith, *Sounds in the Dark: All Night Radio in American Life* (Ames: Iowa State University Press, 2001); Eric W. Rothenbuhler, "Commercial Radio as Communication," *Journal of Communication* 46, no. 1 (1996): 125–43.

[105] Elmer E. Smead, *Freedom of Speech by Radio and Television* (Washington, DC: Public Affairs Press, 1959); Louise Benjamin, *Freedom of the Air and the Public Interest: First Amendment Rights in Broadcasting to 1935* (Carbondale: Southern Illinois University Press, 2001).

9

Television Broadcast Records

Craig Allen

Arizona State University

Television has many advantages for historians and historians-to-be. Not only is television a vast area with numerous valuable topics, all of its questions are tied to one innovation, the broadcasting of pictures. Its main idea is easy to tame. Hardly the least of its attractions is its pervasiveness and appeal. Just as everyone is fascinated by TV, they want to know more about it. Add to this a field unsurpassed in social implications, public interest, and debate, and easily seen is a subject ripe with possibilities.

Yet television historiography is not what many newcomers may think. Gone are the days when authors gave a nostalgic look at the medium's great moments as captured in Edward R. Murrow kinescopes and *I Love Lucy* reruns. Profound changes in the concept of television have come from cable, satellite, and digital delivery, which have diversified its process of production; as well as from on-demand services, home video, and interactive platforms, which have altered its use and effects. For decades, historians had been safe in assuming that the destiny of television lay in three identical and easily studied national networks. Now, they must explain a medium that has turned out differently. When "big television" declined, with it went most of the field's "low hanging fruit." Whether to trace the roots of CNN, MTV, or Tivo, or to bring forth insights from TV's more distant past, information is the paramount concern. In most cases today, historical data must be pulled, shaken, and dredged.

Thus television especially is appropriate for more discussion on sources, records, and the collection of historical evidence. Here we will look more closely at television's changing historical environment. Our examples of old and new history can help authors develop ideas on topics they might choose to pursue. Our larger theme is how authors convert topics into sustained and documented historical works. While television's binding feature, the picture screen, does center thinking, TV's video record is not the bonanza that first-time authors often assume. Nor does an easy task await the author attracted to TV's developmental breakthroughs, its colorful individuals, and its behind-the-scenes intrigue. Television is not a public but a private enterprise. Its "inside story" may be locked in someone's vault. Whatever the topic, no more can TV history simply be "looked up." To document TV's past the modern way, strategies must be employed.

Despite its challenges, television historiography is neither impossible nor beyond the capabilities of history writers. Historians advance projects, and find the sources they need, practically every day. Most will attest that few experiences are more exhilarating than tailing new evidence on some facet of television that no one else has explored. Of all the electronic media, television may best illustrate what by now has been stated many times, that historiography is not a rundown of old events but use of the past to promote something brand new. Particularly in television, the delight of every project is not what an author can propose—but what they can prove.

THE TV RECORD AND CHANGING PERSPECTIVES

Anyone who recently has watched TV can relate to its changing dimensions. Why this change beckons historians is just as easily grasped. The "past" that exists in older works now may be less important. The "past" still to be uncovered may hold the key to explaining what TV became. Often when perspectives change, historians apply the term *revisionism* to authors' attempts to reinterpret events. In the case of television, revisionism approximates but too strongly characterizes that to which we refer. Television historiography remains very new. Even the oldest works anticipate many of televisions modern features. Above all, television is not conducive to "orthodox-revisionist" historical debates that teem in more mature fields. It is good to keep in mind that television was an offshoot of radio. Most critical questions that involve TV, such as why private control did emerge, are historically traced to the radio era. In both its "old" and "new" contexts, TV historiography is "developmental" in form and value.[1] Regardless of changing circumstances, television broadcast

---

[1] William David Sloan, *Perspectives on Mass Communication History* (Hillsdale, NJ: Lawrence Erlbaum Associates, 1991), 5–7.

records are used to address enduring questions. Today's historians are still fundamentally interested in processes and outcomes that came when pictures were added to radio broadcasting.

Even so, a volume of older historiography is a point of departure for most newer historical works. Change is visible in two impulses that most modern writings reflect. First, historians have responded to that which is our main appeal here : better source work. Widely felt, it's a need to instill rigor and depth in a literature dominated by arm-chair accounts. Somewhat of a clarion call in 1981 was David Paul Nord's indictment of media history as "hagiography," that is, that media historians had sought not to analyze but to entertain. They merely had celebrated, in Nord's words, a "glorious, progressive, and just institution."[2] This tendency brims in older TV history. Scholars awoke to works comprised almost entirely of "great people" and "big events." The first classic histories of television, Erik Barnouw's 1970 and 1975 books, were loosely documented panoramic works that referred readers not to original sources but to other books, newspaper articles, and magazine reports.[3] Far more numerous have been popular press television histories with no cited source work at all. Television's story is most widely inscribed in popular works, the largest number memoirs and autobiographies. Almost every prominent person who worked in television, from William Paley and Ted Turner to Walter Cronkite and Captain Kangaroo, has contributed to TV's historical literature.[4] They comprise televisions largest contingent of published "historians."

The other impulse is to loosen television history from its big-network moorings. To account for television's multichannel environment, no longer suitable is history confined to ABC, NBC, and CBS. Unquestionably important yet easy to write about, the "Big Three" networks have grooved numerous historical traditions. Chief among these is the notion that television became

---

[2] David Paul Nord and Harold L. Nelson, "The Logic of Historical Research," in *Research Methods in Mass Communication*, eds. Guido H. Stempel III and Bruce H. Westley (Englewood Cliffs, NJ: Prentice-Hall, 1981), 299.

[3] Erik Barnouw, *The Image Empire: A History of Broadcasting in the United States from 1953* (New York: Oxford University Press, 1970); Erik Barnouw, *Tube of Plenty: The Evolution of American Television* (New York: Oxford University Press, 1975).

[4] William S. Paley, *As It Happened: A Memoir* (Garden City, NY: Doubleday, 1979); Ted Turner, *Ted Turner Speaks: Insight from the World's Greatest Maverick* (New York: Wiley, 1999); Walter Cronkite, *A Reporter's Life* (New York: Knopf, 1996); Robert Keeshan, *Growing Up Happy* (New York: Doubleday, 1989).

one singularly pervasive and power-concentrated bulwark. Bearing on research into television programming are older histories that relate only what came from the three network studios.[5] New probes of television technology must wrestle with older works that define all on-air technical strides as network telecasting feats.[6] Television's image as a "monolithic" institution grew from books and articles on TV's internal affairs that considered only those of ABC, NBC, and CBS.[7] Particularly influential is a torrent of early literature on the history of network news. Still deeply rooted is the idea that television news is governed by half-hour ABC, CBS, and NBC newscasts that grip the nation and join Americans in one nightly news-viewing ritual.[8]

Three works have had much to do with expanding television's historical horizons. One of these was the 1990, *Stay Tuned* by Christopher Sterling and John Kittross, the first large-scale history of television to be written from the perspective of diminished network influence.[9] These authors alerted scholars to new historical pathways that became evident in the 1980s when cable television burgeoned, technology accelerated, and FCC policy because of deregulation had taken a right-angle turn. A second work, the 1990 *Fifties Television*, stirred more historical thinking when William Boddy's archival research revealed that during network television's "Golden Age" more loosely managed and venturesome grassroots entities were those which looked ahead.[10] While

---

[5] Alex McNeil, *Total Television: A Comprehensive Guide to Programming from 1948 to 1980* (New York: Penguin Books, 1980).

[6] Robert Sobel, *RCA* (New York: Stein and Day, 1986); Kenneth Bilby, *The General: David Sarnoff and the Rise of the Communications Industry* (New York: Harper & Row, 1986).

[7] Laurence Bergreen, *Look Now, Pay Later: The Rise of Network Broadcasting* (Garden City, NY: Doubleday, 1980); Jeff Greenfield, *The First Fifty Years* (New York: Abrams, 1977); Robert Metz, *CBS: Reflections in a Bloodshot Eye* (Chicago: Playboy Press, 1975).

[8] Barbara Matusow, *The Evening Stars: The Making of the Network News Anchor* (Boston, MA: Houghton Mifflin, 1983); David Halberstam, *The Powers That Be* (New York: Knopf, 1979); William J. Small, *To Kill a Messenger: Television News and the Real World* (New York: Hastings House, 1970).

[9] Christopher H. Sterling and John M. Kittross, *Stay Tuned: A Concise History of American Broadcasting*, 2nd ed. (Belmont, CA: Wadsworth, 1990).

[10] William Boddy, *Fifties Television: The Industry and Its Critics* (Urbana: University of Illinois Press, 1990).

well-studied network shows, such as those of Milton Berle and Dinah Shore, did not survive the period, local stations had filled time and found audiences with telethons, call-in talk formats, quirky kids concepts, and "extreme" sports such as wrestling and roller derby. These ideas would blossom when cable channels like QVC, CNN, MTV, and ESPN finally arrived. A final historiographical lightning bolt came in the 1991 *Three Blind Mice*, in which the interviews of author Ken Auletta culminated in the first exposure of the ABC–CBS–NBC decline.[11] By probing events of the 1980s, when network ratings had plummeted because of multichannel delivery, Auletta suggested that the network system never had been strong but, in fact, was inherently weak. As viewers were lost, the networks fell to the demands of affiliate stations that the networks never had owned or controlled. Auletta also questioned whether the networks ever had had "great people." None could be found at the most critical moment—the moment when they finally faced competition.

One means for traversing new themes and source work lies in what might be called the "contemporary" approach. Here, in the manner of Auletta, authors leave intact television's "prehistory" and use the record to investigate the "postnetwork" world. Generally speaking, research of this type dates TV's "beginning" at around 1980. Because this period is so recent, its historical record is substantially incomplete. Internal documents still may be active and thus unavailable to researchers. The same is true of the personal papers of contemporary figures. While as a rule the more contemporary the subject the less enduring will be its interpretation, clearly needed are historical studies that account for new technology, channel proliferation, television deregulation, and the impact of audience fragmentation. As we will see, such subjects can be documented through written and video collections, professional and public reportage, and an author's historical interviews. The contemporary approach usually enables the most comprehensive video record. Its obvious advantage is the "gut-level" proximity of its many potential topics. Even the youngest historians have lived through television's whirlwind of changing events.

Limitations of the contemporary historical record have confined its historiography mostly to popular and semischolarly works. Yet considerable has been their role in broadening television's historical base. Tom McGrath's

---

[11] Ken Auletta, *Three Blind Mice: How the TV Networks Lost Their Way* (New York: Random House, 1991).

history of music video reinforces television's developmental links to radio.[12] Alex Block's account of televisions fourth network, Rupert Murdoch's Fox system, recounts the admixture of Hollywood influence, internationalization, and network ownership of affiliates in TV's new organizational scheme.[13] Numerous authors, including Robert McChesney and Edward Herman, trace the intertwining of new technology, television deregulation, and the emergence of corporatism and monopolization.[14] Andrew Davidson's post-1980 history of British television heralds the privatization of foreign TV and its conversion to an American-influenced multichannel system.[15] All-news television was the first area to attract what topic-seeking historians most savor: conflicting explanations. A first wave of authors including Porter Bibb and Robert Goldberg honored Ted Turner's Cable News Network as a breakthrough in television.[16] This view then was confronted by former CNN director Reese Schonfeld who, in a memoir backed by internal documents, argued that Turner's poor management and lack of realistic vision were the factors that sealed Turner's loss of CNN to Time Warner's corporate "suits."[17]

By no means does the recent past dictate research possibilities. More enriching and stimulating can be attempts to re-explain television in the manner of Boddy, by uncovering influences and pathways that trace from TV's inception. This "begin from the beginning" approach requires an author's immersion into time periods and events of which he or she may have no first-hand knowledge. With this follows heavy demands for reading, thesis

---

[12] Alex Block, *Outfoxed: Rupert Murdoch and the Inside Story of America's Fourth Television Network* (New York: St. Martin's Press, 1990).

[13] Tom McGrath, *Video Killed the Radio Star* (New York: Villard, 1994).

[14] Robert W. McChesney, *Our Media, Not Theirs: The Democratic Struggle against Corporate Media* (New York: Seven Stories, 2002); Edward S. Herman and Robert W. McChesney, *The Global Media: The New Missionaries of Corporate Capitalism* (Washington, DC: Cassell, 1997); Jack Banks, *Monopoly Television: MTV's Quest to Control the Music* (Boulder, CO: Westview Press, 1996).

[15] Andrew Davidson, *Under the Hammer: The Inside Story of the 1991 ITV Franchise Battle* (London: Heinemann, 1992).

[16] Porter Bibb, *It Ain't as Easy as It Looks* (Boulder, CO: Johnson, 1997); Robert Goldberg, *Citizen Turner: The Wild Rise of an American Tycoon* (New York: Harcourt Brace, 1995).

[17] Reese Schonfeld, *Me and Ted against the World: The Unauthorized Story of the Founding of CNN* (New York: Cliff Street, 2001).

building, and digging. Yet because distant perspectives are the most sure-footed, the best television history usually results. The greatest attraction of distant history is the opportunity it affords for visiting television's most-prized and often seminal sources. It is here that television's historical record is best set forth.

Television's prehistory includes the events between TV broadcasting's inception in the 1920s and its splintering and diversification in the 1980s. Not surprisingly, the "Big Three" networks act on this period with tidal force. Difficult to imagine is any early interpretation that does not in some way involve ABC, NBC, and CBS. For example, in the battle among the television pioneering corporations of the De Forest Company, Jenkins Laboratories, the Farnsworth Television and Radio Corporation, and the DuMont Company — RCA/NBC is the ultimate victor. ABC, NBC, and CBS are rightfully portrayed at the vortex of early television. At their peak in the 1970s, just these three entities commanded 95 percent of the total viewing audience. Still, it cannot be said too many times that historians have painted a big network picture. The purpose of distant TV research is to work between broad historical brush strokes and magnify gaps, holes, and inconsistencies. Questions that intrigue historians are these: Can television be explained without great people and big events? Why did just three network systems originally emerge? Finally, What from the past foreshadowed their ultimate decline?

The value of the "begin from the beginning" approach is illustrated in research recently opened on what has remained a black hole in network historiography: ABC. Here it is useful to note that traditional history does not equally treat the three original networks. It is told almost entirely through CBS and to some extent through NBC. That ABC brought up the rear, and thus seldom was probed, is precisely the reason it is of interest today. By revealing the affairs of ABC, Marc Gardner and Huntington Williams both have challenged the view that television began in monolithic form. Splintering and diversification had been indicated from a very early stage, when CBS and NBC with mainstream concepts had flourished while ABC had struggled to survive.[18] Not only is an ABC concept called "counter programming" now projected as a modern television strategy. Modern figures such as Ted Turner and Rupert Murdoch no longer are seen as television's first "mavericks." The

---

[18] Marc Gunther, *The House that Roone Built: The Inside Story of ABC News* (Boston, MA: Little, Brown, 1994); Huntington Williams, *Beyond Control: ABC and the Fate of the Networks* (New York: Atheneum, 1989).

"maverick" label applied to just about everyone at ABC, who kept the network from bankruptcy by siphoning niche audiences from the same CBS and NBC programs older histories celebrate. A significant source is the 1991 memoir of Leonard Goldenson, ABC's longtime chair, who demonstrated that modern sports telecasting, and modern television's emphasis on programs aimed at the 18 to 34 age group, grew out of ABC's continuing battle against last-place ratings.[19]

Not only have authors recharacterized the first networks. They have removed from obscurity those institutions recessed in older history that today dominate the television industry. This line of research has a modern appeal in light of today's critical concerns about corporatism and monopolization. Of interest is the firm that began as Time, Inc., but today, as Time Warner, it is the world's largest media provider. By reinterpreting this "magazine company" as a television institution, Connie Bruck and Richard Clurman both have exposed Time as a formidable force in TV's early period.[20] Not only did Time take ground from the major networks by rushing to develop cable TV. It weakened the networks still further with its movie channel Home Box Office, which heralded inexpensive satellite interconnection. Still other institutions opened for television study are Disney, the holder of ABC; Paramount, the main holding of Viacom, the owner of CBS; Universal, half of NBC Universal; and Twentieth Century Fox, which upon its takeover by Murdoch launched Fox television. These Hollywood studios had predated television. From TV's inception they had eyed television delivery. Today, virtually all national television is under their control. All this raises the possibility that TV founders William Paley and David Sarnoff had merely "warmed the seats" for television's true and destined owners, those from Hollywood.[21]

---

[19] Leonard H. Goldenson and Marvin J. Wolf, *Beating the Odds: The Untold Story behind the Rise of ABC* (New York: Scribner, 1991).

[20] Connie Bruck, *Master of the Game: Steve Ross and the Creation of Time Warner* (New York: Simon & Schuster, 1994); Richard M. Clurman, *To the End of Time: The Seduction and Conquest of a Media Empire* (New York: Simon & Schuster, 1992); George Mair, *Inside HBO: The Billion Dollar War between HBO, Hollywood, and the Home Video Revolution* (New York: Dodd, Mead, 1988).

[21] Grant Tinker and Bud Rukeyser, *Tinker in Television: From General Sarnoff to General Electric* (New York: Simon & Schuster, 1994); Kim Masters, *The Keys to the Kingdom* (New York: W. Morrow, 2000); Sumner Redstone with Peter Knobler, *A Passion to Win* (New York: Simon & Schuster, 2001).

Newer use of television's more distant record has been no more effective than in efforts to illuminate another dark area: local TV. A neglect of local television is partially an effect of traditional history's "top-down" perspective, which portrays local stations merely as instruments of network transmission. Yet even older histories had acknowledged local programming innovations. They also had conceded that while networks had provided national programming, local broadcasters had owned all of the TV licenses. All along, the differing and often conflicting interests of networks and stations had lingered as a possible historical focal point. But blocking local historiography were fears that what had unfolded at local stations never could be generalized. The stations, of course, had numbered in the hundreds. They had operated even in the most far-flung locales. Yet by the 1990s, historians widely were engaged in local projects. That decade, the roots of local television assumed significance when stations formed into large groups, canceled and switched network affiliations, and compelled each network to rebuild. This demonstration of local station prerogative finally gave historians a central theme. Suddenly important was local TV's huge yet untapped historical record, which in the era of top-down thinking had had value only in parochial localized accounts.

Craig Allen's study of local television news is one example of "bottom-up" historiography.[22] In this research, previously unseen internal materials piece together years of local unrest with "Olympian" newscasting standards set by the major networks. The documentaries of Edward R. Murrow and the serious newscasts of Walter Cronkite, which had lost money, became passe when local stations introduced friendly newscasters, eyewitness reporting, and "action" news. These materials further attest that the high ratings and huge profits generated by local news shifted the TV news paradigm and instilled techniques visible throughout newscasting today. Of additional interest in this particular research is the further theme of conflict not just between networks and stations but within ABC, NBC, and CBS. While network "greats" fought to preserve their news legacies, they were undermined by the networks' owned-and-operated local stations. The networks' own stations were the vanguard of the movement against network news.

Scarcely are local television's early themes limited to news. The 1997 *Television in America* by Michael D. Murray and Donald G. Godfrey is a collection of local station histories, all documented through archival sources,

---

[22] Craig Allen, *News Is People: The Rise of Local TV News and the Fall of News from New York* (Ames: Iowa State University Press, 2001).

which together confront the traditional view that television's philosophy, organization, process, and effects all were functions of the major networks.[23] Works in this anthology capture that theme mentioned earlier, that while straight-lace and conservatism had reigned at the major networks, more venturesome if less refined concepts had percolated from television's grassroots. This idea is amplified in works by Sherrie Mazingo and Mark Williams, which trace turning-point technological strides, such as electronic newsgathering, to the garage-like tinkering and experimentation that local TV permitted.[24] Adding insight are the additional works of Steve Smethers, whose research focuses on the Midwestern local stations that were the last to be served by AT&T.[25] Well into the 1950s they did not have network connections. These stations became crucibles for programming inventions and techniques. On their own, they generated fanfare and large audiences long before they were able to broadcast network shows. Smethers speculates that television would have thrived had networks never been created.

OPENING CHALLENGES AND TASKS

By now it should be clear that television's meaningful questions have an almost unlimited range. Yet once an idea is floated, the real work begins. Most of the time, authors choose to investigate an aspect of television because it interests them. By virtue of that interest, they have an inkling that some new insight exists. One who might write the history of *Entertainment Tonight* may know that this programming sensation taps a function once served by movie magazines and Hollywood gossip columnists. An author drawn to the history of kid's cartoons might be aware that some of the very first televised images were of Felix the Cat. It would be easy to propose that Hedda Hopper prepared Mary Hart and that the invention of television with Felix pointed to Buzz

---

[23] Michael D. Murray and Donald G. Godfrey, eds., *Television in America: Local Station History from across the Nation* (Ames: Iowa State University Press, 1997).

[24] Sherrie Mazingo, "Home of Programming Firsts," *Television/Radio Age*, March 1987, A1–A62; Mark J. Williams, "From Remote Possibilities to Entertaining Difference: A Regional Study of the Rise of Television Industry in Los Angeles, 1930–1952" (PhD diss., University of Southern California, 1993).

[25] J. Steven Smethers, "Unplugged: Developing Rural Midwestern Television Audiences without Live Network Service, 1949–1952," *Southwestern Mass Communication Journal* 12, no. 1 (1996): 44–60.

Lightyear and Scooby Doo. While such conjecture is precisely what inspires seminal historical works, nothing is accomplished without proof. Unless authors can connect the dots and verify the connections, their research will be short lived.

Television is unique for the obstacles historians must confront. In the several examples of newer historiography just discussed, authors were not able to write off the "top of their heads." They had to troll for information, reduce television's visual element to worded accounts, and sometimes deal not just with the word-picture conundrum but with the additional abstraction of physical objects such as early cameras and tape machines. These often peculiar challenges magnify the first-step tasks historians must fulfill. While such measures enter into all electronic media historiography, and are discussed in other chapters, here we orient needs around television. As much as an author's tendency may be to "jump in," planning can save time and frustration. If an idea cannot sustain the 20 or more pages that a paper or article demands, or the hundreds of pages a book writer would need to compose, it is good to know of this ahead of time. More often than not, ideas must be revised. In some cases they are scrapped. In all cases, ideas that are planned will advance more rapidly.

Developing Foundations: Reading

To begin, historians should take stock in the admonition of historical methodologists Jacques Barzun and Henry Graff, that "it is as impossible for the historian as for anybody else to decide: 'I will now have a great idea.'"[26] Suffice it to say that research questions germinate from the readings authors conduct. While all works must acknowledge a literature review, in television this need is especially acute. Earlier we noted that most television historiography is "developmental" in orientation. This means that historians seek seminal moments and TV "firsts" that base understanding of succeeding events. If what an author thinks is a "first" already has been established, time is wasted in reinventing the wheel. Only through readings can truly new concepts be discerned.

The challenge in television is twofold. First, its literature is voluminous. Its books, articles, and published accounts number in the thousands. No other

---

[26] Jacques Barzun and Henry F. Graff, *The Modern Researcher* (New York: Harcourt Brace and World, 1970), 215.

component of the electronic media has a body of knowledge nearly as large. Second, this literature not only lacks convenient bounds, but trails into nonmedia disciplines. Television is at the forefront of interdisciplinary pursuits media scholars increasingly urge.[27] An author attracted to the origins of political TV can expect to read from general history, political science, and sociology. One who might write the history of Univision would need to read works in Hispanic and minority affairs, culture studies, international policy, and Latin American history.

Internet searches of library holdings can help locate essential readings.[28] Yet this can lead to another problem, one alluded to earlier, that most off-the-shelf TV histories are popular books. For better history and firmer guidance, worthwhile time can be spent combing the indices of scholarly journals. The largest cache of formal if variegated television history is found in conference papers, dissertations, and theses. These unpublished works, their titles and abstracts available on line, likewise should not be overlooked. Always to be kept in mind is the literature review's purpose, that of honing research questions. In many cases, the citations found in one or two good works can comprise most of an author's reading list.

Fortuitously and oddly enough, if well managed, the crush of television literature will work to an author's advantage. One might assume that with so much having been written authors are bound to find their new idea in someone else's article or book. To the contrary, as David Sloan has observed, as a field's literature expands, its interest areas expand even more.[29] As large as it is, the literature on television is stretched. Authors are often amazed finding that which they propose is halfway treated, tangentially mentioned, or not covered at all. Thus in television, the reading process is to be welcomed, not feared.

Situating the Sources

No less critical than the literature review, and frequently an important part of it, is assessing one's odds of finding those records, documents, papers, and

---

[27] Nord and Nelson, "The Logic of Historical Research," 291–94.

[28] Kathleen W. Craver, *Using Internet Primary Sources to Teach Critical Thinking Skills in History* (Westport, CT: Greenwood, 1999); Carol Collier Kuhlthau, M. Elspeth Goodin, and Mary Jane McNally, eds., *The Virtual School Library: Gateway to the Information Superhighway* (Englewood, CO: Libraries Unlimited, 1996).

[29] Sloan, *Perspectives on Mass Communication History,* ix–x.

video transcriptions that original history demands. Shortly, we elaborate on this objective with a "hierarchy" of potential source work. For now, it is helpful to establish some of the issues involved simply in acquiring these materials. Herein lies television's greatest misconception: Most assume that because TV has lifted a literary Mt. Everest, it has an equally mountainous store of research materials. Many young historians turn to this huge field thinking its resource is boundless. In reality, no component of the electronic media has greater resource constraints.

Previously we observed that as a private enterprise television is distanced from the public record. A biographer attracted to the careers of Walter Cronkite, Oprah Winfrey, or Rupert Murdoch will have difficulties. These figures' personal papers are not in the public domain. Cronkite's papers have been donated to the University of Texas, Austin, but they are closed. Similarly, none of the medium's central institutions have either the written or video archives that researchers might expect. The newer the institution, the less likely its owners will deem its documents as "historical." A historian may be chased away. Ironically, an author interested in the very largest TV institutions, such as Time Warner, Viacom, or Comcast, may have shards and snatches of original documentation from which to work.

Yet numerous television archives, and their listings in archive directories, do exist. Not only can the National Archives be a powerful source. New interest in local television is spurred by materials seldom used but long gathered by local historical societies. Moreover, television can give practical meaning to the historiographical bromide, as worded by Barzun and Graff, that a historian's "greatest proof of merit is to find a packet of letters in an attic."[30] Vast quantities of TV's best primary source work are privately kept personal files preserved as family "heirlooms" by broadcast pioneers and their descendants. Ahead, we will stress the interviewing of such individuals. Alert historians use interview encounters to request papers and documentation.

Situating the Artifacts

Television presents the further complication—the prospect of locating tools, devices, and other physical objects that are known as artifacts to historians. Artifacts have special value as "unpremeditated transmitters of facts."[31] First

---

[30] Barzun and Graff, *The Modern Researcher,* 111.

[31] John Martin Vincent, *Historical Research* (New York: Peter Smith, 1929), 17.

and foremost a technology, television especially, leads to artifact investigation. As material sources, kinescopes, films, and video are not artifacts per se. Yet they become artifacts when, as often will be the case, their technology bears on an author's reconstruction of events. For example, an author drawn to the inception of electronic newsgathering would be hard pressed to effectively interpret ENG without having seen and examined its hardware. One who might trace the progression of big-signal telecasting, in which tower technology led to the construction of the world's very tallest structures, would need to visit and study one of these "big sticks." Technology is not the only artifact-inscribed area. Bearing on histories of television production, advertising, and promotion are the studio relics, implements, and displays that these functions have left.

Artifact problems all too often rear up after an author has committed to a subject and interpretation already has begun. Yet what is true in the interpretation of papers and manuscripts also is true of artifacts: Someone else's portrayals do not substitute for original work. Numerous artifacts are situated in the nation's many television museums. Others can be found mingled with written and visual records in television archives. Television stations, technology companies, and private collectors may make artifacts available.

Weighing Costs and Benefits

After readings are conducted and research needs are assessed, one more onerous task remains. An author must decide whether the labor involved in completing a project is within his or her time frame and financial means. Costs will be incurred in the time and effort an author must exert. They accrue most inexplicably in the money an author must spend. Something approaching a business plan is encouraged. Particularly those in television bear the historian's true pedigree not as a bookworm but as an airline-savvy, hotel-hardened "road warrior." Finances may be needed for travel just to one television archive or artifact site. Yet as sobering as such costs may be, the payoff from a promising idea also must be weighed. A project which advances knowledge and changes thinking may be well worth the toll it extracts. A common strategy is to start with small steps, perhaps with a topic made viable by local records, or records known and immediately available. As benefits emerge—costs will seem less daunting.

TELEVISION'S HIERARCHY OF SOURCES

When we spoke of the importance of situating sources, we made the strange point that while television's published literature is voluminous, only a fraction of its historical data have been exposed. How is it that authors have managed to so prodigiously write about a subject so constrained by its available evidence? This is because television magnetizes the anecdotal account. Owing to television's pervasiveness is literature that feeds all levels of public taste. In preparing a literature review, an author will discover relatively few probing histories. As we've discussed, renditions of TV's past accumulate in mass-market biographies and loosely researched popular books. Their lone themes of "great people" and "big events" appear again and again. An author also will find that scholarly writings on television are not predominately histories. They are empirical studies, statistical surveys, essays, and contemporary analyses, which nevertheless require and promote historical perspectives. Even these serious works may reinforce a conventional historical wisdom as handed down in anecdotal works.

All of this raises the big question: How do TV historians maximize the quality of the projects they finally choose to pursue? Or, put another way: What does it take to ensure a project's publishability, if it advances from a conference paper, or a journal, to its acceptance upon challenges from peer research? The answer is source work. Because so many authors are drawn to television, this medium's source work expectations continue to rise. When professors and academic jurors receive a submitted historical work, they will read the first page and then beeline to the endnotes and references. Their most frequent lament is the rejecting of a good idea by references that show only secondary sources—library books, articles from *Broadcasting Magazine*, and pickups from *Time*, *Newsweek*, and *The New York Times*.

Particularly in television, new ideas demand the uncovering of historical data that no one else has seen. The objective is to peel back TV's visible effects and processes of production in order to discover less visible historical truths. Source work not only determines whether the "core" will be reached. It prepares the reader either for new insights or a "been there–done that" encounter. What constitutes "gold," "silver," and "lead" research sources, generally is the same in television as in other electronic media. We begin at the highest level with TV's "most golden" source, written records. Video records, interviews, memoirs, and reportage then are examined. Each level of research pits effort and cost against yield and contribution. Knowing these trade-offs can clarify the source-and-fact decisions an author must make.

Written Records

Although television is a visual medium, original written materials almost always comprise its best and most penetrating store of evidence. Located in archives, company files, and personal collections, these also are the sources most difficult to obtain. They include founding documents, private memoranda and correspondence, diaries, appointment records, meeting notes and transcripts, and all types of personal papers. In television, these sources also can include concept statements, treatments, production scripts, program transcripts, monitoring studies, planning and consulting reports, corporate audience research data, technology blueprints, license renewal files, and television construction permits. Often a definitive primary source in television are the audience ratings reports privately circulated to virtually all broadcasters by Nielsen and Arbitron.

As is true in all historical analysis, written records must be evaluated for accuracy and relevance (see chapter 2). The people who populated the TV field largely were ostentatious and spotlight-driven individuals who even in their personal communication sought notoriety and recognition. The correspondence of Sumner Redstone, the head of Viacom, on the success of MTV may seem a prize historical catch. Yet Redstone may have been far removed from the creation of MTV and motivated to correspond in order to brag. Almost always, historians can verify interpretations by comparing separate sets of historical materials. This strategy is similar to that used by investigative reporters, who do not accept the facts of one person until they are confirmed by at least one other. A historian may seek to argue that the inception of Fox TV propelled sex and violence on all of the other networks. A historian may seek to argue that Fox TV's acquisition of the NFL football telecasts in 1993 was the reason numerous key local stations left ABC, CBS, and NBC and became Fox affiliates. The Fox documents, which may show this, can be verified through the contemporaneous documents of ABC, NBC, and CBS, their affiliate stations. Similarly, the written records of ESPN, which may reveal the influence of ESPN's billionaire benefactor J. Paul Getty, can be checked through the examination of Getty's personal papers.

Television historians have major advantages in setting their sights on these most precious of historical materials. Written record collections do need to be located and opened, but they are extremely large in number. Indeed, television was the electronic media's most collective enterprise. All of its participants produced and likely left much available evidence. For example, that biographer drawn to Oprah Winfrey, whose private materials are unavailable, might write an illuminating Winfrey work through the letters, memoranda, and files of her many friends and associates.

Television's written source work has the further benefit of detail. In only a few grassroots enclaves was television a "mom-and-pop" endeavor. As one of society's largest enterprises, television generated copious and meticulous behind-the-scenes paperwork. The study of just one television program, such as the global "Live Aid" charity spectacular in 1985, can lead an author to comprehensive and exacting production plans, talent procurement budgets, point-of-broadcast transcripts, and follow-up reports. In addition to these advantages, television's written sources are complemented by a unique and often-vital back channel, the video record, which we discuss shortly.

Yet as other chapters have stressed, the written record never is air tight and definitive. Because many individuals participated in TV's breakthroughs and innovations, they may disagree on what occurred. In other cases, interpretations can be skewed by inaccuracies and biases in what participants wrote at the time and what they chose to keep. An author, like a courtroom jury, must weigh a preponderance of evidence. For clarification, an author may be moved to personally contact and interview those pioneers and innovators who still may be alive, a strategy that, as we will see, can help bolt a historical work.

Moreover, the delving of the written record can provoke unanticipated questions. This dilemma can be a blessing. New revelations might ensue. Yet more often than not, unexpected findings are the "fly in the ointment" that marginalize an author's original theme. One case relates to the presumed role of Walter Cronkite in rallying public opposition to President Lyndon Johnson and Johnson's handling of the Vietnam War. Although Johnson personally testified and wrote that "If I've lost Walter Cronkite, I've lost the American public," Nielsen records testify that, at the time, Cronkite's CBS newscast trailed NBC's newscast in the ratings and that at no point did Cronkite reach more than 25 percent of Americans. In this example of television effects, which surely would bear on a truthful biography of Cronkite, an author would have to evaluate whether Johnson or Nielsen was right, or whether the truth lay somewhere in between.

Video Records

Television research literally archives "face" validity in those materials which exactly attest to what broadcasters delivered and what people saw. The video record is most widely rendered in videotapes and, more recently, in computer files. It also includes films and kinescopes. Kinescopes are special films that were used prior to 1956, when videotape was invented, to record live broadcasts. These sources are most easily acquired through archives, historical societies, and private collectors. That they are not easily acquired through the obvious source, the networks and stations that are the subjects of studies, is one of the major challenges in television historiography.

The video record is slightly less important than the written record. While history is crafted entirely from written records, projects based strictly on video, and nothing else, will be deemed incomplete. Yet like the written record, the video record is "gold." Few historical materials more accurately recreate the past than the rolling record of what unfolded in front of a camera lens. General historians tend to regard film and video as artifacts. In television, these are among the most primary of all primary sources.

As we have mentioned several times, television's video record has an inherent constraint. An author must reduce a video's sights, sounds, and sequences to the abstraction of words. Both analytical insight and writing skill are needed to pull this off. One strategy is quantification. An author who traces permissiveness on late night television could review tapes of the *Tonight Show* and count the number of times Johnny Carson worked double entendre into his monologues and interviews. An author interested in the roots of payola in music TV might examine recordings of Dick Clark's *American Bandstand* and enumerate Clark's on-air plugs and promotions. Another strategy is play-by-play. An author might write, "With President Kennedy on his death bed, thirty million anxious viewers watched as NBC's Frank McGee and Chet Huntley tinkered with parts of a telephone, the network's only link to Robert MacNeil's live report from the hospital. For fifteen minutes this comedy of errors continued. Then, technicians switched to WBAP in Fort Worth, where anchor Charles Murphy appeared for five seconds. Suddenly, a blast of sound was heard and the picture blacked out." All too often an author must fall back on description. Safe is language such as: "The coverage was staged in the WOI transmitter building, with the control panels of the station's transmitter providing a rather unusual background. A station announcer appeared on camera to read the latest election results, while noisy fans designed to cool the noisy components of the transmitter whirred in the background."[32]

Picture–word conversion is not the only challenge. Usually a much larger problem, and one which if not confronted can reduce a study's validity, stems from difficulties authors can expect in acquiring video items. For an included item to have validity, clear must be its profundity. If the item is a presidential debate, or the very first broadcast of CNN or ESPN's "Sports Center," profundity is self-evident. Yet rarely will the video record afford such easy opportunities. In most cases, an author will find miscellaneous examples. One who anticipates the acquisition of a seminal broadcast may instead receive, for example, one random recording from David Letterman's early years as an Indianapolis weathercaster or snippets from Jerry Springer's first television experiences while mayor of Cincinnati. Many original television recordings have no dates. An author often must use his or her wits to validate an item's inclusion, finding collaborative evidence. A common strategy is to concede the anecdotal nature of a video source with words such as: "Videotape was a four-year-old toy when the 1950s ended and not available for archiving newscasts." Only a handful of stations filmed their newscast with kinescope reproduction. One 1959 edition of KGW's 11 o'clock news called "Nightbeat," was a glimpse of what viewers encountered when they turned to 1950s local news.[33]

Despite the techniques technological uses may require, recorded materials always should be pursued. When investigating topics that do not overtly relate to programming, such as FCC deregulation and TV's corporate affairs, an author will be surprised at the extent even these subjects connect to the video record. A historian should keep in mind that just as the "proof of the pudding" is the eating, the proof of television is what appeared on TV.

Interviews

Less precious than written and video records yet high on the source work hierarchy are interviews with principals who appear in historical research. While constrained by after-the-fact recollections of often very distant events, interviews are valuable for the control they enable. Through direct contacts with those of whom they write, historians can sharpen perspectives, reduce grey areas, and tie loose ends. Within this category, and in a sense a "written

---

[32] Smethers, "Unplugged," 50.

[33] Allen, *News Is People*, 17–18.

record," are collections of "oral history" interviews performed by specialists from archives, universities, historical societies, and interest groups. Booklike transcripts are placed in the public domain and can be located through Internet searches. Many oral histories can be obtained through interlibrary loan (see chapter 3).

But also within this broader category are interviews authors themselves conduct. Although archived oral history interviews are professionally conducted and publicly available, they encompass only a small selection of TV's many past "players." A frequent experience is to acquire a prospective oral history transcript and find that the interviewer's questions and the subject's answers are not the questions and answers an author needs addressed. Regardless of whether oral histories are used, authors should plan to make at least some contacts on their own. This especially is true in a contemporary field such as television, in which large numbers of past "movers and shakers" still are alive. An author's own historical interviews can conducted by telephone at nominal cost. Not only can authors "go to the source" and directly pose research questions. The inclusion of historical interviews dramatically can enhance a project's prospects for success. Those who review television-related manuscripts will look for interview references. Their absence may cause a reviewer to question an author's proximity to a topic.

Direct contact with subjects can be most worthwhile at two junctures in an author's research. The first comes at the beginning, perhaps soon after the literature review, when key individuals have been identified and a "first" quantity of original information must be mined. One might ask Sam Zelman, the No. 3 person in CNN's original chain of command, "I've read that Ted Turner and Reese Schonfeld disagree on how CNN started. What do you recall?" The second moment comes midway or toward the end of the research, when unexpected questions threaten to snarl or block parts of the writing. An author well along in a history of TV manipulation by President Ronald Reagan, and who may have found confirming evidence in the Reagan Library and in videotapes, still may be vague on whether "manipulation" really was at issue. An interview with one of Reagan's presidential advisors, such as Michael Deaver, might clarify and bring perspective to what the "great communicator" had attempted to achieve on TV.

For the benefits historical interviews provide, authors should keep in mind that their yield rests not only on a subject's memory, but on what a subject chooses to say. Few interview subjects will follow an author's question with a response that places them in a bad light. As well, in the presence of significant individuals, an author may shy from difficult areas. Usually the best historical interviews are those arranged in a project's later stages. An author more in command of the facts will better hold ground in an interview. In turn, the interview subject will be more compelled toward candor.

Historical interviews have one final constraint. This is the matter of verification. In most cases, verification is a procedural rather than a philosophical concern. Authors who have located and engaged important individuals almost always want this known. Indeed, an author's likely impulse will be to offer their interview transcripts to someone's collection or archive, thus giving the interview a perceived greater value, because it is open and available for additional research. Yet working materials may not be suitable for public dissemination. Accordingly, authors may store their notes, transcripts, any accompanying tapes, and computer files. When these are used in finished works, references explicitly must state "in the author's possession," or cite the repository where the documents are available.

Memoirs and Autobiographies

Lower on the historical totem pole is another valid primary source. This is the direct testimony of key individuals as recorded in their memoirs and autobiographies, as well as in their authored articles and other published works. These sources have two outstanding advantages. They are conveniently accessed, and they almost always are supported by a subject's original files, documents, and records. Their main shortcoming—bias, limits their use. Yet in numerous situations, memoirs and autobiographies provide substantial insight and information.

These first-person published accounts warrant special attention in television because of their abundance. The public's fascination with television history is reflected in publishers' willingness to commission the memoirs not just of celebrities and entertainers but of founding figures, managers and executives, producers and directors, and legions of news personnel. While all memoirs are one-sided accounts, and in that respect antithetical to good history, they nevertheless can assist a historian. Even the most self-serving portrayals reveal original facts, anecdotes, and perspectives. These nuggets can spice and sometimes shape an author's final interpretation. Furthermore, a memoir can shed light on events and developments beyond the scope of a person's life story. In the cases in which an individual has died, his or her memoirs may be the only source of information on matters an author may seek, or be forced, to recount.

The discovery of memoirs and autobiographies usually comes during the literature review. Those which have received notice may headline a historian's initial reading list. Much general historiography is inspired by the publication of memoirs. A presidential memoir is a gathering point for historians, whose subsequent work may be devoted to refuting or affirming what a president has claimed. The memoirs of major television figures, when recognized in a litera-ture review, can base similar lines of analysis. Yet memoirs do contain building blocks of historical data—not just autobiographical explication. Thus, they should be considered not just in the readings but in the research stage. A review of literature in local television news likely would not include the mem-oirs of network celebrity Geraldo Rivera. Yet as an author carries through with research on local TV news, and learns that Rivera once was prominent in that field, he or she would have reason to investigate Rivera's memoirs as a possible source. In this case, an author happily would discover that although Rivera's personal story does culminate with his national role, almost one half of his memoirs detail his period in local news.[34]

Reportage

Lowest on the hierarchy of sources but very commonly plied in television research is the reporting of events as recorded in newspapers, magazines, trade periodicals, and other regular publications. Reflecting the weakness of report-age is disagreement among historians on whether it qualifies as a primary source. Some historians maintain that because it consists of other authors' published material and, more notably, because it compresses and reduces events, reportage should be confined to an author's readings and used only for reference.[35] Others point out that because it is timely, and because it bears eyewitness portrayals, reportage is sufficiently valid for the basing of historical works.[36] Here the issue is moot. In television and throughout the mass media, reportage is a well-accepted and routinely used historical tool. Rare is the

---

[34] Geraldo Rivera, *Exposing Myself* (New York: Bantam, 1991).

[35] Barzun and Graff, *The Modern Researcher*, 89–95, 140–41.

[36] MaryAnn Yodelis Smith, "The Method of History," in *Research Methods in Mass Communication*, eds. Guido H. Stempel III and Bruce H. Westley (Englewood Cliffs, NJ: Prentice-Hall, 1981), 311–12.

television history that is not at least partially built from the notices, articles, blurbs, and in-depth coverage circulated in period press.

Reportage has both obvious and discreet advantages. Easily accessible through library holdings and Internet retrieval, it is, to be sure, the most convenient and least costly historical resource. Yet in television, reportage can provide often essential depth, flavor, and dimension. An author who recounts television's first-day response to the September 11th terrorist attacks could add interest to this subject by relating second-day press reports. Post-September 11th quotes and summaries might dramatize the public impact of the horrific scenes shown on TV. An often overlooked further benefit of reportage is its rigid chronological arrangement. Often a foremost challenge in historiography is piecing together a chain of evidence. For this, no source can be more indispensable than television's record of reportage.

Yet a history too rich in reportage will provoke a reader's questions. Newspaper- and magazine-based histories are common because they provide information when time, flexibility, and financial means restrict access to higher levels of historiographical evidence. Reportage often grows in the minds of new authors when, for example, written records are not nearby and travel to archive sites is precluded. Even so, the fact remains that newspaper and magazine articles, like library books, already have been written, edited, and processed. No matter how they are managed, they force authors to comply with someone else's interpretations.

That reportage is questionably original is not its only pratfall. Relatively little reportage embodies a true record of television's development. While usually reliable are television schedules as published in *TV Guide* and ratings tables as journaled in Television/Radio Age, these records still are second hand. This matter opens a broader reportage problem, that within television no "medium of record" ever emerged. In the innumerable student-written television histories in which Broadcasting is the only source, unsuspecting authors often lash themselves to interpretations slanted toward this magazine's probusiness bias. Similarly, the many who form history from newspaper accounts often fail to realize that newspapers and television were philosophically at odds. Authors should always consider newspapers as a source possibly biased against television itself. Meanwhile, a different drawback parallels that often encountered in use of television's video record, that the record is incomplete. An author likely will find no reporting on such television turning points as Walter Cronkite's very first newscast, the maiden telecast of HBO, the first demonstration of HDTV, and the first streamed telecasts on the Internet.

One strategy can redeem a historical study in which only reportage can be used. This is narrowing a project's research questions so that they focus on the reportage itself. While a historian's impulse is to reconstruct events, with this strategy an author would stipulate an event and analyze only its coverage. For example, if only reportage is available, a planned study of newspaper–television cross-ownerships might be reworked so that traced are not cross-ownerships but their reporting in the newspapers that were involved. Similarly, a proposed history on maligned television artists, from Lawrence Welk to Howard Stern, might be reworked into a history not of artists but of the published criticism artists generated.

Reportage is most effective as a supplement to higher priority source work. In many cases, a study exclusively based on reportage can be elevated with a modicum of richer materials. A budget-minded author is encouraged to consider at least one enriched source, historical interviews, which, as was noted, can be conducted by telephone at little cost. By considering other television sources, and working one step at a time, an author still steeped in reportage often can transcend it.

CONCLUSION: TELEVISION
BROADCAST RECORDS AND MORE

As we've said, television is a large and changing field that is unique for the interest it generates and the opportunities it provides. On that note, it is good to highlight two final points.

First, historical research in television can be performed as effectively with numbers and statistics as with files and manuscripts. Here we have assumed that most authors will ply the standard historical method of interpreting culled materials and writing narrated accounts. History, of course, is known for its "qualitative" approach. Yet with the arrival of personal computers, historians found value in long-forgotten statistical data, such as those compiled by government agencies like the FCC or by companies in the course of preparing annual reports. By using computers to analyze older stores of statistical information, what comes off as an empirical study also is a historical work. While still new to television research, "quantitative" history has much to offer. Television's antiquarian databases are many in number, and much of its statistical data can be found in reports and periodicals in libraries. Financial data have been used to better pin the advent of the Fox network, while Nielsen data have tested the impact of 1990s network affiliation changes.[37] Quantitative history may appeal to authors leery of narrative writing and who might prefer the more regimented empirical form of literature review, methodology, findings, and conclusion.[38]

The second point, briefly noted at the start, is that television historiography is not limited to the strict call of "mass media" research. Not only has television become an established domain in general historiography, but no other media subject has so permeated research subfields and nonmedia disciplines. Business, economics, and political sciences, as well as culture, ethnic, and international affairs studies, are just a few of the disciplines in which television history is welcome. This author's studies of local television news, which focused on the advent of class stratified audience research by news consultants, were carried away from the media and into the fields of cultural anthropology and sociology. A new and increasingly vibrant line of historical research, one which bridges media studies, human communication, and political science, is "rhetorical" historiography. This subfield, which examines the communicative nuances of modern political leaders, is one more illustration of TV history's expanding interdisciplinary reach.[39]

Whatever direction an author chooses, a TV historian's work always will rest on the television broadcast records he or she accumulates. It is by applying these records that TV watchers become TV writers. Although diverse interests draw authors to television, this medium's vast and untapped resource is what keeps them coming back.

---

[37] Laurie Thomas and Barry Litman, "Fox Broadcasting Company, Why Now? An Economic Study of the Rise of the Fourth Broadcast Network," *Journal of Broadcasting & Electronic Media* 35, no. 2 (1991): 139–57; and Marianne Barrett, "The Relationship of Network Affiliation Change to Prime Time Program Ratings," *Journal of Broadcasting & Electronic Media* 43, no. 1 (1999): 98–109.

[38] Loren Haskins and Kirk Jeffrey, *Understanding Quantitative History* (New York: McGraw-Hill, 1990); Konrad H. Jarausch and Kenneth A. Hardy, *Quantitative Methods for Historians: A Guide to Research, Data, and Statistics* (Chapel Hill: University of North Carolina Press, 1991).

[39] Ira Chernus, *General Eisenhower: Ideology and Discourse* (East Lansing: Michigan State University Press, 2002); Davis W. Houck, *Rhetoric as Currency: Hoover, Roosevelt, and the Great Depression* (College Station: Texas A&M University Press, 2001).

10

New Media and Technical Records

Marvin R. Bensman
University of Memphis

The "new media" that the communication scholar has to deal with are the outgrowth of past technologies. From the written word, papyrus to paper, moveable type, the telegraph, the phonograph, the wireless telegraph, the telephone, the radio, still photography, the motion picture with sound, television and now, digital means of storage and delivery via cable, satellite, computer, internet, CD, DVD, and so on—all media rest on the science and innovation of the past.[1]

Engineers and scientists are constantly inventing and innovating ahead of what society is often ready to adopt. But it is not solely the technology, the devices, and the delivery systems that are of importance as much as the software—the "killer application," such as the Milton Berle *Texaco Star Theatre* selling TV sets, HBO selling cable and email, and the World Wide Web selling computers.

There is some concern about the scholar of media history learning more and more about less and less. The scholar needs to understand science, politics, social change, economics, and the arts and humanities. The study of political or intellectual philosophy has always been deemed to have intrinsic value, whereas the study of technological history was considered irrelevant. It is apparent today that such study requires broad interdisciplinary knowledge.

---

[1] See Christopher H. Sterling and George Shiers, *History of Telecommunications Technology: An Annotated Bibliography* (Lanham, MD: Scarecrow Press, 2000). These entries trace the history of major telecommunications technologies over the past 175 years.

The factor that limited interest in such study was that technology moves so rapidly that scholar and student cannot keep up with all the changes taking place.

Our grandfathers lived with the horse and buggy. Our fathers saw within their lifetimes autos and air travel and the radio tube and then the transistor, and in our lifetime we have the integrated circuit and digital communication from space. The science fiction of a communicator on *Star Trek* is today the ubiquitous cell phone. The study of the ever-increasing pace of change is the heart of the examination of the history of modern communication media.

Harold Innis (the mentor of Marshal McLuhan) early on asked the questions:

1. How do specific communication technologies operate?

2. What assumptions do they take from and contribute to society?

3. What forms of power do they encourage?

For Innis, a key to social change was the development of communication media. He claimed that each medium embodies a bias in terms of the organization and control of information. If we consider that a society has a network of communications systems, we can see that there are key junctures where significant information is stored and from where it is transmitted to other parts of the system.[2]

The enormous difference in information storage and the means to access this data has fundamentally changed the way we do research because, increasingly, the resources used for research are stored on computer servers. Most of the catalogs and periodical indexes and reference sources have been converted from print to electronic formats. Much research can be done on the Internet searching periodical indexes, reference works, and even periodical articles themselves. The library catalog has expanded to become the place to access a great number of databases through the Internet. The World Wide Web provides the means to access almost everything.[3]

---

[2] Harold A. Innis, *The Bias of Communication*, (1951; repr., Toronto: University of Toronto Press, 1964); Harold A. Innis, "Roddy Flynn's Teaching Webpage: Harold Innis," October 23, 2002, http://www.comms.dcu.ie/flynnr/harold _innis.html.

[3] See *The Nation* Magazine, *The Nation* Digital Archive, http://www.archive.the nation.com. *The Nation* Digital Archive is a collection of political and cultural writing from 1865 to 2002 and the only database product on the market that provides a complete snapshot of the last 137 years.

While libraries provide a means to access increasingly available information resources electronically, it becomes necessary to evaluate the quality of such resources in the same manner as any other material used in research. There is still much information that is not available by any other means than physically tracking down the primary sources. Proprietary information of companies and corporations will only be accessible with their permission and cooperation. Thus, a truly balanced history of an industry has become difficult, if not impossible.

How does one study the history of new media technology and their content? In the study of scientific progress there are the histories of individuals who invented, created, and made things happen, or almost happen.[4] There are the histories of the organizations that financed, controlled, or attempted to control both technology and its applications.[5] There are studies of particular events and their pivotal nature.[6] The impact of messages and how technology affects the message are all just a part of what can be examined.

There are studies not only on the development of technology, but also on its application, acceptance, and familiarity within the realms of the inventor, corporation, government, and public. What are the constraints (financial, social, ethical, and so on) that provide impetus or slow down the acceptance of the new?

What material is needed by the historian in order to arrive at an understanding of the relationships and currents at work? Our interpretation of the past has always been affected by the primary sources available to the historian. New tools and greater access to information as we have conquered space and time has made the study of history more difficult, not less so. The more information there is, the more complex it becomes to sift and differentiate between what is important to what is pivotal.

Of great concern is how society can preserve information and make it readily available to future historians. How will libraries, archives and other repositories handle this so that data being sought can be found with the same ease that we locate a book on a shelf?

---

[4] Ellison Hawks, *Pioneers of Wireless* (New York: Arno Press, 1974).

[5] Ken Auletta, *Three Blind Mice: How the TV Networks Lost Their Way* (New York: Random House, 1991).

[6] Charles Rolo, *Radio Goes to War: The "Fourth Front"* (London: Faber & Faber, 1943).

Time is the enemy. As time passes so does the evidence upon which histori-cal analysis and criticism rests. Increasingly, much primary source material dis-appears or is modified. There are a number of factors why we have lost content over time. As material is translated into different languages (from Greek to Latin) how much did not survive the transfer? In that process there were judg-ments made as to what should be preserved and what discarded. When papy-rus was transplanted by paper, handwritten copies to printing, how much was not passed on due to changing societal norms? When silent movies were sup-planted by sound how much was discarded and lost? When recorded sound on phonograph records were supplanted by CDs what of the extensive catalog that had been developed since the late 1800s was not translated to the new media? When the CD is copied to MP3—you get the idea.

Ever since digital storage was developed, the way we collect and handle information has fundamentally changed. Prior to 1450 when Johann Guten-berg introduced printing with moveable type, if you wanted to purchase a book, it would be an expensive process to pay for having a handwritten copy created. Ownership of scrolls and books was rare. Today we copy with the click of a button.

The Internet began as the Department of Defense Project ARPANET (1969). It connected Department of Defense and governmentally funded research centers and universities. It was based on the principle of high redun-dancy so information could be transmitted even if some computer systems were destroyed. The development of email (1972), Internet protocol (1974), File Transfer Protocol (FTP), the World Wide Web (WWW), browsers, search engines, E-commerce, wireless Internet, MP3, Internet streaming video, all burst upon not only academia but also on the corporate world and then the individual.

From your home computer you can obtain graphics, sound, and print rep-resentations. The browser along with plug-ins, helper applications or proxies allows the viewing of complex documents from anywhere. PDF files make online documents identical to the print version. There are other formats as well. Browsers handle email and Usenet newsgroups, and browsers even can be used to produce your own html or xtml documents or an entire Website.

Library periodical indexes, full-text periodicals, reference works, directo-ries, and other sources online are linked to other research tools. These primary tools are augmented with a variety of search engines. Some, such as Yahoo.com search general subjects. Other search engines that provide their own protocols for finding material are AltaVista.com, Google.com, HotBot.com, Infoseek

.com, Excite.com, Lycos.com, AskJeeves.com, WebCrawler.com, MetaCrawler. com, Dogpile.com, ProFusion.com, ixquick.com, Vivisimo.com, and others. Technological advances combined with the proliferation of digital information resources are reshaping the landscape for historical research.[7]

Online bibliographies are available at such sites as Argus Clearinghouse and most guides listed are available in hypertext versions.[8] *College & Research Libraries News* Internet Resources lists librarian-researched bibliographies.[9] Archival collections can be searched at the sites of the publishers, such as newspaper files and specific government-agency Web pages.

Conversion to digital formats does not come without both negative and positive effects on the historical researcher. Some advantages of taking paper, sight, and sound recordings to digital floppies, hard drives, CD, DVD, and even newer formats are their ease of use, convenience, reduction in size of the records, greater access, and the ability to collaborate and share anywhere.

Some of the negatives of switching media formats is the need for selective preservation due to costs and time factors of conversion. Libraries and archives have been accused of violating their public trust by destroying traditional books, newspapers, and other paper-based collections while at the same time discarding their card catalogs. Traditional card catalogs contain a wealth of information of value to researchers that is not included in online counterparts.[10]

Data transfer can be an inconvenient and very time-consuming process. But the lack of tools and standards has already caused millions of electronic records and historical documents to be lost through technical obsolescence. The lack of standards for how government agencies should implement preservation is being addressed.[11]

---

[7] Patricia Methven and Sheila Anderson, "Historians and Access to Archives in the Digital Age," Keynote address presented at the 1999 annual conference of the Association for History and Computing, King's College, London, September 14–16, 1999. Abstract available at http://www.kcl.ac.uk/humanities/cch/drhahc/ahc/abst271.htm.

[8] Argus Associates, "The Argus Clearing House," http://www.clearinghouse.net/.

[9] American Library Association, "*College & Research Libraries News* Internet Resources," http://www.ala.org/ala/acrl/acrlpubs/crlnews/internetresources.htm.

[10] See Nicholson Baker, *The Size of Thoughts: Essays and Other Lumber* (New York: Random House, 1996).

[11] National Archives and Records Administration, "Records Management by Federal Agencies," http://www.archives.gov/about_us/basic_laws_and_authorities/

The Electronic Records Archives (ERA) is the National Archives strategic response to the challenge of preserving, managing, and accessing electronic records. "To fulfill its mission, the National Archives needs to respond effectively to the challenge posed by the diversity, complexity, and enormous volume of electronic records being created today and the rapidly changing nature of the systems that are used to create them." The National Archives administration is searching for a way to preserve "virtually any kind of electronic record, free from dependence on any specific hardware or software."[12]

We should learn from history as we embark on the next technological digitization effort. Magnetic storage recordings have a limited life as did nitrate film stock.[13] The transfer from Beta to VHS to DVD is a prime example of the conundrum we face. There are those who remember reel-to-reel magnetic tape to 8-track to cassette to CD. We need to develop repositories, not only for print, but for the many other formats and technical standards that have become analog and digital orphans. The paradox of digitization is that the more you use a book, the less durable it becomes, but when a digital copy isn't used, it has a tendency to disappear from the potential of discovery.

There is a mistaken belief that transfer to digital does not result in any degradation of the original. However, the basic technical nature of a material's fidelity is degraded even as digital duplication takes place. This results often in an almost unperceivable reduction from the quality of the original and at each dubbing more is lost little by little by the process of digital compression.[14]

It would appear to the beginning historian that the more current the topic is, the easier the job of finding root documentation would be. It is also an

---

federal_agencies .html; see also Government Accounting Office, "Information Management: Challenges in Managing and Preserving Electronic Records," June 2002, report, http://www.gao.gov/new.items/d02586.pdf.

[12] National Archives and Records Administration, "Electronic Records Archives," http://www.archives.gov/electronic_records_archives/index.html.

[13] Library of Congress, "Risk Analysis Study for a Representative Magnetic Tape Collection," Preservation Research and Testing Series No. 9808 (Washington, DC: Author, Preservation Directorate, 1998).

[14] Library of Congress, "Digitizing Library Collections for Preservation and Archiving: A Handbook for Curators," Preservation Research and Testing series No. 9705 (Washington, DC: Author, Preservation Directorate, 1997).

accepted assertion that distance of time is necessary for a balanced appraisal of the importance and impact of events. However neither is a truism.[15]

The unique attributes of the Internet are infinite informational sources with no spectrum scarcity. There has developed a general lack of gatekeeping, although some Internet service providers (ISPs), Sysops (system operators) do function as editors, but usually a writer's message is sent unaltered. This is very unlike traditional mass media.

There is confusion as to who is the "media?" Who is a "reporter?" Low cost results in "free" speech, while at the same time low cost is the main reason for invasion of privacy through spam.

Electronic media, especially the Internet, have made it possible for almost anyone to become a "publisher." Therein lies the problem for the historian. How reliable is the information if it can be found? How do we handle email in the context of doing a history of the development of a popular TV program? How do we study how new techniques develop and are used, such as special effects or CGI, as corporations become less transparent and their records are deemed proprietary?[16]

The development and use of communication satellites is a combination of government and private industry, and studies of these mixed contributors are so complex that it is uncertain we will have an understanding of how these interactions have affected so many communication industries.[17]

How will the Intellectual Property Law affect the collection of information for scholarly purposes in the digital age? Article I, Section 8 of the Constitution affords "Authors" and "Inventors" "the Exclusive Right" to copyright "for Limited Times." The "limits" have expanded to the point that no TV program will become public domain in your lifetime.

On the Internet, to read is to "copy" and to "display." An example was the number of *Star Trek* fan sites that proliferated on the Internet. Paramount lawyers went into action against fan sites with letters threatening legal action for their using protected material and even writing about the characters of the show. There was a different result when the producer of *Babylon 5* permitted

---

[15] Gary R. Edgerton and Peter C. Rollins, ed., *Television Histories: Shaping Collective Memory in the Media Age* (Lexington: University Press of Kentucky, 2001).

[16] Ben H. Bagdikian, *The New Media Monopoly* (Boston, MA: Beacon Press, 1997).

[17] See David J. Whalen, "Communications Satellites: Making the Global Village Possible," National Aeronautics and Space Administration, http://www.hq.nasa.gov/office/pao/History/satcomhistory.html.

the use of copyrighted material on fan sites as long as they were nonprofit and his copyright notice was appended.[18]

The Digital Millennium Copyright Act of 1998[19] has libraries concerned with the criminalization of copying digital material. The law does exempt Internet Service Providers (ISPs) that don't know of subscribers' acts as long as the ISPs do not financially gain from the transgressions. An ISP is immune if it has reason to believe a subscriber was only engaging in "Fair Use." Also, ISPs are immune from subscribers' suits if material is removed without cause, because the ISP had reason to believe the subscriber was violating copyright. But the subscriber is not immune to lawsuits.

Online privacy on the job does not really exist as employers generally have access to workers' "private" email messages. There are statutes that often prohibit intercepting messages "during transmission," but email archived on a company's server has already "arrived."

The Electronic Communications Privacy Act[20] requires the government to obtain a search warrant unless the messages sought were sent over 180 days before. Then authorities only need an "administrative subpoena" to have access. The use of encryption technology for online privacy will create considerable difficulties in obtaining historical records in the future.

From this transition period it is hoped there will be a rich, vibrant body of primary evidence safeguarded for the use of the future historian. It will be a daunting task to obtain, sift, and weight what the digital age, in all likelihood, can and will preserve.

---

[18] Michael Oppenheimer, "Copyright and Intellectual Property," Arizona State University, Telecommunications for Instruction, Fall 1997, http://seamonkey.ed .asu.edu/~mcisaac/emc523/work/a8/oppen.html.

[19] U.S. Copyright Office, "The Digital Millennium Copyright Act of 1998," http:// www.copyright.gov/legislation/dmca.pdf.

[20] Department of Energy, "Electronic Communications Privacy Act of 1986," Office of the Chief Information Officer, October, 21, 1986, http://cio.doe.gov/Documents/ ECPA .HTM.

Part IV

New Perspectives in Topical Issues

11

Understanding the Historical Context of Race and Gender in Electronic Media

Rebecca Ann Lind
University of Illinois at Chicago

This chapter provides a brief introduction to investigating the contributions made by people of whom you may not be aware if your readings have thus far included only the usual suspects. Clearly, the contributions by notables such as Lee DeForest, David Sarnoff, and Edward R. Murrow are important. But so are the contributions of Eunice Randall, Judith Cary Waller, Jack L. Cooper, and Rufus P. Turner. This chapter will discuss methods and special considerations of researching race and gender in media history and analysis, and present a brief review of the literature describing the contributions of women and people of color in American broadcasting. It also presents a bibliography that should facilitate efforts to study the contributions of women and people of color in American broadcasting.

When approaching any study of the media, understanding the larger context is valuable. Lind described the three major components of the media system as *production,* "anything having to do with the creation and distribution of mediated messages: how the messages are assembled, by whom, in what circumstances, under what constraints"; *content,* "the mediated messages themselves: what they present, and how; what is included, and by implication, what is excluded"; and *audience,* "the people who engage, consume, or interact with mediated messages: how they use the media, what sense they make of media content, and how they are affected by the media."[1] This chapter primarily emphasizes

---

[1] Rebecca Ann Lind, *Race/Gender/Media: Considering Diversity across Audiences, Content, and Producers* (Boston, MA: Allyn & Bacon, 2004), 3.

production, though many of the items in the bibliography will be helpful in investigating texts.

THE METHODOLOGICAL CHALLENGE

This book covers various methods for conducting historical research into electronic media. Research methods are rarely inextricably linked to topics, however, so when the area of interest has to do with race and gender, the researcher may well use any of the traditional or critical methods. This chapter attempts to supplement the material presented elsewhere in this text (although a bit of duplication is inevitable) and highlights some of the issues that arise when conducting historical analyses of women and people of color in American electronic media.

Researching race and gender in media requires dividing all forms of historical evidence into two main families that can be called *artifacts* and *life stories.* Broadly defined, artifacts include all of the "stuff" of electronic media— scripts, tapes and other recordings, memorabilia, legal documents, business records and letters, photographs, clippings, scrapbooks, props, media coverage, archives, and the like. Life stories include all of the diaries, journals, personal letters, tales, recollections, and other stories told either by or about the people of interest. When the story is told by the person involved, it might be an autobiography, an interview, or a life story; when told by others, it usually takes the form of a case study or biography.

The Challenges of Artifacts

When researching race and gender in electronic media, there is a double hurdle to clear in the quest for artifacts. The first has to do with the nature of broadcasting itself, and the second, with the general social status of women and people of color in the United States.

The Scarcity of Artifacts. As acknowledged elsewhere in this book, broadcasting—especially in the days before recording technology was widely used— is impermanent. As Williams noted, "The vast majority of the textual and material practices in early TV were so ephemeral as to be literally lost in the air, and the status of extant materials and information pertinent to its study is in no way stable or exhaustive."[2] Just as in the early days of radio, the television

---

[2] Mark J. Williams, "Considering Monty Margetts's *Cook's Corner:* Oral History and Television History," in *Television, History, and American Culture: Feminist*

program could not be captured; there could be no artifact of the program itself. But these technological limitations do not preclude historians from investigating race and gender in radio and television. The program, its cast, and its producers can leave other artifacts, such as scripts, contracts, reviews, photographs, sketches, and the like.

Yet such artifacts have frequently been thrown away, or not even collected. Furthermore, now that technology does allow us to capture the broadcast itself, these artifacts are still frequently assigned the same ignoble fate. Radio and television stations are often lax about keeping records other than those required by law, and even legally required files are usually kept no longer than absolutely necessary. Fires, floods, and moves have all destroyed invaluable artifacts. Storage space is an additional enemy of the seeker of media artifacts. Even when copies of programs are made, they are discarded when their perceived value has diminished. Most local stations keep copies of their newscasts only for a limited time, deleting one day's worth of material as each new day's material is added. According to Williams, "individual television stations have paid surprisingly little attention to the history of their programs and practices. The television industry in general generates vast quantities of records (correspondence, proposals, studies, reports, ratings, memoranda, etc.), yet has little space and seemingly less compunction to save or to preserve them."[3]

The well-intentioned station or content producer relying on new media technologies to preserve programs may find it has saved storage expenses because the space requirements are so much less for programs stored on a CD, DVD, or hard drive than on traditional audio- or videotapes. Unfortunately, storage formats are evolving so rapidly that the station is destined to discover it can no longer locate a device capable of reading the storage media. At best, and with sufficient funding, the content can be transferred into another format; at worst, the content will become irretrievable.

The challenges of creating and preserving media artifacts are only made worse when the people involved are too busy "doing" to document what they are doing. This can be particularly evident in radio and television programs and stations with a mission of activism or social improvement, which is especially troubling when studying ethnic or feminist media because so much ethnic and undoubtedly all feminist media content has been rooted in such a

Critical Essays, eds. Mary Beth Haralovich and Lauren Rabinovitz (Durham, NC: Duke University Press, 1999), 38.

[3] Ibid., 36.

mission. Sometimes third-party coverage of relevant media content is all the historian can obtain. Newspaper or trade press coverage may be available, but it will likely provide fairly little in-depth information, and content listings offer even less.

Historians attempting to research media history know all too well the frustration of uncovering the fact that a program of historical import existed, but being unable to learn much about the program at all. Hill, Raglin, and Johnson maintained an objective distance when discussing the lack of information available about the first network series starring an African American.[4] Amanda Randolph starred in *The Laytons,* which—two years before *Beulah* and twenty years before *Julia*—"aired from August to October in 1948 on the DuMont network. The program aired from May to June 1949 on local TV in New York. Vera Tatum costarred in *The Laytons,* but very little is known about the series."[5] Streitmatter, on the other hand, rightfully was passionate when responding to a similar situation. Though Streitmatter's book is about print journalists, the sentiments expressed in the following quote are equally felt by historians frustrated in their quest to study the contributions of women and people of color to broadcast media:

> The challenge of locating primary sources has led to the exclusion of journalists from this book who rightfully deserve their chapters. For example, two scholars have identified Sarah Gibson Jones as the only African-American woman journalist working for a newspaper during the Civil War, arguably the most important event in the history of Black America. I devoted two months piecing together Jones's biography and searching for her original newspaper articles in the *Cincinnati Colored Citizen.* I found only two extant copies of the newspaper—one at the Library of Congress and another at the University of Cincinnati. Jones has been excluded from this book, however, because neither copy of the *Colored Citizen* contains any indication of Jones having written or edited any of the articles in it.[6]

---

[4] George H. Hill, Lorraine Raglin, and Chas Floyd Johnson, *Black Women in Television: An Illustrated History and Bibliography* (New York: Garland Press, 1990), 5.

[5] Ibid.

[6] Rodger Streitmatter, *Raising Her Voice: African-American Women Journalists Who Changed History* (Lexington: University Press of Kentucky, 1994), 6–7.

The Challenge of Studying Subordinated Groups. The difficulties encountered when trying to locate relevant artifacts increase exponentially when the quest involves members of nondominant social groups.

Sometimes the artifacts are unavailable for reasons attributable to the cultural practices of the group under consideration. For example, studies of the Native American press are hampered by what Murphy and Murphy called "the unsettled lives of the tribes."[7] As a result, according to Murphy and Murphy, "back issues of many of their papers have only rarely been preserved."[8]

However, far more frequently, the social status of women and people of color have affected the extent to which their contributions are celebrated, preserved, or even acknowledged. Etter-Lewis noted that "documentation of women's lives has tended to be difficult due to a variety of factors, including women's relatively low social status and marginalization within society."[9] Indeed, the sources of information about women's lives "depend to a large extent on the predilections, interests, prejudices, and values of the collectors and historians of an earlier day, which in this case reflect the indifferent attention given to women in history."[10]

Streitmatter wrote that "searching for information about members of a minority group that has been denied its history can be difficult, frustrating, time consuming—and fruitless."[11] Some scholars attribute this lack of attention to minority groups to anything but benign neglect. Anderson, Armitage, Jack, and Wittner's argument about the status of women in academic disciplines and investigations of social reality can be extended to the status of women in other cultural institutions, including broadcasting:

> women's perspectives were not absent ... simply as a result of oversight but
> had been suppressed, trivialized, ignored, or reduced to the status of gossip

---

[7] James Emmett Murphy and Sharon M. Murphy, *Let My People Know: American Indian Journalism, 1828–1978* (Norman: University of Oklahoma Press, 1981), 17.

[8] Ibid.

[9] Gwendolyn Etter-Lewis, "Introduction," in *Unrelated Kin: Race and Gender in Women's Personal Narratives,* eds. Gwendolyn Etter-Lewis and Michele Foster (New York: Routledge, 1996), 8.

[10] Gerda Lerner, *The Majority Finds Its Past* (New York: Oxford University Press, 1994), 64.

[11] Streitmatter, *Raising Her Voice,* 6.

and folk wisdom by dominant research traditions institutionalized in academic settings and in scientific disciplines.[12]

Whether intentional or unintentional, the truth historians must face is that when investigating members of a subordinated cultural group, information will be that much harder to find. Barlow found that there is just a "small number of scholarly articles, books, and dissertations on African Americans' portrayal and participation in radio broadcasting since the 1920s."[13] Danky and Hady described a "pattern of libraries' paying scant attention to publications produced by Black Americans"[14] and further claimed that "the short lifespans and archival neglect of these publications, both of which still persist, have had profound consequences for anyone interested in African-American history."[15] According to Fishman, "there have been no large archival collections available to draw upon to discuss the role of women either as performers, writers, program directors, or station owners. Unfortunately, existing materials on women in broadcasting have been scattered and difficult to locate."[16]

Another challenge that must be acknowledged is that a relatively high proportion of the limited social discourse about cultural diversity or the social importance of race has focused on African Americans, as has much of the scholarly attention paid to minority groups in our society. As a result, scholars investigating the contributions and history of people of African descent will find one level of difficulty, but scholars investigating other racial/ethnic groups will find the search doubly difficult.

Depending on the topic (and era) being investigated, however, the scarcity of formal archives makes the task difficult but not impossible for historians

---

[12] Kathryn Anderson, Susan Armitage, Dana Jack, and Judith Wittner, "Beginning Where We Are: Feminist Methodology in Oral History," in *Feminist Research Methods: Exemplary Readings in the Social Sciences,* ed. Joyce McCarl Neilsen (Boulder, CO: Westview Press, 1990), 96.

[13] William Barlow, *Voice Over: The Making of Black Radio* (Philadelphia, PA: Temple University Press, 1999), xi.

[14] James P. Danky and Maureen E. Hady, eds., *African-American Newspapers and Periodicals: A National Bibliography* (Cambridge, MA: Harvard University Press, 1998), xxxi.

[15] Ibid, xxxii.

[16] Donald A. Fishman, "Foreword," in *Invisible Stars: A Social History of Women in American Broadcasting,* by Donna L. Halper (Armonk, NY: M. E. Sharpe, 2001), vii.

interested in women and people of color. Vaz, for example, described finding a wealth of artifacts in "personal collections [which] were dispersed throughout the city, housed in nontraditional repositories, remaining some of the best-kept secrets in Philadelphia. They were not housed, for the most part, in libraries, archives, historical societies, or museums."[17] Vaz was able to uncover these treasure troves through the network of social connections she made when engaging in conversations with members of the community she was studying: "Thus I found oral narrative research an essential phase in locating photographs[,] documents[,] and memorabilia."[18]

The Challenges of Life Stories

Biographies, autobiographies, interviews, journals, oral histories, and the like are of particular value when researching women and minorities in media. Broadly classified as "life stories," these forms of evidence are vital when study-ing subordinated groups. Due to space limitations and the importance of per-sonal recollections, my consideration of these methods as pertaining to studying the history of women and people of color will focus on interviews/ oral histories.

According to Williams,

> [P]ersonal interviews are the most immediate alternative method of research for early television ... Although some degree of nostalgia, simple mistaken memory, or perhaps even self-interest is unavoidable, such interviews can provide other-wise unobtainable details and typically lead to new directions for research.[19]

Williams further argued that oral history is particularly valuable when study-ing the contributions made by women, an argument that can easily be extended to people of color:

> As a mode of inquiry and research, oral history responds to various gaps in the understanding of women's lives, the historical disparagement of women's activities, unchallenged generalizations about gender roles and gendered behavior, and the call for history "from below" (which usually

---

[17] Kim Marie Vaz, *Oral Narrative Research with Black Women* (Thousand Oaks, CA: Sage, 1997), 187.

[18] Ibid.

[19] Williams, "Considering Monty Margetts's *Cook's Corner,* 36.

emphasizes issues of class, race, and region). In addition, oral history allows women who might feel unconnected to "official" history (i.e., already understood momentous events) to be empowered to narrate their own lives. It is therefore a useful tool in examining historical discourses and activities assigned to the realm of the everyday, the quotidian, and the marginalized.[20]

To Anderson, Armitage, Jack, and Wittner, oral interviews are helpful because interviews provide the opportunity for people both to describe their experiences and to reflect on the meanings of those experiences. The interview is invaluable because it allows people to examine facts and subjectivities, activities and emotions. Importantly, "the interview is the one historical document that can ask people what they mean."[21] In addition, the stories told by women (and, by extension, minorities) have value in building theory:

> If we are to reconstruct theoretical accounts of society by seriously including women, we must begin to situate each individual woman's life story in its specific social and historical setting and show how women's actions and consciousness contribute to the structuring of social institutions ... We need to show how the conflicts, hopes, and fears of these and other women spurred them to action or kept them from it, and what difference this state of affairs made to them and to the worlds they inhabit.[22]

All research involving interview/oral history methodology raises key questions about "voice." One advantage is that it lets people speak in their own voice—in the case of women and minorities, the method explicitly tries to hear a voice too often denied. Though all methods rooted in conversations require special care be taken that the researcher does not dominate the subject's voice, there is disagreement among scholars regarding how best to protect the subject's voice. Many feminist oral historians, for example, argue that the researcher should merely present the accounts as provided by the subject and refrain from conducting any analysis thereof, thus fully removing the researcher's voice. However, as Reinharz and Davidman noted, even when selecting the subject and recording the account, the historian has a role and is involved in some sort of interpretation. An analysis of an account, therefore, is desirable because it not

---

[20] Ibid., 37.

[21] Anderson, Armitage, Jack, and Wittner, "Beginning Where We Are," 101.

[22] Ibid., 106.

only can bring additional depth to the oral account, but according to Reinharz and Davidman it can allow the reader to understand the researcher's perspective and better interpret the text as a whole.[23]

The challenge relating to voice is exacerbated when studying members of a minority group. Etter-Lewis noted the preponderance of White and/or male interviewers involved in oral history projects, and though she explicitly stated that "matching [the gender and racial/ethnic background of] interviewers and interviewees does not guarantee a bias-free interaction," she also argued that "such a match is more likely to create an empowering environment for the narrator and a more reliable finished product."[24] She posed two questions worthy of consideration: "Can an outsider accurately preserve/translate/interpret the experiences of an insider without betraying constraints of her own culture?" and "How and in what way is the collaborative process influenced when the researcher is from a dominant group and the narrator/subject is from an oppressed group?"[25] There are no easy answers to these questions, but the research can only be made stronger if the interviewer strives to overcome any and all obstacles related to the relative social positions of the participants in the interview process. Vaz recommended that interviewers should "be aware of [their] own cultural assumptions, values, and attitudes; this awareness avoids the danger of interviewer bias. An interview does not call for an impossible neutrality, but it does demand special self-awareness and self-discipline."[26]

LITERATURE REVIEW:
SOME CONTRIBUTIONS BY WOMEN AND MINORITIES

Even though this book is about electronic media, we must acknowledge that broadcasting began in an environment rooted in print media.

In the Beginning, There Was Print

In the Colonial period, women were active in printing and publishing. Mary Katherine Goddard of Baltimore, for example, ran the *Maryland Journal,*

---

[23] Shulamit Reinharz, with Lynn Davidman, *Feminist Methods in Social Research* (New York: Oxford University Press, 1992).

[24] Etter-Lewis, "Introduction," 8.

[25] Ibid, 5–6.

[26] Vaz, *Oral Narrative Research with Black Women,* 86.

considered one of the best newspapers of its day and, in 1777, was selected by the Continental Congress to produce the first official printing of the Declaration of Independence.[27] By the 1800s, however, women were given fewer opportunities in journalism, and the 1870 U.S. Census found only 35 of the reported 5,286 journalists were women.[28]

Wittke claimed that:

> there is scarcely a nationality or language group in the United States, however small, that has not at some time or other supported its own press, and there have been more foreign-language papers and periodicals published and read in America, in proportion to population, than in the home countries from which their readers came.[29]

In general, the foreign-language press is important because it preserves cultural ties with the homeland, brings immigrants together in their new land, keeps the language alive, and acculturates and socializes newcomers. According to Kowalik, "the first foreign language newspaper to appear in the United States was the German *Philadelphia Zeitung,* published on May 6, 1732 in Philadelphia."[30] The year 1853 saw the first Chinese newspaper in the United States, *The Oriental.* Published by Lai Sam in San Francisco, *The Oriental* lasted 20 years.[31]

In 1908, the first Spanish-language newspaper in the United States was New Orleans's *El Misisipí.* Kanellos and Martell described the two main functions of Hispanic press: "As an immigrant press, news of the homeland and its relationship with the United States was of primary concern; as a minority

---

[27] Maurine Hoffman Beasley and Sheila J. Gibbons, *Taking Their Place: A Documentary History of Women and Journalism* (Washington, DC: American University Press, in cooperation with the Women's Institute for Freedom of the Press, 1993), 8.

[28] Maurine Hoffman Beasley and Sheila J. Gibbons, *Women in Media: A Documentary Source Book* (Washington, DC: Women's Institute for Freedom of the Press, 1977), 38.

[29] Carl Wittke, *The German-language Press in America* (Lexington: University of Kentucky Press, 1957), 1.

[30] Jan Kowalik, *The Polish Press in America* (San Francisco: R & E Research Associates, 1978), 28.

[31] Karl Lo and Him Mark Lai, *Chinese Newspapers Published in North America, 1854–1975* (Washington, DC: Center for Chinese Research Materials, Association of Research Libraries, 1977).

press, the protection of civil rights and the monitoring of the community's economic, educational and cultural development came to the fore."[32]

Most historians believe the *Cherokee Phoenix* was the first Native American newspaper. Published by the Cherokee Nation, this bilingual newspaper appeared on February 21, 1828.[33]

The Black press had been born a year earlier. Edited by Samuel Eli Cornish and John Brown Russwurm and appearing on March 16, 1827, "*Freedom's Journal* was the first newspaper owned, operated, edited, and published by Black Americans."[34] It "proposed to be a teacher, a prod, a unifier, and a defender and to pursue a reformist program with the ultimate design for the universal improvement of all people."[35] According to Cairns, the 1920s saw several newspapers published by Black women:

> Mary Ellen Vaughan founded the *Murfeesboro Union* in Alabama in the 1920s, Thelma Childs Taylor published the *Topeka Plaindealer* in Kansas, and Charlotta Bass published the *California Eagle* with her husband, Joseph, in Los Angeles. All aimed to make their newspapers the instruments of social uplift and harsh critics of American apartheid.[36]

An activist (or at least educational and improvement-oriented) mission is one of the hallmarks of many newspapers published by nondominant social groups, especially racial and ethnic minorities. To the extent that such were important in the print media, they frequently carried over into the electronic media—beginning, of course, with radio.

Taking to the Air

According to Fishman, there "was an egalitarian quality to early radio. The low pay and small budgets for programming created equal opportunities for

---

[32] Nicolas Kanellos, with Helvetia Martell, *Hispanic Periodicals in the United States, Origins to 1960: A Brief History and Comprehensive Bibliography* (Houston, TX: Arte Publico Press, 2000), 5.

[33] Murphy and Murphy, *Let My People Know*.

[34] Armistead Scott Pride and Clint C. Wilson II, *A History of the Black Press* (Washington, DC: Howard University Press, 1997), 11.

[35] Ibid., 13.

[36] Kathleen A. Cairns, *Front-page Women Journalists, 1920–1950* (Lincoln: University of Nebraska Press, 2003), 14.

women as vocalists and musicians."[37] The equality of which Fishman wrote extended beyond musical roles, but it was gender equality, not racial equality, and it didn't last long. Once the commercial potential of broadcasting became apparent, both the number and variety of opportunities for women in radio (and later, television) decreased. Racial equality took significantly longer to appear; indeed, some might argue it still eludes us.

This literature review can present only the briefest glimpse into the myriad contributions made by women and people of color to broadcasting. Some contributions are technical; some are managerial; many are rooted in performance. This review will present a few of the "firsts" as well as tell a few of the many interesting stories about women and minorities in the early days of broadcasting. I make no pretense at doing any more than that; the interested reader wishing to gain a fuller understanding of this fascinating area of research is invited to use the bibliography as a starting point to uncover more information.

Both women and people of color were accepted more as performers than as managers, and there were relatively few women or minorities working in technical roles. During wartime, however, women were at least temporarily encouraged to take on technical tasks otherwise reserved for males. But there were women and minorities making technological contributions to broadcasting, even in the earliest days of radio.

In 1918, Eunice Randall was the first woman hired by the American Radio and Research Company, or AMRAD.[38] Working alongside the male engineers, Randall learned to build ham radio equipment and to announce. Eventually, she became equal to the men who had welcomed her on board, and was herself an engineer.

Minority contributions to radio began at the same early date. Pride and Wilson argued that "Blacks were instrumental in radio's technological and engineering advancements" and presented as an example the significant contributions of Rufus P. Turner.[39] Not only radios but also most contemporary wristwatches benefit from Turner's engineering breakthroughs. In the early 1920s, when still a teenager, Turner "was awarded an amateur radio license for station 3LF in Washington, D.C., the first of his race to obtain

---

[37] Fishman, "Foreword," viii.

[38] Donna L. Halper, *Invisible Stars: A Social History of Women in American Broadcasting* (Armonk, NY: M. E. Sharpe, 2001).

[39] Pride and Wilson, *A History of the Black Press,* 254.

licensing in the United States."[40] He later became the first Black member of the Institute of Radio Engineers. Among other things, Turner invented "a device in which quarts crystals act as stabilizers, allowing stations to maintain their assigned frequencies without drift and signal interference."[41]

The first woman to own a radio station was Marie Zimmerman. "Her husband was fascinated by ham radio and engineering, while she became interested in business," so in 1922 she launched station WIAE in Vinton, Iowa.[42] It wasn't one of the big success stories of radio, according to Halper, it "lasted barely a year."[43] Several years later, in 1925, Mary Costigan started a station in Flagstaff, Arizona. In 1928 Blanche Virgin inherited a station upon her husband's death. "Rather than sell it, she decided to operate it herself. For six months, she ran the station alone, before hiring an assistant and then gradually expanding the staff of station KMED."[44]

But, as Halper put it, "nobody else was doing anything to equal the work of Ida McNeil, who ran a one-woman radio station for several decades."[45] McNeil operated station KGFX in Pierre, South Dakota:

> as a friendly, folksy hometown station that broke every rule of so-called "professional" broadcasting. Mrs. McNeil gave birthday greetings over the air, said hello to various listeners, took requests, talked about what was going on in the local stores ... talked about how various patients at local hospitals were doing ... and made sure the farmers got the most up-to-date weather available. It should not have worked; when the networks came along, the audience should have insisted on the big-name stars and smooth announcers. But they did not. They insisted on Ida McNeil, who was the entire staff of KGFX (except for a chief engineer), and who became one of the most beloved people in town.[46]

The first Black-owned radio station didn't appear for more than two decades after the first woman-owned station. In 1949, WERD in Atlanta,

---

[40] Ibid.

[41] Ibid., 255.

[42] Halper, *Invisible Stars,* 18.

[43] Ibid., 18.

[44] Ibid., 68.

[45] Ibid.

[46] Ibid., 69.

Georgia was licensed to J. B. Blayton.[47] The first Black-owned television station in the United States was WGPR-TV (UHF channel 62) in Detroit (Grosse Pointe), Michigan. WPGR, which to owner William V. Banks seemed a logical extension of a successful FM radio station, began broadcasting on September 29, 1975. In practice, however, Dr. Banks quickly learned that programming Black-appeal television was much more difficult than programming Black-appeal radio.[48] Johnson's case study of the first three years of WGPR revealed that the station was overly ambitious and its audience became dismayed with what was offered. "WGPR-TV fell victim to its own enthusiasm and inexperience. Its unreal programming goals set up levels of expectation within its audience that could only mean disillusionment with anything less."[49] The station "promised innovated programming produced by Blacks for Blacks. It delivered old movies, westerns, and cartoons now in syndication from decades gone by."[50] WGPR was more successful at realizing its goal of serving as a training ground for minorities, though not as much as if it had more revenues. Still, the station survived, and ultimately thrived. It stayed in Black control until 1995 when it was sold to CBS for $24 million.[51]

Although a national radio program "about tribal history, culture and current affairs" was launched by the Commissioner of Indian Affairs on January 1, 1937, and was carried by 170 stations, the first Native American-owned radio station didn't begin broadcasting until April 1972.[52] The station, KTDB-FM, is a Najavo public radio station in Ramah, New Mexico. The first commercial radio station owned and operated by Native Americans in the United States is KMDX-FM, in Parker, Arizona.[53] The station, owned by Gilbert Leivas, was launched on December 10, 1977. According to Trahant, most Native American radio stations can be considered community radio:

---

[47] Pride and Wilson, *A History of the Black Press.*

[48] Mary H. Johnson, *A Case History of the Evolution of WGPR-TV, Detroit: First Black-owned Television Station in the U.S., 1972–1979* (Master's thesis, University of North Carolina at Chapel Hill, 1979).

[49] Ibid., 98.

[50] Ibid., 99.

[51] Pride and Wilson, *A History of the Black Press.*

[52] Mark N. Trahant, *Pictures of Our Nobler Selves: A History of Native American Contributions to News Media* (Nashville, TN: Freedom Forum First Amendment Center, 1995), 21.

[53] Murphy and Murphy, *Let My People Know.*

People call the station and share information about local government, funerals and even traditional ceremony announcements. Perhaps it is that notion of community broadcasting that best characterizes all tribal stations, rich or poor.[54]

It is difficult to select which of the many fascinating stories to focus on in a limited review such as this one, but I will conclude this discussion with a brief glimpse into the careers of Judith Cary Waller and Jack L. Cooper.

Judith Cary Waller is mentioned in most histories recognizing women's contributions to the broadcasting industry. Waller was named station manager of WGU, in Chicago, despite having no experience with the medium. That was no drawback, according to the men who hired her. They said they didn't know anything about running a radio station, either![55] WGU, Chicago's second radio station, signed-on on April 13, 1922, and later that same year changed its call letters to WMAQ. Even though the station was on the air only two hours a day, it was a constant challenge to find programming to fill that slot. According to O'Dell,

If talent ran short, [Waller] herself often turned announcer and, on more than one occasion, played a classical composition on the song bells in order to fill airtime. From time to time she even found it necessary to fill in playing the drums.[56]

Waller was committed to public service broadcasting, and aired coverage from both national political conventions in 1924. Many broadcasting "firsts" resulted from Waller's programming decisions. She was the first to produce, in 1924, a play-by-play broadcast of a college football game. She was the first to put baseball games on the air, with the Chicago Cubs. She founded radio's first organized drama company, the WMAQ Players. In 1931, she "initiated the radio show *University of Chicago Roundtable*, which brought together the best scholars from the university for lively debates on philosophical issues. The program would air for more than twenty years nationally on the NBC

---

[54] Trahant, *Pictures of Our Nobler Selves*, 22.

[55] Leora M. Sies and Luther F. Sies, *The Encyclopedia of Women in Radio, 1920–1960* (Jefferson, NC: McFarland, 2003).

[56] Cary O'Dell, *Women Pioneers in Television: Biographies of Fifteen Industry Leaders* (Jefferson, NC: McFarland, 1997), 197.

network."[57] According to O'Dell, Waller was committed to an educational mission. Besides becoming associated with both the University of Chicago and Northwestern University, Waller

> founded at WMAQ the largest children's radio club in history. At its peak its membership consisted of 275,000 children. Its primary purpose was to assist area schools with their lessons; several times a week WMAQ carried children's radio programming specially designed to complement whatever subject was currently being taught. By 1928 over one hundred schools within a radius of fifty miles of Chicago were taking advantage of the service.[58]

After WMAQ was bought by NBC, Waller served as public affairs and education director for the network from 1931 to 1957. Sies and Sies called her "a gifted broadcast executive, a radio pioneer who made a significant contribution to American broadcasting."[59] Among other programming firsts, Waller pioneered the strategy of stripping, or airing multiple episodes of a program at the same time across multiple days.

Waller's contributions extended beyond radio, into television. According to Carey, Waller produced television's first educational show for children "three years before *Captain Kangaroo,* thirty years before *Sesame Street,* and decades before *Barney.*"[60] Carey argued that "Waller's work, *Ding Dong School,* dared to treat children—and television—seriously. Unlike many of her contemporaries she realized the medium's inherent power and responsibility."[61]

However, not all of Waller's contributions were so prosocial. After CBS turned it down, it was Judith Waller who brought *Amos 'n' Andy* to WMAQ and the NBC network. Despite her personal misgivings about the show, she accepted it, and after the show's debut on March 19, 1928 it became the biggest hit in the station's history.[62] Indeed, it was this show's phenomenal, unanticipated success that led Waller to air it six nights a week—a programming practice that has become the core of most broadcast scheduling today.

---

[57] Ibid., 200.

[58] Ibid.

[59] Sies and Sies, *The Encyclopedia of Women in Radio, 1920–1960,* 222.

[60] O'Dell, *Women Pioneers in Television,* 203.

[61] Ibid.

[62] Ibid.

Although successful, *Amos 'n' Andy* was nothing if not racist. Its images of Blacks as bumbling and incapable, as crooks, clowns, or cheats, have often been discussed. Newman described early radio as "divided by a color line. On one side of the line was network broadcasting; on the other independent, Black-appeal narrowcasting. The result was that Blacks had two very distinct and different radio experiences. At the same time [as listeners were gritting their] teeth over the Black image *Amos 'n' Andy* presented to the world via network broadcasting, listeners in Chicago received an opposite Black image via Jack L. Cooper's pioneering Black-appeal programs narrowcast on station WSBC."[63]

Jack L. Cooper was a pioneer of Black radio in the 1920s and 1930s, and created many programming strategies still in use today. According to Newman, Jack L. Cooper is "the starting point of any analysis" of Black-appeal radio, but when he first got on the air, nobody knew he was Black.[64] His first job at WCAP, Washington, was an act featuring all sorts of accents including Black dialect. "For all intents and purposes it appeared that Blacks still did not talk on the air."[65]

Because Cooper wanted to be a Black voice on the air, programming for a Black audience, he left Washington for Chicago and constantly pitched the idea of a Black program to radio stations. Finally, he got a deal, and at 5:00 p.m. on Sunday, November 3, 1929, WSBC premiered *The All-Negro Hour* starring Jack L. Cooper and his gang. The show wasn't highly promoted but it was well received in the Black community. Through the early to mid-1930s, the Black-appeal schedule grew on WSBC, but in off-times—late evenings, weekends. By 1935, Cooper controlled about 9½ of the station's 56 hours of weekly airtime. Still, Newman argued, it was only after Cooper was able to break into prime time in 1938, coupled with his expansion into providing about 40 hours of material weekly for at least four stations that he became more successful.[66] As before, Cooper was still narrowcasting, but in a multitude of categories—religious services from many churches, gospel and other music programs, quiz shows, serials, dramas, and more. At one point he had 154 programs on the air, and controlled 19.5 out of the 56 total weekly hours

---

[63] Mark Newman, *Entrepreneurs of Profit and Pride: From Black-appeal to Radio Soul* (New York: Praeger, 1988), x.

[64] Ibid., 52.

[65] Ibid., 56.

[66] Ibid.

WSBC broadcast.[67] He produced these programs through the first successful Black radio production company, Jack L. Cooper Presentations, which he'd founded in 1932.[68] Cooper also launched an advertising agency bearing his name, with the motto: "When we get 'em told, you got 'em sold."[69]

Cooper's success was rooted in his combination of radio talent and entrepreneurial drive. All of the financial risks associated with producing the show lay squarely on Cooper's shoulders; in a time-brokering arrangement, he bought blocks of time from the station and in turn sold advertising to local merchants targeting the Black community. According to Newman, Cooper's goal was to make his show a 100 percent Black effort.[70] He worked to replace the White announcer who introduced the show with a Black one (himself); he worked to become the official announcer of all Black shows and commercial announcer of all advertisements airing during Black segments. He wanted to build a new studio solely to produce and air Black shows. He made great inroads but the show never was an all-Black effort; the station remained White-owned and operated, the engineers were White, and much of the advertising came from White-owned businesses in the Black community. Jack L. Cooper's contributions to American radio were by any measure pivotal, and crossed racial lines. His popularity became so great that "In 1951 he was voted the top radio man in Chicago."[71]

CONCLUSION: REACHING FOR SYNTHESIS

In her attempts to understand how our culture makes sense of women's contributions, Lerner identified four stages of conceptualization in women's history.[72] Lerner's stages are easily extended to include conceptualization of the history of racial and ethnic minorities. Compensatory history identifies and describes the accomplishments of significant women (and people of color), thus closing some of the gaps in the historical record. Contribution history describes women's achievements and status in a male-defined society (and, similarly, the contributions of minorities in a White-defined society). A

---

[67] Ibid., 67.

[68] Barlow, *Voice Over.*

[69] Newman, *Entrepreneurs of Profit and Pride,* 73.

[70] Ibid.

[71] Ibid., 74.

[72] Lerner, *The Majority Finds Its Past.*

transitional stage uses recollections and other artifacts presenting women's (and minorities') own words to guide historians in creating new categories for examining material. Finally, in the synthesis stage, everything comes together to create a fuller, richer, and more accurate picture. As Streitmatter described it, when synthesis occurs,

> women's history [and the histories of people of color] blends with men's history to create a history of all people that has been enriched by the exploration of women's [and minorities'] experiences so that new questions are raised about that blended historical record.[73]

We must strive for that synthesis, because only when we achieve it will we have painted a full and accurate picture of our social world. At the very least, we need to make up for lost ground by including women and people of color in our histories, and we need to encourage historians to record their contributions today, which by tomorrow will have become history.

---

[73] Streitmatter, *Raising Her Voice*, 11.

12

Local Broadcasting History Research Methods

Tim Larson
University of Utah

Doing local broadcasting history is akin to listening to the scratchy story that unwinds from the brittle tape of an old radio detective drama. In the beginning, you have only a few precious clues pointing to what really happened. Likewise, in local broadcasting, surviving documents, tapes, and people offer only selected traces pointing to how it was or what happened in the past. It is the historian's job to go beyond these initial traces to tell a local broadcasting story based on facts validated using as many primary sources as possible.

A historian gathers facts about a subject, selects and distills those facts, arranges them in a narrative or story about the past, and subsequently makes the past known to his or her audience(s) through the written word and other media. Whatever the history, it must be written in terms of what was known and believed at the time, not from the perspective of hindsight. As such, the material or facts must precede the thesis if a historian expects to discover how it really was and come to a valid description of the past, measure change over time, or analyze cause and effect. Fiction writers use imagination. History writers use facts and follow the evidence.[1]

Early in the process of researching aspects of Utah broadcasting history, the author asked a University of Utah historian if the information gathered to date was sufficient to tell a valid state history of Utah broadcasting. The material included selected oral histories from Utah broadcasting pioneers,

---

[1] Barbara W. Tuchman, *Selected Essays: Practicing History* (New York: Ballantine Books, 1981), 9.

ELEMENTS AND FLOW OF HISTORY

Historian Barbara Tuchman says the historian's research process has the following elements and flow:

- *Facts* are to the historian what imagination is to the poet.
- *Selection* of important facts tests a historian's exercise in judgment.
- *Arrangement* of facts is the art of the historian.
- *Methodology* for the historian is chronological narrative or story telling.
- *Subject* is the story of man's past.
- *Function* for the historian is to make the past known.

early newspaper articles, program schedules, photographs, recordings, and radio scripts, among other sources of information about Utah broadcasting stations. The Utah historian's answer: "Don't try to stretch a rat's ass over a rain barrel." The message: The evidence was incomplete and from limited sources, insufficient to make the past known, and insufficient to write a valid statewide Utah broadcasting history.

The local broadcasting historian often does not have the necessary information to write a complete history of broadcasting in a given locale or state. Information can reveal only what it is designed to record, and it sometimes can provide only a small part of the history. It is up to the local broadcasting historians to form questions that the data can answer, to reveal small parts of broadcasting's past that are more complex—and often more interesting to the reader—than the whole picture.

Like those old radio-drama detectives, the local broadcasting historian can find and interpret facts that allow him or her to tell it like it was, whether it is the history of a state or market, the history of a certain station, or the history of one broadcast. Using a helpful guide, the historian can process evidence with the skill of a radio cop named O'Brien dusting for fingerprints and come to tell a valid local broadcasting history. Hopefully, this chapter will help in that endeavor.

AN OVERVIEW OF SOURCES AND PROCEDURES

If we choose to collect the oral, written, and mediated memories of local broadcasting, we know we can neither retrieve everything from the past nor save everything in the future. The volume of material is enormous, and the importance of "everything" is highly questionable. If we hope to go beyond parochial local broadcasting compilations to valid histories, local broadcasting historians must seriously collaborate on not only what they collect and preserve from the past, but also on what they collect and preserve in the future. Of the local memories and documents that could be collected, which ones are already being collected in other archives? Of those that are not being collected, which ones should be preserved in order to make each state or local broadcasting history a contributing and coherent part of national, or even international, broadcasting history?

Three sources are particularly helpful for the local broadcasting historian concerned with archival methods and procedures. "Archival Methods" by David Bearman establishes a conceptual framework for arranging and describing historical material and provides a clear and concise guide to common archival procedures.[2] In addition, the *Archival Procedure Manual* by Todd Ellison and Lois Anderton contains sequential essays that address the four fundamental activities involved in managing the physical record: selecting an appropriate record from the great volume of evidence, preserving that record against time, describing the record that has been retained, and providing for access and use.[3] Finally, *Digitising History* by Sean Townsend, Cressida Chappell, and Oscar Struijvé is a particularly useful guide to creating digital resources from historical documents. It is intended as a reference for individuals and organizations involved with, or planning, the computerization of historical source documents.[4]

After establishing an archival connection, and before beginning a local broadcasting history project, it is wise to consult general local history research sources. Two books on researching and writing generalized local histories are helpful guides: *Nearby History: Exploring the Past Around You* by David Kyvig and Myron Marty is intended for historians interested in

---

[2] David Bearman, "Archival Methods," in *Archives and Museum Informatics* Technical Report 3, no.1 (Pittsburgh, PA: Archives and Museum Informatics, 1991; orig. pub., 1989).

[3] Todd Ellison and Lois Anderton, *Archival Procedure Manual* (Boulder, CO: Carnegie Branch Library for Local History, Boulder Public Library, 1990).

[4] Sean Townsend, Cressida Chappell, and Oscar Struijvé, *Digitising History: A Guide to Creating Digital Resources from Historical Documents,* Arts and Humanities Data Service Guides to Good Practice (Oxford, England: Oxbow Books, 1999).

exploring local histories.[5] It seeks to bring together historical studies of the family, the community, and the environment. These authors suggest specific local history subjects and offer an extensive list of questions for investigating aspects of local history that can be adapted to local broadcasting histories. Also included are helpful forms to request information from federal agencies, sample gift agreements, sources of archival storage products and information, and URLs for using the World Wide Web in local histories. Another insightful applied source is *On Doing Local History* by Carol Kammen. Kammen challenges local historians to go beyond what has often been done in the past—beyond the undefined local history, lacking in context, in perspective, in judgment. She reflects on what local historians do, why they do it, and what it means.[6]

Because local broadcasting histories typically depend heavily on oral histories and personal interviews, it is advisable for the local broadcasting historian to become skillful with oral history methods if he or she expects to produce a valid local broadcasting history. Possibly, the best way to become skillful is to get a mentor and to study some well-constructed oral history collections compiled by others, and then to practice on some people on the fringes of a research topic. This process will not only make one a more skillful oral history interviewer, but it likely will expand the research database of contacts along with addresses and telephone numbers.

There are dozens of books on how to do oral histories, but two were found to be particularly pertinent for researching local broadcasting histories. *Listening for a Change: Oral Testimony and Community Development* by Hugo Slim and Paul Thompson concentrates on the issues that arise from the collection, interpretation, and preservation of oral testimony.[7] Slim and Thompson maintain that without a thorough understanding of the issues involved in the process, listening to people and recording their words can too easily become a purely archival or voyeuristic pursuit, or an exercise in knowledge extraction. Another helpful oral history guide is *Sounding Boards: Oral Testimony and the Local Historian* by David Marcombe. This book, published in England, relates

---

[5] David E. Kyvig and Myron A. Marty, *Nearby History: Exploring the Past Around You,* 2nd ed. (Walnut Creek, CA: Altamira Press, 2000), 42–50.

[6] Carol Kammen, *On Doing Local History,* 2nd ed., American Association for State and Local History book series (Walnut Creek, CA: AltaMira Press, 2003).

[7] Hugo Slim and Paul Thomson, *Listening for a Change: Oral Testimony and Community Development* (Philadelphia, PA: New Society Publishers, 1995).

the origins of the oral tradition, instructs the interviewer on how to conduct an interview, set goals, find respondents, and store, transcribe and analyze material.[8] In addition, it explains the use and abuse of oral testimony and ends with a discussion of the state of the art in gathering oral testimony.

TYPES OF HISTORIANS AND LOCAL BROADCASTING HISTORIES

Local broadcasting historians vary by background and purpose and fall into at least three overlapping categories based on the type of histories they write: I-was-there historians, active participants, and today's historians. Some selected examples from each of the three categories follow

I-Was-There Historians

This historian chronicles episodes of his or her own age. For example, Jim Ladd in *Radio Waves* provides a contemporary history of life and revolution on the FM dial from 1967 to 1987.[9] Rock and roll abandoned AM for FM during this period. Ladd writes the story of the days and nights he was inside the glass booth at RADIO KAOS in Los Angeles, where "free form," a personalized and spontaneous radio music art form was born and thrived. Ladd writes about an episode of his own time. This type of historian writes from experience and often uses contemporaries as sources. Histories of this type are too numerous to include here, but access Amazon, Google, or another search engine and other examples are found easily.

Active Participants

These historians often shape their accounts through roles they played in local broadcasting, or they compile information from biographies, interviews, oral histories, or from other active broadcasting participants. Unlike the I-was-there historian who writes about a specific station at a specific time, the active participant uses experiences to portray examples of general trends or

---

[8] David Marcombe, *Sounding Boards: Oral Testimony and the Local Historian* (Nottingham, England: Department of Adult Education, 1995).

[9] Jim Ladd, *Radio Waves: Life and Revolution on the FM Dial* (New York: St. Martin's Press, 1991).

industry-wide activity. Bob Doll's *Sparks Out of the Plowed Ground,* a book of personal histories, is an example of this type.[10] Doll wrote this book after 45 years in small market radio as an announcer, station manager, owner, consultant, and newsletter publisher. He proclaims the virtues of small town radio, which he calls a "people business," and is an unapologetic booster of those who run small market stations without help from consultants, home-office support, or high-priced specialists. Doll mentions more than 500 small market stations and as many people in his book.

Another example of an active participant historian is Philip K. Eberly. In *Susquehanna Radio: The First Fifty Years,* he writes about the Susquehanna Radio Corporation's rise from one radio station in 1941, WSBA, in York, Pennsylvania, to become a group owner of nine stations in several states.[11] After a lifelong career at WSBA in jobs ranging from copywriter, to vice president/general manager, Eberly writes about the people of the Susquehanna Radio Group. Depending heavily on interviews of past and present employees and oral histories, he uses what he calls "Instant Replay" to generously quote colleagues and others to further the Susquehanna story.

Doll, Eberly, and other historians of this type use sources ranging from histories written by other people to interviews and informal conversations, but mostly they count on their own experiences and those of colleagues over time to research and write local broadcasting histories.

Today's Historians

Historians usually are not direct participants in the historical events they write about, but they use local station and corporate resources, local newspaper and trade magazine articles, government and other official documents, interviews with living pioneers, and oral histories as sources for their histories. These historians often possess wine that has been allowed to ferment.

A short list of local broadcasting histories includes books and chapters by Banning, Lichty and Topping, Baudino and Kittross, Baker, Cantor, Hinds,

---

[10] Bob Doll, *Sparks out of the Plowed Ground* (West Palm Beach, FL: Streamline Press, 1996).

[11] Philip K. Eberly, *Susquehanna Radio: The First Fifty Years* (York, PA: Susquehanna Radio Corporation, 1992).

Nash, and Hilmes.[12] *Television in America,* edited by Michael D. Murray and Donald G. Godfrey, provides some recent, if not typical, examples of this type of historian.[13] These histories document pioneering local television stations in regions around the country. Each chapter includes references specific to each station history, and the editors provide a selected bibliography of books, articles, unpublished material, archives, and special collections. Historians writing about stations in *Television in America* used an abundance of interviews, newspaper articles, and national and local trade sources for their histories. Several also used FCC, station, and corporate records for their documentation. Unpublished papers, dissertations, and documents from personal collections and state archives were also used. No matter what other documents or support data were used, all but a few station historians in *Television in America* depended on oral histories from station principals and employees.

A search of Dissertation Abstracts using ProQuest, an electronic database (http://www.umi.com/), listed more than 50 dissertations and theses over the last ten years dealing with aspects of local broadcasting history. Some are station histories or biographies of important station principals. Others deal with program genre or individual programs, and still others deal with ownership, regulatory, and diversity issues. A number deal with local stations in the United States, in U.S. territories and in foreign countries. There are representative works from each of three history types, with the vast majority in the

---

[12]William P. Banning, *Commercial Broadcasting Pioneer: The WEAF Experiment, 1922–1926* (Cambridge, MA: Harvard University Press, 1946); Lawrence W. Lichty and Malachi C. Topping, eds., *American Broadcasting: A Source Book on the History of Radio and Television* (New York: Hastings House, 1975); Joseph E. Baudino and John M. Kittross, "Broadcasting's Oldest Station: An Examination of Four Claimants," *Journal of Broadcasting* 21 (1977): 61–83; John C. Baker, *Farm Broadcasting: The First Sixty Years* (Ames: Iowa State University Press, 1981); Louis Cantor, *Wheelin' on Beale: How WDIA–Memphis Became the Nation's First All-Black Radio Station and Created the Sound that Changed America* (New York: Pharos, 1992); Lynn Boyd Hinds, *Broadcasting the Local News: The Early Years of Pittsburgh's KDKA-TV* (University Park: Pennsylvania State University Press, 1995); Francis M. Nash, *Towers over Kentucky: A History of Radio and TV in the Bluegrass State* (Lexington, KY: Host Communications, 1995); Michele Hilmes, *Radio Voices: American Broadcasting, 1922–1952* (Minneapolis: University of Minnesota Press, 1997).

[13]Michael D. Murray and Donald G. Godfrey, eds., *Television in America: Local Station History from across the Nation* (Ames: Iowa State University Press, 1997).

today's historian category, as one might expect from graduate students dissertations and theses.

Although the three historian types discussed earlier certainly make useful contributions to local broadcasting history, methods used by today's historian are the primary focus of discussion here.

LOCAL BROADCASTING HISTORICAL RESEARCH METHODS

Several types of traces, as Kyvig and Marty call them, provide facts and evidence for the local broadcasting historian. The type most useful for a particular history depends, of course, on the historian's purpose for doing the history, the nature of available information, and on the audience or reader for whom the history is intended. However, information from all trace categories is essential in distilling, interpreting, and verifying, evidence used to get at how it was in the past.

Kyvig and Marty categorize traces into several overlapping categories adaptable to local broadcasting history research:[14]
- Written and transcribed traces
- Immaterial traces
- Material traces
- Representational traces
- Electronic traces

Written and Transcribed Traces

Traces in this category usually fall into primary and secondary sources and arguably provide the evidence that is most valuable to the local broadcasting historian. Examples of primary sources include letters, personal diaries, journals, manuscripts, business and financial records, and government documents such as license applications, legal papers, court records, and tax returns. Station principals and their professional representatives and employees usually produce these traces. Typical of secondary traces or sources are newspapers, books, magazines, newsletters, and other written materials usually produced by reporters and other outside observers of local broadcasting operations.

Primary traces give contemporary accounts of events in original words or form, and largely determine the validity of the ultimate product. Everything

---

[14] Kyvig and Marty, *Nearby History.*

else is secondary data. We distill primary data for facts and evidence to drive the story, and use secondary data as guides to find out the scheme of what happened. Unlike primary sources, secondary sources are already preselected. The historian selects from available primary sources to determine, for instance, which diaries, letters, journals, and meeting minutes, among other traces advance the history.

Primary traces sometimes are unexpected. For example, the author found station payroll and employee records dating back decades in an abandoned AM transmitter building, near where the mythical painter of urban legends had decades before been electrocuted when he urinated from high on a radio tower. Usually, however, primary documents are found in established archives.

Original documents from the beginnings of wireless and broadcasting to contemporary times are available from several private and public sources; the most complete is the National Archives. The National Archives houses documents covering the regulated activities of all U.S. broadcasting stations. In addition, people in unique positions to relate what was known and believed at the time the documents were produced usually prepared such documents.

Amateur and commercial radio license documents are available in the National Archives from as early as 1912 and before, and documents from the 1920s, 1930s, and 1940s provide especially rich radio broadcasting records. For example, in the 1930s, after lower-power radio station applications were encouraged, the FCC took a direct interest in competing applications and required applicants to answer probing questions under oath in either in-person interviews or depositions. Thus, most station application files from the 1930s and early 1940s provide personal information about every competing applicant for a frequency, not just the successful one. The documents expose the applicants' feelings, reasons for applying, financial records, programming plans, thinking abilities, and character, in most cases. The original documents and the interview transcripts and depositions give the local broadcasting historian primary documents with which to validate other source data.

In the initial stages of research, the author copied important primary documents and brought them from the National Archives to Utah. In order not to "stretch" the data, it was advisable to bring the archives to Utah so the documents could be studied at length, to see who signed them, understand what equipment was being licensed, who was asking questions or being questioned, and how carefully documents were prepared. In addition, an artifact of locally available archives is that they attract graduate students and other researchers interested in researching local broadcasting history.

Over a three-year period, in five trips to the National Archives located in Suitland, Maryland at the Federal Records Center and later at the new National Archives on the perimeter of the University of Maryland campus in College Park, the primary Utah broadcasting records were copied and brought back to the state. Among other documents, these included the original license applications for every radio and television station in Utah. Of particular interest were the very early radio broadcasting license applications dating back to 1922.

As an aside, in a visit to the new National Archives just after it opened in College Park, it was found that the FCC documents recently transferred from Suitland had not been completely processed, the accession numbers were different for those before the transfer, and no public index was yet available. It likely is not allowed today, but the National Archives staff allowed the author unsupervised access to the stacks to retrieve needed FCC documents. It was daunting to go into a cavernous room, with electronically equipped movable shelves situated in rows that parted and compressed to maximize storage space. The author imagined being entombed in the stacks, never to be found, if somebody electronically moved the shelves in search of documents in another row.

No matter the source, the local broadcasting historian must know the analytics of the libraries and archives that house his or her documents. The historian needs to know the accession system at the National Archives and other archives and have a very good idea of what is available in each. For instance, normally, the researcher has no direct access and must depend on runners employed by the National Archives to retrieve documents that may take hours to obtain after they are requested. If a mistake is made, a whole day can be wasted. In addition, access to some documents requires permission from the governmental agency that deposited the documents.

Oral history transcripts also fit the broad written traces category, but their designation as either primary or secondary depends on how close to the event the interviewee was and how long after the event the interview took place. Oral interviews of people who were close to the event in time and space, and who are competent and can describe the event and their involvement, are primary sources. For instance, former local broadcasting players and eyewitnesses are more likely to be primary sources than are their relatives or surviving acquaintances. Oral histories, especially those from primary sources, are essential to a local broadcasting history. Usually, oral history interviewees represent willing participants in local broadcasting history because they often are at an advanced age and are receptive to sharing their lifetime of stories and treasures.

Written traces, among other uses, help collaborate or sort out exaggerated or incorrect claims such as those sometimes made in oral history interviews. For example, oral interviews often bring out fond and faulty memories, especially as regards answering "firsts" questions in local broadcasting. Which radio station was "first" on the air? Who did the "first" man-on-the-street broadcast? Who was the "first" woman announcer?

Beware of the temptation for people in oral history interviews, and in other traces for that matter, to:

- see themselves as more important than they were,
- place themselves closer to the center of action than they were,
- protect a friend or family member in their recollections,
- carry a grudge or have a reason to exaggerate or discredit the accomplishments of others, and/or
- be unable to sort out fact from legend or fiction.

Immaterial Traces

No negative connotations are associated with the *immaterial* label. These traces include institutions, organizations, customs, traditions, beliefs, principles, and practices of the broadcasting trade. The local broadcasting historian must rationally distill immaterial traces that normally are perceptually and emotionally sensed.

Immaterial traces are helpful in providing explanations for early radio station operations, policies, and programming practices, and in reading organizational cultures. Questions that immaterial traces inform might include: Who started the stations? Who owned the stations? Did ownership make a difference in station operations? Did ownership play a part in shaping the organizational culture? Did ownership affect programming?

For example, except for a couple of years since 1922, the Church of Jesus Christ of Latter-day Saints (LDS) has owned Salt Lake's KSL radio. Station operations and programming have reflected the conservative beliefs, customs, traditions, principles, and practices of its owner, whose worldwide headquarters were and are within walking distance of the KSL studios. In the early decades, the owner monitored local programming using LDS standards, and most employees in the early decades were LDS and did not work on Sundays except to air the Mormon Tabernacle Choir. With its hierarchical structure and strict oversight, LDS ownership has affected KSL programming and shaped its organizational culture throughout its history.

Similarly, in early decades, ownership of Salt Lake's KDYL radio affected its operations and culture. It was owned by a savvy promoter whose Jewish believes did not brand the station. He cared little about radio station daily operations, but hired highly qualified people for strategic positions and gave many young people their start in the business in other positions. He became a radio legend in his own time, and in present day, stories still abound concerning his inspired promotional efforts and quirky personal habits. Clearly, immaterial traces answer many important research questions and are vitally important in understanding more fully how it was at local stations as they evolved.

Material Traces

Included here are artifacts, objects, signage, and products of human doing such as buildings, studios, tower and transmitter sites, landscapes, equipment, and other things one can touch or readily see and which may still be in use. Traces in this category are the most easily grasped, not to mention the most fun to explore, and are the tools of the trade or the places where a series of broadcasting activities took place, culminating in the production of the broadcasting product.

There are numerous research questions material traces can help answer. Where were radio station transmitters and towers originally located and why? What brands of equipment were used? How long did stations stay in their original locations, and if relocated, where did they go and why? How was studio space used? Where did the people who originally owned or worked in local broadcasting live? Who were the contractors and workers who constructed the buildings and raised the towers? What expertise did they have?

Sometimes answers to the *why* questions are apparent. For example, wet, sandy, salty soil suited AM's propagation requirements. Likewise, FM and TV transmitters were located in high places, on buildings, on hills, mountains and tall towers, to satisfy the unique line-of-sight propagation requirements of those broadcasting services.

Material traces also help answer less apparent *why* questions. For instance, one of the questions in Salt Lake City was why some television stations relocated their studios in buildings on the same street? Visits to the buildings long after the television stations had moved to other locations revealed that the television studios were put in buildings that had previously housed car dealer-ships. Buildings with unobstructed space, large overhead doors, and heavy-duty elevators well served the needs of the television stations whose major advertisers included car and heavy appliance dealers, and whose early local, live programming required audience space for kid shows and wrestling match-es, among other things.

Other material traces can help the local broadcasting historian tie station activities to wider happenings. For instance, an old promotional sign at radio station KMON in Great Falls proclaimed that KMON was "Color Radio" with "Now Music." This simple 1960s sign signaled an era in which radio was threatened by television. This sign was the only surviving evidence found of this major struggle at KMON. That one piece of evidence gives credence and perspective to why format and ownership changes took place at the station. The sign, although only a material trace, also helped the local broadcasting historian develop the station's time line.

Visiting sites and buildings after the original studios or towers are long gone often provides clues to what was known and believed at the time. For instance, in the 1930s, one Salt Lake radio station was built on land adjacent to what became a uranium tailings dump site. When it came time to build other broadcasting facilities on the same site, construction was not allowed due to health and safety concerns, although the AM radio station remained on the site for decades until chemical seepage from the chemical dump rotted the concrete and metal tower footings. Questioning people who worked at the sta-tion when it was located near the dump site long after it was deemed unsafe could reveal some strong opinions about station management and owners.

Sometimes visiting facilities still in use also provides unexpected and useful information. For example, in 2004, KCBS-TV in Los Angeles completed a new complex miles away from its existing studios. Even though the existing station had been vastly remodeled from its days as the Columbia Square radio headquarters of the Columbia Broadcasting System, a local broadcasting his-torian, Craig Wirth, who contributed to this chapter found evidence of the past. For instance, there was a balcony above an old wooden studio floor. With the knowledge that Columbia Square had been the home of the Jack Benny Radio Program, the historian deducted that CBS placed the audience in the balcony above the floor, and above the actor's microphones, so audience sneezes and coughs would not be heard. The historian also saw a double win-dow between what in present day was the news director's office and the news-room. When installed, the window was slanted so the actors' voices or the band music did not cause microphone feedback. Windows in newly constructed studios are not slanted because microphones are technically more sophisticated and discriminating, obviating the need for slanted glass. The opportunity to make such observations in the old studio was lost when KCBS moved to its new location.

Another example of a material trace visit included a drive up the road to one of Utah's mountaintop television transmitter sites with the engineer who 30 years before had constructed the road and the facility. The engineer had not been on the road for 20 years. On the way up, he showed a series of photographs taken during actual construction. The road by law could not exceed a six-percent grade, so it thus wound up the mountain for five miles to the transmitter site. The author experienced this precarious 45-minute drive only one time, but came to appreciate what some station engineers endured for decades getting to their mountaintop jobs.

At the transmitter building, the old-time engineer was delighted to see that the original transmitter he installed 30 years before was still in back-up operation. This prompted a story about the blowout problems he had with the large, water-cooled, transmitter tubes when they were first installed. The problem, he said, was solved when he discovered that the tubes needed to be filled with distilled rather than tap water to prevent their burning up.

At a station in Southern Utah, a radio announcer related how in the 1950s he provided news coverage from an airplane, of atomic bomb tests taking place just west of his station in Nevada. He had pictures of the distant mushroom clouds he took from the airplane. Thirty years later, like so many of his fellow downwinders in Southern Utah, he had thyroid cancer linked to exposure to the nuclear blasts. This prompted questions about working conditions and about what information the radio and television stations in Utah and elsewhere reported to listeners and viewers at the time of the nuclear blast.

There is a remarkable example of material traces producing helpful and unexpected primary data. In the mid-1980s, important documents were discovered at the boyhood home of a prominent early Utah broadcaster. As a ten-year-old radio amateur in the 1920s, he tuned-in distant amateur radio stations and then confirmed that he had done so with the stations. Sixty years after he pinned 100 D-Xing cards on the wall of his parents' garage in which he operated his amateur station, they were retrieved, fragile but clearly readable. His family had moved from the house decades before, and subsequent owners had left the D-Xing cards in place behind some boards and lawn equipment.

Material traces, though not essential in writing the history of a station, may help explain why things were done the way they were, and how problems now considered routine or nonexistent were not routinely solved in early television days. Questions about the environment, studio and transmitter construction, signage, the working conditions for station employees, distant signal reception, and amateur activities, among other things, can be richly informed using material traces. Discovering this information helps the local historian know more about how it was for people in their times and better prepares him or her to tell a valid local broadcasting history story by following and interpreting the evidence.

Representational Traces

The best examples of representational traces are photographs and other visual traces (such as films and video recordings). In addition, orally transmitted legends, music, and other audio materials are representational traces of the past. These are things perceived with the senses, but often they also are capable of being written down or recorded on electrical transcriptions (ETs), records, tapes, discs, CDs, and other storage devices. Photographs, ETs, scripts, and audio and video tapes symbolically reveal the past when meticulously examined. For example, photographs of early studios, transmitter sites, and people at work show the facilities and working environment of early broadcasters. Other photographs show formal meetings and informal gatherings, indicating who may have worked or socialized together. Electrical transcriptions (ETs) from early radio and kinescopes from early television also are immensely helpful representational traces in analyzing and evaluating early programming.

Representational traces are things in themselves, but they are also symbols of something else and can answer important questions for the discerning local broadcasting historian. Family and business scrapbooks are valuable sources for representational traces about local broadcasting. In Utah, local individuals, families, or institutions owned early Utah broadcasting, as they likely did in most other states. More often than not, children and grandchildren followed their parents and grandparents into the business, and the early radio pioneers became television and cable pioneers. Family collections are not to be ignored as a rich source of representational traces. For example, one roll of film from a very early news show at a Salt Lake TV station was saved only because the penny-pinching, TV photographer took a picture of his dog and mother at the end of the reel and thus by chance kept the attached program.

Representational traces often result from the investigation of material traces, as was the case when the engineer and announcer discussed above gave the original blueprints and photographs of the mountaintop transmitter site and pictures taken from an airplane of the mushroom cloud to the author to archive.

Electronic Traces

This type overlaps with all of the above and refers to electronic traces interactively captured or discovered using computers and the Internet. Email, chat rooms, teleconferencing, the World Wide Web, search engines, personal and organizational web sites, and virtual reality all provide electronic traces. Primary and secondary data, photographs, documents, video and audio recordings, live conferences, and virtual tours are all available electronically. Use caution, however, when using electronic traces because there are no universally accepted standards for posting local broadcasting and other historical information on the Internet, and the qualifications of persons or organizations posting information are difficult to evaluate.

VALIDATION

Information obtained through the traces needs to be validated using other sources, preferably primary sources. If one can't validate information using primary data, it is possible triangulate it using the several categories and attached questions listed that follow.

For example, the validation process below was used to validate information about a popular pioneer Utah station owner, Sid Fox, who was never without a good cigar in one hand and a woman in the other as he gambled away a fortune in Las Vegas. Each survivor from Fox's time adds to the legend about this man who in old age, virtually penniless, lived in a small hotel room paid for by his old broadcasting cronies. He dressed in his 1930's suits, hitched rides to Las Vegas to gamble away his Social Security check, and smoked big cigars. But a local broadcasting history needs more than legends and anecdotes, it needs evidence to tell a valid history. In the case of Sid Fox, professional validation was found in his FCC testimony in Washington, D.C., and in legal correspondence with his lawyer. One of Fox's grandchildren was located, and she filled in a valuable piece of her grandfather's personal story and family history and provided photographs that helped validate some important information.

LOCAL HISTORY CATEGORIES AND QUESTIONS

About the People

- Life story of growing up
- Got into broadcasting how and why?
- Broadcasting career details
- Colleagues, mentors or adversaries who affected his or her career
- Anecdotal information, the stuff of legends
- Any photographs, documents, tapes, equipment, and other memorabilia to share?
- Closely follow the conversation and the thread of evidence to generate more questions

Area Around the Station

- Was the station located downtown?
- Why did the station locate where it did?
- What other businesses were in the neighborhood of the station?
- What was the general economic condition or cultural make-up of surrounding businesses?
- Were there restaurants or other "hang outs" for media people in the area?
- Did the station own the building in which it was housed?

Station History

- Who founded the station?
- What are the important events in the station history?
- What was the station's relationship with other stations in the market?
- How did the station either grow or decline?
- How did the station compare to other stations in the market in terms of audience size and demographics? In terms of financial success?

Employees

- What did the station organizational chart look like?
- Who were the key employees? Why were they key employees?
- How were employees recruited?

- How did managers treat employees? What did employees think of managers?
- Were there any gender considerations in the manner employees were hired or treated?
- Who terminated employees, why was it done, and did it make a difference in station operations?
- Did terminations provide some insight into station personalities?
- How were the "old" and "new" guard treated after a merger, sale, or expansion?

Family Connections

- Were employees related or connected to the managers or owners?
- Was advancement from within? Was it based on merit or family ties?
- What beliefs—political, religious, and cultural—did the owners and managers have and how did these shape policy or affect programming and operations?
- How long did employees tend to work for the station, and why did they leave?
- Where did employees go after leaving? Same market? Same medium?
- Did transfer of power take place in the family line? Was it successful?

Daily Operations

- What was the daily routine in conducting business?
- How were people trained or mentored?
- How were successes rewarded and failures dealt with?
- How did changing technology affect the station?
- How did the changing business climate—recession, inflation, depression, and mergers—affect the station?
- What were the station's attitudes—through programming or employment—toward various ethnic, racial, or religious groups in the community?
- What crisis situations did the station face, and how were they handled?

Education

- What educational level did employees obtain?
- What educational or training programs were provided by the station or encouraged among the employees?
- What schools did the employees attend?
- What happened to those who had either more or less education than others?
- What attitudes did the management have toward education in terms of those with less education versus those with more education?
- Did the station pay for employee education or encourage it?

Public Affairs

- To what extent were station employees involved in public or community affairs?
- Were there political, social, or religious reasons the station employees were or were not involved in community affairs?
- Were there specific projects or programs station employees participated in or not because of gender, religious, political, racial, or social considerations?
- Did the station benefit from its mission marketing?

Marketing

- How did the station promote itself?
- What was its target audience?
- How did the station position itself in the market?
- What brand identity did the station have?
- What slogans or marketing concepts did the station use?
- Who were the station's major advertisers?

Adapted from Kyvig and Marty, *Nearby History*, 20–39.

Of course, like a radio drama, characters and traces associated with Fox took researchers on journeys through the shadows to produce more documents or dusty boxes of memorabilia and personal belongings. For Sid Fox, there were income tax records spanning 30 years, 900 photos, an unfinished autobiography, some informative legal correspondence, eye glasses, an ashtray, and a double-breasted suit found, among other places, in the attic of a uniform store owned by a Fox friend. These articles were all that remained from Fox's 30-year broadcasting career when he died at age 92 in 1991. Each piece of evidence, however, helped to validate other data and reveal how it was and what was known and believed in Fox's time.

Traces are validated by asking questions of the information they provide. Obviously, not all categories or questions are useable in every local broadcasting history, but one or more of the categories and questions above should aid the validation process and serve as a template for oral history interviews and for the evaluation and verification of trace evidence.[15]

CONCLUSIONS

The challenge that the local broadcasting historian faces comes not from the past, but the present. Broadcasting is and was a business of the present and future, never of the past. As commercial radio reached its eighth decade and television reached its fifth decade, there were massive mergers and ownership changes. Few markets have local owners, nor even local managers as the station groups combine to achieve the economies of large-scale operations.

A local historian discovered from old station memos that the curious call letters from L.A.'s KHJ stood for "Kindness, Happiness, and Joy" from the days of the old Don Lee Network. As business records are destroyed and filing cabinets of what appear to be meaningless old correspondence are discarded, much is lost. More important, as broadcasting's neon signs end up in the dump and its oldtimers from stations all over the country retire during consolidation or die, the stories of "Kindness, Happiness, and Joy" disappear.

All local broadcasting activity leaves some recorded memory, and that memory will disappear without intervention by some preserving agent. It is essential that we as local broadcasting historians serve that purpose and establish archival partnerships or strategic alliances as we do local broadcasting histories. The archival partnerships, individually and collectively, will not only help local and state broadcasting historians determine what to collect and retain from the past, but they assure that the material will be preserved for its useful life and be made accessible to future users.[16]

---

[15] Material adapted from Kyvig and Marty, *Nearby History,* 20–39.

[16] The research methods discussed in this chapter were used to produce two Utah television history documentaries, both available from the author at tim.larson@utah.edu.

13

Exploring Biography

Dale Cressman
Brigham Young University

D ouglass Daniel began work on a biography of the late Harry Reasoner by searching for primary documents. He quickly learned that the late television-news anchorman's papers had already been placed at the Center for American History at the University of Texas. Nevertheless, Daniel was not shy about asking Reasoner's friends and relatives if they had any additional correspondence related to his subject. Daniel's queries paid off when one of Reasoner's daughters asked if he would be interested in seeing some letters that her father had written while he was in the army. *Some* letters turned out to be nearly 300, Daniel remembered. The letters were still in envelopes and even in chronological order. The letters provided Daniel with a sense of Reasoner's voice and outlook as a 19-year-old draftee contemplating a trip to the battlefields of Europe. The serendipitous find encouraged Daniel to ask other sources for materials, leading him to acquire such things as high-school commencement programs, even a letter Reasoner's ex-wife had written about the couple's failed marriage. The materials provided valuable insight into Reasoner, enabling Daniel to evoke the late broadcaster's personality and character in a way that the already archived materials could not.[1]

The purpose of this chapter is to define biography, its historical context, and provide the researcher with the basic procedures common to biographical and historical research in general—the selection of the subject, the gathering of evidence, and, finally, the construction of a biographical narrative.

---

[1] Douglass K. Daniel, correspondence with author, 26 March 2004.

DEFINING BIOGRAPHY

The very essence of biography, to bring history's people back to life, has not changed through the centuries, even though the methods have changed. Ancients hoped to remain immortal by going into the hereafter with their life stories carved in stone, while medievals put to parchment the stories of the church's saints and traveling minstrels sang the praises of their kings. Despite a preoccupation with man's inability to control his fate and an Aristotelian belief in modesty as virtue, the Greeks made notable contributions to biography: Isocrates is believed to have produced the first autobiography when he wrote a thinly veiled fictional account of an elderly rhetorician who is forced to defend himself in a legal dispute;[2] Plutarch provided an early definition that distinguished biography from history. According to the Greek philosopher, biography is meant to examine humans as individuals, while history examines their deeds.[3] Nevertheless, biography did not develop into a fully developed and distinct form of literature until the eighteenth century, when writers extended their scope beyond monarchs and saints. The word "biography," which draws from the Greek roots *bios* (life) and *graphein* (to write) did not even appear until at least 1660.[4]

Even as biographers began to put a greater emphasis on accuracy, novels and the theater influenced their writing, injecting a sense of drama and artistic detail. Rather than a raw recitation of facts, the great English biographer James Boswell aimed for a "higher truth."[5] His biography of Samuel Johnson, published in 1791, was considered the greatest biography of its time and it has since earned Boswell the reputation of a "Shakespeare of biographers."[6] Subsequent biographies either suffered in comparison to Boswell's work, or were

---

[2] Isocrates, *Antidosis I,* trans. David Mirhady and Yun Lee Too (Austin: University of Texas Press, 2000), 201–64; John A. Garraty, *The Nature of Biography* (New York: Knopf, 1957), 38.

[3] Alexander Plutarch, *Greek Lives,* trans. Robin Waterfield (Oxford: Oxford University Press, 1998), 312; Catherine N. Parke, *Biography: Writing Lives* (New York: Twayne, 1996), 6.

[4] Parke, *Biography,* 1; Garraty, *Nature of Biography,* 70.

[5] James Boswell, *The Life of Samuel Johnson,* vol. 1, ed. Roger Ingpen (Bath, England: Bayntun Press, 1925), 1–5; Garraty, *Nature of Biography,* 95.

[6] Adam Sisman, *Boswell's Presumptuous Task: The Making of the Life of Dr. Johnson* (New York: Farrar, Straus, and Giroux, 2001), xv.

largely forgettable all on their own. Self-censorship and hagiography were the order of the day during the Victorian era. Biographies served to "inculcate morality and patriotism," noted historian Scott Casper.[7] Not only did the biographies of the time make for bad literature, according to Casper, but also bad history. For example, the first notable American biography, Mason Locke Weems's 1800 account of George Washington was later judged as "a mixture of fairy stories and outrageous panegyric."[8] Sixty-four years later, James Parton's book continued in the tradition of the Romantic interpretation of history, in which historians favored elite editors and conservative values.[9] Parton, who has been called the father of American biography, heaped praise on Benjamin Franklin, while criticizing Franklin's brother, James, for challenging the status quo.[10]

By the beginning of the twentieth century, Victorian restraint and the Romantic interpretation gave way to scientific objectivity, leading writers to search for larger historical truths. Such inductive reasoning tended to result in the depersonalizing of biography, robbing it of human warmth. The determinism of Hegel, Darwin, and Marx further diminished biography's relevance: After all, if humans had little control over their environment, there was little need to study the lives of individuals. Sigmund Freud, for example, drew from psychology to explain the personality of Leonardo DaVinci. While many biographers dismissed Freud's influence as psychobiography, Freud blunted the influence of determinism by claiming that not all humans react to external stimuli in the same manner. By drawing from Freud, and striving to "lay bare the facts," writers such as Lytton Strachey helped advance biography beyond the weaknesses of the Victorian Era.[11] Nevertheless, science's intrusion into biography produced a backlash in the artistic literary community, as some

---

[7] Scott E. Casper, *Constructing American Lives: Biography and Culture in Nineteenth-century America* (Chapel Hill: University of North Carolina Press, 1999), 10.

[8] Garraty, *Nature of Biography*, 100.

[9] James Parton, *Life and Times of Benjamin Franklin* (New York: Mason Brothers, 1864).

[10] James D. Startt and William David Sloan, *Historical Methods in Mass Communication* (Hillsdale, NJ: Lawrence Erlbaum Associates, 1989), 24.

[11] Lytton Strachey, *Eminent Victorians* (New York: Harcourt, Brace & World, 1969), ix; Parke, *Biography*, 27; Michael Holroyd, *Lytton Strachey: A Biography* (New York: Penguin Books, 1971), 609; Thomas Elliott Berry, ed. *The Biographer's Craft* (New York: Odyssey Press, 1967), 90.

writers rejected a heavy emphasis on facts. Novelist George Gissing believed that genuine biography was only novels.[12] Rather than confine oneself to available facts, preserved by a "capricious fate" and subjectively chosen, Lewis Mumford encouraged writers to "fill in the gaps out of his imagination," to "restore the missing nose in plaster, even if he does not find the original marble."[13]

An increased reliance on fiction was an untenable position for academic historians, who clearly valued the integrity of traditional scholarship. Thus, in the 1940s, a new approach emerged, which Catherine Drinker Bowen called the "narrative" method. Bowen's book typified the narrative biography in that historical facts were built into a dramatic plot.[14] Thus, the values of traditional scholarship were combined with the artistic writing techniques popular with writers and readers in the 1920s and 1930s. As such, biography was thought to be a "noble and adventurous art"[15] and the "most delicate and humane of all the branches of the art of writing."[16] This model remains popular for much of biography, a "strange coupling between old-fashioned history and the traditional novel," writes biographer Michael Holroyd, "though many suspect the real father to have been journalism."[17]

Indeed, journalism's influence on biography could be clearly seen in the 1970s, as journalists such Robert A. Caro, David Halberstam, Bob Woodward, and Carl Bernstein combined their investigative reporting techniques with biography's narrative literary style to produce best selling books. Woodward and Bernstein helped dethrone a president and then wrote about his

---

[12] Michael Holroyd, *Works on Paper: The Craft of Biography and Autobiography* (Washington, DC: Counterpoint, 2002), 20; Carol Shields, *Jane Austen* (New York: Viking, 2001), 10.

[13] Lewis Mumford, "The Task of Modern Biography," *English Journal* 23 (1934): 1–9; Garraty, *Nature of Biography,* 129.

[14] Catherine Drinker Bowen, *John Adams and the American Revolution* (Boston, MA: Little, Brown, 1950); Garraty, *Nature of Biography,* 145.

[15] Leon Edel, "The Figure under the Carpet," in *Biography as High Adventure: Life Writers Speak on Their Art,* ed. Stephen B. Oates (Amherst: University of Massachusetts Press, 1986), 20.

[16] Strachey, *Eminent Victorians,* viii.

[17] Holroyd, *Works on Paper,* 20.

demise.[18] Woodward continues to write instant histories in the biographical narrative style, which has, in turn, influenced journalism itself to a degree. Halberstam discredited government officials that allowed the country to become mired in the Vietnam War, sarcastically titling his book *The Best and the Brightest.*[19] For his part, Caro focused his investigative skills on Robert Moses, the long-time urban planner of New York City,[20] and then spent more than a quarter century researching and writing three large volumes on Lyndon Johnson. His accounts of Moses and Johnson were condemned as being overly critical, but earned the writer two Pulitzer Prizes—most recently in his third volume on Lyndon Johnson.[21] Meanwhile, Robert Dallek, an academic, has written a largely sympathetic two-volume biography of Johnson that some observers believe was written to offset the critical nature of Caro's biography of the former president.[22]

At the end of the twentieth century, one prominent and controversial work challenged journalism's influence on biography. Edmund Morris, author of a biography on Theodore Roosevelt, had been chosen to be an authorized biographer of Ronald Reagan. Morris's stated hope to "make literature out of Ronald Reagan"[23] along with his bafflement with the former president's complex personality, led the author to take the certain creative liberties: Feeling that his years of research had made him feel as though he knew Reagan as a young man, Morris placed himself inside the narrative as a fictitious character. Even while endorsing the biographical imagination,

---

[18] Bob Woodward and Carl Bernstein, *The Final Days* (New York: Simon & Schuster, 1976).

[19] David Halberstam, *The Best and the Brightest* (Greenwich, CT: Fawcett Publications, 1973).

[20] Robert A. Caro, *The Power Broker: Robert Moses and the Fall of New York* (New York: Vintage Books, 1975).

[21] Robert A. Caro, *The Years of Lyndon Johnson: Master of the Senate,* vol. 3 (New York: Alfred A. Knopf, 2002). See also Caro's earlier two volumes on Johnson: *The Years of Lyndon Johnson: The Path to Power,* vol. 1 (1982) and *The Years of Lyndon Johnson: Means of Ascent,* vol. 2 (1990).

[22] Robert Dallek, *Lone Star Rising: Lyndon Johnson and His Times 1908–1960* (New York: Oxford University Press, 1991) and *Flawed Giant: Lyndon B. Johnson, 1960–1973* (New York: Oxford University Press, 1998).

[23] Edmund Morris, *Dutch: A Memoir of Ronald Reagan* (New York: Modern Library, 1999), v–vi.

most academics charged that Morris's method would erode the credibility of biography.

Thus remains the tension within biography between artistic, academic, and journalistic approaches. While echoing the sentiment that twentieth-century biographers are "profitably picnicking 'round the tombstones of the newly dead, sucking the bones clean and flinging them over their shoulders,'" Holroyd characterizes biographers as being "simply jumped-up journalists" who are neither "proper writers" nor legitimate descendants of Boswell; "the ambitious professor" with "one foot in a university, the other ... on television; or literary or artistic biographers who are thought of by their fellow novelists and poets as 'parasites.'"[24]

Neither is biography viewed highly by traditional journalism history scholars. In a groundbreaking essay that stressed the need for researchers to adopt a cultural approach to journalism history, James Carey complained that the discipline was "needlessly preoccupied with the production of biographies of editors and publishers."[25] Similarly, David Paul Nord argued that the history of journalism and mass communication should focus on organizational and cultural aspects, rather than on individuals.[26] Carey and Nord are historians; mass communication researchers, who largely tend to gravitate toward disciplines such as sociology and psychology, are even less sympathetic to biography.[27] One need only browse the past quarter century's editions of *Journalism and Mass Communication Quarterly* or the *Journal of Broadcasting & Electronic Media* to arrive at the conclusion that communication research is dominated by the social sciences. Indeed, Nord argued that historians "not leave social sciences to the social scientists."[28] In response to such criticisms, historians have

---

[24] Holroyd, *Works on Paper,* 4–6.

[25] James W. Carey, "The Problem of Journalism History," in *James Carey: A Critical Reader,* eds. Eve Stryker Munson and Catherine A. Warren (Minneapolis: University of Minnesota Press, 1997), 87.

[26] David Paul Nord, "Intellectual History, Social History, Cultural History, and Our History," *Journalism Quarterly* 67, no. 4 (1990): 647.

[27] Guido H. Stempel III and Bruce H. Westley, "The Systematic Study of Mass Communication," in *Mass Communication Research and Theory,* eds. Guido H. Stempel III, David H. Weaver, and G. Cleveland Wilhoit (Boston, MA: Allyn & Bacon, 2003), 2.

[28] David Paul Nord, "The Nature of Historical Research," in *Research Methods in Mass Communication,* eds. Guido H. Stempel III and Bruce H. Westley (Englewood Cliffs, NJ: Prentice-Hall, 1989), 314.

in recent decades discovered ways in which social science theory and method-ology can enrich the biographic tradition, particularly in the areas of compara-tive and economic histories (see chapter 7, "Quantitative Methods").[29] Methodologies once seen as an either–or proposition are today seen as com-plementary. While remaining rooted in the humanistic tradition, biographers are increasingly borrowing from social scientific methodology.

Regardless of orientation, however, most historians follow a standard research regimen designed for, as Donald Godfrey puts it, "the discovery of supportable truths."[30] William David Sloan and James Startt proscribe the his-torical research process as follows: An immersion in available literature to gain an understand of what others have written about the subject under consider-ation; the location of all available sources applicable to the inquiry, to include such sources as family documents, archives, museums, databases, and other repositories of information; the extrapolation and evaluation of primary source evidence; and finally, the construction of a narrative in which evidence is placed into historical context, answer questions related to "causation, gener-alization, interpretation, and the establishing of significance."[31]

SELECTING A SUBJECT

The first and most important—not to mention the most obvious—step is selecting a subject. Foremost among the considerations should be whether the person is worth writing about. This is not to say that the person necessarily needs to be prominent; in recent decades academics have tried to steer away from the "Great Man" biographies that have been so prevalent since ancient times. In fact, it is fair to say that the unknown also have important stories. People love to read about the experiences of others—be they celebrities, men-tors, industry leaders, or simply their families. Furthermore, biographies pro-vide readers with a picture of what it was like to live in a specific period of time. Nevertheless, it would be reasonable to consider whether the person under consideration has had substantial experiences and a story that is inter-esting enough to justify the research. An even stronger justification can be

---

[29] Ibid, 300.

[30] Donald G. Godfrey, "Broadcast Archives for Historical Research: Revisiting the Historical Method," *Journal of Broadcasting & Electronic Media* 46, no. 3 (2002): 493.

[31] William David Sloan and James D. Startt, eds., *The Media in America: A History*, 4th ed. (Northport, AL: Vision Press, 1999), xiii–xiv.

found if a study of the subject under consideration would shed light on important issues of the day.

Perhaps the most important consideration in this regard is whether the author is interested in writing about a particular individual. As in other types of history, researching and writing is time consuming—in most cases authors spend years working on a biography. For the late Stephen E. Ambrose, writing a biography on Richard Nixon was "an exhausting process."

> More often than not I'd get no exercise in the course of a day—and there were altogether 2,920 days I devoted to the project. I spent probably a sixth of them, or about 500 days, writing, an average of five pages per day. The other days I was reading memoirs, documents, newspaper articles, all the material that goes into a big book. Sometimes—it can't be as long as it seems in retrospect—I was just sitting, thinking about who had done what, or said what, or why.[32]

Clearly, a deep interest—if not a long attention span—is required of the biographer.

Writers should also know what has already been written about the individual under consideration. For historical figures in broadcasting like Edward R. Murrow, there is plenty to be found. Ann M. Sperber published a massive volume on Murrow in 1986.[33] More recently, Bob Edwards wrote a slim volume.[34] Murrow also is mentioned in many other biographies, autobiographies, and general histories of broadcasting. By contrast, a lesser-known figure that went largely unnoticed for many years is Philo T. Farnsworth, one of the inventors of television. Several books have come forth recently on Farnsworth, beginning with a scholarly study by Godfrey.[35] Similarly, David Weinstein has profiled Allen Du Mont, the largely forgotten founder of the Du Mont

---

[32] Stephen E. Ambrose, *To America: Personal Reflections of an Historian* (New York: Simon and Schuster, 2002), 185.

[33] Ann M. Sperber, *Murrow: His Life and Times* (New York: Freundlich Books, 1986).

[34] Bob Edwards, *Edward R. Murrow and the Birth of Broadcast Journalism* (Hoboken, NJ: Wiley, 2004).

[35] Donald G. Godfrey, *Philo T. Farnsworth: The Father of Television* (Salt Lake City: University of Utah Press, 2001); Evan I. Schwartz, *The Last Lone Inventor: A Tale of Genius, Deceit and the Birth of Television* (New York: HarperCollins, 2002).

television network.[36] Examples of other broadcaster-related biographies include Reginald Fessenden, Lee DeForest, Vladimir Zworykin, and David Sarnoff.[37] In addition, there are numerous historical studies that contain biographical information on multiple figures. For example, Stanley Cloud and Lynne Olson profile Murrow and the broadcasters he hired during the Second World War. Cloud and Olson also profile an often-ignored member of the "Murrow Boys," Mary Marvin Breckinridge.[38]

Other notable examples include Tom Lewis, Jeff Alan, Irving E. Fang, and Erik Barnouw. Most of the literature focuses on White men, a group Catherine Parke terms "majority biography."[39] Meanwhile, what Parke describes as "minority biography"—works profiling women and minorities—are given only sparing attention, appearing mostly in encyclopedic works.[40] For example, Mal Goode, the first Black reporter on network television news, is profiled in Murray and in history books, but not in a book-length biography.[41]

---

[36] David Weinstein, *The Forgotten Network: Du Mont and the Birth of American Television* (Philadelphia, PA: Temple University Press, 2004).

[37] Ormond Raby, *Radio's First Voice: The Story of Reginald Fessenden* (Toronto: Canadian Communications Association, 1970); James A. Hijiya, *Lee de Forest and the Fatherhood of Radio* (Bethlehem, PA: Lehigh University Press, 1992); Albert H. Abramson, *Zworykin: Pioneer of Television* (Urbana: University of Illinois Press, 1995); Kenneth Bilby, *The General: David Sarnoff and the Rise of the Communications Industry* (New York: Harper & Row, 1986).

[38] Stanley Cloud and Lynne Olson, *The Murrow Boys: Pioneers on the Front Lines of Broadcast Journalism* (Boston, MA: Houghton Mifflin, 1996).

[39] Tom Lewis, *Empire of the Air: The Men Who Made Radio* (New York: HarperCollins, 1991); Jeff Alan, *Anchoring America: The Changing Face of Network News* (Chicago: Bonus Books, 2003); Irving E. Fang, *Those Radio Commentators* (Ames: Iowa State University Press, 1977); Erik Barnouw, *Media Marathon: A Twentieth-Century Memoir* (Durham, NC: Duke University Press, 1996); Parke, *Biography,* xvii.

[40] Michael D. Murray, ed., *Encyclopedia of Television News* (Phoenix, AZ: Oryx Press, 1999); Les Brown, The New York Times *Encyclopedia of Television* (New York: Times Books, 1977); Joseph P. McKerns, ed., *Biographical Dictionary of American Journalism* (Westport, CT: Greenwood, 1989); Stanley L. Harrison, *Cavalcade of Journalists, 1900–2000: Chroniclers of an American Century* (Miami, FL: Wolf Den Books, 2002).

[41] Edward Bliss Jr., *Now the News: The Story of Broadcast Journalism* (New York: Columbia University Press, 1991).

Likewise, women were not hired in the early days of broadcasting because radio owners—nearly all men—presumed that listeners preferred masculine voices. Despite this, Mary Beadle and Michael Murray argue that women made valuable contributions to the development of American broadcasting.[42] Three other books among the few that celebrate the contribution of women broadcasters are by one by Marlene Sanders and Marcia Rock and two by Judith Marlane.[43]

If biographies have already been written, the research must decide if anything could be added that would make an intellectual contribution. As Asa Briggs wrote, a writer considering a biography should undergo an intensive period of immersion, reading and analyzing all existing literature.[44] By paying particular attention to the sources already used in the existing literature, a researcher can consider whether additional documentary evidence has become available to justify a new publication.

The matter of available evidence cannot be taken too lightly. Researchers must find out whether material exists in archives and whether that material is available for examination. What about documentary material that may potentially exist outside of archives? Occasionally, researchers make serendipitous finds by contacting a subject's descendants and inquiring whether the deceased had left letters, diaries, or other materials. Great consideration should be given to whether one should write about a subject who is still living. The benefit, of course, is the opportunity to interview the subject and ask for clarification when questions arise from documentary evidence. Clearly, this necessitates the subject to be willing to cooperate, which is not always the case (see chapter 3, "Oral History"). Often, subjects do not wish to cooperate with a biographer unless a certain level of comfort and trust has been attained. However, there are also some reasons to be cautious when selecting a living subject. For one thing, some authors find it difficult to be objective or to write about

---

[42] Mary E. Beadle and Michael D. Murray, eds., *Indelible Images: Women of Local Television* (Ames: Iowa State University Press, 2001), 11.

[43] Marlene Sanders and Marcia Rock, *Waiting for Prime Time: The Women of Television News* (Urbana: University of Illinois Press, 1994); Judith Marlane, *Women in Television News Revisited: Into the Twenty-first Century* (Austin: University of Texas Press, 1999); Judith Marlane, *Women in Television News* (New York: Columbia University Press, 1976).

[44] Asa A. Briggs, *Social History and Human Experience* (Cedar City, UT: Grace A. Tanner Center for Human Values, 1984), 8–10.

unpleasant matters if the subject is alive and cooperating with the research. Biographer James Veninga believes it is easier to write about historical figures who have been dead for many years because "You don't encounter problems with family, problems with lawsuits, problems with trying to get access to letters and archival materials."[45]

GATHERING EVIDENCE

Because primary documentary evidence is most valued in academic research, biographers seek out archives. To the uninitiated, this may seem to be an arduous task. However, many biographers find it to be an enjoyable experience. John Stacks, author of Scotty Reston's biography, describes archive work as "voyeuristic" because researchers are able to read memoranda not intended for publication. Such work seems "totally illicit, and a great amount of fun," according to Stacks.[46]

There are a number of archives that specialize in the materials of broadcasters. The Wisconsin State Historical Society in Madison, Wisconsin, maintains a large collection that includes papers of the National Broadcasting Company (NBC), as well as those of prominent figures such as David Brinkley, Charles Collingwood, and Howard K. Smith. Sig Mickelson is an example of a lesser-known figure whose papers are contained in the Wisconsin collection. However, because Mickelson was the first president of CBS News, the collection contains many items of interest to those researching other CBS News figures. Similarly, the Media History Archive at the Center for American History at the University of Texas at Austin holds an impressive collection of broadcaster-related documents. All of Walter Cronkite's documents are contained there, for example. The archive also has custody of the CBS Evening News archives. However, that collection is not available as of this writing. The University of Maryland's Archives include various collections, including the National Public Broadcaster's Association Archives. And the Fletcher School of Law and Diplomacy at Tufts University has a large collection of Edward R. Murrow's papers.

---

[45] James F. Veninga, ed., *The Biographer's Gift: Life Histories and Humanism* (College Station: Texas A&M University Press, 1983), 17.

[46] John Stacks, Remarks to the AJHA-AEJMC Spring meeting, March 13, 2004, New York City.

Writing in the area of broadcast history affords researchers the opportunity to view films and kinescopes, and listen to audiotapes. While such material must be used with caution,[47] they may also provide historical clues and texture. Examples of such archives include the News Film Library at the University of South Carolina, which contains a large portion of Fox Movietone newsreels, as well as the Museum of Television and Radio and the Museum of Broadcast Communications. Network television newscasts may also be obtained from the Vanderbilt Archives in Nashville. Some sources may be viewed online. For example, the Canadian Broadcasting Corporation and the British Broadcasting Corporation maintain Websites with historical broadcast material.

Before traveling to an archive, researchers typically want to find out what they can expect to find there. This information can be found in a document called a "finding aid." This document lists the archive's holdings, sometimes down to the contents of folders. Usually, archives will make finding aids available to researchers for a nominal cost. It is also advisable (and sometimes required) that researchers call an archive before visiting. Some archive collections will not yet be organized and, thus, not have a finding aid available. In such cases, Stacks advises researchers to examine everything available, to "go to the bottom of the box" in search of clues that may become useful at some point in the project.[48]

University, government, and corporate archives are not the only places to find documents. It was not uncommon for the Federal Bureau of Investigation (FBI) to keep files on many broadcasters and broadcast journalists during the twentieth century. Thus, authors should, as a matter of routine, file a request with the FBI, according to the guidelines of the Freedom of Information (FOI) Act. It takes considerable time for requests to be granted, and information is often redacted from documents, in accordance with privacy laws. However, such requests may result in finding useful documents that cannot be found elsewhere. Most government agencies have Websites that provide information on how to file FOI requests.

As important as archival material is, Douglass Daniel advises researchers to begin their research with human sources. Often, such sources are elderly and may not be available for long, whereas archival material will always be available. Daniel suggests that researchers begin their project by listing available

---

[47] Godfrey, "Broadcast Archives," 494–95.

[48] Stacks, Remarks.

human sources by age, then approaching the oldest people first. Human sources may provide documentary and oral evidence. Before asking sources for documents or interviews, Daniel first asks for their addresses so he can tell them more about his project. After sending potential sources a short, well-crafted letter that describes his project, Daniel requests an opportunity to interview them. In order to get sources to talk about difficult subjects, Daniel found it useful to first offer information he already had. For example, sources would only talk about Harry Reasoner's reputation, if Daniel mentioned it first. After conducting successful interviews with sources, Daniel then asks them for letters, photographs, or other pieces of physical evidence. Finally, Daniel suggests that unknown sources may be found if researchers are not shy about telling people about their project.[49]

Some historians distrust information gained through oral history interviews. However, oral history has gained credibility as a methodology since the emergence of the oral history research project at Columbia University in the late 1950s. As a methodology it has some clear advantages for biography, such as allowing the researcher to ask questions raised by other documents—questions that might not be answered if the source were dead.[50] Oral history also allows the subject of the biography to have a part in recreating history. Scholar Bonnie Brennan argues for oral history's emancipatory potential by allowing official history to be challenged by more realistic and fair reconstructions of history.[51]

Nevertheless, as with any type of evidence, there are concerns about the reliability and validity of oral history interviews. Some critics point to memory decay, often evidenced by a subject's account changing over time. Such decay would compromise a source's reliability.[52] However, research suggests that as much memory decay takes place over the first nine months after an event as over the next 40 years; furthermore, the elderly typically have sharper long-term than

---

[49] Douglass Daniel, Remarks to the AJHA-AEJMC Spring meeting, March 13, 2004, New York City.

[50] Alice Hoffman, "Reliability and Validity in Oral History," *Today's Speech* 22 (1974): 25.

[51] Bonnie Brennan, "Toward a History of Labor and News Work: The Use of Oral Sources in Journalism History," *The Journal of American History* 83, no. 2 (1996): 571–79.

[52] William L. Lang and Laurie K. Mercier, "Getting It Down Right: Oral History's Reliability in Local History Research," *Oral History Review* 12 (1984): 82–83.

short-term memories.[53] Even when a subject's memory is not perfect, researchers should refrain from discounting the interview's overall reliability; most people remember life's experiences by events rather than by time sequences and, as time increases between an experience and its recounting, people tend to condense the sequence of events and omit critical actions.[54]

Meanwhile, sources may have recollections which conflict with other primary sources, thus compromising the validity of the oral history document.[55] Many people intentionally give a version of history favorable to themselves—succumbing to a fond and faulty memory.[56] However, this may not necessarily impeach a source's validity, as oral historians not only seek historical facts, but also memory claims—information that conveys a sense of the past as it was actually lived and how it is remembered.[57]

Problems of reliability and validity are not peculiar to oral history. Historical research typically privileges the written archival documents, but it still places the same requirement on all sources. In other words, most documents are subject to the same potential problems with validity as oral history interviews. Diaries will often contain a biased view of history. Collections of documents can be manipulated by the very act of selecting which documents go into a collection and which do not. Even statistics, normally regarded as empirical facts, can be fraught with distortions. In fact, oral history interviews may instill more confidence than archival material—particularly if they are produced through a biographer's own field work—because the credibility of the source can be more accurately judged.[58]

Wherever possible, oral historians should verify an account of events with other primary sources, such as letters, newspaper accounts, or other interviewees. Furthermore, interviewers should be familiar with what interviewees have experienced since the event they are recounting, as those experiences can change an individual's perspective and color his or her recollection. Fatigue, interview settings, and the subject's willingness to submit to questions are also

---

[53] Paul Thompson, *The Voice of the Past: Oral History,* 3rd ed. (New York: Oxford University Press, 2000), 92.

[54] Ibid., 157; Lang and Mercier, "Getting It Down Right," 96–97.

[55] Hoffman, "Reliability and Validity," 25.

[56] Ibid., 27; Lang and Mercier, "Getting It Down Right," 83–85.

[57] Thompson, *Voice of the Past,* 162.

[58] Ibid., 119–24; James E. Fogerty, "Filling the Gap: Oral History in the Archives," *American Archivist* 46, no. 2 (1983): 148–47.

potential factors contributing to an interview's validity. Ultimately, a researcher must ensure, through critical evaluation, that oral history interviews, like other forms of evidence, are fundamentally honest accounts of the past.[59]

Another concern historians have had with conducting oral history interviews is that they have required, in recent years, to undergo a human subjects review protocol. However, in 2003, the Department of Health and Human Services, the American Historical Association, and the Oral History Association ruled that "oral history interviewing activities, in general, are not designed to contribute to generalizable knowledge and, therefore ... do not need to be reviewed by an institutional review board (IRB)."[60]

Another type of evidence that is closely related to interviewing human sources is for researchers to visit the places in which a subject lived and worked. In order to learn more about Lyndon Johnson, Robert Caro moved his family to the part of Texas where Johnson grew up. It was not to be a short visit: Caro lived there for three years in an effort to get the Texans of Hill Country to trust him and to get a feel for the influences on Johnson's life. By learning of the harsh living conditions residents there endured, he was able to learn something of Johnson's personality, as well as the relationship Johnson had with voters there.[61] Likewise, Edmund Morris had become so familiar with Ronald Reagan's early homes by frequent visits to Illinois that he found himself playing the role of tour guide to the 40th president of the United States.[62]

It was this familiarity that made it possible for Morris to know Reagan well enough that he could write himself into the biography as a fictitious character—an achievement, however ethically questionable the method.

---

[59] Jacques Barzun and Henry F. Graff, *The Modern Researcher,* 5th ed. (New York: Harcourt Brace Jovanovich, 1992), 96–133; Anthony Seldon and Joanna Pappworth, *By Word of Mouth: Elite Oral History* (London: Methuen, 1983), 80–84.

[60] American Historical Association, "Oral History Excluded from IRB Review," From the News column of the December 2003 *Perspectives,* http://www.historians .org/Perspectives/Issues/2003/0312/0312new5.cfm.

[61] Steve Weinberg, *Telling the Untold Story: How Investigative Reporters Are Changing the Craft of Biography* (Columbia: University of Missouri Press, 1992), 56; Random House, "About the Author: Robert A. Caro," http://www.randomhouse.com/ knopf/authors/caro/.

[62] Morris, *Dutch,* xxvii.

Although a popular pastime, genealogical research—the historical method used in the study of family history—is largely overlooked by biographers. As Asa Briggs, the eminent British historian and author, describes it, genealogy is a method "to obtain a knowledge of the English [people] … morality, fertility, marriage patterns and the reconstruction for the first time of the family life of our ancestors."[63] Genealogical research not only helps biographers place their subjects within a larger context of human existence, but will also yield valuable primary documentation. Birth certificates, for example, help establish birth dates, birthplaces, and parentage. In some cases, such information will merely document what is already known. However, there have been cases in which historical figures have lied about their age and background. Similarly, records related to marriage, divorce, and probate produce documents that might not be obtainable otherwise.

CONSTRUCTING THE NARRATIVE

Just as in other forms of historical writing, biography is written in narrative form[64] and, most authors agree, in chronological order. Chronology is important because it recreates for the reader the sense of a life being lived. To do otherwise runs the risk of confusing the reader and robbing the biography's subject of his or her humanity. According to Weinberg, Dwight D. Eisenhower's biographer Stephen Ambrose was inclined to organize his second volume on Eisenhower by subject, rather than by chronology. However, he ultimately decided that, although topically appropriate, it would have placed the primary subject, Eisenhower, as a secondary subject.[65] Adhering to a chronology means writers must resist the temptation to indulge in hindsight or in foreshadowing. As the eminent historian Barbara W. Tuchman put it, the story should be told "as if the outcome were still in the balance."[66] Typically, the two defining events of a life, and thus a biography, are the events of birth

---

[63] Briggs, *Social History and Human Experience,* 8–10.

[64] Startt and Sloan, *Historical Methods in Mass Communication,* 45, 160.

[65] See Steve Weinberg, *Telling the Untold Story,* 20; Stephen Ambrose, *Eisenhower: The President,* vol. 2 (New York: Simon and Schuster, 1985).

[66] Barbara W. Tuchman, "Biography as a Prism of History," in *Biography as High Adventure: Life Writers Speak on Their Art,* ed. Stephen B. Oates (Amherst: University of Massachusetts Press, 1986), 96.

and death.[67] This rule is ignored, of course, if the subject of the biography is still alive.

Although historians are expected to analyze evidence and provide interpretation, it is vital that biography be true to the life it portrays. As Paul Murray Kendall put it, biography is neither a dry recitation of cold facts nor a work of fiction: "The one fails truth; the other fails art. Between the two lies the impossible craft of true biography."[68] Biography that is true to a subject's life may require the author to "surrender" to the evidence. John Milton Cooper, Jr. said biographers also need "to retain the capacity for surprise and the willingness to follow our subjects down paths that we did not foresee or even down paths that take us in the opposite direction from the one in which we originally intended to go."[69]

In order to be "true to a life," biography must be proportional. Often, gaps will exist in the documentary evidence available to the researcher. For example, there may be an abundance of documents for a person's adult life, but a dearth of physical evidence for the period covering the subject's childhood. To ignore that time period for which there is little documentary evidence creates the possibility of biographical disproportion. Paul Murray Kendall insists that "biographic space-time ... approximate the weight of significance of the moment."[70] In other words, if that portion of a person's life for which there is little evidence is not significant, a lack of evidence may not present a problem. On the other hand, ignoring a significant portion of a subject's life because documents are not available would, according to Frederick B. Tolles, produce a "queer, even a grotesque portrait."[71] In such cases, biographers can use oral history or any other possible method to overcome the documentary shortage.

---

[67] André Maurois, "Biography as a Work of Art," in *Biography as High Adventure: Life Writers Speak on Their Art,* ed. Stephen B. Oates (Amherst: University of Massachusetts Press, 1986), 5.

[68] Paul Murray Kendall, "Walking the Boundaries," in *Biography as High Adventure: Life Writers Speak on Their Art,* ed. Stephen B. Oates (Amherst: University of Massachusetts Press, 1986), 40.

[69] John Milton Cooper Jr., "Conception, Conversation, and Comparison: My Experiences as a Biographer," in *Writing Biography: Historians and Their Craft,* ed. Lloyd E. Ambrosius (Lincoln: University of Nebraska Press, 2004), 87–88.

[70] Kendall, "Walking the Boundaries," 43.

[71] Frederick B. Tolles, "The Biographer's Craft," in *The Craft of American History: Selected Essays,* ed. A. S. Eisenstadt (New York: Harper & Row, 1954), 80.

If the challenge cannot be overcome, authors need to be honest with their readers about the existing gaps.

Being *true to a life* means researchers must use caution in their interpretations—particularly in succumbing to oversimplifying cause and effect implications. While the individual "makes history," John Garraty reminds us that "so does chance" and "so do social forces."[72]

Biographical subjects must also be placed in the context of the times in which they lived. As Leon Edel puts it, "No biography is complete unless it reveals the individual within history, within an ethos and a social complex."[73] In so doing, historians are afforded the opportunity to find commonalities between men and women at particular times, as well as those factors that differentiate them.[74] Without understanding the times in which an individual has lived it is impossible to truly know that individual, nor understand how that person thinks or why he or she reacted in a particular way. Conversely, by learning about an individual, readers can learn about society in other periods of time. In fact, historian Barbara Tuchman said she wrote biography "less for the sake of the individual subject than as a vehicle for exhibiting an age."[75] Because readers like to read about other people, biography is a popular way to tell history.

Perhaps the toughest balance a biographer must find is that between empathy and objectivity. Biographers may be empathetic toward their subject in order to understand the subject's point of view, yet they must not be blinded by hero worship. On one hand biographers play the role of participant; on the other, they assume that of the observer.[76] According to Paul Murray Kendall, the biographer "does not trust his witnesses, living or dead."

> He may drip with the milk of human kindness, believe everything that his wife and friends and his children tell him, enjoy his neighbors and embrace the universe—but in the worship he must be as ruthless as a board meeting smelling out embezzlement, as suspicious as a secret agent riding the Simplon-Orient Express, as cold-eyed as a pawnbroker viewing a leaky

---

[72] Garraty, *Nature of Biography,* 6.

[73] Leon Edel, *Writing Lives: Principia Biographica* (New York: Norton, 1984), 4.

[74] Holroyd, *Works on Paper,* 22.

[75] Tuchman, "Biography as a Prism of History," 93.

[76] Shirley A. Leckie, "Biography Matters": Why Historians Need Well-crafted Biographies More than Ever," in *Writing Biography: Historians and Their Craft,* ed. Lloyd E. Ambrosius (Lincoln: University of Nebraska Press, 2004), 8–9.

concertina. With no respect for human dignity, he plays off his witnesses one against the other, snoops for additional information to confront them with, probes their prejudices and their pride, checks their reliability against their self-interest, thinks the worst until he is permitted to think better.[77]

While relying upon facts—and the interpretation of those facts—a biographer relies upon his imagination in order to bring back to life what Leon Edel called "the figure under the carpet."[78] After working with the evidence, the biographer must be able to, in Frank Vandiver's words, "shape a person from the past—more than that, to evoke a person into being."[79]

In order to "evoke a person into being," it helps to allow the subjects of the biography to speak for themselves. "They were there," said Stephen Ambrose, "I wasn't. They saw with their own eyes, they put their own lives on the line. I didn't. They speak with an authenticity no one else can match."[80]

"Pure biography," according to Stephen B. Oates, brings "people alive again, eliciting from the coldness of fact the 'warmth of a life being lived,' as Paul Murray Kendal expressed it."[81]

John A. Garraty calls biography a "reconstruction of a human life"[82] in which it is neither possible nor desirable for the writer to be objective. Instead, its purpose is to evoke and to create the sense and warmth of "a life being lived."

The biographer does not need to love his subject, but should at least identify with him, according to Catherine Drinker Bowen.[83] Stephen B. Oates spent five years writing a biography of Martin Luther King.

> During that time, I came to know King so intimately that I spoke to him in my dreams ... in a strange and miraculous way, the very man I re-created

---

[77] Kendall, "Walking the Boundaries," 45.

[78] Edel, "Figure under the Carpet," 25.

[79] Frank E. Vandiver, "Biography as an Agent of Humanism," in *Biography as High Adventure: Life Writers Speak on Their Art,* ed. Stephen B. Oates (Amherst: University of Massachusetts Press, 1986), 51.

[80] Ambrose, *To America,* 196.

[81] Stephen B. Oates, ed., *Biography as High Adventure: Life Writers Speak on Their Art* (Amherst: University of Massachusetts Press, 1986), 124.

[82] Garraty, "Nature of Biography," 70.

[83] Catherine Drinker Bowen, "The Biographer: Relationship with His Hero," in *Biography as High Adventure: Life Writers Speak on Their Art,* ed. Stephen B. Oates (Amherst: University of Massachusetts Press, 1986), 66.

became a warm, sympathetic friend. When King died in my story, I was stricken with an overwhelming sense of loss, as though a member of my family had been killed. After I sent him home to Atlanta, to be buried near his Grandmother Williams whom he had loved so as a boy, I left my typewriter and staggered into my living room, unable to believe or to bear what had happened. And I cried.[84]

Such an act, according to Vandiver, is "the highest biographical art." When the subject of a biography "seems to come off the pages in full force," said Vandiver, "then the biographer has truly succeeded."[85]

CONCLUSION

The craft of biography has a long history, dating back to ancient times. Since then, it has evolved into a distinct, yet eclectic, form of literature that is based on verifiable facts and written in narrative form. Biography arises from a tension between academic, artistic, and journalistic approaches. There is an abundance of biographies of White men, so many that such works have come to be known as "Great Man" biographies. Media historians are recognizing the need to write about women, minorities, and lesser-known figures about whose lives are worth writing. Biographies are popular, in part, because they provide readers with a vivid picture of what life was like in other times. Thus, strong biographical subjects are also capable of shedding light on important historical issues. After selecting a biographical subject, writers must then immerse themselves in existing literature and locate archival material. Not all documentary evidence is formally archived, so writers must also ask human sources, such as the subject's survivors for additional documentation. Oral history and genealogical research methods help fill the inevitable gaps in archival collections, although they are subject to problems of reliability and validity. Biography is typically written in narrative form and in chronological order. Rather than providing readers with a dry recitation of facts, biographies are meant to evoke the subject and bring them to life once again. Such a reconstruction of a human life requires writers to draw on the traditional and nontraditional sources, while remaining anchored in verified facts and maintaining a balance between empathy and objectivity.

---

[84] Oates, *Biography as High Adventure,* 137.
[85] Vandiver, "Biography as an Agent of Humanism," 51.

Part V

For the Record …

14

Dealing with the Archive Records

Chuck Howell
University of Maryland

In the evolution of human communication from the spoken to the written word and eventually to print, the twentieth century brought dramatic technological advances that profoundly altered the way information is disseminated. For the first time it became possible for people all over the world to experience the same event simultaneously. From Marconi's successful trans-Atlantic broadcasting experiments in 1901 to live, global, satellite-linked coverage of the turn of the new millennium, the twentieth century was truly a "broadcast century." Preserving the history of this century is the purpose of our archives.

In the twenty-first century, more information is available, in more delivery modes, than ever before. The amount of material available online is staggering. The popular Google search engine seeks results across more than 8 billion Web pages at this writing. Searching for archives using key words yields surprising addresses: *radio archives,* 189,000; *television archives,* 67,800; *radio clubs,* 53,600; *television clubs,* 1,360; and so forth. With numbers like that, the researcher might begin to think that all information is on the Web. However, even with a medium like broadcasting (barely more than 100 years old by the most generous estimate), Web resources may lead you to important archival addresses, but online sources barely scratch the surface of the vast amounts of material waiting for the scholar. Going deeper requires access to archived, primary-source materials and, most often, a trip to an archive or special collection devoted to broadcasting and electronic media.

As explained in chapter 2 ("Historical Evidence"), primary-source materials are any firsthand, or eyewitness, accounts of an event, and these are the foundations of our archives. In the past, such historical sources were mostly confined to paper—diaries, correspondence, published accounts of events by participants, handwritten manuscripts, and the like. In the mid-nineteenth century, beginning with the advent of photography, followed by sound recording and the motion picture, historical-record sources broadened. People not only read of the horrible cost of the Civil War, they could see it through the pioneering work of photographer Matthew Brady. Rather than merely read about the Great Caruso, the opera buff in the hinterlands could hear him at home on the gramophone. Early motion pictures actually frightened audiences with their realism, causing them to shriek at the image of an oncoming train.

With the arrival of radio, listeners were able to sit in their homes and hear President Roosevelt calm a frightened nation during the worst of the Great Depression, Herb Morrison give an on-the-spot report of the destruction of the dirigible *Hindenburg,* Hitler in all his oratorical bombast during the Munich Crisis, and Edward R. Murrow and other correspondents reporting from the various fronts of World War II. The age of mass communication had arrived and the audience had a front-row seat to the world. What people were seeing and hearing was history. Today the researcher often can access the same broadcasts, and a great deal more—it only requires a trip to an archive or special collection.

WHAT ARE ARCHIVES?

In the strictest sense of the word, archives are *records* created—by an individual, institution, or organization—in the course of operations and preserved because of their continuing value. An archive or special collection organization then acquires and stores these records for research and preservation purposes. The building block of the archives is the document, which is any discreet piece of information. It can be a single sheet of correspondence, an annotated radio program script, or a DVD containing an episode of a favorite television series. The format of the information does not matter.

There are two types of archives—in-house archives and collecting archives. In-house archives are administrative units of larger organizations and are responsible for the records of the parent organizations alone. Though such archives may allow access to individuals unaffiliated with the organizations, their primary responsibility is to facilitate the work of the parent organizations—such as the news archives of a newspaper, the networks, or a broadcast station. The U.S. National Archives and Records Administration (NARA) is this type of archive; though, its access rules (for nongovernmental employees) are less restrictive than most in-house corporate archives—due to its special nature and the contrasting proprietary nature of the corporate archives.

Collecting archives contain records and documents acquired by an often-unrelated organization, such as a university or historical society. Such archives usually accumulate material centered on a particular subject or area of study. The special collections departments of many college and university libraries are such archives and often contain papers of prominent professors and alumni, material related to the city or state in which the institution is located, or collections that support the scholarly interests of the academy—literary and historical manuscripts and rare books for example.

Media Materials

The types of material available for the researcher in electronic-media collections vary widely. Basically, they fall within seven broadly descriptive categories: programming, oral histories, personal papers, industry papers, program production material, still photographs, and artifacts. Some facilities, like the Museum of Television and Radio in New York, deal strictly with programming. The Vanderbilt Television News Archives are more specialized, making network newscasts since 1969 their focus. Others, like the Library of Congress and the University of California, Los Angeles's (UCLA's) Film and Television Archive, have wider collection policies. Differing kinds of information and resources are available in various archives and special collections around the country. The specialization of any particular archive may depend on its geography, the focus of the institution governing it, or the intended use of the materials.

Programming. Surviving radio programs, broadcast prior to 1930, are quite scarce. Recording technology was beyond the means of many stations and was considered somewhat superfluous. This attitude changed as technology improved and the further into the radio era one goes the more material becomes accessible. Early recordings were made first on wax or soft aluminum discs. These materials allowed only a limited number of playbacks and soon gave way to aluminum discs coated with acetate. This blank disc was then "cut" with a recording of a program or event in real time. Known as electrical or instantaneous transcriptions (ETs), discs of this kind became the primary means of capturing live radio for future listening or later rebroadcast. They came in a variety of sizes, but the most common in radio was 16 inches in diameter. In the period before microgroove, long-play, record technology, records of this size would allow for 15 minutes per side when played or recorded at 33⅓ rpm. This allowed for the disc to be flipped at the commercial break halfway through a half-hour program. In a practice frowned upon by the networks, discs of this kind also were used by stations for an early form of time shifting.

During World War II, aluminum was in great demand for defense purposes and glass was used for a time in the production of recording blanks. Discs of this type are extremely fragile.

In addition to the different disc-based recording methods used throughout radio's "Golden Age" (1930–1960), audiotape was introduced in the late 1940s. Coexisting with ETs throughout the 1950s, it eventually supplanted them entirely.

Television also is preserved via differing technologies. Prior to the invention of videotape, live television programming was recorded for later viewing by the kinescope process. A special 16mm, motion picture camera was pointed at a high-quality television monitor, filming the program as it was broadcast live. This accounts for the inferior quality of much of what remains from television's early days. Additionally, television programs were filmed in a manner similar to motion pictures, as well as by the three-camera process pioneered on the *I Love Lucy* show. That program is still watched around the globe, at least in part because of the picture's high quality.

Videotape was introduced in 1956 by the AMPEX Corporation and soon began to change the industry. Starting with a broadcast of *Douglas Edwards and the News* on CBS, over time it supplanted film in many areas of television production and, by the early 1970s, was ubiquitous on the local and national level. The number of videotape formats introduced since 1956 are almost too numerous to count. Media archives eventually see many of them, which makes playback of multiple formats a goal, if not a reality. If a tape you are desperate to see happens to be in an obsolete format, be prepared to help defray the cost of its transfer by an outside vendor (see chapter 10, "New Media and Technical Records").

Oral Histories and Interviews. This form of first-hand account usually consists of an interviewer and a subject, though sometimes the subject alone has recorded them. Most institutions that archive oral histories have transcripts of the recordings made as time and money allow. Transcripts are much easier to work with than the raw interview on tape, especially when an oral history is of considerable length. If the researcher wants to hear the voice of the subject at a particular point in the interview, the transcript can at least speed the search process.

Oral histories can be of great historic worth though, as with any account by a participant or observer, the researcher should bear in mind the potential for human error. This is especially true when the subject is recounting events from many years earlier. There is also the chance that the subject will, perhaps inadvertently, put the best possible light on their own role in events being discussed. When possible, corroboration of information in oral histories is a good policy, especially if dealing with a controversial issue (see chapter 3, "Oral History Records").

Personal Papers or Collections. Personal papers are private documents generated and accumulated by an individual over the course of their life. The unifying principal in this case is the person just as the unifying principal in an archive is the organization. Collections of this type can be of great value to the researcher. They can paint a picture of an individual's entire career, indeed their life, if the collection is comprehensive.

Industry-Produced Pamphlets, Reports, Press Releases, Sales and Publicity Materials, Annual Reports, Newsletters, and Magazines. From the earliest days of commercial broadcasting, stations produced material about their programs and activities. Some were intended for public consumption, while others—usually dealing with audience research, ratings, ad rates, and the like—were not. Whatever its original purpose, printed material of this kind is now an invaluable historical resource. Items in this category cover every aspect of the broadcasting industry, from a richly produced commemorative program for the opening of a radio station in the early 1920s, to a press packet for the most recent network "upfronts" for the new TV season.

Program Production Material, Including Scripts, Ad Copy, Notes, Set Designs, Lighting Plots, Continuity, Shot Lists, Rundown Sheets, and Cast Lists. Documents of this type can help the researcher understand program production's mechanics in the so-called "Golden Ages" of radio and television and beyond. One look at the personal script of a radio actor or director—in all its dog-eared, hand-edited, heavily annotated glory—conveys the pressure of live radio as little else can. Television documentation can be even more detailed, reflecting the complex nature of this visual medium. Intricate master plots–showing lighting, sets, and camera placement; color wheels and costume designs; diagrams outlining the elaborate linkages required for live coast-to-coast broadcasts in the days before satellites–are all valuable sources of information. Unfortunately, because many actual broadcasts were never recorded in the first place or were destroyed or otherwise disposed of, this sort of material is required as a stand in for a sizeable number of programs.

Still Photographs. Photographs are important tools in studying broadcasting history, especially radio. Radio is a medium of sounds, not images, and photographs provide a necessary visual resource. Images illustrate more than just the history, however; they also document many of the historical events that have shaped twentieth-century American culture.

Artifacts. Giveaways and premiums, radio and television equipment (receivers, cameras, microphones, tubes, and so on), banners, awards, and memorabilia—a tremendous amount of what may be termed *material culture*—has grown up around the radio and television industries. From an early autographed picture of a favorite radio star, like the "Silver-masked Tenor," to the hundreds of licensed items that are produced in the wake of a successful kid's TV show today, items like this help us understand the interaction between the audience and the medium.

Web-Based Resources

As mentioned previously, the World Wide Web (WWW) is not the most comprehensive resource for serious mass-media research. This is not to say that there is nothing worth surfing for. Such sites as Thomas White's United States Early Radio History (http://earlyradiohistory.us/), Barry Mishkind's The Broadcast Archive (http://www.oldradio.com/), Lou Genco's The Original Old Time Radio (OTR) WWW Pages (http://www.old-time.com/), and The Generic Radio Workshop's Old Time Radio Script Collection (http://www.genericradio.com/) all contain programs and documents of interest to the researcher. These are some of the best, but by no means the only, such sites on the Web. A concerted search will reveal a great deal of material, especially in the area of programming. Still, it is only a fraction of what is contained in collections around the country. One of the best uses of the Web is as a tool to find out where those resources are.

SOME U.S. REPOSITORIES CONTAINING RADIO- AND TELEVISION-RELATED ARCHIVAL MATERIAL

The following alphabetical list, by states, concerns major collections of broadcast-related material, with (in almost every case) the institution's Web address.

Arizona

Arizona State University Libraries. The *Newsweek* Video Archive includes copies of all programs produced by *Newsweek* magazine's video department from 1971 to 1982. It contains productions taped for network and cable programming, such as *Newsweek Feature Service, Today's Woman, Cartoon-a-torial, Newsweek Woman,* and others. The collection also holds the accompanying press releases and scripts from *Bureau Report, Cartoon-a-torial, Newsweek Feature Service, Sports Week, Today's Woman, What's Cookin', You and the Law,* and submissions for *Cartoon-a-torial* not chosen for animation. A card catalog provides a listing of subjects found in *Newsweek Feature Service* and *Today's Woman.* These materials are for educational use only. The George Everson and Philo Taylor Farnsworth Papers detail the early history of television. See http://www.asu.edu/lib/speccoll/.

There are more than 200 archival collections documenting the history and culture of central Arizona and the Phoenix metropolitan area. Broadcasting-related materials are present in several audio, film, and video formats, as well as scripts, correspondence, and photographs. Most are derived from the political papers of several Arizona congressmen, governors and state legislators, such as Governor Howard Pyle, Senator Carl Hayden, and Congressman John Rhodes. The I. N. Shun, Meredith Harless, Stuart-Tovrea Family, Jack Murphy, and Tom Chauncey collections specifically document the history of broadcasting in Arizona, 1930 to 2004. See http://www.asu.edu/lib/archives/arizona.htm.

KAET-TV. Several institutional record series document the history of broadcasting at Arizona State University. University archives preserve the records and local productions of KAET-TV, the local PBS affiliate (1960–present), including some reporter's notes and all production versions of the nightly news analysis television show *Horizon.* Archives also hold scripts, audio recordings, and photographs from the *Western Business Roundup* radio show from 1955 to 1967. Student television and radio stations also are documented. See www.asu.edu/lib/archives/arizona.htm.

California

Stanford University Archive of Recorded Sound—Pryor Collection. Housed at Stanford, this collection comprises more than 1,000 aluminum and acetate transcription discs recorded off the air by Roy Pryor. The majority were recorded between 1940 and 1942 and contain both network and local programming. Local programming from this era is especially rare, making this an important resource. See http://www-sul.stanford.edu/depts/ars/index.html.

University of California, Los Angeles (UCLA), Film and Television Archive. This is another archive of major significance for the broadcast researcher. UCLA is especially important for scholarship in radio and television humor—because it houses the papers of comedian Jack Benny. The papers of Jack Benny were donated to UCLA by Mr. Benny's family after his death and include correspondence and business records, publicity material, scripts, and recordings of his radio and television programs. The archive's television collection documents the entire course of broadcast history; it includes the Academy of Television Arts and Sciences/UCLA Collection of Historic Television, donations from the *Hallmark Hall of Fame,* Milton Berle, Loretta Young, and many milestones in the history of television technology. The news collections, including the Hearst Newsreels and the News and Public Affairs collections, offer the researcher coverage of events from newsreels and national and local television news broadcasts. See http://www.cinema.ucla.edu/.

The American Radio Archive, Thousand Oaks. This was established in 1984 by the California Library Foundation and contains manuscripts, sound recordings, scripts, books, photographs, and other materials that vividly reflect the history of radio and radio broadcasting. Rudy Vallee, Norman Corwin, Robert Q. Lewis, and the Pacific Pioneer Broadcasters have all donated material to this collection. See http://www.tol.lib.ca.us/pages/new/screens/listcollections.html#ara.

Pacifica Radio Archives, Berkeley. Founder Lewis Hill's mission was to create a new kind of radio, supported by listeners, owing nothing to sponsors, providing an outlet for creative expression, and a safe haven for artistic experiments with the radio medium. Beginning in 1949 with KPFA-FM in Berkeley, the Pacifica network added four stations (in New York City, Washington, D.C., Houston, and Los Angeles), over the next 28 years. This large and important collection is the oldest U.S. public-radio programming collection. http://www.pacificaradioarchives.org/index.html.

San Francisco Bay Area Television Archives, San Francisco State University, Archives/Special Collections Department, J. Paul Leonard Library

KQED Film Archive. The KQED (PBS affiliate) Film Archive is a collection of approximately 1.2 million feet of 16mm local newsfilm created between 1967–1980, as well as selected documentaries and other footage. When using this collection, allow at least one day for retrieval of materials. Newsfilm, created between 1966–June, 1970, has been transferred to videotape reference copies and is available in the Media Access Center with authorization from Archives/Special Collections Department staff.

Over Easy. This is a KQED-produced program of over 600 half-hour programs concerning issues of aging, ca. 1977–1983. This collection has been transferred to ½ videotape-reference copies and viewing copies are available in the Media Access Center with authorization from Archives/Special Collections Department staff.

KPIX Film Library. The KPIX (CBS affiliate) Film Library is a collection of approximately 5–7 million feet of 16mm local newsfilm created between 1955–1980, as well as selected documentaries. This collection is being processed and is accessible as time and staffing permits.

KTVU Selected Newsfilm. This is a collection of selected local newsfilm from the 1960s. When using this collection, allow at least one day for retrieval of materials.

Local Emmy Award Winners. This collection consists of the 1974–present winners of local Emmy Awards presented by the San Francisco/Northern California Chapter of the National Academy of Television Arts and Sciences. This collection is available on a limited basis, subject to the condition/fragility of the videotape and availability of equipment on which to use it. Copyright is held by the individual station/production company that produced the award-winner. Local Emmy-Award winners were donated by the National Academy of Television Arts and Sciences, San Francisco/Northern California Chapter. For more information about the provenance of the collection, visit The Emmy Collection. See http://www.library.sfsu.edu/special/sfbata.html.

Colorado

The Cable Center, Denver

Barco Library. This library holds a distinctive place as the primary re-source for information on the rich heritage that the cable industry has gen-erated. Its television programming, technology, business models, and its entrepreneurs are all represented through a wide variety of print collec-tions, current electronic resources and databases, and archival and special collections. The Barco Library is intended for use as a tool for the industry, academia, and the public. It holds large collections of equipment, oral his-tories, memorabilia, photographs, and programming. It also has several important special collections, including the archives of Telecommunica-tions, Inc. (TCI).

The TCI Archive. This archive consists of the Photograph Collection, the Records Collection, the Media Collection, and the Ephemera Collection. There are close to 3,000 photos in the Photograph Collection, covering the thirty-one years of the company's existence. The Records Collection contains categories such as Business Units, Employee Relations, General History, Legal & Financial Mergers, Partnerships, Acquisitions & Ven-tures, Programming, Promotional Materials, Press Kits, Press Releases, and Clippings. The TCI Media Collection is comprised of more than 2,000 videotapes and audiotapes. The majority of the videotapes cover the last decade of TCI's existence and include investor meetings, FCC proceed-ings, promotional spots, interviews with executives, and programming promotions. The Ephemera Collection contains promotional objects such as mugs, t-shirts, and caps. There are also awards, plaques, and framed stock certificates. See http://www.cablecenter.org/library/index.cfm.

Connecticut

Yale University. The purpose of the Yale Collection of Historical Sound Recordings (HSR) is to collect, preserve, and make available for study histori-cal recordings of performers important in the fields of Western classical music, jazz, American musical theater, drama, literature, and history (including ora-tory). Mr. and Mrs. Laurence C. Witten II founded it with their collection of early vocal recordings devoted to styles and practices of nineteenth-century singing—considered among the finest of such collections—and it has been extended into the other subjects areas mentioned. The recordings in HSR now number over 160,000, in a variety of formats. The Collection holds a large library of printed materials and microforms, which provide information about composers, performers, and the recording industry, and include discographical data useful for locating and dating recordings. The books have been cataloged in Orbis. Staff-accessible finding aids have been prepared for many of the recordings. Researchers should arrange to be interviewed concerning their needs for service. See http://www.library.yale.edu/musiclib/collections.htm.

District of Columbia

National Museum of Natural History, Smithsonian Institution. Among the edited films in the Human Studies Film Archive (HSFA) collection–both sound and silent–are independent documentaries and ethnographic films, instructional media (educational and industrial films), local and network television broadcasts, theatrical and nontheatrical exploration documentaries, and pre-1920s actuality films. There also are a few fiction films and quasi-documentaries suitably placed in the HSFA collections because of their content. See http://www.nmnh.si.edu/naa/guide/film_toc.htm.

National Museum of American History Archives Center, Smithsonian Institution. Holdings include the N. W. Ayer Advertising Agency Collection. Records include business records, but consist primarily of print advertising created for thousands of clients between 1869–1996. The Walter Landor/Landor Associates Collection and the Frances Mair Collection document their groundbreaking work in packaging design and in developing corporate identity programs. The Maidenform and Hills Bros. Coffee Collections have exceptionally complete advertising and marketing records. The Krispy Kreme Doughnut Corporation Records and the Carvel Ice Cream Company Records reveal the early history of prepared foods, franchising, and the role of marketing in their success. Other collections include the Breck Girls Collection. In addition, the Archives Center has documented through oral history the creation of important advertising campaigns for products such as Pepsi, Alka-Seltzer, Marlboro, Federal Express, Cover Girl, Campbell Soup, Nike, and Kraft Television Theatre. See www.si.edu/nmah/archives/ac-i.htm.

The Library of Congress. As in so many other areas of scholarship, the Library of Congress is an extremely important resource for the study of radio and television, certainly the most important one in the study of NBC. The Library of Congress's Motion Picture, Broadcast and Recorded Sound Division

(M/B/RS) houses more than 150,000 acetate discs of NBC radio programming, as well as voluminous paper records of the network's activities. The Library is also the home of the papers of radio and television legend Bob Hope, among other notables. The Library of Congress's television collections deserve special mention:

NBC Television Collection. This is an historic collection of 18 thousand television programs broadcast, preserved and, for the most part, produced by NBC. With programs dating from the beginning of U.S. network television (1948–1977), the NBC Television Collection includes not only performances by major actors and musical talents, but also numerous events featuring significant individuals in public affairs. This acquisition significantly supplements M/B/RS's holdings of television not acquired via copyright deposit: programs from the late 1940s–early 1950s and genres such as sports, game shows, children's programs, and daytime television. Kinescopes comprise the majority of the NBC Television Collection, while M/B/RS holds mostly picture negatives with separate sound tracks. Viewing copies are presently available for only a few titles. Researchers with enough lead-time may request that video viewing copies be produced for in-house use only.

NET (National Educational Television) Programs. NET programs held by the Library of Congress probably total over 10,000 titles and date from 1955–1969. NET became PBS (Public Broadcasting Service) in 1969 and a few PBS programs, from the early 1970s, are included in this group of NET programs. The programs are instructional or educational, including the series *Touristen-deutsch* (14 programs teaching elementary conversational German, produced in 1957 by WTTW, Chicago); the *Nature of Communism* (60 lectures coproduced by Vanderbilt and Notre Dame Universities in 1964); and *Two Centuries of Symphony* (20 programs teaching music appreciation, produced by WGBH, Boston in 1960). The broadening interests of educational television also are reflected in such series as *Casals Master Class,* international acquisitions such as *Civilization,* and programs documenting the social revolution of the 1950s and 1960s such as *Escape from the Cage* (on mental illness), *History of the Negro,* and *Net Journal.*

PBS (Public Broadcasting Service) Collection. The Library will continue to acquire a broad range of public television through PBS's gift of programs to which its distribution rights have expired. It is one of the largest of M/B/RS's television acquisitions—some 30,000 master videotapes were available for transfer at the time of the agreement and will be preserved by the Library of Congress. *Leontyne Price at the White House, 3-2-1 Contact,* and James Burke's *The Day the Universe Changed* are just a few examples from the full range of cultural and informative programming PBS has made available in this country since 1969. PBS will continue to transfer additional programs annually.

Television News. The only example of "early" television news in M/B/RS is a noncopyright deposit, television news series, *Douglas Edwards and the News* (CBS) (40 issues, September 26–November 11, 1960), comprised primarily of coverage of the Kennedy–Nixon presidential election campaign. The Division holds nearly complete weeknight broadcasts of *ABC Evening News* (1977–1992) and numerous issues of *Nightline* (beginning in 1987); nearly all CBS news programs (1975–1993); and an extensive collection of *MacNeil-Lehrer Newshour*; but there are no *NBC Evening News* deposits. See http://www.loc.gov/rr/record/rsfind.htm and http://www.loc.gov/rr/mopic/tvcoll.html.

National Archives and Records Administration (NARA). NARA is the depository for all Federal records. It therefore chronicles (among other things) the government's involvement with broadcasting, from policy and regulation (the records of the Federal Radio Commission and Federal Communications Commission), to actual broadcasting and program production (the records of Armed Forces Radio and Television, The Office of War Information, and Voice of America). The KIRO-CBS Milo Ryan Phonoarchives at the NARA also contain all the CBS Radio News broadcasts from WWII. See http://www.archives.gov/index.html.

Presidential Libraries. Administered by NARA, the Presidential Libraries contain a plethora of material of interest to broadcasting scholars looking at (among other things) the intersection of politics and media in the United States. The Presidential Library system is made up of ten Presidential Libraries. Each Presidential library contains a museum and provides an active series of public programs.
- **George Bush Library** (http://www.archives.gov/presidential_libraries/addresses/george_bush.html)
- **Jimmy Carter Library** (http://www.archives.gov/presidential_libraries/addresses/jimmy_carter.html)

- **William J. Clinton Presidential Library and Museum**
  (http://www.archives.gov/presidential_libraries/addresses/
  william_clinton.html)
- **Dwight D. Eisenhower Library** (http://www.archives.gov/
  presidential_libraries/addresses/dwight_eisenhower.html)
- **Gerald R. Ford Library and Museum** (http://www.archives.gov/
  presidential_libraries/addresses/gerald_ford.html)
- **Herbert Hoover Library** (http://www.archives.gov/
  presidential_libraries/addresses/herbert_hoover.html)
- **Lyndon B. Johnson Library** (http://www.archives.gov/
  presidential_libraries/addresses/lyndon_johnson.html)
- **John F. Kennedy Library** (http://www.archives.gov/
  presidential_libraries/addresses/john_kennedy.html)
- **Ronald Reagan Library** (http://www.archives.gov/
  presidential_libraries/addresses/ronald_reagan.html)
- **Franklin D. Roosevelt Library** (http://www.archives.gov/
  presidential_libraries/addresses/franklin_roosevelt.html)
- **Harry S. Truman Library** (http://www.archives.gov/
  presidential_libraries/addresses/harry_truman.html)

Also included in the Presidential Library system is the Nixon Presidential Materials Staff, which administers the Nixon Presidential materials under the terms of the Presidential Recordings and Materials Preservation Act. See http://www.archives.gov/presidential_libraries/addresses/richard_nixon.html.

The Office of Presidential Libraries is a nationwide network of libraries, which is part of the NARA, located in College Park, Maryland. See http://www.archives.gov/presidential_libraries/addresses/addresses.html.

Florida

Louis Wolfson II Florida Moving Image Archive, Miami

Wolfson Archive. This archive contains millions of feet of film and thousands of hours of videotape, spanning over nine decades of Florida's past. Together, these materials provide the opportunity to re-live, or see for the first time, the issues and events that have shaped the history and culture of this region. The archive also contains newsfilm, scripts, photos, and so on from WTVJ-TV Miami. See http://www.fmia.org/.

Georgia

The Walter J. Brown Media Archives and Peabody Awards Collection, University of Georgia

Peabody Awards Collection. This archive, of its prestigious namesake, holds more than 40,000 titles, both radio and television. The collection represents not only the winners, but includes all entries in the categories of news, documentary, entertainment, educational, children's, and public-service programming. Many of these are the only surviving copies of the work. Reference copies are available for much of the collection in the University of Georgia Libraries Media Department, while press kits, scripts, and correspondence submitted with the entries are housed at the Hargrett Rare Book and Manuscript Library.

WSB Television Newsfilm Collection. More than five million feet of newsfilm from this Atlanta station, dating from 1949–1981, represent a visual history of Atlanta and the southeast during a period of growth and social change. No other Atlanta area television stations saved their newsfilm, making this collection a unique historical resource. This collection is indexed in a database located in Media Archives. See http://www.libs .uga.edu/mediadept/index.html.

Georgia State University Libraries

Don Naylor Papers. These papers include scrapbooks, sound recordings, correspondence, and scripts from Mr. Naylor's service at WGST and WAGA radio and WAGA-TV in Atlanta.

WSB Collection. This collection includes photographs, sound recordings, artifacts, program logs, and other materials related to WSB Radio, Atlanta's first radio station.

WSB Radio Collection. Approximately 75 cubic feet, this collection includes 25 document cases, 3 record-center cartons, artifacts, oversize documents and log books, 16 reels of microfilm, 14 inches of film cans, and the card index to portions of the sound-recording library. It has nearly 55,000 disc-sound recordings; approximately 300 transcription discs, primarily of political programs, speeches and events; reel-to-reel tape recordings of WSB programs; approximately 10 cubic feet of photographs; artifacts,

including microphones, headsets, and WSB banners. See http://www
.library.gsu.edu/spcoll/Collections/Music/index.htm#radio.

Illinois

Museum of Broadcast Communications (MBC), Chicago. Though primarily a museum, the MBC does house programming as well. The A.C. Nielsen Jr. Online Research Center allows access to the MBC's large catalog of
radio and television shows. See http://www.museum.tv/index.shtml.

WPA Film Library. A stock footage outlet, they handle material from
WETA in Washington, DC (Public TV) and also have some early TV ads. See
http://www.wpafilmlibrary.com/.

Ronald Colman (1891–1958). This archive of the screen (and radio) legend does not have a Web site (yet). Call George E. Schatz at 708-432-8556 for
more information.

Chicago Historical Society

Sound Collections. The collection includes a large number of sound
recordings of radio programs, oral-history interviews, speeches, and proceedings. These include *Problems of the City* radio programs, 1970–1991
and Bill Cameron's *The Reporters* radio shows, 1978–1993.

The Studs Terkel/WFMT Oral History Archives. The archives include
audio-recordings of interviews, readings, and musical programs created by
Studs Terkel and aired during his tenure at WFMT Radio from the early
1950s–1999. During a radio career spanning five decades, Terkel interviewed individuals from every walk of life—from public figures like Martin Luther King, Jr. and U.S. president Jimmy Carter to the proverbial
"man on the street." As a result, the archives include a wide range of discussions that narrate the cultural, literary, and political history of Chicago and
the United States in the second half of the twentieth century.

Burr Tillstrom Collection and Archives. The Tillstrom collection and archives at the Chicago Historical Society constitute the primary extant
holdings of papers, films, artifacts, and memorabilia relating to the career
of Burr Tillstrom—master puppeteer and creator of the Kuklapolitan
Players and the long-running television program *Kukla, Fran and Ollie.*

These materials were transferred to the Society by Burr Tillstrom through a series of gifts made during his lifetime and by bequest following his death in 1986.

WGN Newsfilm Collection. This collection includes aircuts and outtakes from WGN television newscasts from about 1948–1977. Chicago news includes accidents, disasters, fires; education; public, cultural, and sports events; the Chicago Transit Authority, mass transit, and O'Hare International Airport; public housing, Mayor Richard J. Daley, politics and government; the civil rights movement, and Martin Luther King Jr. National news includes NASA and the space program, primarily related to the Apollo missions. See http://www.chicagohs.org/.

Chicago Public Library, Harold Washington Library Center, Visual and Performing Arts Division

Music. A significant collection of more than 150,000 recordings from 78 rpms to CDs (including the Arnold Jacobsen Recorded Sound Collection) has been developed for research and use in the Library's listening facilities. Special strengths lie in popular music, jazz, and blues. Unique collections include the Frank McNulty/WLS-TV Collection and Dick Buckley's WNPR series *Archives of Recorded Jazz* (400 hours).

The *Jubilee Showcase* Archives. One of the longest-running programs in Chicago television history, *Jubilee Showcase* was aired for 21 years, January 10, 1963–January 8, 1984, on WLS-TV, Chicago. Presenting a wide variety of gospel and inspirational music, this pioneering program reached a vast audience every Sunday morning and featured America's greatest gospel artists. See http://www.chipublib.org/001hwlc/hwvpa.html.

University of Illinois-Urbana-Champagne (UIUC). The Communications Library supports the instructional and research programs of the UIUC College of Communications, including the Department of Advertising, the Department of Journalism, and the Institute of Communications Research. Its collections contain more than 16,000 volumes of books, journals, and newspapers, as well as materials in other formats, on advertising, journalism, media studies, radio and television broadcasting, telecommunications, popular culture, and polling and public opinion.

National Association of Farm Broadcasters (NAFB). Official NAFB Historian's Records (1937, 1943–1995) document the origin and growth of the National Association of Farm Broadcasters through summaries of the organization's yearly activities, biographical sketches of officers, programs, minutes, and reports of national and regional meetings, constitution and bylaws, official correspondence, photographs and clippings showing members at work, with visiting dignitaries, attending meetings and conventions, receiving honors and awards, and engaging in social pursuits. Most of the photographs were published in *Chats* (RS 8/3/88). The following records are also included: NAFB Subject File, 1941–2002 and NAFB Audio and Video Recording, 1952–2001. See http://web .library.uiuc.edu/ahx/Nafb/nafb.htm.

WILL-AM-FM and TV Materials

Harry J. Skornia Papers, 1937–1991. The papers of Harry Jay Skornia (1910–1991), professor of journalism and communications (1953–1975), include published articles and books, manuscripts, radio scripts, notes, clippings, course materials, reports, and records of trips. The series includes materials on Skornia's role in setting up the West German broadcasting system (1948–1949), operating the U.S.-controlled Austrian Red-White-Red radio network (1951–1953), as well as his service as radio director at Indiana University (1942–1951); executive director/president of the National Association of Education Broadcasters (1953–1960), and vice president of the National Association for Better Broadcasting (1968–1991).

Advertising Council Archives. The Ad Council's early campaigns covered the crisis in education, world trade, Army prestige, the Red Cross, car accidents, and forest fire prevention. It has been instrumental in encouraging people to vote, use zip codes, and participate in the census, as well as in promoting involvement in volunteer projects such as the Peace Corps, VISTA, and the National Guard and Reserve. Among the hallmark images of the past fifty years that it has introduced are Smokey the Bear, McGruff the Crime Dog, and the Crash Test Dummies. The archive houses both the finished advertisements themselves and materials on policy and campaign formation. Materials include both print and television and radio advertisements and holdings are in a number of formats—including 35mm film, videocassette, reel-to-reel, and compact disc, as well as print proofs and posters. The collection also includes minutes, notes, and correspondence. See http://web.library.uiuc.edu/ahx/adcouncil/default.asp.

Other Advertising Materials. http://web.library.uiuc.edu/ahx/advert.htm.

Billy Graham Center Archives, Wheaton College, Wheaton. Highlights include the Papers of Percy and Ruth Crawford (early televangelists). Films, videos, audio tapes, correspondence, a book manuscript, sermon notes, and other materials documenting the evangelistic ministry of Percy and Ruth Crawford, particularly their radio and television work.

Little Country Church of Hollywood **Collection.** The *Little Country Church of Hollywood* radio program was a daily religious broadcast founded by Dr. William B. Hogg. The program first aired over Radio Station KFAC at 8:00 a.m. on January 2, 1933. Broadcasting studios were located in the building in the center of Hollywood, at the corner of Argyle and Yucca Streets. On September 30, 1934, the program was broadcast coast to coast over the Columbia Broadcasting System (CBS). Airings of the program continued at least until Hogg's death January 14, 1937. A rural community before and during "meetin' time" provided the program's setting.

The *Hour of Decision Radio* **Program Collection.** Recordings of the Billy Graham Evangelistic Association's weekly radio program, which included music, announcements about evangelistic meetings, and a sermon by Graham, an associate, or guest. Many programs make references to then-current political or social events. Also includes the Spanish *Momentos de Decision* program on compact discs and digital audio tapes, 2000–2003.

Records of the *Hour of Freedom* **Radio Program.** Copies of 455 broadcasts of a weekly radio program titled *Hour of Freedom,* featuring evangelist Howard O. Jones, continuation of a program broadcast for years both in Africa and the United States. Each program consists of a half hour of music, scripture readings, and an evangelistic sermon; also includes sermons of guest speakers, such as Ralph Bell.

Records of the Billy Graham Evangelical Association (BGEA). Films and video-films, and videotapes, primarily of television broadcasts of evangelistic crusades, produced by the BGEA. This collection does not include productions by the BGEA subsidiary World Wide Pictures. There are restrictions on the use of this collection.

Records of the Billy Graham Evangelical Association, World Wide Pictures, Inc. Films and files relating to the production and distribution of evangelistic movies and television programs, and to publicity for Billy Graham's crusades. Several of the publicity and crusade clippings scrapbooks in the collection are on microfilm. There are restrictions on the use of this collection. http://www.wheaton.edu/bgc/archives/archhp1.html.

Indiana

The Lilly Library-Film, Radio and Television Collections, Indiana University. Though it holds only one collection with significant radio-related material, the Lilly Library is still an important destination for the radio historian. The reason—the collection in question is that of Orson Welles. Welles's place in the medium's history is assured and his radio work is well documented with correspondence, scripts, and recordings all available for scholarly use.

The Lilly Library also houses the Papers of John McGreevey, which contains an impressive collection of early television scripts. Representative programs include *Armstrong Circle Theatre, Lux Video Theatre, Westinghouse Studio One,* and *Climax!.* Additional scripts in the collection include a variety of series such as *The Farmer's Daughter, My Three Sons, General Electric Theatre, Hazel, Ironside, Laredo, The Name of the Game, Wagon Train,* and *The Waltons.*

Other holdings of note related to television include the entire run of annotated production scripts for *Laugh In,* as well as scripts for such landmark series as *I Love Lucy, Star Trek, Mission Impossible, Wild Bill Hickok, The Addams Family, All in the Family, Gunsmoke, The Mary Tyler Moore Show, Maude, Perry Mason, Room 222,* and *The Wild Wild West.* See http://www .indiana.edu/~liblilly/overview/film.shtml.

Indiana Historical Society

WRTV-6 (McGraw-Hill Broadcasting, Inc.) Film Collection, 1920– 1980 (bulk 1949–1980). The WRTV collection consists of 574 canisters of film representing 434 film titles, almost all of them 16mm film in format. In addition, the collection includes two copies each of 17 VHS videotape-user copies of 88 titles in the collection. More of these VHS-user copies may be made in the future in response to researcher requests. The films include documentaries produced by WFBM/WRTV-6, commercials, political campaign spots, public service announcements, and promotional films for companies or organizations. Some film titles include different film elements such as A-and B-roll material, soundtracks, and outtakes. See http://www.indianahistory.org/.

The C-SPAN Archives. The C-SPAN Archives record, index, and archive all C-SPAN programming for historical, educational, research, and archival uses. The archives began within the Purdue University, School of Liberal Arts in 1987. In July 1998, C-SPAN assumed responsibility for the archival operations and the facilities were moved from the Purdue University campus to the Purdue Research Park in West Lafayette, Indiana.

The C-SPAN Archives collection begins in September 1987 with the Robert Bork nomination to the Supreme Court. All programs that have aired since October, 1987 are recorded, indexed, abstracted, and archived. Duplicate copies of most of these programs are available for purchase. The collection includes all House and Senate proceedings, call-in programs, committee hearings, speeches, forums, conventions, rallies, *BookTV* programming, and other special programming, such as *Lincoln-Douglas Debates, Tocqueville, American Presidents,* and *American Writers.* Prices are set by the length, age, and type of programs. See http://www.c-spanarchives.org/Info/aboutarchives.php.

Iowa

Sioux City Public Museum. The museum contains news and information programming along with newsfilm from local station KCAU-TV. See http:// www .sioux-city.org/museum/.

Kansas

University of Kansas, Archive of Recorded Sound. This is an exceptional collection of recordings of great historical significance. Containing some 160,000 items, it is one of the ten largest sound archives in the country and many of its recordings are among the rarest in the world. The archive includes the Wright Jazz Collection, the Seaver Opera Collection, and Bierley Early Band Collection. It also contains all equipment necessary for playback of its various early recording technologies, including Pathe, Edison, and cylinder players. The archive is a tremendous resource for performers and scholars. See http://www.ku.edu/~sfa/mad/jazzarchive/.

Kentucky

The University of Kentucky, Audiovisual Archives. The broadcasting-related portion of the archives consist of extensive holdings of local television and radio programming. Currently, the television collection includes Louis-ville stations WAVE-TV (Channel 3) and WLKY-TV (Channel 32) and WKYT-TV (Channel 27, Lexington). It generally span the dates from 1965 to 1988. The Broadcasting Archive also contains selected programs from Ken-tucky Educational Television, such as the "Distinguished Kentuckians" series and gubernatorial debates. The news material in these collections is stored on 16mm film and ¾-inch videotape.

The radio collections include selected programs from WBKY/WUKY (University of Kentucky Radio), WHAS (Louisville), WAVE (Louisville), WVLK (Lexington), WBLG (Lexington), and WLAP (Lexington). Also fea-tured in these radio collections, the Al Smith collection contains the public affairs program, *Primeline*. The WHAS collection is a major collection of public affairs and political programming dating primarily from the 1930s and 1940s. The WVLK and WLAP collections consist primarily of public-affairs programming from the 1970s and 1980s. See http://www.uky.edu/Libraries/Special/av/collections/broadcast.htm.

Louisiana

New Orleans Public Library, Louisiana Division

Joseph Culotta Jr. Collection. The collection consists of audiotapes, pri-marily of the radio call-in/interview program *Let's Talk It Over* (1965–1990). Also included are several tapes of *The American Legion Hour* (1962–1965) radio program and scattered tapes of *Mid-Month in New Orleans* (1969–1981)—a taped program heard on approximately the mid-dle Sunday of each month. See http://nutrias.org/~nopl/culotta/ltio.htm.

WVUE -TV Newsfilm Collection, 1969–1979. Four-reel microfilm ver-sion of original 5,000 card index available onsite. See http://nutrias.org/~nopl/spec/speclist.htm.

Maine

Northeast Historic Film. Northeast Historic Film has a large and growing collection of unique moving-image materials relating to the history and cul-ture of northern New England. See http://www.oldfilm.org/.

WAGM-TV Collection, 1970–1995. The collection contains news stories produced by station WAGM-TV, including many public-affairs programs dealing with topics such as local construction of public housing in the 1970s, agriculture, public utilities, community celebrations, and fairs. See http://www.oldfilm.org/ocg/publicMainView.cfm?id=589.

WCBB Collection, 1986–1990. Collection contains documentaries and other factual works. "Remember the Maine" (1986) brings together historians to discuss the Spanish-American War and destruction of the battleship Maine. *Establishment of a Maine Film Commission* (1987) is a television feature report on the Commission and includes a short history of film production in Maine. See http://www.oldfilm.org/ocg/publicMain View.cfm?id=471.

WCVB Collection, 1989–1996. Collection contains documentaries and factual works. *Mount Katahdin* is about Maine's highest peak and Baxter State Park. *Welcome to the Maine Grange* shows the history of agricultural organizations in rural communities. See http://www.oldfilm.org/ocg/public MainView.cfm?id=569.

WLBZ Collection, 1970–1995. Collection contains news, advertising, and documentaries. Each week from 1975–1980 is represented by several 400-ft. cans of news film with sound. The videotapes include news, promotional spots, sports, natural disasters, local series and documentaries, and coverage of community events. See http://www.oldfilm.org/ocg/public MainView.cfm?id=615.

WMTW Collection, 1938–1990. Collection contains promotional films produced by the Maine Department of Economic Development, Anheuser Busch, American Hardwood Association and others, with titles such as *Downeast Dairymen.* Used as filler on the station until 1991. See http://www.oldfilm.org/ocg/publicMainView.cfm?id=492.

Maryland

The University of Maryland (UM). The UM's broadcasting archives contain two separate media collections.

The Library of American Broadcasting. This library is a wide-ranging collection of material devoted exclusively to the history of broadcasting in the United States. In addition to several thousand linear feet of manuscript material (including the WNET–Thirteen/Arthur Godfrey Collection), the Library is also home to nearly 200 linear feet of subject files, 6,000 books, 1,100 oral histories, interviews and speeches, 7,000 pamphlets, 300 periodical titles, 225,000 photographs, 10,000 recorded discs, 5,000 scripts, and a growing collection of video and film material. See http://www.lib.umd.edu/LAB/.

The National Public Broadcasting Archives (NPBA). The NPBA brings together the archival record of the major U.S. entities of noncommercial broadcasting, including the Public Broadcasting Service, National Public Radio (NPR), the Corporation for Public Broadcasting, NPR precursor the National Educational Radio Network, National Educational Television, the Children's Television Workshop, and much more. http://www.lib.umd.edu/NPBA/index.html.

The Golden Radio Buffs of Maryland. Golden Radio Buffs of Maryland is a nonprofit association of volunteers dedicated to the celebration of old-time radio. Specifically, they seek to recognize the many contributions of the radio stations, broadcasts, and on-air and behind-the-scenes personalities that brought us the news, drama, comedy, music, and other aspects of radio from the 1920s–1950s, which the members consider to be *The Golden Age of Radio.* Club maintains tape lending library. See http://members.aol.com/grbmd/.

National Library of Medicine (NLM), Bethesda. The NLM maintains a large collection of educational and PBS programming on medical and health topics, including programs produced by WGBH, WETA, WHYY, Thirteen/WNET, KCET, MacNeil-Lehrer Productions, the CBC, and the BBC. An online searchable database is available. http://www.nlm.nih.gov/.

Langsdale Library, University of Baltimore, WMAR-TV News Archives, 1948–1987. This archive contains news film and video, as well as stock footage from the Baltimore station. Online index is available at http://archives.ubalt.edu/wmar/table.htm.

Massachusetts

Mount Holyoke College, South Hadley, Archives and Special Collections, The Edward R. and Janet Brewster Murrow Papers. These papers contain correspondence, published and unpublished writings, subject files, financial and legal records, biographical material, memorabilia, and Brewster and Murrow family papers and photographs, chiefly dating from 1929–1965.

Of particular note are letters written by and to the Murrows while they were in Great Britain during World War II that reflect his work as director of European broadcasting for CBS, Inc. and her duties as executive director of the London Committee of Bundles for Britain, Inc. Also includes letters and other documents concerning his service as director of the United States Information Agency (1961–1964). See http://www.mtholyoke.edu/lits/library/arch/col/index.shtml.

The WGBH Educational Foundation—Boston, Media Archives and Preservation Center. Researchers may have access to the archives' processed collections at the WGBH Educational Foundation in Boston. Archival materials are restricted to on-site use only. In order to use any of WGBH's archival materials, individuals must contact the center directly via mail or email with a specific research request before visiting. To learn more about the archives, contact archive_requests@wgbh.org or visit http://www.wgbh.org/resources/archives. The WGBH Archives offers online access to three former TV series:

New Television Workshop. WGBH produced this experimental video art series from 1974 to 1993.

Say Brother. WGBH's longest-running public-affairs TV program that was by, for, and about African Americans. It first aired in 1968 and changed its name to *Basic Black* in 1998.

Ten O'Clock News. WGBH produced this nightly news program from 1976 to 1991.

Michigan

Michigan State University, G. Robert Vincent Voice Library. This is the largest academic voice library in the nation. It houses taped utterances (speeches, performances, lectures, interviews, broadcasts, and so forth) by more than 50,000 persons from all walks of life recorded over 100 years. The Vincent Voice Library contains more than 1,100 collections of spoken-word, audio recordings. Each collection is described by an online finding aid that contains information about the collection in general and provides a description of and access information for each recording. In total, there are close to 10,000 individual recordings described. Online collections of interest to the broadcast scholar include news, popular culture, radio programs, U.S. presidents and vice presidents, sound recording history, sports, U.S. politics,

military, women speakers, and World Wars I and II. See http://www.lib
.msu.edu/vincent/.

Minnesota

Minnesota Historical Society. It owns 3 million feet of news film from
KSTP-TV in Minneapolis/St. Paul, dating from 1948 to 1980. It is not
yet ready for prime time, but when the reels are transferred from film to video
for reference use, this collection will be an invaluable document of life in
the Twin Cities. See http://www.mnhs.org/library/collections/movingimages/
movingimages.html.

Mississippi

*Mississippi Department of Archives and History, William F. Winter Ar-
chives and History Building, WLBT Newsfilm Collection, 1954–1971.* The
Newsfilm Collection contains the following materials from WLBT in Jackson, Mississippi: unedited 16mm news film (black-and-white and color),
news scripts, photographs, and audio tapes. The 635 reels of news film in the
database contain approximately 550,000 feet of film. The collection has been
transferred to 8mm videocassettes, which can be viewed in the library. The
subject content varies widely—legislative activities, election campaigns and
procedures, education, crime, entertainment, weather disasters, segregation,
human interest, sports events, and civil rights movement activities. The collection consists of unedited news film, the footage shot by the film crews in the
field [not the station's edited news broadcasts]. See http://mdah.state.ms.us/
arlib/contents/newsfilm.html.

Missouri

Kansas City Broadcasting Oral History Collection. There are numerous
interviews with local broadcast journalists represented in this collection. They
were taped between 1985 and 1993. Although they are part of a private collection yet to be housed in an archive, arrangements can be made to work with
the tapes at Rockhurst College. Contact: William J. Ryan, Associate Professor,
Departments of Communication and Fine Arts, Rockhurst College, Kansas
City, Missouri 64110, Phone 816-333-2159. Interviewees include:
- Anschutz, Wendell (reporter and news anchor)
- Bodine, Walt (reporter, news director, talk show host)

- Butler, David (news director)
- Dorsey, Claude (transradio reporter, news director, news anchor)
- Gray, Charles (reporter and news director)
- Grove, Harold Mack (reporter, news director, anchor)
- Heckerson, Noel S. (reporter, announcer, anchor)
- Mullins, Reverdy L. (news reporter)
- Smith, Allen D. (news reporter, news director)
- Thornberry, John (news announcer and anchor)
- Whiting, Pam (reporter, announcer, news director)
- Williams, Lafe (announcer, reporter)

University of Missouri, Kansas City, The Miller-Nichols Library

Marr Sound Archives. This unit of the Special Collections Department holds nearly 250,000 sound recordings in formats that include LPs, 78 rpms, 45 rpms, cylinders, transcription discs, instantaneous cut discs, and open-reel tapes. The focus of the collection is the American experience as reflected in recorded sound, with very substantial and significant holdings in the following areas: historic voices; American popular music, jazz, blues, and country; vintage radio programs; authors reading their own works; and historic classical and operatic recordings.

Wilder Wylie Collection. The Wylie Collection consists of radio scripts for KIDO-NBC, *The Bob Hope Show,* various radio plays produced by the National Broadcasting Company (NBC), as well as scripts for several television shows. In addition, there are several television commercials for the Borden Company and three broadcast schedules.

Arthur Church Collection. The Collection documents Church's approximately thirty years in radio and television. Included in the collection are photos, published sheet music, scrap books, advertising brochures, contracts, telegrams, station newsletters, and broadcast recordings. The collection of recordings is comprised of 16-inch instantaneous and transcription discs as well as the metal parts used to manufacture the transcription discs.

The Raymond Scott Collection. A pianist, bandleader, and composer, Raymond Scott (1908–1994) is noted for his eccentric compositions written in the late 1930s for his six-piece quintette. Quirky pieces such as "Twilight in Turkey," "Powerhouse," and "Dinner Music for a Pack of Hungry Cannibals" have been used in over one hundred Warner Brothers cartoons. Scott also served as a conductor for the CBS radio orchestra and the television show, *Your Hit Parade.* The Raymond Scott Collection includes open-reel tapes, instantaneous discs of Scott's network programs, engineering workbooks, diaries, LPs, scores and band arrangements, photos, and music manuscripts. Sound recordings from this collection are housed in the Marr Sound Archives on the ground floor of the Miller Nichols Library. See http://www.umkc.edu/lib/MNL/index.html.

New Jersey

Princeton, The David Sarnoff Library. It actually consists of a museum, an archives, and a library. Besides Mr. Sarnoff's papers and memorabilia, the Library's holdings include 25,000 photographs and thousands of notebooks, reports, publications, and artifacts related to the histories of RCA Laboratories and RCA. See http://www.davidsarnoff.org/index.htm.

New York

New York Public Library. One of the largest of its kind in the nation, the Donnell Media Center contains important film and video collections, as well as extensive audio holdings. The outstanding collection of predominantly circulating material includes: 3,000 popular home videos and 2,200 videotapes ranging from video art to independently produced documentaries and exemplary television programs; 8,500 16mm films, including independent experimental films, documentaries; and more than 250 feature films ranging from classics to current releases. The audio collection contains nearly 35,000 music and nonmusic CDs and audiocassettes, including: musical recordings ranging from classical to jazz; instruction in languages other than English; and literature recordings featuring critical discussion and readings from the classics. See http://www.nypl.org/branch/central/dlc/dmc/.

Columbia University Oral History Research Office. One of this program's many oral history projects was a series of recorded sessions with radio pioneers. Interviews were conducted with Walter Damrosch, David Sarnoff, Bertha Brainerd, Frank Conrad, Al Jolson, Owen D. Young, Henry Ford, Fred Waring, William S. Paley, George F. McClelland, Merlin H. Aylesworth, Erik Barnouw, and others. See http://www.columbia.edu/cu/lweb/indiv/oral/.

Museum of Television and Radio (MTR). With branches in New York and Los Angeles, the MTR serves both the serious scholar and the casual visitor. It not only mounts exhibits and satellite seminars but also has one of the largest programming archives in the world. Research must be done on site. See http://www.mtr.org.

The Television Advertising and Culture Archive at Brooklyn College. At present, the department is only able to make available the Diamant Classic Television Commercials Collection and the Niedermeyer Collection to qualified researchers and scholars. See http://academic.brooklyn.cuny.edu/tvradio/ commarch.htm. Resources include:

Celia Nachatovitz Diamant Classic Television Commercials Collection. Volume one and volume two together comprise 87 classic television commercials (about 114 minutes of material) that were created, both live and on film, between 1948–1964.

Fred Niedermeyer Collection. This is a collection of 55 cigarette commercials from the late 1960s and early 1970s that was donated in 1999.

Ted Bates Collection. More than 7,000 commercials produced from the early 1950s–early 1980s, were donated to the department in 1994.

Seagram Collection. Advertising for products of the Seagram Company.

Ithaca College Library

Rod Serling Archives. Emmy-winning, television writer and producer Rod Serling is best known today for his anthology program *The Twilight Zone,* but his collection at the Ithaca College Library covers a career much more varied than the fantasy genre work for which he is remembered. The archives consist of television scripts, movie screenplays, stage play scripts, films, published works by Serling, unproduced scripts, and secondary materials. There is an online finding aid to the Rod Serling Archives' television scripts.

Milton Cross Collection. Radio announcer Milton Cross was known as "The Voice of The Met." He became the announcer for the Metropolitan Opera in New York on December 25, 1931 and would continue until his death 43 years later. Cross broadcast every Saturday matinee performance, giving plot synopsis, notes on costuming, staging, and acting. Radio scripts and other memorabilia comprise the collection. See http://www .ithaca.edu/library/archives/ArchivesHome.html.

Columbia University. Alfred I. du Pont awards are regarded widely as the most prestigious awards in television and radio journalism, the broadcast equivalent of the Pulitzer Prizes. The awards have been presented annually since 1942. Their purpose is to bring the best in television and radio journalism to professional and public attention and to honor those who produce it. The Center houses an extensive archive of award winners reaching back several decades and available for student and faculty use. See http://www.jrn .columbia.edu/events/dupont/.

The Clio Awards—New York and Chicago. Since 1960 the mission of the Clio Awards is to provide the international advertising and design industry with the world's best-judged creative competition in the areas of TV, Print, outdoor, radio, integrated campaign, innovative media, design, internet, content & contact, and student work—and, in so doing, to honor advertising and design excellence worldwide. The Website features a database of past award winners at http://www.clioawards.com/html/main.isx.

New York City Municipal Archives, WNYC, 1936–1981. Films (1949– 1981) and lacquer discs (1936–1963) produced by municipal radio and television station WNYC. Dating from 1947–1981, the moving-image portion of this collection includes mayoral press conferences, national and international dignitaries visiting City Hall, luminaries from the worlds of culture, science and art; government operations; and City Council and Police and Fire Department activities. Rare, unseen footage of New York City in the 1950s, plus important city events over three decades—rallies, riots, ocean liners, parades, and the World's Fair are a few highlights. See http://www.nyc.gov/ html/records/html/about/archives.shtml.

George Eastman House, Rochester. Though known primarily as a motion picture repository, George Eastman House does have a number of kinescopes in its holdings. See http://www.eastmanhouse.org/.

Syracuse University, Belfer Audio Archive and Laboratory. The archives total approximately 340,000 recordings in all formats, primarily cylinders, discs, and magnetic tapes. The late nineteenth and early twentieth centuries are well represented in the commercial classical, popular, and jazz genres, with additional resources of spoken-word materials, broadcasts, and university events. Donations from broadcast notables like Mike Wallace of *60 Minutes* and radio playwright Norman Corwin also are housed here. No online catalog is available at this time. Call or write for more information: Belfer Audio Archive and Laboratory, Syracuse University, Syracuse University Library, 222 Waverley Ave., Syracuse, NY 13244-2010, 315-443-3477, email: ststinso @syr.edu. Also see http://libwww.syr.edu/information/belfer/.

North Carolina

The John W. Hartman Center for Sales, Advertising, & Marketing History, Rare Book, Manuscript, and Special Collections Library, Duke University, Durham

J. Walter Thompson Co. Archives. This archive stands alone as the single, most complete and informative corporate record of the history of modern advertising. It consists of more than 2,000 linear feet of printed and manuscript materials, including some 2 million items, half of which are advertisements. A sampling of collections included within the archives are the following materials:

- Thompson advertisement tear sheets and proofs 1875–1990s, arranged by client;
- Advertisement tear sheets of competing agencies 1916–1990s, arranged by product category;
- Company publications: more than 1,887, including newsletters 1916–1990s, and annual reports;
- Biographical files for Thompson employees 1914–1990s;
- Personnel files 1910s–1950s;
- Speeches and writings of Thompson executives 1908–1990s;
- Internal staff memoranda 1924–1990s;
- Verbatim staff meeting minutes 1927–1938;
- Market and product research reports 1916–1949;
- Radio-Television Department files, including microfilm of scripts of most of the agency-produced radio and television shows 1930–1960—including *Kraft Music Hall, Lux Radio Theatre,* and *Lux Video Theatre*;
- Board of Directors' minute books from 1896–1980s;
- Photographs of staff, offices, and activities;
- Records relating to the agency's offices abroad especially in Latin America and Europe;

- Tapes and transcripts of oral interviews with Company staff and officers, 1963–1979; and
- Press clippings and press releases.

D'Arcy Masius Benton & Bowles (DMB&B) Archives. The collection consists of advertising-agency records spanning the years 1929–1989. The bulk of the material dates from the 1950s to the mid-1980s. The archives include material that documents aspects of three advertising agencies: DMB&B, Benton & Bowles (B&B), and D'Arcy-MacManus & Masius (D-MM). The archives as a whole provide a comprehensive overview of B&B's advertisements (1932–1984) and commercials (1950s–1970s), primarily those created by the agency's New York office. Other major topics include William B. Benton's and Atherton W. Hobler's advertising careers; Gordon Webber's and Frank Smith's research and publication about the history of B&B; B&B-created television programs in the 1950s; aspects of employee training, recruitment, and management; and marketing research. The Archives also document the merger of the D-MM agency with B&B to form DMB&B in 1985. See http://scriptorium.lib.duke .edu/hartman/.

North Dakota

State Historical Society Archives of North Dakota, North Dakota Heritage Center. This center has manuscript material and audio and video recordings from a number of North Dakota broadcasting outlets—including KBOM and KVHF-AM radio; KTHI, KXMB, and KXJB television; and Prairie Public Radio and Television. See http://www.state.nd.us/hist/hcenter.htm.

Ohio

Browne Popular Culture Library/The Music Library and Sound Recordings Archives, Bowling Green State University. One of the most important U.S. centers for pop culture studies, Bowling Green State University is home to a wealth of material of interest to the radio historian. Scripts, books, and sound recordings can be found in these two facilities. The Browne Library also allows the genre researcher to delve into collections focusing on mystery, science fiction, westerns, comedy, and romance. See http://www.bgsu.edu/ colleges/library/.

Northeast Ohio Broadcast Archives, John Carroll University, Cleveland. Northeast Ohio Broadcast Archives were established in 1988 to provide a permanent home for radio, television, and print material related to this geographic area. It currently holds more than 150,000 films, audio and video recordings, and still photographs. Major contributors to the archives include WEWS, Channel 5, WKYC, Channel 3, and WGAR radio. Many other stations and individuals have added to the collection, including a major gift by retired news photographer William Wynne. See http://www.jcu.edu/communications/Archives.htm.

Oklahoma

Political Communication Center, University of Oklahoma, Julian P. Kanter Political Commercial Archive. This archive serves as repository for political radio and television commercials. The major purpose of the archive is to preserve these valuable historical materials and to make them available for scholarly and professional use. Originally founded in 1956, by private collector Julian P. Kanter, and housed at the University of Oklahoma since 1985, the archive collects, preserves, and catalogs an ever-increasing number of political commercials and related materials. The archive is now home to approximately 70,000 spots dating back to 1936 for radio and 1950 for television and representing candidates for offices ranging from the U.S. Presidency to school boards throughout the United States. The archive also contains commercials by political action committees—advertisements sponsored by corporations and special interest groups on public issues and ballot initiatives—and commercials done for elections in foreign countries. See http://www.ou.edu/pccenter/archive.htm.

Oklahoma Historical Society, Research Division, Motion Picture and Broadcasting Collections. The broadcasting collection spans from 1920–present and includes information on KSWO, KSWO-TV, KRHD, KOMA, KTUL, KGEO-TV, KADA, KFJK, KVOO, KOTV, KWTV, KOCO-TV, KTVQ, KTEN, KWSH, KTOK, KNOR, KGWA, KNED, OETA, WKY, WKY-TV, KTVY, KFOR, and many more radio and television stations in Oklahoma. Broadcasting collections include: film , video, oral histories, photographs, manuscripts, microfilm, newspapers and more. A "Timeline of Oklahoma Broadcasting" is available. See http://www.ok-history.mus.ok.us/arch/filmvideo.htm.

Oregon

Oregon Historical Society. The Society has recorded discs and audiotapes from a number of Oregon radio stations, including:

KOIN Collection. Local and national news programs (CBS network), including reports on World War II, the Korean War, and the Cold War, as well as the speeches of Franklin Roosevelt, Harry Truman, Winston Churchill, and others. Local programs include live reports on Kaiser shipyard launchings (1941–1945); reports on the Vanport Flood (1948); *Northwest Neighbors* radio talk show; *Who Killed Dr. Drew?*, the award-winning documentary on African-American physician Dr. Charles Drew; and *Kid Critics*, featuring Portland-area grade school children reviewing books.

The KBPS Collection. This station broadcast educational programs produced under the auspices of the Portland Public Schools, as well as programming produced by KGW or released from other affiliates. Programs include *The American Challenge*, a U.S. history series; *Bill Scott, Forest Ranger*, a conservation program sponsored by the U.S. Forest Service; live coverage of the 1941 Benson High School dance; and a drama (1939) from Reed College. See http://www.ohs.org/collections/index.cfm.

Pennsylvania

The Annenberg School for Communication Library, University of Pennsylvania

Annenberg Television Script Archive. This archive includes the *TV Guide* Collection (20,000 scripts and growing), Agnes Nixon Collection, and the new ABC Soap Opera Collection (a few hundred scripts from *All My Children*). In total, there are more than 29,000 television scripts.

Pat Polillo Archive. This archive consists of video, scripts, speeches, interviews, notes, and memos of local television news innovator Pat Polillo. Polillo was a pioneer of television news at the local level for almost 40 years, from 1961 to 1998. After serving as news director at stations in Philadelphia, Boston, San Francisco, and Atlanta, he served as vice president and general manager at KPIX-TV in San Francisco and from 1980 to 1984 at KYW-TV in Philadelphia. He gained a reputation in the business for transforming sagging news operations into market leaders everywhere he went.

Media Events Archive. A video collection of important historic events covered by the media on television and film in the twentieth century. Many of the videos show news coverage of media events; others are documentaries about those events. These videos are available for viewing in the Annenberg Library.

The Annenberg/Pew Archive of Presidential Campaign Discourse. This archive houses transcripts of speeches, television ads, and debates of twelve United States presidential campaigns, 1952–1996. It includes the work of the two major-party nominees—with the exception of Barry Goldwater. Collection of materials begins on September 1 of each election year and ends on election eve or day. Nomination acceptance speeches are also included. See http://www.library.upenn.edu/annenberg/.

Archives of Industrial Society, University of Pittsburgh, Archives Service Center. This archive contains historical collections related to the development of the urban industrial society, with an emphasis on Pittsburgh and Western Pennsylvania. Collections of interest to the broadcast historian include:

Papers of Harry Phillips Davis, 1915–1944. Harry Phillips Davis was a mechanical and electrical engineer that worked for the Westinghouse Electric and Manufacturing Company. He eventually rose to the position of vice president in charge of manufacturing and engineering for Westinghouse. During his tenure, Davis helped bring about the first commercial radio station in the United States, KDKA. His efforts to promote radio extended to his participation in creation the Public Broadcasting Company. This company combined the radio stations of Westinghouse, General Electric, and the Radio Corporation of America. Davis was serving as chairman of the board of directors of the National Broadcasting Company at the time of his death.

Guide to the Papers and Recordings of Local News Television in Pittsburgh: An Oral History Project, 1987–1991. This oral history collection consists of transcripts, cassette tapes, and release forms of the 29 interviews conducted during the Oral History Project. The Oral History Project documents Pittsburgh's early television history and its pioneers. The content of the interviews spans the late 1940s to the early 1960s. Other resources include the WQED-TV, Three Mile Island Nuclear Accident Video Collection (1979), KDKA coverage of the Pitt Parade and Eyewitness News footage, WQED Newsroom, and The Editors Series tapes.

South Carolina

University of South Carolina (USC). USC has been the recipient of several film collections. The most significant of these is a local television newsfilm collection. Columbia's NBC affiliate, WIS-TV, has donated their existing 16mm newsfilm covering the years 1959 to 1978. This footage provides an excellent record of local broadcast coverage regarding South Carolina events and personalities of the period. Other local television stations have followed suit by donating their materials as well, although these collections (WBTW, WLTX) are significantly smaller and not as well documented as the WIS-TV donation. See http://www.sc.edu/newsfilm/. In addition to the newsfilm collections, USC also houses the McKissick Museum and the Newsfilm Library.

McKissick Museum, South Carolina Broadcaster's Association Archives. The archives document the history of broadcasting in South Carolina by collecting and interpreting photographs, papers, videos, film, and knowledge of radio and TV's development, entertainment, and community activities in the state. The collection includes personal papers of industry leaders, original broadcasts and scripts, equipment, a music library, and station materials. The archives also collect materials that document the activities of the South Carolina Broadcasters Association and include audio, moving image, and print material. See http://www.cla.sc.edu/MCKS /broadcast/index.html.

The Newsfilm Library. The Newsfilm Library owns 11 million feet of Twentieth Century Fox Movietonews reels and their associated outtakes. Included are all reels from 1919 to 1934, as well as the complete newsreels and all associated outtakes from the important World War II period of September 1942 through August 1944.

Tennessee

Radio Archive of the University of Memphis. This programming archive has a 77-page, single-spaced catalog. This collection is the work of Dr. Marvin Bensman, who built it up over a 35-year period. Programs can be ordered from the archive by mail. See http://www.people.memphis.edu/~mbensman/ welcome.html.

Vanderbilt University Television News Archive. This archive, at Vanderbilt University, holds more than 30,000 individual network evening news broadcasts and more than 9,000 hours of special news-related programming. These special reports and periodic news broadcasts cover presidential press conferences and political campaign coverage, as well as national and international events such as the Watergate hearings, the plight of American hostages in Iran, and both the wars in the Persian Gulf. See http://tvnews.vanderbilt .edu/.

Texas

The Center for American History, University of Texas at Austin, Media History Archives. Collection highlights include:

Sig Mickelson Papers, 1930–1994 (30 ft.). Research materials, speeches, correspondence, audio and video tapes, photographs, film, and literary productions reflecting Mickelson's career as a broadcast executive and educator and his interest in telecommunications legislation, the role of television in politics, and the impact of television on public policy. Sig Mickelson held positions at CBS for nearly 20 years beginning in 1943. When CBS News became an autonomous corporate division in the mid 1950s, Mickelson became its first president.

Walter Cronkite Papers, 1931–present (287 ft.). Includes scripts, correspondence, research files, photographs, film, videotape, and printed materials, as well as Cronkite's oral history life memoir, a transcript produced from taped interviews with Cronkite made by CAH director Dr. Don Carleton in 1990–1993, which served as the basic text for Cronkite's published memoir *A Reporter's Life* (1996). The papers document Cronkite's career as a United Press wire reporter and war correspondent before joining CBS in 1950 as the network's Washington correspondent and news anchor at WTOP-TV. In 1962, Cronkite became the managing editor and anchor of *The CBS Evening News,* a position he held until his retirement in 1981.

CBS Evening News **Archive, 1962–1981 (75 ft.).** News scripts, memoranda, publicity materials, photographs, view mail, and miscellaneous materials generated during the years in which Walter Cronkite served as managing editor of *The CBS Evening News,* 1962–1981. This collection is closed to use pending lifting of restrictions by CBS News.

Steve Carlin Papers, 1950–1954 (50 ft.). These papers document Carlin's career in television entertainment for both children and adults during the 1950s, including the popular children's show *The Rootie Kazootie Club* on NBC. The collection contains near complete documentation of *The Rootie Kazootie Club,* including correspondence, scripts, contestant files, and advertising, and documents Carlin's pioneering work in marketing spin-off products from television shows. See http://www.cah.utexas.edu/collectioncomponents/media.html.

Hamon Arts Library, Southern Methodist University, Dallas, G. William Jones Film and Video Collection. This collection contains more than 9,000 film prints and negatives in all formats, and more than 3,000 videotapes. Other holdings include an extensive collection of antique projectors (some dating to 1905), cameras, and hundreds of film scripts, press kits, and production stills. Among the films that have been acquired and preserved are *The Pleasure Garden* (1926), Alfred Hitchcock's first film as director; *The Runaway* (1926), starring Koko the Clown in the Fleischer Bros.' first real mixing of live action with animation; *President John F. Kennedy* (1963) delivering his last speech on the morning of his assassination. See http://www.smu.edu/cul/hamon/collections/jonescollection.htm.

Principal Holdings:
- Tyler, Texas, Black Film Collection
- Benchmarks of Animation Film Collection
- Gene Autry Film Collection
- Belo Newsfilm Collection
- Canadian Film Collection
- Documentary Classics Film Collection
- Pre-Nickelodeon Short Films
- Dallas Theater Center Videotape Collection
- NorthPark Theatrical Trailer Collection

Utah

Arts and Communication Archives, Harold B. Lee Library, Brigham Young University, L. Tom Perry Special Collections. This collection is more heavily weighted toward film personalities, but several of its donors had significant broadcasting careers as well. Cecil B. DeMille (director of *The Lux Radio Theater*), Andy Devine (a regular on Jack Benny's program), Robert Cummings (numerous radio guest spots as well as starring on his own TV programs), and Jimmy Stewart (*The Six Shooter*) have all placed their papers here. Early television is documented by the collection of director Henry S. Kesler, which includes episodes of *I Led Three Lives* and other TV dramas, and the collection of screenwriter Art Arthur. See http://sc.lib.byu.edu/collections/arts.html.

University of Utah, Marriott Library, Manuscripts Division, Special Collections, Guide to the Broadcast Collections. This guide was created as a reference tool to provide a general overview. Most of the materials covered are personal collections, but some are organizational. Nearly all the collections relate to the broadcast industry in Salt Lake City and throughout Utah, although some materials concern broadcasting on the national and international levels, including the papers of Philo T. Farnsworth.

Subjects covered in the guide include radio and television stations, federal and private broadcast organizations, programming, advertising, promotion, performers, announcers, and engineering and technological developments. References to each subject are found in various forms: correspondence, scripts, business ledgers, company newsletters, reports, research papers, program schedules, corporate and financial records, oral-history interviews, newspaper and magazine clippings, subject files, biographical materials, engineering notebooks, photographs, and recordings. See http://www.lib.utah.edu/spc/index.html.

Washington

Gonzaga University, Spokane, Foley Center Library Special Collections Department, Bing Crosby Collection. The collection is the largest public Crosby collection, containing his 1944 Oscar for *Going My Way*, gold and platinum records, trophies and awards, photographs, correspondence, newsclippings, radio disks, records and cassettes, and other memorabilia. For a complete inventory, contact the Special Collections Department through their Website at http://www.gonzaga.edu/Academics/Libraries/default.htm. Categories include:

Original Manuscripts. Materials such as correspondence by Crosby, his family; friends, and contemporaries such as Bob Hope, Al Rinker, Rosemary Clooney, and Frank Sinatra. Also includes materials relating to Crosby organizations, such as the Bing Crosby Historical Society.

Photographs. Pictures of Bing, his family, friends, contemporaries, and places associated with him—such as his boyhood home in Tacoma.

Audiovisual. Recordings of his music, including phonograph records (33⅓ rpms and 78 rpms), Compact disks, and cassettes; radio show broadcasts. Commercial copies of his movies on video tapes or laser disks.

Realia. Includes three-dimensional objects relating to Crosby, such as Bing Crosby ice cream cartons, Crosby coloring books, buttons, Crosby clothing, and so forth.

Bing Crosby Historical Society Collection. In 1993 Gonzaga University received the entire collection of the Bing Crosby Historical Society of Tacoma, Washington. This collection includes materials relating to the life and career of Bing Crosby, business files of the Bing Crosby Historical Society, as well as correspondence, newsclippings, photographs, and Crosby memorabilia. The inventory to this collection is available to researchers who contact the Special Collections Department.

Bing Crosby Radio Shows. Gonzaga University has a large collection of Bing Crosby radio discs including:
* *The Bing Crosby Show:* 1949–1954
* *Kraft Music Hall:* 1943–1946
* *Minute Maid Fresh Squeezed Orange Juice:* 1949–1950
* *Philco Radio Time:* 1946–1949
* Miscellaneous: 1936–1960

Western Washington University. Center for Pacific Northwest Studies collects private papers and organizational and institutional records documenting economic, social, cultural, and political trends significant to the study of the Pacific Northwest.

The Rogan Jones Collection. The collection consists of business, legal, financial, and personal records of Lafayette Rogan Jones (1895–1972). Jones was a pioneer in radio and television broadcasting. During the 45 years he was active in the field, his contributions were widely recognized. He owned and operated four radio stations and one television station in Washington and the International Good Music Corporation. The collection contains a group of radio and oral history interviews that Jones and others recorded on 32 seven-inch and two five-inch, open-reel audiotapes and three cassette tapes. This group also includes a ten-inch reel of KGMI's 40th anniversary show (November 15, 1967).

KVOS Documentary Film Collection. A valuable collection of short documentary films made for or by KVOS and broadcast by the company between 1961–1968. The collection includes most of the *Webster Report* by Jack Webster, Vancouver newsman and radio columnist. The collection also includes numerous "Channel 12 Specials." See http://www.acadweb .wwu.edu/cpnws/default.htm.

West Virginia

Marshall University, Huntington James E. Morrow Library—Special Collections. Collections of interest include:

WPBY (Television Station), Huntington. Transcript of a videotaped program, "The Comstock Load" and a series of interviews with Jim Comstock, editor and publisher of the *West Virginia Hillbilly.*

WSAZ (Television station), Huntington. Film; videotape, 1953–1982 including 1,036 reels of film; 240 videocassettes; 57 cubic ft. other; sound, black-and-white, and color 16mm film and half-inch videotape. Newsfilm and tape of local National Broadcasting Company affiliate evening news broadcast; includes scripts and an index. See http://www.marshall.edu/ speccoll/mss.asp.

Wisconsin

Marquette University, Milwaukee, Department of Special Collections and University Archives. Search for collections at http://www.mu.edu/library/collections/archives/Finding.html.

Catholic Broadcasters Association Records 1947, 1955–1972. Records of a network of Catholic communications professionals which established the Gabriel Awards to recognize programs that "uplift and nourish the human spirit," including correspondence, newsletters, pamphlets, photographs, press releases, and proceedings of general assemblies and awards banquets. See http://www.marquette.edu/library/collections/archives/Mss /CBA/mss-CBAmain.html.

Catholic Film and Television Programs Collection 1952–1953, 1955, 1959. A collection of films from the 1950s relating to the Catholic faith, including *Christopher Programs* with James Cagney, Danny Thomas, and Robert Young; a *Catholic Hour* program on corrupt practices in U.S.

politics; and a film of a Midnight Pontifical High Mass at St. Patrick's Cathedral in New York City.

Al McGuire Film and Videtape Collection, 1953–present. A collection of audio, video, and 16mm film relating primarily to McGuire's second career in broadcasting. A large portion of the gift collection consists of master videotape interviews with prominent college basketball coaches and players. Highlights include McGuire's own interview with WTMJ the day he was hired by Marquette (April 11, 1964) and 15-minute, half-time (NBC) shows with Digger Phelps, Bobby Knight, and Michael Jordan. The collection also documents McGuire's civic contributions with many reels of "Al's Run" for Children's Hospital. See http://www.marquette.edu/library/collections/archives/Mss/McG/MCG.html.

Donald T. McNeill Collection, 1928–1969. Records of the long-running ABC Network radio program *The Breakfast Club* (1933–1968) and *Don McNeill's TV Club* (1950–1951), and related personal papers of their host, Don McNeill. Included are program scripts and outlines; publicity and advertising material; photographs; clippings and scrapbooks; films of *Breakfast Club* simulcasts, *TV Club* programs, and other television programs featuring McNeill; audiotape and phonograph recordings of *Breakfast Club* programs from the 1940s and 1950s; and master audiotapes for the last seven months of the *Breakfast Club,* May 30–December 27, 1968. See http://libus.csd.mu.edu/record=b1767960.

Hildegarde Sell Papers, 1921–1982. Correspondence, photographs, press clippings, programs, and ephemera documenting the career of internationally celebrated cabaret and café singer/pianist Hildegarde Loretta Sell (known professionally as "The Incomparable Hildegarde"), a native of Adell, Wisconsin who attended the Marquette University School of Music in 1924–1925. Most of the documents are contained in 49 scrapbooks. See http://libus.csd.mu.edu/record=b1833565.

Wisconsin Historical Society/University of Wisconsin-Madison, Wisconsin Center for Film and Theater Research. Cosponsored by the University of Wisconsin-Madison and the Wisconsin Historical Society, the Wisconsin Center for Film and Theater Research (WCFTR) is one of the world's major archives of research materials relating to the entertainment industry. It maintains more than 300 manuscripts collections from outstanding playwrights, television and motion picture writers, producers, actors, designers, directors, and production companies. In addition to the paper records, materials preserved include 15,000 motion pictures, television shows, and videotapes; 2 million still photographs and promotional graphics; and several thousand sound recordings. WCFTR's collections are richest in records of the American film industry between 1930 and 1960, popular theater of the 1940s and 1950s, and television from the 1950s through the 1970s.

The center's television collections are especially rich for the pre-videotape era, when programs were either broadcast live and copied onto kinescope or produced and broadcast using film. The anthology dramas telecast live from New York City are well documented in the moving-image and manuscripts portions of the Fred Coe and David Susskind Collections. Numerous episodes of *Armstrong Circle Theatre, Philco Television Playhouse, Goodyear Playhouse, Playhouse 90, Playwrights '56,* and many of the other weekly drama series are available for viewing on original kinescope.

The largest of WCFTR's television collections is comprised of 3,500 shows produced by Ziv Television, the most successful producer of action-adventure programming filmed for first-run syndication from 1948 to 1962. The Ziv library includes viewing copies and printing elements for every episode of *Boston Blackie, I Led Three Lives, Mr. District Attorney, Highway Patrol, Sea Hunt, Bat Masterson,* and 32 other series. Scripts, production, and promotional materials for these and additional Ziv series can also be examined at the center.

Other collections contain viewing prints, scripts, production, and legal information from the immensely popular television documentary series *Victory at Sea, Project XX, The 20th Century* and *The 21st Century.* WCFTR's Ed Sullivan Collection holds copies of many episodes from *The Ed Sullivan Show,* as well as manuscripts and photographs documenting his entire career. The center also holds film and manuscript documentation of other television variety shows, such as *The Bell Telephone Hour* and *The Martha Raye Show.*

Nearly complete runs of the early 1960s groundbreaking, dramatic programs *Eastside/Westside* and *The Defenders,* popular programming like *Bonanza,* and seminal comedies such as *You'll Never Get Rich* and *Car 54, Where Are You?* can be viewed at the Center. Again, the viewing prints of these programs are accompanied by complete pre- and postproduction and broadcast information in the collections of David Susskind, Reginald Rose, Nat Hiken, and others. The MTM Enterprises Collection consists of film and videotape copies of pilots and selected episodes from series such as *The Mary Tyler Moore Show, Rhoda, Bob Newhart, Paris,* and *Lou Grant.* Scripts for the entire run of virtually all of the MTM series, from *St. Elsewhere* to *Remington Steele,* can be studied in the Archives Research Room.

Documentation of television milestones and the evolution of entire broadcast genres can be found in the manuscript collections of pioneer television writers and producers Alvin Boretz, Paddy Chayevsky, Hal Kanter, Loring Mandel, E. Jack Neuman, Irna Phillips, Howard Rodman, Sy Salkowitz, and many others. Information about WCFTR manuscript collections is available in ARCAT, the online catalog. See http://www.wisconsinhistory.org/wcftr/.

15

Assessing the Record:
A Century of Historical Research

Christopher H. Sterling
George Washington University

Today's historians are building upon more than a century of published electronic media research, ranging from the earliest histories of wireless telegraphy technology to studies of the rise (and occasional failure) of modern electronic media. Nearly all of these have used a traditional narrative approach, providing varied levels of both documentation and evidence of reliable research.

Four of those studies can be seen as watersheds, helping to set new directions in electronic media historical writing. For example, Fahie initiated two decades of technical wireless histories, most written by engineers.[1] Archer's two radio business histories were among the earliest attempts to describe how the new industry had developed—and suggested a growing research interest in that story.[2] Barnouw's masterful trilogy was the epitome of graceful writing as well as a highwater mark of traditional narrative history based on interviews and existing literature, and on which so much work since has been based.[3]

---

[1] John J. Fahie, *A History of Wireless Telegraphy 1838–1899* (New York: Dodd, Mead, 1899, repr. New York: Arno Press, in the series *History of Radio and Television,* 1971).

[2] Gleason L. Archer, *A History of Radio to 1926* (New York: American Historical Society, 1938; repr., New York: Arno Press, in the series *History of Broadcasting,* 1971).

[3] Erik Barnouw, *A Tower in Babel: A History of Broadcasting in the United States to 1933,* vol. 1 (New York: Oxford University Press, 1966); Erik Barnouw, *The Golden*

Reflecting the growing academic interest in the field, Aitken's two studies of radio's early technical development brought us full circle back to the baseline technology underlying broadcasting, though now applying the full panoply of modern historical research methods based on a growing cornucopia of source material.[4] Many more recent studies cited below show a growing trend toward more focused and detailed research.

This final chapter assesses the growing number of serious analytical historical books—most of them products of the past couple of decades—and their use of source material, modes of analysis, and application of context. For want of space, this survey must be selective, generally excluding most work done elsewhere (other than to make usually invidious comparisons with weaker American efforts), important studies published in other languages (chiefly French, German, and Japanese), international (including propaganda) or comparative studies, historical textbooks, popular history, and most of the growing scholarly journal literature. Rather than assessing the canon chronologically, this chapter reviews it by topical categories: technology, industry and economics, programming, audience, policy, concluding with some suggestions of what is still needed.

TECHNOLOGY

Histories of wireless technology were the earliest—and for years made up by far the best and most precise historical work on radio. These first histories were all British and drew on a tradition of detailed telegraph and telephone histories. Fahie set a high standard of accuracy in what was the first history of wireless theoreticians and inventors, published on the eve of the first commercial application of radio technology.[5] Working directly with patents, articles, and interviews (Marconi, for example, was not yet 30), Fahie provided an

---

Web: A History of Broadcasting in the United States 1933–1953, vol. 2 (New York: Oxford University Press, 1968); Erik Barnouw, *The Image Empire: A History of Broadcasting in the United States from 1953,* vol. 3 (New York: Oxford University Press, 1970).

[4] Hugh G. J. Aitken, *Syntony and Spark: The Origins of Radio* (New York: Wiley, 1976; repr., Princeton, NJ: Princeton University Press, 1985); Hugh G. J. Aitken, *The Continuous Wave: Technology and American Radio, 1900–1932* (Princeton, NJ: Princeton University Press, 1985).

[5] Fahie, *A History of Wireless Telegraphy,* 1899.

intricately documented survey of the experimental beginnings of radio. Among the many writers who followed his path, Fleming is of special interest in that the engineer author played a central role in some of the history he relates, thus drawing on direct experience as well as documentary research.[6] Blake wrapped up the first generation of wireless development with a highly detailed survey down to citing specific patents and events.[7] Nearly two decades later McNicol provided a broader survey of radio's development from the vantage point of a distinguished radio engineer, accurate though undocumented as it was written for nontechnical readers.[8] The study of early radio wave detectors predating vacuum tubes is well documented in Phillips.[9] Written largely for collectors, but invaluable as detailed and carefully documented history are two studies of the development of vacuum tubes by Tyne and Stokes.[10] Aitken's studies of wireless to 1900 and radio in the first three decades of the twentieth century are models of historical research, careful assessment, and clear writing about often complex topics—all of it extremely well documented.[11] Douglas covers much of the same ground skillfully combining technology, industrial developments, and developing government policy.[12] Hers is a fine and widely cited example of dissertation research standards translated to a published book. Finally, the important role of the Navy in developing both technology and government policy in the period leading up to broadcasting is the subject of the well-researched Howeth book, an admirable study based

---

[6] John A. Fleming, *The Principles of Electric Wave Telegraph and Telephony,* 2nd ed. (New York: Longmans, Green, 1910).

[7] George G. Blake, *History of Radio Telegraphy and Telephony* (London: Chapman & Hall, 1928; repr., New York: Arno Press, in the series *Telecommunications,* 1974).

[8] Donald McNicol, *Radio's Conquest of Space: The Experimental Rise in Radio Communication* (New York: Murray Hill Books, 1946; repr., New York: Arno Press, in the series *Telecommunications,* 1974).

[9] Vivian J. Phillips, *Early Radio Wave Detectors* (London: Peter Peregrinus, 1981).

[10] Gerald F. J. Tyne, *Saga of the Vacuum Tube* (Indianapolis, IN: Howard W. Sams, 1977); John W. Stokes, *70 Years of Radio Tubes and Valves* (Vestal, NY: Vestal Press, 1982).

[11] Aitken, *Syntony and Spark;* Aitken, *The Continuous Wave.*

[12] Susan J. Douglas, *Inventing American Broadcasting, 1899–1922* (Baltimore, MD: Johns Hopkins University Press, 1987).

heavily on primary documentation and still considered definitive four decades later.[13]

Research-based biographies of radio's innovators are generally few and disappointing. Of the several Marconi biographies published since the first appeared in 1937, Jolly provides the closest approach in both tone and analysis—and he does so again in his later study of Britain's Sir Oliver Lodge.[14] MacGregor-Morris offers the only biographical study of vacuum-tube inventor (and prolific author) Ambrose Fleming, based in part on the latter's extensive papers, his 1934 autobiography, and the author's knowledge of him as a former teacher.[15] Brittain's study of engineer E. F. W. Alexanderson was years in preparation, and is perhaps the best researched model of what is needed for so many other figures.[16] Seitz's brief monograph on Fessenden approaches what is sorely needed for others.[17] At the opposite extreme, Maclaurin's study of the more important radio inventors (including those noted here), innovations, and patent fights to about 1940 set a standard for careful research and judgment yet to be superceded more than a half century later.[18]

Only more recently has television's technical history been subjected to serious analysis. By far the best overall histories, filled with detail and carefully documented, are those by Abramson, a television engineer himself, and Burns comparing developments in Britain, Germany, France, and the United States

---

[13] Linwood S. Howeth, *History of Communications-electronics in the United States Navy* (Washington, DC: Government Printing Office, 1963).

[14] W. P. Jolly, *Marconi* (New York: Stein & Day, 1972); W. P. Jolly, *Sir Oliver Lodge: Psychical Researcher and Scientist* (Cranbury, NJ: Associate University Presses, 1974).

[15] John T. MacGregor-Morris, *The Inventor of the Valve: A Biography of Sir Ambrose Fleming* (London: Television Society, 1954).

[16] James E. Brittain, *Alexanderson: Pioneer in American Electrical Engineering* (Baltimore, MD: Johns Hopkins University Press, 1992).

[17] Frederick Seitz, *The Cosmic Inventor: Reginald Aubrey Fessenden (1866–1932)*, transactions of the American Philosophical Society, 89 (Philadelphia, PA: American Philosophical Society, 1999).

[18] W. Rupert Maclaurin, *Invention and Innovation in the Radio Industry* (New York: Macmillan, 1949; repr., New York: Arno Press, in the series *History of Broadcasting*, 1971).

to about 1940.[19] Fisher and Fisher provided a generally accurate study (largely of U.S. work) designed for general readers and based largely on secondary sources, though it must be used with care for some details.[20] Udelson combined discussion of business, regulatory, and technical developments in American television before World War II—a fairly sketchy study still widely cited given the continuing dearth of much else.[21] Kurylo offers a solidly researched life of cathode-ray tube inventor Ferdinand Braun.[22] Of the key American inventors, Abramson's biography of Zworykin, and Godfrey's study of Philo T. Farnsworth set the standard, being carefully based on primary sources and reaching measured conclusions.[23] (Somewhat surprisingly, given the likely market, at least four further popular biographies of Farnsworth have also appeared in the past few years, though they all stress the inventor as embattled hero, adding little to the record.)

Relevant consumer technologies have also begun to generate solid historical research. Schiffer's 1991 history of the changing radio receiver refocused scholarly attention on the audience with its pioneering assessment of changing portable radio design from crude sets of the 1920s to modern solid state equipment (see also the several manufacturing company histories discussed later under "economics").[24] Although there is no comparable history of television receivers, Abramson (noted previously) provides some material. Both audio and video recording methods have been well recorded in an excellent

---

[19] Albert H. Abramson, *The History of Television, 1880–1941* (Jefferson, NC: McFarland, 1987); Albert H. Abramson, *The History of Television, 1942–2000* (Jefferson, NC: McFarland, 2003); Russell W. Burns, *Television: An International History of the Formative Years* (London: Institute of Electrical Engineers, 1998).

[20] David E. Fisher and Marshall John Fisher, *Tube: The Invention of Television* (New York: Harcourt Brace, 1996).

[21] Joseph H. Udelson, *The Great Television Race: A History of the American Television Industry, 1925–1941* (Tuscaloosa: University of Alabama Press, 1982).

[22] Friedrich Kurylo, *Ferdinand Braun: A Life of the Nobel Prizewinner and Inventor of the Cathode-ray Oscilloscope,* trans. and adapted by Charles Susskind (Cambridge, MA: MIT Press, 1981).

[23] Albert H. Abramson, *Zworykin: Pioneer of Television* (Urbana: University of Illinois Press, 1995); Donald G. Godfrey, *Philo T. Farnsworth: Father of Television* (Salt Lake City: University of Utah, 2001).

[24] Michael Brian Schiffer, *The Portable Radio in American Life* (Tucson: University of Arizona Press, 1991).

(though little known) anthology of original technical history edited by Daniel, Mee, and Clark.[25] The rise of video recording is related in Abramson's history, as well as in Nmungwun and Marlow and Secunda, both of which focus usefully on the rise (and sometimes fall) of specific approaches to video tape recording technologies.[26] Newer technologies are less well served—understandable given their very recency. The short-lived story of teletext is analyzed, and the reasons for its short life are explained, by Graziplene, while the often-labored initial steps toward adopting digital television standards around the world are detailed in Dupagne and Seel, a model of comparative research.[27]

Perhaps most difficult to write is broadly integrated history of electronic media technology. One of the earliest attempts, Harlow, equally treated the development of telegraph, telephone, and radio, providing solid history though lacking in documentation.[28] Sadly, there is little in the American literature to match Pawley's excellent history of a half century of BBC engineering.[29] One attempt, Inglis, offers a generally accurate account of both radio and television development, though reflecting an RCA bias (where the author once worked), and suffering from a sometimes confusing organization.[30] Winston offers his unique model of technological innovation to frame a well-researched and documented study of telecommunication, computer, and

---

[25] Eric D. Daniel, C. Denis Mee, and Mark H. Clark, eds., *Magnetic Recording: The First 100 Years* (New York: Institute of Electrical and Electronics Engineers, Inc. [IEEE] Press, 1999).

[26] Aaron Foisi Nmungwun, *Video Recording Technology: Its Impact on Media and Home Entertainment* (Hillsdale, NJ: Lawrence Erlbaum Associates, 1989); Eugene Marlow and Eugene Secunda, *Shifting Time and Space: The Story of Videotape* (Westport, CT: Praeger, 1991).

[27] Leonard R. Graziplene, *Teletext: Its Promise and Demise* (Bethlehem, PA: Lehigh University Press, 2000); Michael Dupagne and Peter B. Seel, *HDTV: High-definition Television, A Global Perspective* (Ames: Iowa State University Press, 1998).

[28] Alvin F. Harlow, *Old Wires and New Waves: The History of the Telegraph, Telephone, and Wireless* (New York: Appleton, 1936; repr., New York: Arno Press, in the series *History of Radio and Television,* 1971).

[29] Edward Pawley, *BBC Engineering: 1922–1972* (London: British Broadcasting Corporation [BBC], 1972).

[30] Andrew F. Inglis, *Behind The Tube: A History of Broadcasting Technology and Business* (Boston, MA: Focal Press, 1990).

media invention and application.[31] Chandler's history provides an insightful broad view, comparing and contrasting consumer electronics and computer industry development from the 1920s into the 1990s.[32] Additionally, Rohlfs provides a fascinating study of what he terms the "bandwagon" effect of adoption of new technologies, many of his examples being drawn from electronic media.[33]

Journals are especially important for technical history, exemplified by the massive golden anniversary issue of the Institute of Radio Engineers (IRE) with its dozens of deeply documented surveys on the development of most aspects of radio technology.[34] Likewise occasional and well-documented historical articles in journals published by the Institution of Electrical Engineers (IEE) and Institute of Electrical and Electronics Engineers (IEEE) and, especially, the Society of Motion Picture and Television Engineers (SMPTE), as well as the quarterly *Technology and Culture* add social context to the canon. Too little of this material migrates to book publication.

ECONOMICS

There is nothing in the American literature that comes close to the British models of what can and should be accomplished with institutional history: First, Asa Briggs wrote five volumes on BBC history taking it as far as 1975 (another volume by other authors is in preparation to continue from where Briggs stopped).[35] Meanwhile, independent television in Britain was documented over four volumes by Bernard Sendall and Jeremy Potter, beginning with its origin and foundation in 1946 and continuing through its expansion

---

[31] Brian Winston, *Media Technology and Society: A History from the Telegraph to the Internet* (New York: Routledge, 1998).

[32] Alfred D. Chandler, *Inventing the Electronic Century: The Epic Story of the Consumer Electronics and Computer Industries* (New York: Free Press, 2001).

[33] Jeffrey H. Rohlfs, *Bandwagon Effects in High-technology Industries* (Cambridge, MA: MIT Press, 2001).

[34] Institute of Radio Engineers, "The Fiftieth Anniversary Issue," *Proceedings of the Institute of Radio Engineers* 50 (May 1962): 529–1,448.

[35] Asa Briggs, *The History of Broadcasting in the United Kingdom:* vol. 1, *The Birth of Broadcasting;* vol. 2, *Golden Age of Wireless;* vol. 3, *The War of Words;* vol. 4, *Sound & Vision;* vol. 5, *Competition* (London: Oxford University Press, 1961, 1965, 1970, 1979, and 1995).

and change, politics and control, and companies and programs up to 1980; Paul Bonner (with Leslie Aston) contributed a fifth volume taking the ITV history from 1981 to 1992.[36]

The complex story of pre-World War I American wireless companies is well traced and documented in Mayes, rescuing their precise detail before all the evidence disappeared.[37] Archer laid the groundwork for the study of American broadcasting companies with his considerable detail on RCA and NBC (and somewhat less on CBS), drawn from interviews and company documents.[38] His was perhaps the first radio history based on such access to both people and archives, but it suffers from confusing organization and its RCA bias, offers little on programs or their effects, and relies upon an old-fashioned "great men" approach to industry leaders and their roles. Aside from two surveys aimed largely at general audiences and offering minimal documentation (Bergreen, written before cable competition created huge inroads in their audiences; and MacDonald), U.S. broadcast network "history" has largely consisted of coffee-table picture books.[39]

Scholarship at the station level is better served. While many outlets have published brief popular surveys emphasizing programs and personalities, research-based efforts are less common—in considerable part this appears due to scattered resources of an industry not known for retaining records or even being interested in its past. Greb and Adams have plumbed the records to rescue and document Charles Herrold, the pioneer San Jose, California creator of radio broadcasting (but, reflecting another problem, they had a difficult time

---

[36] Bernard Sendall and Jeremy Potter, *Independent Television in Britain:* vol. 1, *Origin and Foundation, 1946–62;* vol. 2, *Expansion and Change, 1958–68;* vol. 3, *Politics and Control, 1968–1980;* vol. 4, *Companies and Programmes, 1968–1980* (London: Macmillan, 1981, 1982, 1989, 1990); Paul Bonner with Leslie Aston, *Independent Television in Britain:* vol. 5, *ITV and the IBA 1981–92: The Old Relationship Changes* (London: Macmillan, 1998).

[37] Thorn L. Mayes, *Wireless Communication in the United States: The Early Development of American Radio Operating Companies* (East Greenwich, RI: New England Wireless and Steam Museum, 1989).

[38] Gleason L. Archer, *Big Business and Radio* (New York: American Historical Company, 1939; repr., New York: Arno Press, in the series *History of Broadcasting*, 1971).

[39] Laurence Bergreen, *Look Now, Pay Later: The Rise of Network Broadcasting* (Garden City, NY: Doubleday, 1980); J. Fred MacDonald, *One Nation under Television: The Rise and Decline of Network TV* (New York: Pantheon, 1990).

finding a publisher).[40] Banning's classic study of AT&T's station WEAF and the inception of radio advertising in New York in the 1920s stands almost alone more than a half century after its appearance.[41] He wrote as a former AT&T employee with access to people and records. Evans's study of Chicago station WLS from 1922 to 1960 is another example of carefully documented scholarly research.[42] Godfried traces another Chicago outlet, in this case labor union-owned WCFL.[43] Difficult to find as it appeared only in a limited number of paper-bound copies is Pusateri's well-documented history of WWL in New Orleans.[44] Murray and Godfrey edited a very useful anthology of original research-based essays—really case studies—of local commercial television stations from different parts of the country.[45] Few serious statewide broadcasting histories have appeared, Schroeder being one example tracing both early radio and television stations in Texas.[46] Finally, while Jaker, Sulek, and Kanze is more a directory of individual New York City AM station brief histories, it indicates the level of valuable detail that can be rescued with diligent (if largely undocumented in this case) effort.[47]

Of equipment manufacturers, Baker's history of the Marconi Co. is one of only a handful of available histories though it sadly lacks documentation.[48]

---

[40] Gordon Greb and Mike Adams, *Charles Herrold: Inventor of Radio Broadcasting* (Jefferson, NC: McFarland, 2003).

[41] William P. Banning, *Commercial Broadcasting Pioneer: The WEAF Experiment, 1922–1926* (Cambridge, MA: Harvard University Press, 1946).

[42] James F. Evans, *Prairie Farmer and WLS: The Burridge D. Butler Years* (Urbana: University of Illinois Press, 1969).

[43] Nathan Godfried, *WCFL: Chicago's Voice of Labor, 1926–78* (Urbana: University of Illinois Press, 1997).

[44] C. Joseph Pusateri, *Enterprise in Radio: WWL and the Business of Broadcasting in America* (Washington, DC: University Press of America, 1980).

[45] Michael D. Murray and Donald G. Godfrey, eds., *Television in America: Local Station History from across the Nation* (Ames: Iowa State University Press, 1997).

[46] Richard Schroeder, *Texas Signs On: The Early Days of Radio and Television* (College Station: Texas A&M University Press, 1998).

[47] Bill Jaker, Frank Sulek, and Peter Kanze, *The Airwaves of New York: Illustrated Histories of 156 AM Stations in the Metropolitan Area, 1921–1996* (Jefferson, NC: McFarland, 1996).

[48] W. J. Baker, *A History of the Marconi Company* (New York: St. Martin's Press, 1972).

Bryant and Cones's studies of Zenith Radio are already one of the best company histories, though the third volume has yet to appear.[49] It is written primarily for receiver collectors, and provides a wealth of text and illustration detail found nowhere else. Even more focused on the radios themselves is the Ramirez and Prosise study of the prewar Philco company's huge output.[50] A final example of what dedicated collectors–researchers can produce are two studies of Atwater Kent (the important radio maker in the 1920s and early 1930s) by Williams, though again the emphasis here is more on the actual equipment.[51]

Far more typical of what is available is Sobel's rather shallow business history of RCA written just as that company was disappearing into General Electric, aimed at a general audience, and providing little documentation.[52] There is no scholarly biography of long-time RCA head and industry leader David Sarnoff, though Bilby, who worked with "the general," comes the closest of the several published studies with his balanced account that ends several long-standing myths.[53] Cowie, on the other hand, demonstrates what can be accomplished in his careful analysis of RCA labor policies over 75 years and two countries.[54] Likewise, Graham's case study of RCA's disastrous management experience with home video recording drew on unprecedented access to company records, and offers a rare documented record of senior management attempting but failing to manage fast-changing technology.[55]

---

[49] John H. Bryant and Harold N. Cones, *Zenith Radio: The Early Years, 1919–1935* (Atglen, PA: Schiffer, 1997); Harold N. Cones and John H. Bryant, *Zenith Radio: The Glory Years, 1936–1945:* vol. 1, *History and Product;* vol. 2, *Illustrated Catalog and Database* (Atglen, PA: Schiffer, 2003).

[50] Ron Ramirez, with Michael Prosise, *Philco Radio 1928–1942* (Atglen, PA: Schiffer, 1993).

[51] Ralph Williams, "The Atwater Kent Radios," *The Antique Wireless Association Review* 12 (1999); Ralph Williams, *A. Atwater Kent: The Man, The Manufacturer, and His Radios* (Chandler, AZ: Sonoran Publishing, 2002).

[52] Robert Sobel, *RCA* (New York: Stein and Day, 1986).

[53] Kenneth Bilby, *The General: David Sarnoff and the Rise of the Communications Industry* (New York: Harper & Row, 1986).

[54] Jefferson Cowie, *Capital Moves: RCA's Seventy-five Year Quest for Cheap Labor* (Ithaca, NY: Cornell University Press, 1999).

[55] Margaret B. W. Graham, *RCA & the Videodisc: The Business of Research* (New York: Cambridge University Press, 1986).

There are markedly few scholarly biographies or historical studies of broadcast or cable industry leaders, personnel in general, or organizations. Only Koenig traces and assesses the role of craft and technical unions in broadcasting.[56] Although several network figures have written autobiographies (and there are three popular biographies of CBS founder William S. Paley), these lack scholarly value given their usual lack of balance and total lack of research apparatus. A stellar exception in this desert is Garay, a careful biography drawn from Gordon McClendon's papers and interviews.[57]

Histories of the development of advertising support for broadcasting are also very spotty (here again the British excel as there are several scholarly analyses of the rise of television—and later radio—advertising in that country). Hettinger recorded the initial decade of commercials on U.S. radio with a level of detail and documentation not reached since.[58] Barnouw's history of sponsorship is wonderfully written and based on considerable research but carries a strong point of view and limited documentation.[59] Smulyan is the first scholarly analysis of the decisions that led to the "acceptance" of advertising on the air—carefully researched, documented, and written.[60] Streeter applies "critical" analysis in both viewpoint and method, going over some of the same ground as previous writers, but arguing that advertising support for radio was not the foregone conclusion generally assumed.[61]

The development of noncommercial broadcasting has naturally attracted academic authors over the years, given that many of the stations were and are administered by colleges and universities. Frost wrote the first detailed history and still provides a baseline today, with its recording of individual pioneering

---

[56] Allen E. Koenig, *Broadcasting and Bargaining: Labor Relations in Radio and Television* (Madison: University of Wisconsin Press, 1970).

[57] Ronald Garay, *Gordon McLendon: The Maverick of Radio* (Westport, CT: Greenwood, 1984).

[58] Herman S. Hettinger, *A Decade of Radio Advertising* (Chicago: University of Chicago Press, 1933; repr., New York: Arno Press, in the series *History of Broadcasting,* 1971).

[59] Erik Barnouw, *The Sponsor: Notes on a Modern Potentate* (New York: Oxford University Press, 1978).

[60] Susan Smulyan, *Selling Radio: The Commercialization of American Broadcasting 1920–1934* (Washington, DC: Smithsonian Institution Press, 1994).

[61] Thomas Streeter, *Selling the Air: A Critique of the Policy of Commercial Broadcasting in the United States* (Chicago: University of Chicago Press, 1996).

stations, many of which have long since left the air.[62] Both Blakely and Day provide overall histories of the noncommercial sector (radio and television by the former; television only in the latter) as seen, in part, by the players inside.[63] These are measured accounts, though written in a sympathetic tone. Stone traces the conflict of the new public broadcasting system and the Nixon administration, centering on the battle over "long-range" funding.[64] Land and the more detailed Lasar assess the often contentious history of the liberal Pacifica Foundation stations, and some of their key personnel from founder Lewis Hill to the present.[65] Both studies are based on interviews and archival source material.

PROGRAMMING

Of the huge number of books on radio or television entertainment programming or stars, the vast majority are written for a general audience, and few have lasting research value or demonstrate much contextual insight. There is yet no overall scholarly history of broadcast (or even of radio or television) programming—admittedly a daunting task. But useful studies have appeared —some of the most interesting scholarship has centered on specific entertainment program genres. Stedman initiated this effort with his gracefully written study of serial drama across the decades in three media—film, radio, and television.[66] Others have since followed similar pathways.

---

[62] S. E. Frost Jr., *Education's Own Stations: The History of Broadcast Licenses Issued to Educational Institutions* (Chicago: University of Chicago Press, 1937).

[63] Robert J. Blakely, *To Serve the Public Interest: Educational Broadcasting in the United States* (Syracuse, NY: Syracuse University Press, 1979); James Day, *The Vanishing Vision: The Inside Story of Public Television* (Berkeley: University of California Press, 1995).

[64] David M. Stone, *Nixon and the Politics of Public Television* (New York: Garland, 1985).

[65] Jeff Land, *Active Radio: Pacifica's Brash Experiment* (Minneapolis: University of Minnesota Press, 1999); Matthew Lasar, *Pacifica Radio: The Rise of an Alternative Network* (Philadelphia, PA: Temple University Press, 1999).

[66] Raymond W. Stedman, *The Serials: Suspense and Drama by Installment,* 2nd ed. (Norman: University of Oklahoma Press, 1977).

Turning first to radio, Greenfield provides what is essentially an annotated guide to research available on different radio program genres.[67] Two scholars, Michele Hilmes and Michael C. Keith, have focused their efforts —and considerable output—on radio programming, hugely assisting a revival in serious attention to the senior medium. Hilmes ranges over three decades of radio network programming in her well-documented analysis of what was on the air.[68] Keith is amazingly productive: His 1995 study appears to be the first book on Native American radio; his 1997 study of underground radio in the 1960s is also the first serious study of that movement and its later impact, as is his 2000 analysis of radio talk in an era of television, and his informal 2001 history of all-night radio in American life.[69] Keith's books are based on extensive interviews and documentary work, and demonstrate a fine editing hand to tie the pieces together.

Wertheim's analysis of comedy formats on radio—published three decades after the subject programs left the air—remains a standard scholarly study as does Ely who focused on the long-running *Amos 'n' Andy* series on both radio and television.[70] Religious programs (and stations) are traced by Howard Dorgan, who examines the Appalachian region specifically, and by Tona Hangen who places such broadcasts in a broader cultural context.[71] Howard

---

[67] Thomas Allen Greenfield, *Radio: A Reference Guide* (Westport, CT: Greenwood, 1989).

[68] Michele Hilmes, *Radio Voices: American Broadcasting, 1922–1952* (Minneapolis: University of Minnesota Press, 1997).

[69] Michael C. Keith, *Signals in the Air: Native Broadcasting in America* (Westport, CT: Praeger, 1995); Michael C. Keith, *Voices in the Purple Haze: Underground Radio and the Sixties* (Westport, CT: Praeger, 1997); Michael C. Keith, *Talking Radio: An Oral History of American Radio in the Television Age* (Armonk, NY: M.E. Sharpe, 2000); Michael C. Keith, *Sounds in the Dark: All-night Radio in American Life* (Ames: Iowa State University Press, 2001).

[70] Arthur F. Wertheim, *Radio Comedy* (New York: Oxford University Press, 1979); Melvin Patrick Ely, *The Adventures of Amos 'n' Andy: A Social History of an American Phenomenon* (New York: Free Press, 1991).

[71] Howard Dorgan, *The Airwaves of Zion: Radio and Religion in Appalachia* (Knoxville: University of Tennessee Press, 1993); Tona J. Hangen, *Redeeming the Dial: Radio, Religion, and Popular Culture in America* (Chapel Hill: University of North Carolina Press, 2002).

Blue reviews radio's domestic role during World War II.[72] Baker surveys the rapidly disappearing format of agricultural radio over six decades.[73]

In television, Rose offered the first broad-ranging handbook of the development of different types of television program genre (entertainment and public affairs) with contributions from nearly two-dozen scholars.[74] He followed this up with a more focused analysis of television coverage of the performing arts.[75] Hawes has recorded the rise and expansion of American network television drama from the experiments of the late 1930s to the dominance of film by the late 1950s, based on a careful analysis of surviving recordings and documents.[76] Edgerton and Rollins review in 16 original scholarly papers how well or poorly entertainment and documentary programs depict history.[77]

Not surprisingly, there is far more serious study of news and public affairs programming. Bliss made the first attempt at an overall scholarly history of broadcast news—more than six decades after its inception.[78] The author combined traditional research with his own knowledge of key people from years of network news work. The birth and golden years of radio commentators and the impacts of news in the 1930s are carefully described in five books by Culbert, Hosley, Brown, Craig, and Miller that overlap to some degree,

---

[72] Howard Blue, *Words at War: World War II Era Radio Drama and the Postwar Broadcasting Industry Blacklist* (Lanham, MD: Scarecrow Press, 2002).

[73] John C. Baker, *Farm Broadcasting: The First Sixty Years* (Ames: Iowa State University Press, 1981).

[74] Brian G. Rose, *TV Genres: A Handbook and Reference Guide* (Westport, CT: Greenwood, 1985).

[75] Brian G. Rose, *Television and the Performing Arts: A Handbook and Reference Guide to American Cultural Programming* (Westport, CT: Greenwood, 1986).

[76] William Hawes, *American Television Drama: The Experimental Years* (Tuscaloosa: University of Alabama Press, 1986); William Hawes, *Live Television Drama, 1946–1951* (Jefferson, NC: McFarland, 2001); William Hawes, *Filmed Television Drama, 1952–1958* (Jefferson, NC: McFarland, 2002).

[77] Gary R. Edgerton and Peter C. Rollins, eds., *Television Histories: Shaping Collective Memory in the Media Age* (Lexington: University Press of Kentucky, 2001).

[78] Edward Bliss Jr., *Now the News: The Story of Broadcast Journalism* (New York: Columbia University Press, 1991).

although all five authors provide useful insight and documentation.[79] A related topic that is well covered with scholarly work is the use of radio and television by presidents and candidates to be president—see, for example, Chester, Gilbert, and Diamond and Bates—as well as the seemingly countless journalistic books on individual campaigns.[80] The once important network television documentary was best defined and described in Bluem who covered the 1950s and early 1960s "golden age," and was updated by Hammond to cover programs of the 1970s.[81]

More recent analyses that benefit from the passage of time, tighter focus, and often the availability of more records and memoirs include Murray's analysis of the first two decades of CBS documentary broadcasts, Rosteck who focuses on the pioneering role of Murrow and Friendly at CBS in the early 1950s, and Curtin who relates network documentary content to cold war pressures.[82] Television's coverage of the Vietnam war has been carefully assessed in Braestrup—a massive two-volume content study of press and television coverage of the early 1968 "Tet" offensive—and the broader historical

---

[79] David Holbrook Culbert, *News for Everyman: Radio and Foreign Affairs in Thirties America* (Westport, CT: Greenwood, 1976); David H. Hosley, *As Good as Any: Foreign Correspondence on American Radio, 1930–1940* (Westport, CT: Greenwood, 1984); Robert J. Brown, *Manipulating The Ether: The Power of Broadcast Radio in Thirties America* (Jefferson, NC: McFarland, 1998); Douglas B. Craig, *Fireside Politics: Radio and Political Culture in the United States, 1920–1940* (Baltimore, MD: Johns Hopkins University Press, 2000); Edward D. Miller, *Emergency Broadcasting and 1930s American Radio* (Philadelphia, PA: Temple University Press, 2003).

[80] Edward W. Chester, *Radio Television and American Politics* (New York: Sheed and Ward, 1969); Robert E. Gilbert, *Television and Presidential Politics* (North Quincy, MA: Christopher Publishing, 1972); Edwin Diamond and Stephen Bates, *The Spot: The Rise of Political Advertising on Television*, 3rd ed. (Cambridge, MA: MIT Press, 1992).

[81] A. William Bluem, *Documentary in American Television: Form, Function, Method* (New York: Hastings House, 1965); Charles M. Hammond Jr., *The Image Decade: Television Documentary 1965–1975* (New York: Hastings House, 1981).

[82] Michael D. Murray, *The Political Performers: CBS Broadcasts in the Public Interest* (Westport, CT: Praeger, 1994); Thomas Rosteck, See It Now *Confronts McCarthyism: Television Documentary and the Politics of Representation* (Tuscaloosa: University of Alabama Press, 1994); Michael Curtin, *Redeeming the Wasteland: Television Documentary and Cold War Politics* (New Brunswick, NJ: Rutgers University Press, 1995).

surveys of the coverage and its impact on the home front opinion by McDonald and Hallin.[83] The slow decline of the importance of network news and concomitant rise of local station journalism is framed well in Allen who explores factors behind the shift.[84] Edgerton provides the first serious study of history documentary filmmaker Ken Burns, based on the oeuvre itself as well his own analyses.[85] There is even a history of television weather programs and people by Henson.[86]

Aside from the many popular biographies of radio and television "personalities" is a growing number of research-based biographies of key figures. Radio's early demagogues and charlatans are more clearly defined in studies authored by Juhnke, Lee, and Warren.[87] Hilliard and Keith have tackled the controversial development of sexual content on both radio and television.[88] Their volume, focusing substantially on radio's "shock jocks," includes nearly 100 pages of important relevant documents.

The rise of television talk shows is assessed by Timberg who defines and compares a series of talk program cycles over several decades.[89] Johnson and

---

[83] Peter Braestrup, *Big Story: How the American Press and Television Reported and Interpreted the Crisis of Tet 1968 in Vietnam and Washington,* 2 vols. (Boulder, CO: Westview Press, 1977; reissued in abridged form by Yale University Press, 1983); J. Fred MacDonald, *Television and the Red Menace: The Video Road to Vietnam* (New York: Praeger, 1985); Daniel C. Hallin, *The "Uncensored War": The Media and Vietnam* (New York: Oxford University Press, 1986).

[84] Craig Allen, *News Is People: The Rise of Local TV News and the Fall of News from New York* (Ames: Iowa State University Press, 2001).

[85] Gary R. Edgerton, *Ken Burn's America* (New York: St. Martin's Press, 2001).

[86] Robert Henson, *Television Weathercasting: A History* (Jefferson, NC: McFarland, 1990).

[87] Eric S. Juhnke, *Quacks & Crusaders: The Fabulous Careers of John Brinkley, Norman Baker & Harry Hoxsey* (Lawrence: University Press of Kansas, 2002); R. Alton Lee, *The Bizarre Careers of John R. Brinkley* (Lexington: University Press of Kentucky, 2002); Donald Warren, *Radio Priest: Charles Coughlin, The Father of Hate Radio* (New York: Free Press, 1996).

[88] Robert L. Hilliard and Michael C. Keith, *Dirty Discourse: Sex and Indecency in American Radio* (Ames: Iowa State University Press, 2003).

[89] Bernard M. Timberg, *Television Talk: A History of the TV Talk Show* (Austin: University of Texas Press, 2002).

Keith provide the only scholarly history of gay and lesbian broadcasting.[90] The generally overlooked role of women in this field is somewhat rescued in O'Dell who reviews the role and impact of selected leaders, Beadle and Murray who portray 20 examples of local television station female personalities and news people, and the broader historical survey by Halper.[91] The development of African-American radio since the 1950s is recorded in Newman as well as Barlow.[92] Black-oriented television programming is reviewed by MacDonald and Bogle who both find many gains and successes since the 1960s, but numerous shortcomings as well.[93] All of these studies provide fairly detailed documentation.

Scholarly biographies of broadcast news figures are surprisingly uncommon—Sperber on Murrow and Schroth on Sevareid are two standout examples for their wealth of detail and analysis.[94] Serious study of key creative personnel in radio also is relatively rare, two examples include Bannerman on producer/playwright Norman Corwin and Cox on the program factory of Frank and Anne Hummert.[95] Of the plethora of books on radio's top

---

[90] Phylis A. Johnson and Michael C. Keith, *Queer Airwaves: The Story of Gay and Lesbian Broadcasting* (Armonk, NY: M. E. Sharpe, 2001).

[91] Cary O'Dell, *Women Pioneers in Television: Biographies of Fifteen Industry Leaders* (Jefferson, NC: McFarland, 1997); Mary E. Beadle and Michael D. Murray, eds., *Indelible Images: Women of Local Television* (Ames: Iowa State University Press, 2001); Donna L. Halper, *Invisible Stars: A Social History of Women in American Broadcasting* (Armonk, NY: M. E. Sharpe, 2001).

[92] Mark Newman, *Entrepreneurs of Profit and Pride: From Black-appeal to Radio Soul* New York(: Praeger, 1988); William Barlow, *Voice Over: The Making of Black Radio* (Philadelphia, PA: Temple University Press, 1999).

[93] J. Fred MacDonald, *Blacks and White TV: African Americans in Television since 1948,* 2nd ed. (Chicago: Nelson-Hall, 1992); Donald Bogle, *Prime Time Blues: African Americans on Network Television* (New York: Farrar, Straus, & Giroux, 2001).

[94] Ann M. Sperber, *Murrow: His Life and Times* (New York: Freundlich Books, 1986); Raymond A. Schroth, *The American Journey of Eric Sevareid* (South Royalton, VT: Steerforth Press, 1995).

[95] R. LeRoy Bannerman, *Norman Corwin and Radio: The Golden Years* (Tuscaloosa: University of Alabama Press, 1986); Jim Cox, *Frank and Anne Hummert's Radio Factory: The Programs and Personalities of Broadcasting's Most Prolific Producers* (Jefferson, NC: McFarland, 2003).

comedians, only Havig and Taylor—both on Fred Allen's life and work—are noteworthy as research-based scholarly studies.[96]

Many reference books on radio and television programming provide detailed information though little or no analysis, seemingly aimed at those who collect program recordings as well as the scholarly market. These include seasonal listings of network radio programs (Summers), detailed descriptions of network radio programs including many useful and insightful mini-essays on radio genre (Dunning), and annotated directories of nationally distributed television programs over more than a half century (Brooks and Marsh; McNeil).[97] Shapiro has taken a different approach with book-length diagrams illustrating network schedules in radio to 1967 and in network television to about 1990.[98] All of these surely provide valuable input for future program history research. While there have been several popular books on various cable television program services, Mullen offers the first research attempt to relate the overall story of programming on cable television.[99]

---

[96] Alan Havig, *Fred Allen's Radio Comedy* (Philadelphia, PA: Temple University Press, 1990); Robert Taylor, *Fred Allen: His Life and Wit* (Boston, MA: Little, Brown, 1989).

[97] Harrison B. Summers, comp., *A Thirty-year History of Programs Carried on National Radio Networks in the United States, 1926–1956* (Columbus: The Ohio State University, Department of Speech, 1958; repr., New York: Arno Press, in the series *History of Broadcasting,* 1971); John Dunning, *On the Air: The Encyclopedia of Old-time Radio* (New York: Oxford University Press, 1998); Tim Brooks and Earle Marsh, *The Complete Directory to Prime-time Network TV Shows, 1946–Present* (New York: Ballantine Books, 1995); Alex McNeil, *Total Television: The Comprehensive Guide to Programming from 1948 to the Present,* 4th ed. (New York: Penguin Books, 1997).

[98] Mitchell E. Shapiro, *Television Network Prime-time Programming, 1948–1988* (Jefferson, NC: McFarland, 1989); Mitchell E. Shapiro, *Television Network Daytime and Late-night Programming, 1959–1989* (Jefferson, NC: McFarland, 1990); Mitchell E. Shapiro, *Television Network Weekend Programming, 1959–1990* (Jefferson, NC: McFarland, 1992); Mitchell E. Shapiro, *Radio Network Prime Time Programming, 1926–1967* (Jefferson, NC: McFarland, 2002).

[99] Megan Gwynne Mullen, *The Rise of Cable Programming in the United States: Revolution or Evolution?* (Austin: University of Texas Press, 2003).

AUDIENCE/EFFECTS

This is the subject area most lacking in historical work—there are huge holes in what we know. For whatever reason, markedly few scholarly histories of commercial audience research exist. The prime exception is Beville, which remains the standard resource on the development of commercial electronic media audience research.[100] The author knew many of the people about whom he writes and was himself an important methodological pioneer in audience research methods. He draws on both company (e.g., Nielsen, Arbitron) research and that of academics to place different methods and firms in context. Luke sets a very useful example with its review of four decades of research findings on the impact of children's television.[101]

Histories of scholarly research into communication effects are, on the other hand, more common. Rogers takes a biographical approach though only his final few chapters relate to electronic media work.[102] Lerner and Nelson were devoted substantially to the important work of Wilbur Schramm and his compatriots.[103] Lowery and DeFleur, though designed for text use, is a valuable record of important research studies undertaken by academics (as well as a few industry studies), all of it well documented.[104]

REGULATION

With a tradition of concern for legal precedent and long-accepted methods of legal history research, scholarly studies of policy are among the most consistent type of electronic-media history. For example, legal treatises offering considerable history include one of the earliest, Socolow; one of the best that included both radio and early television, Warner; and the ongoing (updated twice a year) Ferris, Lloyd, and Casey that focuses largely on cable and newer

---

[100] Hugh Malcolm Beville Jr., *Audience Ratings: Radio, Television, and Cable,* 2nd ed. (Hillsdale, NJ: Lawrence Erlbaum Associates, 1988).

[101] Carmen Luke, *Constructing the Child Viewer: A History of the American Discourse on Television and Children, 1950–1980* (Westport, CT: Praeger, 1991).

[102] Everett Rogers, *A History of Communication Study* (New York: Free Press, 1994).

[103] Daniel Lerner and Lyle M. Nelson, *Communication Research: A Half-century Appraisal* (Honolulu: University of Hawaii Press, 1977).

[104] Shearon A. Lowery and Melvin L. DeFleur, *Milestones in Mass Communication Research,* 3rd ed. (White Plains, NY: Longman, 1995).

services.[105] All of these are copiously annotated with legal history as is the norm with such studies. Based on his dissertation, Edelman provided a still-valuable history of the development of the licensing function at the FCC.[106] Bensman reviews the rise of American radio regulation through the 1927 Radio Act, while Benjamin offers a broader study of First Amendment rights in radio through 1935.[107] Rosen surveys the relationship of radio to the federal government from 1920 to the Communications Act of 1934. Each of these is carefully documented.[108] Only Brinson offers a carefully researched biography of a key FCC member.[109]

Several works of legal reference provide a useful historical resource for researchers. The Kahn anthology was the first attempt to pull together key broadcasting regulatory documents in one place. Designed as a text, it went through several editions.[110] Paglin headed a team (with Rosenbloom and Hobson) that assembled the legislative history of the Communications Act of 1934 and a second volume gathering the primary amendments to the law passed from the 1930s to the major 1996 amendments.[111] Both included introductory essays based on historical research that place the documents in context.

---

[105] A. Walter Socolow, *The Law of Radio Broadcasting,* 2 vols. (New York: Baker & Voorhis, 1939); Harry P. Warner, *Radio and Television Law* (Albany, NY: Matthew Bender, 1948); Harry P. Warner, *Radio and Television Rights* (Albany, NY: Matthew Bender,1953); Charles D. Ferris, Frank W. Lloyd, and Thomas J. Casey, *Cable Television Law: A Video Communications Practice Guide* (Washington, DC: Matthew Bender, 1983).

[106] Murray Edelman, *The Licensing of Radio Services in the United States, 1927 to 1947* (Urbana: University of Illinois Press, 1950).

[107] Marvin R. Bensman, *The Beginning of Broadcast Regulation in the Twentieth Century* (Jefferson, NC: McFarland, 2000); Louise M. Benjamin, *Freedom of the Air and the Public Interest: First Amendment Rights in Broadcasting to 1935* (Carbondale: Southern Illinois University Press, 2001).

[108] Philip T. Rosen, *The Modern Stentors: Radio Broadcasters and the Federal Government, 1920–1934* (Westport, CT: Greenwood, 1980).

[109] Susan L. Brinson, *Personal and Public Interests: Frieda B. Hennock and the Federal Communications Commission* (Westport, CT: Praeger, 2002).

[110] Frank J. Kahn, ed., *Documents of American Broadcasting,* 4th ed. (Englewood Cliffs, NJ: Prentice-Hall, 1984).

[111] Max D. Paglin, ed., *A Legislative History of the Communications Act of 1934* (New York: Oxford University Press, 1989); Max D. Paglin, Joel Rosenbloom, and

There is a growing shelf of historical policy case studies available. A very insightful collection of six case studies of technical regulation is found in Slotten, a landmark book for the breadth and quality of its historical analysis.[112] One of the earliest policy histories was Robinson, tracing the rise and regulation of radio networks, based on his dissertation and appearing just as the Supreme Court agreed with relevant FCC regulations.[113] Foust relates the long-running battle over "clear channel" AM radio station policies, an industry conflict that raged from the inception of such stations in the late 1920s into the 1970s.[114] Braun provides an insightful analysis over the fight concerning AM stereo technical standards—from the late 1970s into the early 1990s—and why the FCC's "marketplace" shibboleth failed in this case.[115] Einstein assesses the rise, fall, and impact of the financial interest and syndication rules in television over nearly four decades.[116] Gibson and Engelman carefully review changing government policy toward (and politics concerning) the noncommercial/public system, based largely on open documents.[117] The only histories of cable policy are now three decades old and, thus, miss the vital changes in the years since. Phillips and Le Duc both assess the struggle to develop a policy regime for the technology.[118]

James R. Hobson, eds., *The Communications Act: A Legislative History of the Major Amendments, 1934–1996* (Washington, DC: Pike & Fischer, 1999).

[112] Hugh R. Slotten, *Radio and Television Regulation: Broadcast Technology in the United States, 1920–1960* (Baltimore, MD: Johns Hopkins University Press, 2000).

[113] Thomas Porter Robinson, *Radio Networks and the Federal Government* (New York: Columbia University Press, 1943).

[114] James C. Foust, *Big Voices of the Air: The Battle over Clear Channel Radio* (Ames: Iowa State University Press, 2000).

[115] Mark J. Braun, *AM Stereo and the FCC: Case Study of a Marketplace Shibboleth* (Norwood, NJ: Ablex, 1994).

[116] Mara Einstein, *Media Diversity: Economics, Ownership, and the FCC* (Mahwah, NJ: Lawrence Erlbaum Associates, 2004).

[117] George H. Gibson, *Public Broadcasting: The Role of the Federal Government, 1912–76* (New York: Praeger, 1977); Ralph Engelman, *Public Radio and Television in America: A Political History* (Thousand Oaks, CA: Sage, 1996).

[118] Mary Alice Mayer Phillips, *CATV: A History of Community Antenna Television* (Evanston, IL: Northwestern University Press, 1972); Don R. Le Duc, *Cable Television and the FCC: A Crisis in Media Control* (Philadelphia, PA: Temple University Press, 1973).

SURVEY HISTORIES

In many ways histories that range over a medium's whole history are perhaps the hardest books to research and write. There is so much available material that the task looks forbidding to most scholars. As noted earlier, Barnouw set the stage for modern historical writing with his classic trilogy, which provided the basis for his later one-volume history of television.[119] Douglas broadly assesses the role of radio within changing American culture.[120] Somewhat easier to take on are shorter periods and useful work of this nature is appearing. In addition to the many studies of radio's golden years noted earlier, Boddy surveys television's first decade in America; Watson assesses the news and public affairs role of television in the Kennedy years of the early 1960s; and Bodroghkozy reviews the same decade by focusing on cultural aspects of specific program examples reflecting the youth rebellion of that era.[121]

A few history texts also have appeared, but these are naturally based largely on secondary sources (see Hilliard and Keith, that is brief and well-illustrated; Hilmes, that centers on cultural history; and Sterling and Kittross, that detail the story in a thousand pages with extensive appendices).[122] Readers or anthologies that gather both primary and useful modern historical research pieces (usually for student use) include Lichty and Topping, a pioneering effort that

---

[119] Barnouw, *A Tower in Babel*; Erik Barnouw, *Tube of Plenty: The Evolution of American Television,* 2nd rev. ed. (New York: Oxford University Press, 1990).

[120] Susan J. Douglas, *Listening in: Radio and the American Imagination from Amos 'n' Andy and Edward R. Murrow to Wolfman Jack and Howard Stern* (New York: Times Books, 1999).

[121] William Boddy, *Fifties Television: The Industry and Its Critics* (Urbana: University of Illinois Press, 1990); Mary A. Watson, *The Expanding Vista: American Television in the Kennedy Years* (New York: Oxford University Press, 1990); Aniko Bodroghkozy, *Groove Tube: Sixties Television and the Youth Rebellion* (Durham, NC: Duke University Press, 2001).

[122] Robert Hilliard and Michael C. Keith, *The Broadcast Century and Beyond: A Biography of American Broadcasting,* 3rd. ed. (Woburn, MA: Focal Press, 2001); Michele Hilmes, *Only Connect: A Cultural History of Broadcasting in the United States* (Belmont, CA: Wadsworth, 2002); Christopher H. Sterling and John M. Kittross, *Stay Tuned: A History of American Broadcasting,* 3rd ed. (Mahwah, NJ: Lawrence Erlbaum Associates, 2002).

offered both breadth and depth with a good deal of original material;[123] Hilmes, which ranges over all of broadcasting and cable development;[124] and two recent readers focusing on radio's cultural impact and providing collections of recent research work: Hilmes and Loviglio and Squier.[125]

A subset of writing, focusing on critical studies approaches to history, centers on the work of McChesney, who provides a useful counter to the usual historical perception of the rise of the broadcast industry and its regulation into the 1930s; likewise, Streeter.[126]

There is a slowly growing number of valuable research-based references—dictionaries and encyclopedias—dealing with electronic media. Of the multivolume works, Newcomb was the pathmaker with three volumes on television history here and abroad—a new edition published in 2005.[127] Sterling followed with a reference on radio along the same lines.[128] Though broader in coverage, many of the lengthy essays filling the four volumes of Johnston are devoted to histories of electronic media both here and abroad.[129] Each of these benefits from a variety of contributors. Of the briefer one-volume approaches, Godfrey and Leigh survey program, organization, and biographical highlights of American radio; while Sies and Sies provide two large volumes of thousands

---

[123] Lawrence W. Lichty and Malachi C. Topping, eds., *American Broadcasting: A Source Book on the History of Radio and Television* (New York: Hastings House, 1975).

[124] Michele Hilmes, *Connections: A Broadcast History Reader* (Belmont, CA: Wadsworth, 2003).

[125] Michele Hilmes and Jason Loviglio, eds., *Radio Reader: Essays in the Cultural History of Radio* (New York: Routledge, 2002); Susan Merrill Squier, ed., *Communities of the Air: Radio Century, Radio Culture* (Durham, NC: Duke University Press, 2003).

[126] Robert W. McChesney, *Telecommunications, Mass Media and Democracy: The Battle for the Control of U.S. Broadcasting, 1928–1935* (New York: Oxford University Press, 1993); Streeter, *Selling the Air*.

[127] Horace Newcomb, ed., *Encyclopedia of Television*, 3 vols. (Chicago: Fitzroy Dearborn, 1997; 2nd ed., 4 vols., 2005).

[128] Christopher H. Sterling, ed., *Encyclopedia of Radio*, 3 vols. (New York: Fitzroy Dearborn, 2004).

[129] Donald H. Johnston, ed., *Encyclopedia of International Media and Communications*, 4 vols. (San Diego, CA : Academic Press, 2003).

of sometimes brief entries on people and programs.[130] Slide and Brown both offer useful historical dictionaries of television,[131] the former with extensive bibliographic references. Sterling assembled an annotated statistical abstract of electronic media development with tables and supporting text.[132]

A few scholarly historical studies have begun to explore the changing relationships between radio and television and other media. Jackaway reviews radio's impact on the press, focusing on the famous press–radio "war" over news.[133] Hilmes assesses the impact of radio and television broadcasting on the film industry while Wasser reviews the more recent impact of the home video recorder on Hollywood.[134]

TAKING STOCK

Electronic media history has come a long way, especially in the past two decades. The appearance of such focused journals as *Journal of Broadcasting* (1956), and *Journal of Radio Studies* (1991), to cite only two, has helped immensely. So has university press interest, as well as that of a few commercial houses, notably Greenwood and McFarland.

Already some subject areas seem overdone. There is plenty of (generally popular) material on old-time radio, as well as early political and news radio in the 1930s. While the flood is unlikely to abate, we have a lot of material on the political role of radio and television, more coming with each election cycle.

---

[130] Donald Godfrey and Fritz A. Leigh, eds., *Historical Dictionary of American Radio* (Westport, CT: Greenwood, 1998); Luther F. Sies, *Encyclopedia of American Radio, 1920–1960* (Jefferson, NC: McFarland, 2000); Leora M. Sies and Luther F. Sies, *The Encyclopedia of Women in Radio, 1920–1960* (Jefferson, NC: McFarland, 2003).

[131] Anthony Slide, *The Television Industry: A Historical Dictionary* (Westport, CT: Greenwood, 1991); Les Brown, *Les Brown's Encyclopedia of Television*, 3rd ed. (Detroit: Gale, 1992).

[132] Christopher H. Sterling, *Electronic Media: A Guide to Trends in Broadcasting and Newer Technologies, 1920–1983* (New York: Praeger, 1984).

[133] Gwenyth L. Jackaway, *Media at War: Radio's Challenge to the Newspapers, 1924–1939* (Westport, CT: Praeger, 1995).

[134] Michele Hilmes, *Hollywood and Broadcasting: From Radio to Cable* (Urbana: University of Illinois Press, 1990); Frederick Wasser, *Veni, Vidi, Video: The Hollywood Empire and the VCR* (Austin: University of Texas Press, 2001).

What then, after decades of historical research, is still lacking? Where should new work be focused? A few suggestions:

Technology

Despite their central importance, we still lack analytic scholarly appraisals of the work and impact of Guglielo Marconi, Edwin Howard Armstrong, Lee de Forest, or Reginald Fessenden—to cite just four examples. Few researchers have tackled the complex story of "new[er]" media and their impact on broadcasting and cable. There is no solid history of FM radio, for example, perhaps the first such "new" medium. Though satellites have been central in program distribution for more than two decades, historical studies are sparse. Only a few published works relate the growing impact of the Internet and cyberspace generally on radio and television, though it is clearly too soon for a "history."

Industry and Economics

We generally lack well-documented histories of important electronic media companies, or their leaders. This is partially due to a dearth of company archives—or a reluctance to provide access to those that do exist—but also to a lack of a tradition of such historical work in this field and in this country. More recently worries about competitive information or legal liabilities have also restricted access to the needed records. Finally, few media economics books are written to be historical, tending to focus more on current issues or controversies. Thus we have markedly little institutional history of electronic media—no scholarly assessment of either radio or television network development and impact, for example. Yet the networks have largely defined the commercial services for decades. There is no overall history of cable television's more than half century of existence. There are almost no critical biographies of key industry figures in radio or television. There is little consistent and reliable historical statistical information on the electronic media.

Programming

There are few genre histories of the standard set by Stedham and Wertheim. While the situation comedy has been a television standard for decades, for example, there is no scholarly assessment of the format. Most of the writing about televised sports is current and shallow, or focused on the economic relations between teams and television—we lack much of historical value. While we have begun to see some serious work in the cultural history of radio, thus far there is markedly little of the larger and longer impact of television.

Audience

We know markedly little of how the audience has changed over the years. Other than some useful data issued by the ratings firms (chiefly Nielsen), there is little longitudinal research tracing major trends in audience listening patterns. As to the devices that make that listening possible, we still lack a scholarly historical assessment of the radio (except for the portable set) or television receiver. Totally lacking is an audience-centered study of the historical impact of broadcasting.

Policy

We lack a history of the FCC (70 years old in 2004), and only a few books devoted to specific regulatory issues or important policy people. The legal literature (chiefly law review articles) offers well-documented surveys of some issues, though little of this has been expanded to book form.

Clearly there is still plenty for future researchers to chose from.

Appendix

Adapting Historical Citations to APA Style

In many of the communication journals APA is the published style. In the mainstream historical journal the published style is Chicago. A review of APA style can frustrate the historian as there are no APA directives for historical research. APA does, however, advise that when researchers have references that do not match the examples presented in the *APA Publications Manual,* they can modify an existing form in order to properly document the work. It also directs that it is better to provide more information than not enough. The purpose of this appendix is to offer ways for historians, submitting their work to the journals requiring APA, to document their historical sources in the APA style.

What is important for historical documentation? First, that enough information is given so that future researchers can locate the documentary evidence; and second, that the references are presented in a consistent style. In suggesting these guidelines the editor has analyzed the *Publication Manual of the American Psychological Association, Writing With Style: APA Style Made Easy* by Lenore T. Szuchman, the *Pocket Guide to APA Style* by Robert Perrin—the latter is most helpful in providing categorized ready-made examples with minimal narrative, the *Oral History Review,* and the 14th edition of *The Chicago Manual of Style.* Examples utilized are from the editor's own research, so that any errors can be properly attributed and corrected.

The historical citation, particularly a reference from broadcast material such as primary documents, must include all of the information necessary to enable future researchers to locate and examine the document. This is critical in establishing the credibility of the source. The examples below are from historical documents where these elements are clear, readily accessible, and easily adapted from *Chicago* to *APA*. Variations are noted from those unpublished archived materials and personal records that are often the challenge. The citations may look a little different at first, but they contain the elements that comprise full documentation thus establishing the validity of the source and the value of the evidence.

General Example

The common reference requirements include and are set out as follows:

> Author, Director, Producer, Reporter—the content responsible person or agency. (The exact date, where possible). *Title or descriptive information in italics* (filing information, such as box and file numbers, not italicized). Collection and/or archival information, city and state.

At the first mention of an archive the researcher may indicate "hereafter referred to as," thus shortening the extended information on the name and location of the collection as citations from the same collection continue, but refer to different documents and/or authors, etc. The author should pay particular attention to how the library/archive/museum itself wants the collection cited.

In-text Example (Author, Year/Date)

The in-text citation is merely the author/content responsible person or agency, followed by the year of origin. If more than one document some the same source/author/year is utilized then the full date is presented.

Archival Source Examples

> **Correspondence:** The general correspondence between parties is presented with full names of each party, date, and location information. The in-text reference refers only to the author of the information.
>
> > Farnsworth, P. T. (1927, February 27). *Correspondence from Philo T. Farnsworth to George Everson.* (Box 2, File 1). University of Utah, Marriott Library Special Collections, Salt Lake City, UT.
>
> **In-text:** (Farnsworth, 1927)

Business Records: Business records, where possible, should include the name of the author/content control person and an exact date. If, however, the author and the exact date are uncertain, the record can be identified by the title of the work and the approximate date.

> *The history of Farnsworth.* (circa 1948–1952). Business Pamphlet. (ITT Library Farnsworth Papers). ITT Aerospace/ Communications Division, International Telephone and Telegraph Corporation, Fort Wayne, IN. Hereafter referred to as ITT Papers.

In-text: (The history of Farnsworth, 1948–1952)

Proceedings of Meetings:

> Proceedings of annual meetings of stockholders. (1931, May 5). *Annual RCA Stockholders Report,* p. 7. (Sarnoff Corporation Library). Princeton, NJ.

In-text: (Proceedings of the Annual Meetings of Stockholders, 1931)

Newspaper or Magazines: Newspapers or magazine citations follow the traditional APA style especially in major newspapers that might readily be available for research online or via library access. However, where the article and/or reference material are incomplete, for example, those coming from a clipping service or an archival file, then the reference location information must be provided, such as from the Library of Congress, Newspaper and Current Periodical Reading Room, where records from the past centuries are found.

> Postman, N. (1999, March 29). Electrical engineer: Philo Farnsworth, *Time 100 Special Issue,* 153:12, 92–94.

In-text: (Postman, 1999)

Newspaper/Magazine from Archival Source:

> True electrical scanning radio television step. (1928, September). Unidentified newspaper clipping. *Christian Science Monitor.* (Box No. ___, File No___.). University of Utah, Marriott Library Special Collections, Salt Lake City, UT.

In-text: (True Electrical Scanning Radio Television Step, 1928, September)

Films, Television, Audio and Visual Sources: Citations for these documents are drafted as directed in *APA*. However, in historiography it is important for the researcher to identify the content control person, beyond the over generalized designation of "producer," or "director," as well as differentiate the source itself. In the example below, Murrow is identified as the "reporter." In the descriptive portion of the citation (see the general example above as well as below) the author needs to provide sufficient detail so the reader knows when the information has passed through a diversity of creative filters. For example, an unedited live broadcast has more evidential value than an edited report. Similarly, film/video out takes, scripts, and printed documents surrounding the creation of the content could be considered primary evidence and should be identified within the citation. The reel, disc, or transcript page number should also be noted where it is available.

Murrow, E. R. (Reporter.) (1941, June 1). *CBS radio news.* Unedited
live broadcast report. (Electronic Transcription Disc no. 23,
Audio reel 1181a). National Archives, CBS-KIRO Milo Ryan
Phonoarchive, Washington, DC.

In-text: (Murrow, 1941)

Oral Histories: Oral histories are challenging for the historian. While these interviews reflect wonderful color and at times represent primary participants, the information is also suspect enough that they often require supportive verifiable documentation. There is something of an unspoken hierarchy within the utilization of the oral history records as evidence. For example, a reference from an oral history within the Columbia School of Journalism's Oral History Collection has more credibility than a recorded phone conversation between the author and the subject. The question within this question of an oral history source appears to be *access* as well as accuracy. So it behooves the author/interviewer to provide information relative to the interview for future research, such as tape recording, transcript, and location information. In the following example, the latter provides the weakest source of evidence, simply because it is unavailable for future research and examination.

The minimal information in a full oral history interview (OHI) includes: (1) the name of the interviewee (commonly called narrator in oral history); (2) the name of the interviewer; (3) the date of the interview; the full date if there have been more than one interview within a given year;

(4) the place of the interview; and, (5) the repository that houses the transcript and/or recording. The in-text citation could include the last name of the narrator, OHI (indicating this is from an *oral history interview,* and the year.

> Hoover, H. (n.d.). *The reminiscences of Herbert Clark Hoover.* Oral History Research Office, Radio Pioneers, Fiche (1) Series II, pp. 10-11. Columbia University, New York.

In-text: (Hoover OHI, n.d.)

> Lindsay, Agnes (1985). Oral history interview conducted by Timothy Larson. (Transcript Box No.___, File No.___ and/or reel/ transcript information). University of Utah, Marriott Library Special Collections, Salt Lake City, UT.

In-text: (Lindsay OHI, 1985)

> Eberhardt, Edward (1995). Oral history interview conducted by Samuel G. Godfrey. Recorded interview (and/or transcript/notes) in possession of the author.

In-text: (Eberhardt OHI, 1995)

Editor's Note

Many historians who desire to preserve history as well as promote research have created collections or donated materials from their own works. Erik Barnouw's interviews for his trilogy on American broadcast history are in the Columbia University Oral History Research Office. The original electronic transcription disks providing the foundation for Milo Ryan's *History in Sound* are now housed at the National Archives. Donald Godfrey's work on broadcast pioneers has been placed in the Arizona State University and the University of Utah Library Special Collections units. Thus full documentation can be disclosed and future access is provided.

Bibliography

Abrams, Janet H. "Little Photoshop of Horrors: The Ethics of Manipulating Journalistic Imagery." *Print* November/December (1995): 24–45, 159–64.

Abramson, Albert H. *The History of Television, 1880–1941.* Jefferson, NC: McFarland, 1987.

———. *The History of Television: 1942–2000.* Jefferson, NC: McFarland, 2003.

———. *Zworykin: Pioneer of Television.* Urbana: University of Illinois Press, 1995.

Ackerman, William C. "The Dimensions of American Broadcasting." *Public Opinion Quarterly* August (1945), 283–304.

Adams, Robert C. *Social Survey Methods for Mass Media Research.* Hillsdale, NJ: Lawrence Erlbaum Associates, 1989.

Adorno, Theodor W. "Sociology and Empirical Research." In *The Adorno Reader,* edited by Brian O'Conner. Malden, MA: Blackwell Publishers, 2000.

Aitken, Hugh G. J. *The Continuous Wave: Technology and American Radio, 1900–1932.* Princeton, NJ: Princeton University Press, 1985.

———. *Syntony and Spark: The Origins of Radio.* New York: Wiley, 1976. Reprint, Princeton, NJ: Princeton University Press, 1985.

Alan, Jeff. *Anchoring America: The Changing Face of Network News.* Chicago: Bonus Books, 2003.

Allen, Craig. *News Is People: The Rise of Local TV News and the Fall of News from New York.* Ames: Iowa State University Press, 2001.

Allison, Alida, and Terri Frongia. *The Grad Student's Guide to Getting Published.* New York: Prentice-Hall, 1992.

Altschull, J. Herbert. "The Journalist and Instant History: An Example of the Jackal Syndrome." *Journalism Quarterly* 50 (Fall 1973): 389–96.

Alwood, Edward. *Straight News.* New York: Columbia University Press, 1998.

Amar, Akhil Reed. *The Bill of Rights: Creation and Reconstruction.* New Haven, CT: Yale University Press, 1998.

Ambrose, Stephen E. *Eisenhower: The President.* Vol. 2. New York: Simon and Schuster, 1985.

———. *To America: Personal Reflections of an Historian.* New York: Simon and Schuster, 2002.

American Historical Association. "Oral History Excluded from IRB Review." *Perspectives,* News column. December 2003. http://www.historians.org/Perspectives/Issues/2003/0312/0312new5.cfm.

American Psychological Association. *APA Style: Electronic References.* http://www.apastyle.org/elecref.html.

American Society of Media Photographers. "Code of Ethics." 1993. http://www.asmp.org/culture/code.php.

Anderson, James A. *Communication Research: Issues and Methods.* New York: McGraw-Hill, 1987.

Anderson, James A., and Robert K. Avery. "An Analysis of Changes in Voter Perception of Candidate Positions." *Communication Monographs* 45, no. 4 (1978): 354–61.

Anderson, Kathryn, Susan Armitage, Dana Jack, and Judith Wittner. "Beginning Where We Are: Feminist Methodology in Oral History." In *Feminist Research Methods: Exemplary Readings in the Social Sciences,* edited by Joyce McCarl Neilsen. Boulder, CO: Westview Press, 1990.

Ang, Ien. *Desperately Seeking the Audience.* New York: Routledge, 1991.

Angle, Paul. "The Minor Collection." *Atlantic Monthly,* April 1929, 516–25.

Apostolidis, Paul. *Stations of the Cross: Adorno and Christian Right Radio.* Durham, NC: Duke University Press, 2000.

Appleby, Joyce, Lynn Hunt, and Margaret Jacob. *Telling the Truth About History.* New York: W. W. Norton, 1994.

Archer, Gleason L. *Big Business and Radio.* New York: American Historical Society, 1939. Reprint, New York: Arno Press in the series *History of Broadcasting,* 1971.

———. *A History of Radio to 1926.* New York: American Historical Society, 1938. Reprint, New York: Arno Press in the series *History of Broadcasting,* 1971.

Argus Associates. "The Argus Clearing House." http://www.clearinghouse.net/.

Arkansas Educational Television Commission v. Forbes, 523 U.S. 666 (1998).

Armstrong, Cameron B., and Alan M. Rubin. "Talk Radio as Interpersonal Communication." *Journal of Communication* 39, no. 2 (1989): 84–94.

Association of College and Research Libraries. "College and Research Libraries News." http://www.ala.org/ala/acrl/acrlpubs/crlnews/collegeresearch.htm.

Association of Legal Writing Directors and Darby Dickerson. *ALWD Citation Manual: A Professional System of Citation.* 2nd ed. New York: ASPEN Publishers, 2003.

Atkinson, Carroll. *American Universities and Colleges That Have Held Broadcast License.* Boston, MA: Meador, 1941.

Aufderheide, Patricia. *Communications Policy and the Public Interest.* New York: Gilford Press, 1999.

Auletta, Ken. *Three Blind Mice: How the TV Networks Lost Their Way.* New York: Random House, 1991.

Bagdikian, Ben H. *The Media Monopoly.* 4th ed. Boston, MA: Beacon Press, 1992.

———. *The New Media Monopoly.* Boston, MA: Beacon Press, 1997.

Baker, John C. *Farm Broadcasting: The First Sixty Years.* Ames: Iowa State University Press, 1981.

Baker, Nicholson. *The Size of Thoughts: Essays and Other Lumber.* New York: Random House, 1996.

Baker, W. J. *A History of the Marconi Company.* New York: St. Martin's Press, 1972.

Banks, Jack. *Monopoly Television: MTV's Quest to Control the Music.* Boulder, CO: Westview Press, 1996.

Bannerman, R. LeRoy. *Norman Corwin and Radio: The Golden Years.* Tuscaloosa: University of Alabama Press, 1986.

Banning, William P. *Commercial Broadcasting Pioneer: The WEAF Experiment, 1922–1926.* Cambridge, MA: Harvard University Press, 1946.

Barfield, Ray. *Listening to Radio: 1920–1950.*. Westport, CT: Praeger, 1996.

Barker, David C. *Rushed to Judgment?* New York: Columbia University Press, 2002.

Barlow, William. *Voice Over: The Making of Black Radio.* Philadelphia, PA: Temple University Press, 1999.

Barnhurst, Kevin G. "Queer Political News: Election Year Coverage of the Lesbian and Gay Communities on National Public Radio, 1992–2000." *Journalism* 4, no. 1 (2003): 5–28.

Barnouw, Erik. *Documentary: A History of the Non-fiction Film.* 2nd ed. New York: Oxford University Press, 1993.

———. *The Golden Web: A History of Broadcasting in the United States, 1933–1953.* Vol. 2. New York: Oxford University Press, 1968.

———. *The Image Empire: A History of Broadcasting in the United States from 1953.* Vol. 3. New York: Oxford University Press, 1970.

———. *Media Marathon: A Twentieth-Century Memoir.* Durham, NC: Duke University Press, 1996.

———. *The Sponsor: Notes on a Modern Potentate.* New York: Oxford University Press, 1978.

———. *A Tower in Babel: A History of Broadcasting in the United States to 1933.* Vol 1. New York: Oxford University Press, 1966.

———. *Tube of Plenty: The Evolution of American Television.* New York: Oxford University Press, 1975; 2nd rev. ed., 1990.

Barrett, Marianne. "The Relationship of Network Affiliation Change to Prime Time Program Ratings." *Journal of Broadcasting & Electronic Media* 43, no. 1 (1999): 98–109.

Barsam, Richard. *Non-fiction Film: A Critical History.* 2nd ed. Bloomington: Indiana University Press, 1992.

Barzun, Jacques, and Henry F. Graff. *The Modern Researcher.* New York: Harcourt Brace and World, 1970. 4th ed. New York: Harcourt Brace Jovanovich, 1985; 5th ed. 1992.

Baudino, Joseph E., and John M. Kittross. "Broadcasting's Oldest Station: An Examination of Four Claimants." *Journal of Broadcasting* 21 (1977): 61–83.

Beadle, Mary E., and Michael D. Murray, eds. *Indelible Images: Women of Local Television.* Ames: Iowa State University Press, 2001.

Bearman, David. "Archival Methods." In *Archives and Museum Informatics* Technical Report 3, no. 1. Reprint, Pittsburgh, PA: Archives and Museum Informatics, 1991. Originally published, 1989.

Beasley, Maurine Hoffman. "Oral History." In *Guide to Sources in American Journalism History,* edited by Lucy Shelton Caswell. New York: Greenwood, 1989.

Beasley, Maurine Hoffman, and Sheila J. Gibbons. *Taking Their Place: A Documentary History of Women and Journalism.* Washington, DC: American University Press, in cooperation with the Women's Institute for Freedom of the Press, 1993.

———. *Women in Media: A Documentary Source Book.* Washington, DC: Women's Institute for Freedom of the Press, 1977.

Beasley, Maurine Hoffman, and Richard R. Harlow. "Oral History: Additional Tool for Journalism Historians." *Journalism History* 6 (Fall 1979): 98–102.

Beaver, Frank. *On Film.* New York: McGraw Hill, 1983.

Beck, Debra Baker. "The 'F' Word: How the Media Frame Feminism." *NWSA Journal* 10, no.1 (1998): 139–55.

Benjamin, Louise. *Freedom of the Air and the Public Interest: First Amendment Rights in Broadcasting to 1935.* Carbondale: Southern Illinois University Press, 2001.

———. "In Search of the Sarnoff 'Radio Music Box' Memo: Nally's Reply." *Journal of Radio Studies* 9, no. 1 (2002): 97–106.

———. "In Search of the Sarnoff 'Radio Music Box' Memo: Separating Myth from Reality." *Journal of Broadcasting & Electronic Media* 37, no. 3 (1993): 325–35.

Bennion, Sherilyn Cox. *Equal to the Occasion: Women Editors of the Nineteenth-century West.* Reno: University of Nevada Press, 1990.

Bensman, Marvin R. *The Beginning of Broadcast Regulation in the Twentieth Century,* Jefferson, NC: McFarland, 2000.

———. *Broadcast/Cable Regulation.* Lanham, MD: University Press of America, 1990.

———. *Broadcast Regulation: Selected Cases and Decisions.* 2nd ed. Lanham, MD: University Press of America, 1985.

———. "Foreword." In *ReRuns on File: A Guide to Electronic Media Archives,* edited by Donald G. Godfrey. Hillsdale, NJ: Lawrence Erlbaum Associates, 1992.

Benson, Lee. "Research Problems in American Political Historiography." In *Common Frontiers of the Social Sciences,* edited by Mirra Komarovsky. Glencoe, IL: Free Press, 1957.

Berelson, Bernard. *Content Analysis in Communication Research.* New York: Free Press, 1952.

Bergmeier, Horst J. P., and Rainer E. Lotz. *Hitler's Airwaves: The Inside Story of Nazi Radio Broadcasting and Propaganda Swing.* New Haven, CT: Yale University Press, 1997.

Bergreen, Laurence. *Look Now, Pay Later: The Rise of Network Broadcasting.* Garden City, NY: Doubleday, 1980.

Berry, Thomas Elliott, ed. *The Biographer's Craft.* New York: Odyssey Press, 1967.

Berry, Venise T., and Carmen L. Manning-Miller, eds. *Mediated Messages and African-American Culture: Contemporary Issues.* Thousand Oaks, CA: Sage, 1996.

Berstein, Mark, and Alex Lubertozzi. *World War II on the Air: Edward R. Murrow and the Broadcasts that Riveted a Nation.* Naperville, IL: Sourcebooks, 2003.

Beville, Hugh Malcolm, Jr. *Audience Ratings: Radio, Television, and Cable.* 2nd ed. Hillsdale, NJ: Lawrence Erlbaum Associates, 1988.

———. *Social Stratification of the Radio Audience.* Princeton, NJ: Princeton Office of Radio Research, 1939.

Bibb, Porter. *It Ain't as Easy as It Looks.* Boulder, CO: Johnson, 1997.

Biehl, Kathy, and Tara Calishain. *The Lawyer's Guide to Internet Research.* Lanham, MD: Scarecrow Press, 2000.

Bilby, Kenneth. *The General: David Sarnoff and the Rise of the Communications Industry.* New York: Harper & Row, 1986.

Billington, Ray A., ed. *Allan Nevins on History.* New York: Charles Schribner's Sons, 1995.

Bittner, John R. *Law and Regulation of Electronic Media.* 2nd ed. Englewood Cliffs, NJ: Prentice-Hall, 1994.

Bitzer, Lloyd F. "The Rhetorical Situation." *Philosophy and Rhetoric* 1, no. 1 (1968): 1–14.

Blake, George G. *History of Radio Telegraphy and Telephony.* London: Chapman & Hall, 1928. Reprint, New York: Arno Press in the series *Telecommunications,* 1974.

Blakely, Robert J. *To Serve the Public Interest: Educational Broadcasting in the United States.* Syracuse, NY: Syracuse University Press, 1979.

Bliss, Edward, Jr. *Now the News: The Story of Broadcast Journalism*. New York: Columbia University Press, 1991.

Block, Alex. *Outfoxed: Rupert Murdoch and the Inside Story of America's Fourth Television Network*. New York: St. Martin's Press, 1990.

Blue, Howard. *Words at War: World War II Era Radio Drama and the Postwar Broadcasting Industry Blacklist*. Lanham, MD: Scarecrow Press, 2002.

Bluem, A. William. *Documentary in American Television: Form, Function, Method*. New York: Hastings House, 1965.

Boddy, William. *Fifties Television: The Industry and Its Critics*. Urbana: University of Illinois Press, 1990.

Bodroghkozy, Aniko. *Groove Tube: Sixties Television and the Youth Rebellion*. Durham, NC: Duke University Press, 2001.

Bogle, Donald. *Blacks in American Film and Television: An Illustrated Encyclopedia*. New York: Simon & Schuster, 1989.

———. *Prime Time Blues: African Americans on Network Television*. New York: Farrar, Straus, & Giroux, 2001.

Bonner, Paul, with Leslie Aston. *Independent Television in Britain*. Vol. 5, *ITV and the IBA 1981–92: The Old Relationship Changes*. London: Macmillan, 1998.

Bormann, Ernest G. *Theory and Research in the Communicative Arts*. New York: Holt, 1965.

Boswell, James. *The Life of Samuel Johnson*. Vol. 1. Edited by Roger Ingpen. Bath, England: Bayntun Press, 1925.

Botein, Michael. *Regulation of the Electronic Mass Media: Law and Policy for Radio, Television, Cable and the New Video Technologies*. 3rd ed. St. Paul, MN: West, 1998.

Bowen, Catherine Drinker. "The Biographer: Relationship with His Hero." In *Biography as High Adventure: Life Writers Speak on Their Art,* edited by Stephen B. Oates. Amherst: University of Massachusetts Press, 1986.

———. *John Adams and the American Revolution*. Boston, MA: Little, Brown, 1950.

Braden, Maria. *She Said What? Interviews with Women Newspaper Columnists*. Lexington: University Press of Kentucky, 1993.

Brady, Kathleen. *Ida Tarbell: Portrait of a Muckraker*. Pittsburgh, PA: University of Pittsburgh Press, 1989.

Braestrup, Peter. *Big Story: How the American Press and Television Reported and Interpreted the Crisis of Tet 1968 in Vietnam and Washington*. 2 vols. Boulder, CO: Westview Press, 1977. Reissued in abridged form, New Haven, CT: Yale University Press, 1983.

Braun, Mark J. *AM Stereo and the FCC: Case Study of a Marketplace Shibboleth*. Norwood, NJ: Ablex, 1994.

Brennan, Bonnie. "Toward a History of Labor and News Work: The Use of Oral Sources in Journalism History." *The Journal of American History* 83, no. 2 (1996): 571–79.

Briggs, Asa A. *The History of Broadcasting in the United Kingdom*. Vol. 1, *The Birth of Broadcasting*. Vol. 2, *Golden Age of Wireless*. Vol. 3, *The War of Words*. Vol. 4, *Sound & Vision*. Vol. 5, *Competition*. London: Oxford University Press, 1961, 1965, 1970, 1979, and 1995.

———. *Social History and Human Experience*. Cedar City, UT: Grace A. Tanner Center for Human Values, 1984.

Brinson, Susan L. *Personal and Public Interests: Frieda B. Hennock and the Federal Communications Commission*. Westport, CT: Praeger, 2002.

Brittain, James E. *Alexanderson: Pioneer in American Electrical Engineering.* Baltimore, MD: Johns Hopkins University Press, 1992.

Brooks, Tim, and Earle Marsh. *The Complete Directory to Prime-time Network TV Shows, 1946–Present.* New York: Ballantine Books, 1995.

Brower, Kenneth. "Photography in the Age of Falsification." *The Atlantic Monthly,* May 1998, 92–111.

Brown, Les. *Les Brown's Encyclopedia of Television.* 3rd ed. Detroit, MI: Gale, 1992.

———. The New York Times *Encyclopedia of Television.* New York: Times Books, 1977.

Brown, Robert J. *Manipulating the Ether: The Power of Broadcast Radio in Thirties America.* Jefferson, NC: McFarland, 1998.

Browne, Donald R., Charles M. Firestone, and Ellen Mickiewicz. *Television/Radio News and Minorities.* Queenstown, MD: Aspen Institute, 1994.

Bruck, Connie. *Master of the Game: Steve Ross and the Creation of Time Warner.* New York: Simon & Schuster, 1994.

Brugioni, Dino. *Photo Fakery: The History and Techniques of Photographic Deception and Manipulation.* Dulles, VA: Brassey's, 1999.

Brummett, Barry. *Rhetoric in Popular Culture.* New York: St. Martin's Press, 1994.

Bryant, Jennings, and Dolf Zillmann, eds. *Media Effects: Advances in Theory and Research.* Mahwah, NJ: Lawrence Erlbaum Associates, 2002.

Bryant, John H., and Harold N. Cones. *Zenith Radio: The Early Years, 1919–1935.* Atglen, PA: Schiffer, 1997.

Bulloch, John, and Simon Chapman. "Experts in Crisis: The Framing of Radio Debate about the Risk of AIDS to Heterosexuals." *Discourse and Society* 3, no. 4 (1992): 437–67.

Burgoyne, Robert. *Film Nation: Hollywood Looks at U.S. History.* Minneapolis: University of Minnesota Press, 1997.

Burns, Russell W. *Television: An International History of the Formative Years.* London: Institute of Electrical Engineers, 1998.

Cain, Earl R. "A Method for Rhetorical Analysis of Congressional Debate." *Western Speech* 18 (March 1954): 91–95.

Cairns, Kathleen A. *Front-page Women Journalists, 1920–1950.* Lincoln: University of Nebraska Press, 2003.

Calvert, Clay. "Should You Publish in a Law Review?" *Media Law Notes* 30 (Spring 2002)" 1–2.

Cantor, Louis. *Wheelin' on Beale: How WDIA–Memphis Became the Nation's First All-Black Radio Station and Created the Sound that Changed America.* New York: Pharos Books, 1992.

Cantril, Hadley. *The Invasion from Mars: A Study in the Psychology of Panic.* Princeton, NJ: Princeton University Press, 1940.

Carcasson, Martin, and James Aune. "Klansman on the Court: Justice Hugo Black's Radio Address to the Nation." *Quarterly Journal of Speech* 89, no. 2 (2003): 154–70.

Carey, James W. "A Cultural Approach to Communication." *Communication* 2 (December 1975): 1–22.

———. "The Origins of the Radical Discourse on Cultural Studies in the United States." *Journal of Communication* 33, no. 3 (1983): 311–13.

———. "The Problem of Journalism History." In *James Carey: A Critical Reader,* edited by Eve Stryker Munson and Catherine A. Warren. Minneapolis: University of Minnesota Press, 1997.

Caristi, Dom. *Expanding Free Expression in the Marketplace: Broadcasting and the Public Forum.* New York: Quorum Books, 1992.

Carlson, Scott. "The Uncertain Fate of Scholarly Artifacts in a Digital Age." *The Chronicle of Higher Education* 50, no. 21 (2004): A25.

Carnes, Mark, ed. *Past Imperfect: History According to the Movies.* New York: H. Holt, 1995.

Caro, Robert A. *The Power Broker: Robert Moses and the Fall of New York.* New York: Vintage Books, 1975.

———. *The Years of Lyndon Johnson.* Vol. 1, *The Path to Power.* Vol. 2, *Means of Ascent.* Vol. 3, *Master of the Senate.* New York: Knopf, 1982, 1990, 2002.

Carpenter, Ronald H. *Father Charles E. Coughlin: Surrogate Spokesman for the Disaffected.* Westport, CT: Praeger, 1998.

Carpenter, Sue. *40 Watts from Nowhere.* New York: Scribner, 2004.

Carroll, Raymond L., Michael I. Silbergleid, and M. Beachum. "Meanings of Radio to Teenagers in a Niche-Programming Era." *Journal of Broadcasting & Electronic Media* 37, no. 2 (1993): 159–76.

Carter, J. Barton, Marc Franklin, and Jay B. Wright. *The First Amendment and the Fifth Estate: Regulation of Electronic Mass Media.* 6th ed. University Casebook Series. Westbury, NY: Foundation Press, 2003.

———. *The First Amendment and the Fourth Estate: The Law of Mass Media.* 8th ed. University Casebook Series. Westbury, NY: Foundation Press, 2001.

Carter, Sue J. *Riding the Airwaves: Three Models of Women's Success to Broadcasting.* Unpublished manuscript, from the collection of Emerson College Library, 1991.

Casey, Michael, and Aimee Rowe. "Driving Out the Money Changers: Radio Priest Charles E. Coughlin's Rhetorical Vision." *Journal of Communication and Religion* 19, no. 1 (1996): 37–47.

Casper, Scott E. *Constructing American Lives: Biography and Culture in Nineteenth-century America.* Chapel Hill: University of North Carolina Press, 1999.

CBS News. *Four Days in November.* Peabody Awards Collection, 88202DCT. Aired November 17, 1988.

———. "Woodward Shares War Secrets." *60 Minutes.* Aired April 18, 2004.

Chandler, Alfred D. *Inventing the Electronic Century: The Epic Story of the Consumer Electronics and Computer Industries.* New York: Free Press, 2001.

Chappell, Matthew N., and Claude E. Hooper. *Radio Audience Measurement.* New York: Stephen Daye, 1944.

Chernus, Ira. *General Eisenhower: Ideology and Discourse.* East Lansing: Michigan State University Press, 2002.

Chesebro, James W. "Communication, Values, and Popular Television Series: A Twenty-five Year Assessment and Final Conclusions." *Communication Quarterly* 51, no. 4 (2003): 367–418.

Chester, Edward W. *Radio Television and American Politics.* New York: Sheed and Ward, 1969.

Chinn, Sandra Hardy. *At Your Service—KMOX and Bob Hardy: Pioneers of Talk Radio.* St. Louis, MO: Virginia Publishing, 1997.

Christenson, Peter G., and Peter DeBeneditis. "Eavesdropping on the FM Band: Children's Use of Radio." *Journal of Communication* 36, no. 2 (1986): 27–38.

Clark, David. "Radio in Presidential Elections." *Journal of Broadcasting* 6, no. 3 (1962): 229–38.

Clark, W. R. "Radio Listening Habits of Children." *Journal of Social Psychology* 12 (1940).

Cloud, Stanley, and Lynne Olson. *The Murrow Boys: Pioneers on the Front Lines of Broadcast Journalism.* Boston, MA: Houghton Mifflin, 1996.

Clurman, Richard M. *To the End of Time: The Seduction and Conquest of a Media Empire.* New York: Simon & Schuster, 1992.

Coe, Brian. *The History of Movie Photography.* Westfield, NJ: Eastview Editions, 1981.

Coe, Lewis. *Wireless Radio: A Brief History.* Jefferson, NC: McFarland, 1996.

Cohen, Jeremy, and Timothy Gleason. *Social Research in Communication and Law.* Newbury Park, CA: Sage, 1990.

Cohen, Morris L., and Kent C. Olson. *Legal Research in a Nutshell.* 7th ed. St. Paul, MN: West Group, 2000.

Coleman, Alice White. "Radio in the Alaska Bush: Native Responses to Cultural Diffusion." *Journal of Radio Studies* 6, no. 2 (1997): 7–14.

Cones, Harold N., and John H. Bryant. *Zenith Radio: The Glory Years, 1936–1945.* Vol. 1, *History and Product.* Vol. 2, *Illustrated Catalog and Database.* Atglen, PA: Schiffer, 2003.

Cooper, John Milton, Jr. "Conception, Conversation, and Comparison: My Experiences as a Biographer." In *Writing Biography: Historians and Their Craft,* edited by Lloyd E. Ambrosius. Lincoln: University of Nebraska Press, 2004.

Coville, Gary, and Patrick Lucanio. *Smokin' Rockets: The Romance of Technology in American Film, Radio, and Television, 1945–1962.* Jefferson, NC: McFarland, 2002.

Cowie, Jefferson. *Capital Moves: RCA's Seventy-five Year Quest for Cheap Labor.* Ithaca, NY: Cornell University Press, 1999.

Cox, Jim. *Frank and Anne Hummert's Radio Factory: The Programs and Personalities of Broadcasting's Most Prolific Producers.* Jefferson, NC: McFarland, 2003.

Craig, Douglas B. *Fireside Politics: Radio and Political Culture in the United States, 1920–1940.* Baltimore, MD: Johns Hopkins University, 2000.

Craig, Steve. "The Farmer's Friend: Radio Comes to Rural America, 1920–1927." *Journal of Radio Studies* 8, no. 2 (2001): 330–46.

Craver, Kathleen W. *Using Internet Primary Sources to Teach Critical Thinking Skills in History.* Westport, CT: Greenwood, 1999.

Creech, Kenneth C. *Electronic Media Law and Regulation.* 3rd ed. Boston, MA: Focal Press, 2000.

Creedon, Pamela J., ed. *Women in Mass Communication.* 2nd ed. Newbury Park, CA: Sage, 1993.

Crisell, Andrew. *Understanding Radio.* 2nd ed. London: Routledge, 1994.

Critchlow, James. *Radio Hole-in-the-Head: Radio Liberty, An Insider's Story of Cold War Broadcasting.* Washington, DC: American University Press, 1995.

Cronkite, Walter. *A Reporter's Life.* New York: Knopf, 1996.

Culbert, David Holbrook. *News for Everyman: Radio and Foreign Affairs in Thirties America.* Westport, CT: Greenwood, 1976.

Curtin, Michael. *Redeeming the Wasteland: Television Documentary and Cold War Politics.* New Brunswick, NJ: Rutgers University Press, 1995.

D'Acci, Julie. *Defining Women: Television and the Case of* Cagney & Lacey. Chapel Hill: University of North Carolina Press, 1994.

Dallek, Robert. *Flawed Giant: Lyndon B. Johnson, 1960–1973.* New York: Oxford University Press, 1998.

———. *Lone Star Rising: Lyndon Johnson and His Times 1908–1960.* New York: Oxford University Press, 1991.

Daniel, Eric D., C. Denis Mee, and Mark H. Clark, eds. *Magnetic Recording: The First 100 Years.* New York: Institute of Electrical and Electronics Engineers Press, 1999.

Daniel, Walter C. *Black Journals of the United States.* Westport, CT: Greenwood, 1982.

Danky, James P., and Maureen E. Hady, eds. *African-American Newspapers and Periodicals: A National Bibliography.* Cambridge, MA: Harvard University Press, 1998.

Davidson, Andrew. *Under the Hammer: The Inside Story of the 1991 ITV Franchise Battle.* London: Heinemann, 1992.

Davidson, James West, and Mark Hamilton Lytle. *After the Fact: The Art of Historical Detection.* 4th ed. Boston, MA: McGraw Hill, 2000.

Dawkins, Wayne. *Black Journalists: The NABJ Story.* Sicklerville, NJ: August Press, 1993.

Day, James. *The Vanishing Vision: The Inside Story of Public Television.* Berkeley: University of California Press, 1995.

Delli Carpini, Michael X. "Radio's Political Past." *Media Studies Journal* 7, no. 3 (1993): 23–35.

Demers, David. *Global Media: Menace or Messiah?* Cresskill, NJ: Hampton Press, 1999.

Dennis, Everette E. "Foreword." In *Social Research in Communication and Law,* edited by Jeremy Cohen and Timothy Gleason. Newbury Park, CA: Sage, 1990.

Dennis, Paul M. "Chills and Thrills: Does Radio Harm Our Children?" *Journal of the History of the Behavioral Sciences* 34, no. 1 (1998): 33–50.

Department of Energy. "Electronic Communications Privacy Act of 1986." Office of the Chief Information Officer. October 21, 1986, http://cio.doe.gov/Documents/ECPA.HTM.

Dewey, John. *The Public and Its Problems.* New York: H. Holt, 1927. Reprint, Athens, OH: Swallow Press, 1954.

Diamond, Edwin, and Stephen Bates. *The Spot: The Rise of Political Advertising on Television.* 3rd ed. Cambridge, MA: MIT Press, 1992.

Dicks, Steven J., and Walter McDowell. "Pirates, Pranksters, & Prophets: Understanding America's Unlicensed 'Free' Radio Movement." *Journal of Radio Studies* 8, no 2 (2000): 329–41.

Doherty, Thomas. *Cool War, Cool Medium.* New York: Columbia University Press, 2003.

Doll, Bob. *Sparks out of the Plowed Ground.* West Palm Beach, FL: Streamline Press, 1996.

Dominick, Joseph, and Roger Wimmer. "Training the Next Generation of Media Researchers." *Communication and Society* 6, no. 1 (2003): 3–9.

Dondis, Donis A. *A Primer of Visual Literacy.* Cambridge, MA: MIT Press, 1973.

Dorgan, Howard. *The Airwaves of Zion: Radio and Religion in Appalachia.* Knoxville: University of Tennessee Press, 1993.

Douglas, Susan J. *Inventing American Broadcasting, 1899–1922.* Baltimore, MD: Johns Hopkins University Press, 1987.

———. *Listening In: Radio and the American Imagination.* New York: Times Books, 2000. Minneapolis: University of Minnesota Press, 2004.

———. *Listening In: Radio and the American Imagination from Amos 'n' Andy and Edward R. Murrow to Wolfman Jack and Howard Stern.* New York: Times Books, 1999.

———. *Where the Girls Are: Growing Up Female with the Mass Media.* New York: Times Books, 1994.

Downing, John D. "Ethnic Minority Radio in the United States." *Howard Journal of Communication* 2, no. 2 (1990): 135–48.

Dryer, Sherman Harvard. *Radio in Wartime.* New York: Greenberg, 1942.

Duncan, Jacci, ed. *Making Waves: The 50 Greatest Women in Radio and Television as Selected by American Women in Radio and Television, Inc.* Kansas City, MO: Andrews McMeel Publishing, 2001.

Dunham, Corydon. *Fighting for the First Amendment: Stanton of CBS vs. Congress and the Nixon White House.* Westport, CT: Praeger, 1997.

Dunning, John. *On the Air: The Encyclopedia of Old-time Radio.* New York: Oxford University Press, 1998.

Dupagne, Michael, and Peter B. Seel. *HDTV: High-definition Television, A Global Perspective.* Ames: Iowa State University, 1998.

Duster, Alfreda M., ed. *Crusade for Justice: The Autobiography of Ida B. Wells.* Chicago: University of Chicago Press, 1970.

Eberly, Philip K. *Susquehanna Radio: The First Fifty Years.* York, PA: Susquehanna Radio Corporation, 1992.

Edel, Leon. "The Figure under the Carpet." In *Biography as High Adventure: Life Writers Speak on Their Art,* edited by Stephen B. Oates. Amherst: University of Massachusetts Press, 1986.

———. *Writing Lives: Principia Biographica.* New York: Norton, 1984.

Edelman, Murray. *The Licensing of Radio Services in the United States, 1927 to 1947.* Urbana: University of Illinois Press, 1950.

Edgerton, Gary R. *Ken Burns's America.* New York: St. Martin's Press, 2001.

Edgerton, Gary R., and Peter C. Rollins, eds. *Television Histories: Shaping Collective Memory in the Media Age.* Lexington: University Press of Kentucky, 2001.

Edwards, Bob. *Edward R. Murrow and the Birth of Broadcast Journalism.* Hoboken, NJ: Wiley, 2004.

Edwards, Emily D., and Michael W. Singletary. "Life's Soundtracks: Relationships Between Radio Music Subcultures and Listeners' Belief Systems." *Southern Communication Journal* 54, no. 2 (1989): 144–58.

Ehrlich, Matthew C., and Noshir S. Contractor. "'Shock' Meets 'Community Service': J. C. Corcoran at MOX." *Journal of Radio Studies* 5, no. 1 (1998): 22–35.

Einstein, Mara. *Media Diversity: Economics, Ownership, and the FCC.* Mahwah, NJ: Lawrence Erlbaum Associates, 2004.

Eiselein, Eddie Bill. *Indian Issues.* Browning, MT: Spirit Talk Press, 1993.

Ellison, Todd, and Lois Anderton. *Archival Procedure Manual.* Boulder, CO: Carnegie Branch Library for Local History, Boulder Public Library, 1990.

Ely, Melvin Patrick. *The Adventures of Amos 'n' Andy: A Social History of an American Phenomenon.* New York: Free Press, 1991.

Emanuel, Steven L. *Lexis-Nexis for Law Students.* 3rd ed. Larchmont, NY: Emanuel, 1997.

Engelman, Ralph. *Public Radio and Television in America: A Political History.* Thousand Oaks, CA: Sage, 1996.

Erickson, Hal. *Religious Radio and Television in the United States, 1921–1991: The Programs and Personalities.* Jefferson, NC: McFarland, 1992.

Etter-Lewis, Gwendolyn. "Introduction." In *Unrelated Kin: Race and Gender in Women's Personal Narratives,* edited by Gwendolyn Etter-Lewis and Michele Foster. New York: Routledge, 1996.

Evans, James F. *Prairie Farmer and WLS: The Burridge D. Butler Years.* Urbana: University of Illinois Press, 1969.

Fahie, John J. *A History of Wireless Telegraphy 1838–1899.* New York: Dodd, Mead, 1899. Reprint, New York: Arno Press in the series *History of Radio and Television,* 1971.

Fairchild, Charles. *Community Radio and Public Culture: Being an Examination of Media Access and Equity in the Nations of North America.* Cresskill, NJ: Hampton Press, 2001.

Fajans, Elizabeth, and Mary R. Falk. *Scholarly Writing for Law Students: Seminar Papers, Law Review Notes and Law Review Competition Papers.* 2nd ed. St. Paul, MN: West Group, 2000.

Fallow, Katherine A. "The Big Chill? Congress and the FCC Crack Down on Indecency." *Communications Lawyer* 22, no. 1 (2004): 1, 25–32.

Fang, Irving E. *Those Radio Commentators.* Ames: Iowa State University Press, 1977.

Farnsworth, Elma G. *Distant Vision: Romance & Discovery on an Invisible Frontier.* Salt Lake City, UT: PemberlyKent Publishers, 1999.

Fay, Jennifer. "Casualties of War: The Decline of Foreign Language Broadcasting During World War II." *Journal of Radio Studies* 6, no. 1 (1999): 62–80.

Ferris, Charles D., Frank W. Lloyd, and Thomas J. Casey. *Cable Television Law: A Video Communications Practice Guide.* Washington, DC: Matthew Bender, 1983.

Fisher, David E., and Marshall John Fisher. *Tube: The Invention of Television.* New York: Harcourt Brace, 1996.

Fishman, Donald A. "Foreword." In *Invisible Stars: A Social History of Women in American Broadcasting,* by Donna L. Halper. Armonk, NY: M. E. Sharpe, 2001.

Fleischhauer, Carl. "Looking at Preservation from the Digital Library Perspective." *The Moving Image* 3 (Fall 2003): 96–100.

Fleming, John A. *The Principles of Electric Wave Telegraph and Telephony.* 2nd ed. New York: Longmans, Green, 1910.

Fogerty, James E. "Filling the Gap: Oral History in the Archives." *American Archivist* 46, no. 2 (1983): 148–57.

Foley, Joseph M. "Broadcast Regulation Research: A Primer for Non-Lawyers." *Journal of Broadcasting* 17, no. 2 (1973): 147–57.

Fornatale, Peter, and Joshua E. Mills. *Radio in the Television Age.* Woodstock, NY: Overlook Press, 1980.

Foust, James C. *Big Voices of the Air: The Battle over Clear Channel Radio.* Ames: Iowa State University Press, 2000.

Fowler, Gene, and Bill Crawford. *Border Radio: Quacks, Yodelers, Pitchmen, Psychics, and Other Amazing Broadcasters of the American Airwaves.* Austin: University of Texas Press, 2002.

Francois, William E. *Mass Media Law and Regulation.* 6th ed. Prospect Heights, IL: Waveland Press, 1994.

Franklin, Marc A., David A. Anderson, and Fred H. Cate. *Mass Media Law.* 6th ed. Westbury, NY: Foundation Press, 2000.

Frisch, Michael. *A Shared Authority: Essays on the Craft and Meaning of Oral and Public History.* Albany: State University of New York Press, 1990.

Frizot, Michel, ed. *The New History of Photography.* Köln, Germany: Könemann, 1998.

Frost, S. E., Jr. *Education's Own Stations: The History of Broadcast Licenses Issued to Educational Institutions.* Chicago: University of Chicago Press, 1937.

———. *Is American Radio Democratic?* Chicago: University of Chicago Press, 1937.

Gandy, Oscar. "Foreword." In *The Politics of TV Violence: Policy Uses of Communication Research,* edited by Willard D. Rowland Jr. Beverly Hills, CA: Sage, 1983.

Ganzert, Charles F. "All-Women's Radio at WHER-AM in Memphis." *Journal of Radio Studies* 10, no. 1 (2003): 80–92.

Garay, Ronald. *Gordon McLendon: The Maverick of Radio.* Westport, CT: Greenwood, 1984.

———. "Guarding the Airwaves: Government Regulation of World War II American Radio." *Journal of Radio Studies* 3 (1995): 130–48.

Garner, Bryan A., ed. *Black's Law Dictionary.* 8th ed. Eagan, MN: West Group, 2004.

———. *A Dictionary of Modern Legal Usage.* 2nd ed. New York: Oxford University Press, 1995.

———. *The Elements of Legal Style.* 2nd ed. New York: Oxford University Press, 2002.

———. "Fairness Doctrine." In *Black's Law Dictionary.* 7th ed. Eagan, MN: West Publishing, 2004.

———. "Preface to the First Edition." In *A Dictionary of Modern Legal Usage.* 2nd ed. New York: Oxford University Press, Incorporated, 1995, xiii–xv.

———. *The Redbook: A Manual on Legal Style.* St. Paul, MN: West Group, 2002.

Garner, Ken, ed. *The Radio Journal.* Glasgow, Scotland: Glasgow Caledonian University, 2003–2004.

Garraty, John A. *The Nature of Biography.* New York: Knopf Publishers, 1957.

Gelfman, Judith S. *Women in Television News.* New York: Columbia University Press, 1976.

George, Martha Washington. *Black Radio ... Winner Takes All: America's 1st Black Deejays.* Philadelphia, PA: Xlibris Corporation, 2003.

Gerbner, George, Ole Holsti, Klaus Krippendorff, William Paisley, and Philip Stone. *The Analysis of Communication Content: Developments in Scientific Theories and Computer Techniques.* New York: Wiley, 1969.

Gibson, George H. *Public Broadcasting: The Role of the Federal Government, 1912–76.* New York: Praeger, 1977.

Gilbert, Robert E. *Television and Presidential Politics.* North Quincy, MA: Christopher Publishing, 1972.

Gillmor, Donald M. *Power, Publicity, and the Abuse of Libel Law.* New York: Oxford University Press, 1992.

Gillmor, Donald M., Jerome A. Barron, and Todd F. Simon. *Mass Communication Law.* 6th ed. Belmont, CA: Wadsworth, 1998.

Gillmor, Donald M., Jerome A. Barron, Todd F. Simon, and Herbert A. Terry. *Fundamentals of Mass Communication Law.* St. Paul, MN: West Group, 1996.

Gillmor, Donald M., and Everette E. Dennis. "Legal Research in Mass Communication." In *Research Methods in Mass Communication,* edited by Guido H. Stempel III and Bruce H. Westley. 2nd ed. Englewood Cliffs, NJ: Prentice-Hall, 1989.

Gleason, Timothy W. "Historians and Freedom of the Press since 1800." *American Journalism* 5, no. 4 (1988): 230–47.

Godfrey, Donald G. "Broadcast Archives for Historical Research: Revisiting the Historical Method." *Journal of Broadcasting & Electronic Media* 46, no. 3 (2002): 493–503.

———. "Canadian Marconi: CFCF, the Forgotten First." *Canadian Journal of Communication* 8, no.4 (1982): 56–71.

———. "*CBS World News Roundup:* Setting the Stage for the Next Half Century." *American Journalism* 7, no. 3 (1990): 164–92.

———. *Philo T. Farnsworth: The Father of Television.* Salt Lake City: University of Utah Press, 2001.

———, ed. *ReRuns on File: A Guide to Electronic Archives.* Hillsdale, NJ: Lawrence Erlbaum Associates, 1992.

———. "Senator Dill and the 1927 Radio Act." *Journal of Broadcasting* 23, no. 4 (1979): 477–89.

Godfrey, Donald G., and Louise Benjamin. "Radio Legislation's Quiet Backstage Negotiator: Wallace H. White, Jr." *Journal of Radio Studies* 10, no. 1 (2003): 93–103.

Godfrey, Donald G., and Fritz A. Leigh, eds. *Historical Dictionary of American Radio.* Westport, CT: Greenwood, 1998.

Godfrey, Donald G., and Val Limburg. "The Rogue Elephant of Radio Legislation: Senator William E. Borah." *Journalism Quarterly* 67, no. 1 (1990): 214–24.

Godfrey, Donald G., and Davie R. Spencer, "Canadian Marconi: CFCF Television from Signal Hill to the Canadian Television Network." *Journal of Broadcasting & Electronic Media* 44, no. 3 (2000): 437–55.

Godfried, Nathan. *WCFL: Chicago's Voice of Labor, 1926–78.* Urbana: University of Illinois Press, 1997.

Goldberg, Robert. *Citizen Turner: The Wild Rise of an American Tycoon.* New York: Harcourt Brace, 1995.

Goldenson, Leonard H., and Marvin J. Wolf. *Beating the Odds: The Untold Story behind the Rise of ABC.* New York: Scribner, 1991.

Goldstein, Tom, and Jethro K. Lieberman. *The Lawyer's Guide to Writing Well.* 2nd ed. Berkeley: University of California Press, 2002.

Gomery, Douglas. "Methods for the Study of the History of Broadcasting and Mass Communication." *Film & History* 21, no. 2–3 (1991): 55–63.

Goodale, James C. "Did Janet Jackson Have a Right to Do It?" *New York Law Journal,* April 2, 2004, 3.

Goodlad, Lauren M. E. "Packaged Alternatives: The Incorporation and Gendering of 'Alternative' Radio." In *Communities of the Air: Radio Century, Radio Culture,* edited by Susan Merrill Squier. Durham, NC: Duke University Press, 2003.

Gottschalk, Louis R. *Understanding History: A Primer of Historical Method.* 2nd ed. New York: Knopf, 1969.

Government Accounting Office. "Information Management: Challenges in Managing and Preserving Electronic Records." June 2002. Report. http://www.gao.gov/new.items/d025 86.pdf.

Graham, Margaret B. W. *RCA & the Videodisc: The Business of Research.* New York: Cambridge University Press, 1986.

Grame, Theodore. *Ethnic Broadcasting in the United States.* Washington, DC: American Folklife Center, 1980.

Gray, Herman. "Recodings: Possibilities and Limitations in Commercial Television Representations of African-American Culture." In *Connections: A Broadcast History Reader,* edited by Michelle Hilmes. Belmont, CA: Wadsworth, 2003, 278–88.

———. *Watching Race: Television and the Struggle for "Blackness."* Minneapolis: University of Minnesota Press, 1995.

Graziplene, Leonard R. *Teletext: Its Promise and Demise.* Bethlehem, PA: Lehigh University Press, 2000.

Greb, Gordon, and Mike Adams. *Charles Herrold: Inventor of Radio Broadcasting.* Jefferson, NC: McFarland, 2003.

Greenberg, Bradley S., and Rick Busselle. "Reporting Rape: The Impact of Relationships and Names on Radio Listener Judgments." *Journal of Radio Studies* 4 (1997): 45–59.

Greenfield, Jeff. *The First Fifty Years.* New York: Abrams, 1977.

Greenfield, Patricia, and Jessica Beagles-Roos. "Radio vs. Television: Their Cognitive Impact on Children of Different Socioeconomic and Ethnic Groups." *Journal of Communication* 38, no. 2 (1988): 71–92.

Greenfield, Thomas Allen. *Radio: A Reference Guide.* Westport, CT: Greenwood, 1989.

Grele, Ronald J., ed. *Envelopes of Sound: The Art of Oral History.* Rev. ed. Westport, CT: Meckler, 1990.

Griffin, Leland M. "The Rhetoric of Historical Movements." *Quarterly Journal of Speech* 38, no. 2 (1952): 184–88.

Gross, Lynn. *Telecommunications: An Introduction to Electronic Media.* 6th ed. Madison, WI: Brown and Benchmark, 1997.

Grossman, George S. *Legal Research: Historical Foundations of the Electronic Age.* New York: Oxford University Press, 1994.

Gruenberg, Sidonie Matsner. "Radio and the Child." *Annals of the American Academy of Political Science* 177 (January 1935): 123–38.

Gunther, Marc. *The House that Roone Built: The Inside Story of ABC News.* Boston, MA: Little, Brown, 1994.

Gutiérrez, Félix, and Jorge Reina Schement. *Spanish-language Radio in the Southwestern United States.* Austin: Center for Mexican American Studies, University of Texas at Austin, 1979.

Hackett, Yvette. "The Search for Authenticity in Electronic Records." *The Moving Image* 3 (Fall 2003): 100–107.

Hafner, Katie. "In a Wired Age, Library Stacks Get Dustier." *Register-Guard,* June 21, 2004, A1.

Halberstam, David. *The Best and the Brightest.* Greenwich, CT: Fawcett Publications, 1973.

———. *The Powers That Be.* New York: Knopf, 1979.

Hall, Alice, and Joseph N. Cappella. "The Impact of Political Talk Radio Exposure." *Journal of Communication* 52 (2002): 332–50.

Hall, Kermit L., ed. *The Oxford Companion to the Supreme Court.* New York: Oxford University Press, 1992.

———, ed. *The Oxford Guide to the United States Supreme Court Decisions.* New York: Oxford University Press, 1999.

Hall, Stuart. "Encoding, Decoding." In *The Cultural Studies Reader,* edited by Simon During. New York: Routledge, 1993, 90–103.

Hallin, Daniel C. *The "Uncensored War": The Media and Vietnam.* New York: Oxford University Press, 1986.

Halper Donna L. *Invisible Stars: A Social History of Women in American Broadcasting.* Armonk, NY: M. E. Sharpe, 2001.

Halstead, Dirck. "If You Think Dodging and Burning Is a Problem Now, Just Wait." *The Digital Journalist.* http://www.digitaljournalist.org/issue0310/ dhcommentary.html.

———. "The Importance of Saving Your Photography." *The Digital Journalist.* http://www.digitaljournalist.org/issue0312/halsteadcommentary.html.

Hammond, Charles M., Jr. *The Image Decade: Television Documentary 1965–1975.* New York: Hastings House, 1981.

Hammond, Sharon Lee, Vicki S. Freimuth, and William Morrison. "Radio and Teens: Convincing Gatekeepers to Air Health Messages." *Health Communication* 2, no. 2 (1990): 59–67.

Hangen, Tona J. *Redeeming the Dial: Radio, Religion, and Popular Culture in America.* Chapel Hill: University of North Carolina Press, 2002.

Harlow, Alvin F. *Old Wires and New Waves: The History of the Telegraph, Telephone, and Wireless.* New York: Appleton, 1936. Reprint, New York: Arno Press, in the series *History of Radio and Television,* 1971.

Harris, Chad, Vicki Mayer, Catherine Saulino, and Dan Schiller. "The Class Politics of Rush Limbaugh." *The Communication Review* 1, no. 4 (1996): 545–64.

Harrison, Stanley L. *Cavalcade of Journalists, 1900–2000: Chroniclers of an American Century.* Miami, FL: Wolf Den Books, 2002.

Haskins, Loren, and Kirk Jeffrey. *Understanding Quantitative History.* New York: McGraw-Hill, 1990.

Hattaway, Allison M., and Susan L. Brinson. "Race & Radio: The Albama Negro Extension Service Broadcasts." *Journal of Radio Studies* 8, no. 2 (2001): 372–87.

Havig, Alan. *Fred Allen's Radio Comedy.* Philadelphia, PA: Temple University Press, 1990.

Hawes, William. *American Television Drama: The Experimental Years.* Tuscaloosa: University of Alabama Press, 1986.

———. *Filmed Television Drama, 1952–1958.* Jefferson, NC: McFarland, 2002.

———. *Live Television Drama, 1946–1951.* Jefferson, NC: McFarland, 2001.

Hawks, Ellison. *Pioneers of Wireless.* New York: Arno Press, 1974.

Head, Sydney, Christopher Sterling, and Lemuel Schofield. *Broadcasting in America.* 7th ed. Boston, MA: Houghton Mifflin, 1994.

Heinke, Rex S. *Media Law.* Washington, DC: Bureau of National Affairs, 1994.

Heinz, Catharine. "Women Radio Pioneers." *Journal of Popular Culture* 12 (1979): 305–14.

Hendy, David. *Radio in the Global Age.* London: Polity Press, 2000.

Henige, David. *Oral Historiography.* New York: Longman, 1982.

Henson, Robert. *Television Weathercasting: A History.* Jefferson, NC: McFarland, 1990.

Herman, Edward S., and Robert W. McChesney. *The Global Media: The New Missionaries of Corporate Capitalism.* Washington, DC: Cassell, 1997.

Hermanson, Louise W. "Quality Legal Research Possible Even with Limited Resources." *Media Law Notes* 20 (Fall 1993): 14.

Herzog, Herta. *Children and Their Leisure Time Listening to the Radio: A Survey of the Literature in the Field.* New York: Office of Radio Research, Columbia University, 1941.

Hettinger, Herman S. *A Decade of Radio Advertising.* Chicago: University of Chicago Press, 1933. Reprint, New York: Arno Press, in the series *History of Broadcasting,* 1971.

Heyer, Paul. "A Reassessment of Orson Welles' 1938 War of the Worlds Broadcast." *Journal of Communication* 28, no. 2 (2003): 149–65.

Hijiya, James A. *Lee de Forest and the Fatherhood of Radio.* Bethlehem, PA: Lehigh University Press, 1992.

Hill, George H., and Sylvia Saverson Hill, eds. *Blacks on Television: A Selectively Annotated Bibliography.* Metuchen, NJ: Scarecrow Press, 1985.

Hill, George H., and J. J. Johnson. *Black Radio in Los Angeles, Chicago, New York.* Carson, CA: Daystar, 1987.

Hill, George H., Lorraine Raglin, and Chas Floyd Johnson. *Black Women in Television: An Illus-trated History and Bibliography.* New York: Garland Press, 1990.

Hilliard, Robert L., and Michael C. Keith. *The Broadcast Century and Beyond: A Biography of American Broadcasting.* 3rd. ed. Woburn, MA: Focal Press, 2001.

———. *Dirty Discourse: Sex and Indecency in American Radio.* Ames: Iowa State University Press, 2003.

———. "Farm and Rural Radio: Some Beginnings and Models." *Journal of Radio Studies* 8, no 2 (2001): 321–30.

———. *The Quieted Voice: Rise and Demise of Localism in American Radio.* Carbondale: South-ern Illinois University Press, 2005.

———. *Waves of Rancor: Tuning in the Radical Right.* Armonk, NY: M. E. Sharp, 1999.

Hilmes, Michele, ed. *Connections: A Broadcast History Reader.* Belmont, CA: Wadsworth, 2003.

———. "Desired and Feared: Women's Voices in Radio History." In *Television, History, and American Culture: Feminist Critical Essays,* edited by Mary Beth Haralovich and Lauren Rabinovitz. Durham, NC: Duke University Press, 1999.

———. *Hollywood and Broadcasting: From Radio to Cable.* Urbana: University of Illinois Press, 1990.

———. *Only Connect: A Cultural History of Broadcasting.* Thousand Oaks, CA: Wadsworth, 2002.

———. *Radio Voices: American Broadcasting, 1922–1952.* Minneapolis: University of Minne-sota Press, 1997.

Hilmes, Michele, and Jason Loviglio, eds. *Radio Reader: Essays in the Cultural History of Radio.* New York: Routledge, 2002.

Hinds, Lynn Boyd. *Broadcasting the Local News: The Early Years of Pittsburgh's KDKA-TV.* Uni-versity Park: Pennsylvania State University Press, 1995.

Hocking, John E., Don W. Stacks, and Steven T. McDermott. *Communication Research.* 3rd ed. Boston, MA: Allyn & Bacon, 2003.

Hoffman, Alice. "Reliability and Validity in Oral History." *Today's Speech* 22 (1974): 23–27.

Hoffman-Riem, Wolfgang. *Regulating Media: The Licensing and Supervision of Broadcasting in Six Countries.* New York: Guilford Press, 1996.

Hofstetter, C. Richard, and Christopher Gianos. "Political Talk Radio: Actions Speak Louder than Words." *Journal of Broadcasting & Electronic Media* 41, no. 4 (1997): 501–15.

Hogan, Lawrence D. *A Black National News Service: The Associated Negro Press and Claude Barnett, 1919–1945.* Rutherford, NJ: Associated University Presses, 1984.

Hollander, Barry A. "Talk Radio: Predictors of Use and Effects of Attitudes About Govern-ment." *Journalism and Mass Communication Quarterly* 73, no. 1 (1996): 102–13.

Hollander, Barry A., Robert L. Hilliard, and Michael C. Keith. "Influence of Talk Radio on Political Efficacy and Participation." *Journal of Radio Studies* 3 (1995): 23–31.

———. "Political Talk Radio in the 90s: A Panel Study." *Journal of Radio Studies* 6, no. 2 (1999): 236–45.

Holroyd, Michael. *Lytton Strachey: A Biography.* New York: Penguin Books, 1971.

———. *Works on Paper: The Craft of Biography and Autobiography.* Washington, DC: Counter-point, 2002.

Holsinger, Ralph L., and Jon Paul Dilts. *Media Law.* 3rd ed. New York: McGraw-Hill, 1987.

Hoopes, James. *Oral History: An Introduction for Students.* Chapel Hill: University of North Carolina Press, 1979.

Hopkins, W. Wat, ed. *Communications and the Law.* Mahwah, NJ: Lawrence Erlbaum, forthcoming.

Horkheimer, Max, and Theodor W. Adorno."The Culture Industry: Enlightenment as Mass Deception." In *Dialectic of Enlightenment,* by Max Horkheimer and Theodor W. Adorno. New York: Continuum, 1944, 120–67.

———. *Dialectic of Enlightenment.* New York: Continuum, 1944.

Horten, Gerd. *Radio Goes to War: The Cultural Politics of Propaganda during World War II.* Berkeley: University of California Press, 2002.

Hosley, David H. *As Good as Any: Foreign Correspondence on American Radio, 1930–1940.* Westport, CT: Greenwood, 1984.

Hosley, David H., and Gayle K. Yamada. *Hard News: Women in Broadcast Journalism.* New York: Greenwood, 1987.

Houck, Davis W. *Rhetoric as Currency: Hoover, Roosevelt, and the Great Depression.* College Station: Texas A&M University Press, 2001.

Howell, Martha, and Walter Prevenier. *From Reliable Sources: An Introduction to Historical Methods.* Ithaca, NY: Cornell University Press, 2001.

Howeth, Linwood S. *History of Communications-electronics in the United States Navy.* Washington, DC: Government Printing Office, 1963.

Huntemann, Nina. "A Promise Diminished: The Politics of Low-Power Radio." In *Communities of the Air: Radio Century, Radio Culture,* edited by Susan Merrill Squier. Durham, NC: Duke University Press, 2003.

Hutchby, Ian. *Confrontation Talk: Arguments, Asymmetries, and Power on Talk Radio.* Lawrence Erlbaum Associates, 1996.

Hutton, Frankie. *The Early Black Press in America, 1827 to 1860.* Westport, CT: Greenwood, 1993.

Inglis, Andrew F. *Behind The Tube: A History of Broadcasting Technology and Business.* Boston, MA: Focal Press, 1990.

Innis, Harold A. *The Bias of Communication.* 1951. Reprint, Toronto: University of Toronto Press, 1964.

———. *Empire & Communications.* Toronto: University of Toronto Press, 1972.

———. "Roddy Flynn's Teaching Webpage: Harold Innis." October 23, 2002. http://www .comms.dcu.ie/flynnr/harold_innis.html.

Institute of Radio Engineers. "The Fiftieth Anniversary Issue." *Proceedings of the Institute of Radio Engineers* 50 (May 1962): 529–1,448.

International Association of Library Associations and Institutions. *Library & Information Science: Citation Guides for Electronic Documents.* February 3, 2003, http://www.ifla.org/I/ training/citation/citing.htm.

Iowa Center for Communication Study. *The Iowa Guide: Scholarly Journals in Mass Communications and Related Fields.* 8th ed. Thousand Oaks, CA: Sage, 1999.

Irby, Kenny. "A Photojournalistic Confession." *The Digital Journalist.* http://www.digital journalist.org/issue0309/kirby.html.

Isocrates. *Antidosis I,* trans. David Mirhady and Yun Lee Too. Austin: University of Texas Press, 2000.

Jackaway, Gwenyth L. *Media at War: Radio's Challenge to the Newspapers, 1924–1939.* Westport, CT: Praeger, 1995.

Jackson, David Earl, Marie Dutton Brown, and Linda Tarrant-Reid. *Celebrating Twenty Years: BET Black Star Power.* Washington, DC: BET Books, 2000.

Jaker, Bill, Frank Sulek, and Peter Kanze. *The Airwaves of New York: Illustrated Histories of 156 AM Stations in the Metropolitan Area, 1921–1996.* Jefferson, NC: McFarland, 1996.

Jarausch, Konrad H., and Kenneth A. Hardy. *Quantitative Methods for Historians: A Guide to Research, Data, and Statistics.* Chapel Hill: University of North Carolina Press, 1991.

Jay, Martin. *The Dialectical Imagination: A History of the Frankfurt School and the Institute of Social Research, 1923–1950.* Berkeley: University of California Press, 1973.

Jeter, James Phillip. *Black-oriented Radio: An Audio Documentary.* Master's project, Cornell University, 1973.

Johnson, Frank W., Jr. "The Development of Black Radio Networks in the United States: 1943–1993." *Journal of Radio Studies* 2 (1993): 173–87.

Johnson, Mary H. *A Case History of the Evolution of WGPR-TV, Detroit: First Black-owned Television Station in the U.S., 1972–1979.* Master's thesis, University of North Carolina at Chapel Hill, 1979.

Johnson, Phylis, and Joe S. Foote. "Alternative Radio: Other Voices Beyond the Mainstream." *Journal of Radio Studies* 7, no. 2 (2000): 282–86.

Johnson, Phylis A., and Michael C. Keith. *Queer Airwaves: The Story of Gay and Lesbian Broadcasting.* Armonk, NY: M. E. Sharpe, 2001.

Johnston, Donald H., ed. *Encyclopedia of International Media and Communications.* 4 vols. San Diego, CA: Academic Press, 2003.

Johnstone, Ronald L. "Who Listens to Religious Radio?" *Journal of Broadcasting & Electronic Media* 16, no. 1 (1972): 91–102.

Jolly, W. P. *Marconi.* New York: Stein & Day, 1972.

———. *Sir Oliver Lodge: Psychical Researcher and Scientist.* Cranbury, NJ: Associate University Presses, 1974.

Jones, Alex, exec. dir. *Seeing Is Believing: How Can You Tell What's Real?* Washington, DC: Newseum, 1997. 17 min. videocassette.

Juhnke, Eric S. *Quacks & Crusaders: The Fabulous Careers of John Brinkley, Norman Baker & Harry Hoxsey.* Lawrence: University Press of Kansas, 2002.

Kahn, Frank J., ed. *Documents of American Broadcasting.* New York: Appleton-Century-Crofts 1968. 4th ed. Englewood Cliffs, NJ: Prentice-Hall, 1984.

Kammen, Carol. *On Doing Local History.* 2nd ed. Walnut Creek, CA: AltaMira Press, American Association for State and Local History, 2003.

Kanellos, Nicolas, with Helvetia Martell. *Hispanic Periodicals in the United States, Origins to 1960: A Brief History and Comprehensive Bibliography.* Houston, TX: Arte Publico Press, 2000.

Kay, Jack, George Ziegelmueller, and Kevin Minch. "From Coughlin to Limbaugh: Fallacies and Techniques of Propaganda in American Populist Talk Radio." *Journal of Radio Studies* 5, no. 1 (1998): 9–21.

Keeshan, Robert. *Growing Up Happy.* New York: Doubleday, 1989.

Keith, Michael C. *Signals in the Air: Native Broadcasting in America.* Westport, CT: Praeger, 1995.

———. *Sounds in the Dark: All-night Radio in American Life.* Ames: Iowa State University Press, 2001.

————. *Talking Radio: An Oral History of American Radio in The Television Age.* Armonk, NY: M. E. Sharpe, 2000.

————. *Voices in the Purple Haze: Underground Radio and the Sixties.* Westport, CT: Praeger, 1997.

Kellner, Douglas. *Critical Theory, Marxism and Modernity.* Baltimore, MD: Johns Hopkins University Press, 1989.

————. *Media Culture: Cultural Studies, Identity and Politics Between the Modern and the Postmodern.* New York: Routledge, 1995.

Kendall, Paul Murray. "Walking the Boundaries." In *Biography as High Adventure: Life Writers Speak on Their Art,* edited by Stephen B. Oates. Amherst: University of Massachusetts Press, 1986.

Kerlinger, Fred N. *Foundations of Behavioral Research: Educational and Psychological Inquiry.* New York: Holt, Rinehart and Winston, 1964.

Kessler-Harris, Alice. "Social History." In *The New American History,* edited by E. Foner for the American Historical Association. Philadelphia, PA: Temple University Press, 1990.

King, Julie Adair. *Digital Photography for Dummies.* 2nd ed. Foster City, CA: IGA Books Worldwide.

Knapp, Mark L., and John A. Daly. *A Guide to Publishing in Scholarly Communication Journals.* Mahwah, NJ: Lawrence Erlbaum Associates, 2004.

Kobre, Ken. "The Long Tradition of Doctoring Photos." *Visual Communication Quarterly* 2 (Spring 1995): 14–15.

Koch, Hoard. *The Panic Broadcast: Portrait of an Event.* Boston, MA: Little Brown, 1970.

Koenig, Allen E. *Broadcasting and Bargaining: Labor Relations in Radio and Television.* Madison: University of Wisconsin Press, 1970.

Kowalik, Jan. *The Polish Press in America.* San Francisco, CA: R & E Research Associates, 1978.

Krasnow, Erwin G., and G. Gail Crotts. "Inside the FCC: A Guide for Information Seekers." *Public Telecommunications Review* 3 (July–August 1975): 49.

Krattenmaker, Thomas G. *Telecommunications Law and Policy.* Durham, NC: Carolina Academic Press, 1998.

Kuhlthau, Carol Collier, M. Elspeth Goodin, and Mary Jane McNally, eds. *The Virtual School Library: Gateway to the Information Superhighway.* Englewood, CO: Libraries Unlimited, 1996.

Kurtz, Howard. *Hot Air: All Talk, All the Time.* New York: Crown, 1996.

Kurylo, Friedrich. *Ferdinand Braun: A Life of the Nobel Prizewinner and Inventor of the Cathode-ray Oscilloscope,* trans. and adapted by Charles Susskind. Cambridge, MA: MIT Press, 1981.

Kyvig, David E., and Myron A. Marty. *Nearby History: Exploring the Past Around You.* Nashville, TN: American Association for State and Local History, 1982. 2nd ed. Walnut Creek, CA: AltaMira Press, 2000.

Ladd, Jim. *Radio Waves: Life and Revolution on the FM Dial.* New York: St. Martin's Press, 1991.

Land, Jeff. *Active Radio: Pacifica's Brash Experiment.* Minneapolis: University of Minnesota Press, 1999.

Lang, Kurt, and Gladys Engel Lang. *Television and Politics.* Chicago: Quadrangle Books, 1970.

Lang, William L., and Laurie K. Mercier. "Getting It Down Right: Oral History's Reliability in Local History Research." *Oral History Review* 12 (1984): 82–83.

Larson, Charles U. "Radio, Secondary Orality, and the Search for Community: A Case Study of 'A Prairie Home Companion.'" *Journal of Radio Studies* 3 (1995–1996): 89–105.

Larson, Mary Strom. "Rush Limbaugh: Broadcast Demagogue." *Journal of Radio Studies* 4 (1997): 184–97.

Lasar, Matthew. *Pacifica Radio: The Rise of an Alternative Network.* Philadelphia, PA: Temple University Press, 1999.

Lazarsfeld, Paul F. *Radio and the Printed Page.* New York: Duell, Sloan and Pearce, 1940.

Lazarsfeld, Paul F., Bernard Berelson, and Hazel Gaudet. *The People's Choice: How the Voter Makes Up His Mind in a Presidential Election.* New York: Columbia University Press, 1944.

Lazarsfeld, Paul F., and Patricia L. Kendall. *Radio Listening in America: The People Look at Radio—Again.* New York: Prentice-Hall, 1948.

Le Duc, Don R. *Beyond Broadcasting: Pattern in Policy and Law.* New York: Longman, 1987.

———. "Broadcast Legal Documentation: A Four-dimensional Guide." *Journal of Broadcasting* 17, no. 2 (1973): 131–45.

———. *Cable Television and the FCC: A Crisis in Media Control.* Philadelphia, PA: Temple University Press, 1973.

Leckie, Shirley A. "Biography Matters": Why Historians Need Well-crafted Biographies More than Ever." In *Writing Biography: Historians and Their Craft,* edited by Lloyd E. Ambrosius. Lincoln: University of Nebraska Press, 2004.

Lee, R. Alton. *The Bizarre Careers of John R. Brinkley.* Lexington: University Press of Kentucky, 2002.

Lerner, Daniel, and Lyle M. Nelson. *Communication Research: A Half-century Appraisal.* Honolulu: University of Hawaii Press, 1977.

Lerner, Gerda. *The Majority Finds Its Past.* New York: Oxford University Press, 1994.

Lester, Paul. *Visual Communication: Images with Messages.* Belmont, CA: Wadsworth, 1995.

Levin, Harry Leon. *The Use of Radio in Family Planning.* Oklahoma City, OK: World Neighbors, 1974.

Levin, Murray B. *Talk Radio and the American Dream.* Lexington, MA: Lexington Books, 1987.

Levy, Leonard W., Kenneth L. Karst, and Dennis J. Mahoney, eds. *Encyclopedia of the American Constitution.* 4 vols. New York: Macmillan, 1986 and supp., 1992.

Lewis, Justin. *Constructing Public Opinion.* New York: Columbia University Press, 2001.

Lewis, Tom. *Empire of the Air: The Men Who Made Radio.* New York: HarperCollins, 1991.

———. "Triumph of the Idol: Rush Limbaugh and a Hot Medium." *Media Studies Journal* 7, no. 3 (1993): 51–61.

Lewis, Peter M., and Jerry Booth. *Invisible Medium: Public, Commercial, and Community Radio.* Washington, DC: Howard University Press, 1990.

Library of Congress. *Citing Electronic Resources.* September 12, 2003. http://lcweb2.loc.gov/ammem/ndlpedu/start/cite/index.html.

———. "Digitizing Library Collections for Preservation and Archiving: A Handbook for Curators." Preservation Research and Testing series No. 9705. Washington, DC: Author, Preservation Directorate, 1997.

———. *Library of Congress Motion Picture, Broadcasting, Recorded Sound: An Illustrated Guide.* Washington, DC: Library of Congress, 2001.

———. "Risk Analysis Study for a Representative Magnetic Tape Collection." Preservation Research and Testing Series No. 9808. Washington, DC: Author, Preservation Directorate, 1998.

Lichty, Lawrence W., and Malachi C. Topping, eds. *American Broadcasting: A Source Book on the History of Radio and Television.* New York: Hastings House, 1975.

Lincoln, Yvonna S., and Egon G. Guba. *Naturalistic Inquiry.* Beverly Hills, CA: Sage, 1985.

Lind, Rebecca Ann. *Race/Gender/Media: Considering Diversity across Audiences, Content, and Producers.* Boston, MA: Allyn & Bacon, 2004.

Lipschultz, Jeremy H. *Broadcast Indecency: F.C.C. Regulation and the First Amendment.* Boston, MA: Focal Press, 1996.

———. *Free Expression in the Age of the Internet, Social and Legal Boundaries.* Boulder, CO: Westview Press, 2000.

Littlefield, Daniel F., Jr., and James W. Parins. *American Indian and Alaska Native Newspapers and Periodicals, 1826–1924.* Westport, CT: Greenwood, 1984.

Lively, Donald E. *Essential Principles of Communications Law.* New York: Praeger, 1992.

———. *Modern Communications Law.* New York: Praeger, 1991.

Lo, Karl, and Him Mark Lai. *Chinese Newspapers Published in North America, 1854–1975.* Washington, DC: Center for Chinese Research Materials, Association of Research Libraries, 1977.

London, Barbara, John Upton, Ken Kobre, and Betsy Brill. *Photography.* 7th ed. Upper Saddle River, NJ: Prentice-Hall, 2002.

Lowe, Felicia. "Asian American Women in Broadcasting." In *Making Waves: An Anthology of Writings by and about Asian American Women,* edited by Asian Women United of California. Boston, MA: Beacon Press, 1989.

Lowery, Shearon A., and Melvin L. DeFleur. *Milestones in Mass Communication Research: Media Effects.* 3rd ed. White Plains, NY: Longman, 1995.

Luey, Beth. *Handbook for Academic Authors.* 4th ed. New York: Cambridge University Press, 2002.

Luke, Carmen. *Constructing the Child Viewer: A History of the American Discourse on Television and Children, 1950–1980.* Westport, CT: Praeger, 1991.

Lum, Casey. "An Alternative Voice from Afar: A Brief History of New York's Chinese Language Wireless Radio." *Journal of Radio Studies* 2 (2000): 355–72.

Lummis, Trevor. *Listening to History: The Authenticity of Oral Evidence.* Totowa, NJ: Barnes & Noble Books, 1988.

Lyness, Paul I. "Radio's Young Audience Habits." *Broadcasting* 25 (September 1950).

Lyons, Eugene. *David Sarnoff, a Biography.* New York: Harper & Row, 1966.

MacDonald, J. Fred. *Blacks and White TV: African Americans in Television since 1948.* 2nd ed. Chicago: Nelson-Hall, 1992.

———. *Don't Touch That Dial: Radio Programming in American Life, 1920–1960.* Chicago: Nelson-Hall, 1979.

———. *One Nation under Television: The Rise and Decline of Network TV.* 1st ed. New York: Pantheon, 1990.

———, ed. *Richard Durham's Destination Freedom: Scripts from Radio's Black Legacy, 1948–50.* New York: Praeger, 1989.

———. *Television and the Red Menace: The Video Road to Vietnam.* New York: Praeger, 1985.

Mace, O. Henry. *Collector's Guide to Early Photographs.* Radnor, PA: Wallace-Homestead, 1990.

MacGregor-Morris, John T. *The Inventor of the Valve: A Biography of Sir Ambrose Fleming.* London: Television Society, 1954.

Maclaurin, W. Rupert. *Invention and Innovation in the Radio Industry.* New York: Macmillan, 1949. Reprint, New York: Arno Press, in the series *History of Broadcasting,* 1971.

Mair, George. *Inside HBO: The Billion Dollar War Between HBO, Hollywood, and the Home Video Revolution.* New York: Dodd, Mead, 1988.

Mann, Thomas. *The Oxford Guide to Library Research.* New York: Oxford University Press, 1998.

Marcombe, David. *Sounding Boards: Oral Testimony and the Local Historian.* Nottingham, England: Department of Adult Education, 1995.

Marcus, Sheldon. *Father Coughlin: The Tumultuous Life of the Priest of the Little Flower.* Boston, MA: Little, Brown, 1986.

Marlane, Judith. *Women in Television News.* New York: Columbia University Press, 1976.

———. *Women in Television News Revisited: Into the Twenty-first Century.* Austin: University of Texas Press, 1999.

Marlow, Eugene, and Eugene Secunda. *Shifting Time and Space: The Story of Videotape.* Westport, CT: Praeger, 1991.

Marwick, Arthur. "The Historian at Work: Forget 'Facts,' Foreground Sources." In *The New Nature of History: Knowledge, Evidence, Language.* Chicago: Lyceum Books, 2001, 152–94. [Rev. ed. of *The Nature of History.*]

———. *The Nature of History.* 3rd ed. London: MacMillan Education and Chicago: Lyceum Books, 1989.

Masters, Kim. *The Keys to the Kingdom.* New York: W. Morrow, 2000.

Mata, Marita. "Being Women in the Popular Radio." In *Women in Grassroots Communication,* edited by Pilar Riano. Thousand Oaks, CA: Sage, 1994.

Matelski, Marilyn. *Vatican Radio: Propagation by the Airwaves.* Westport, CT: Praeger, 1995.

Matusow, Barbara. *The Evening Stars: The Making of the Network News Anchor.* Boston, MA: Houghton Mifflin, 1983.

Maurois, André. "Biography as a Work of Art." In *Biography as High Adventure: Life Writers Speak on Their Art,* edited by Stephen B. Oates. Amherst: University of Massachusetts Press, 1986.

Mayes, Thorn L. *Wireless Communication in the United States: The Early Development of American Radio Operating Companies.* East Greenwich, RI: New England Wireless and Steam Museum, 1989.

Maynard, Mary, and June Purvis, eds. *Researching Women's Lives from a Feminist Perspective.* London: Taylor & Francis, 1994.

Mazingo, Sherrie. "Home of Programming Firsts." *Television/Radio Age,* March 1987, A1–A62.

McChesney, Robert W. "Conflict, Not Consensus: The Debate over Broadcast Communication Policy, 1930–1935." In *Ruthless Criticism: New Perspectives in U.S. Communication History,* edited by William S. Solomon and Robert W. McChesney. Minneapolis: University of Minnesota, 1993.

———. *Our Media, Not Theirs: The Democratic Struggle Against Corporate Media.* New York: Seven Stories, 2002.

———. *Telecommunications, Mass Media, and Democracy: The Battle for the Control of U.S. Broadcasting, 1928–1935.* New York: Oxford University Press, 1993.

McGrath, Tom. *Video Killed the Radio Star.* New York: Villard, 1994.

McKerns, Joseph P., ed. *Biographical Dictionary of American Journalism.* New York: Greenwood, 1989.

McLuhan, Marshall. *Understanding Media: The Extensions of Man.* New York: Signet, 1966.

McMahon, Robert Sears. *Federal Regulation of the Radio and Television Broadcast Industry in the United States.* New York: Arno Press, 1979.

McNeil, Alex. *Total Television: A Comprehensive Guide to Programming from 1948 to 1980.* New York: Penguin Books, 1980.

———. *Total Television: The Comprehensive Guide to Programming from 1948 to the Present.* 4th ed. New York: Penguin Books, 1997.

McNicol, Donald. *Radio's Conquest of Space: The Experimental Rise in Radio Communication.* New York: Murray Hill Books, 1946. Reprint, New York: Arno Press, in the series *Telecommunications,* 1974.

Mechling, Elizabeth Walker, and Jay Mechling. "The Atom According to Disney." *Quarterly Journal of Speech* 81, no. 4 (1995): 436–53.

Meckiff, Donald, and Matthew Murray. "Radio and the Black Soldier during World War II." *Critical Studies in Mass Communication* 15, no. 4 (1998): 337–56.

Meehan, Eileen. "Heads of Household and Ladies of the House: Gender, Genre, and Broadcast Ratings, 1929–1990." In *Ruthless Criticism: New Perspectives in U.S. Communication History,* edited by William S. Solomon and Robert W. McChesney. Minneapolis: University of Minnesota, 1993.

Meeker, Heather. "Stalking the Golden Topic: A Guide to Locating and Selecting Topics for Legal Research Papers." *Utah Law Review,* 1996, 917.

Merrick, Beverly G. "Mary McBride, Talk Show Host: The Perfect Proxy for Radio Listeners." *Journal of Radio Studies* 4 (1997): 146–65.

Mersky, Roy M., and Donald J. Dunn. *Fundamentals of Legal Research.* 8th ed. New York: Foundation Press, 2002.

———. *Legal Research Illustrated.* 8th ed. Eagan, MN: Thomson West, 2002.

Methven, Patricia, and Sheila Anderson. "Historians and Access to Archives in the Digital Age." Keynote address presented at the 1999 annual conference of the Association for History and Computing. King's College London, September 14–16, 1999. Abstract is available online at http://www.kcl.ac.uk/humanities/cch/drhahc/ahc/abst271.htm.

Metz, Robert. *CBS: Reflections in a Bloodshot Eye.* Chicago: Playboy Press, 1975.

Meyrowitz, Joshua. *No Sense of Place: The Impact of Electronic Media on Social Behavior.* New York: Oxford University Press, 1985.

Middleton, Kent R., Robert Trager, and Bill F. Chamberlin. *The Law of Public Communication.* 6th ed. Boston, MA: Allyn & Bacon, 2004.

Migala, Joseph. *Polish Radio Broadcasting in the United States.* Boulder, CO: East European Monographs, 1987.

Milam, Lorenzo Wilson. *Original Sex and Broadcasting: A Handbook for Starting a Radio Station for the Community.* San Francisco, CA: Mho & Mho Works, 1988.

Miller, Edward D. *Emergency Broadcasting and 1930s American Radio.* Philadelphia, PA: Temple University Press, 2003.

Mishler, Elliot G. *Research Interviewing: Context and Narrative.* Cambridge, MA: Harvard University Press, 1986.

Mitchell, Caroline. *Woman and Radio: Airing Differences.* London: Routledge, 2001.

Mitchell, William. *The Reconfigured Eye: Visual Truth in the Post-photographic Era.* Cambridge, MA: MIT Press, 2001.

Moore, Roy L. *Mass Communication Law and Ethics.* 2nd ed. Mahwah, NJ: Lawrence Erlbaum Associates, 1999.

Morley, Patrick. *"This Is the American Forces Network": The Anglo-American Battle of the Air Waves in World War II.* Westport, CT: Praeger, 2001.

Morris, Edmund. *Dutch: A Memoir of Ronald Reagan.* New York: Modern Library, 1999.

Morson, Gary Saul. "The War of the Well(e)s." *Journal of Communication* 29, no. 3 (1979): 10–20.

Mosco, Vincent. *The Political Economy of Communication: Rethinking and Renewal.* Thousand Oaks, CA: Sage, 1996.

Mueller, Milton. "Why Communications Policy Is Passing 'Mass Communication' by: Political Economy as the Missing Link." *Critical Studies in Mass Communication* 12, no. 4 (1995): 457–72.

Mullen, Megan Gwynne. *The Rise of Cable Programming in the United States: Revolution or Evolution?* Austin: University of Texas Press, 2003.

Mumford, Lewis. "The Task of Modern Biography." *English Journal* 23 (1934): 1–9.

Murphy, James E. "Alaska Native Communication Media: An Overview." *Gazette* (Fairbanks, AK), 1982.

Murphy, James Emmett, and Sharon M. Murphy. *Let My People Know: American Indian Journalism, 1828–1978.* Norman: University of Oklahoma Press, 1981.

Murray, Michael D. "And That's the Way He Is: Interview with Walter Cronkite." In *The Political Performers.* New York: Praeger, 1994.

———. "Creating a Tradition in TV News: A Conversation with David Brinkley." *Journalism History* 21, no. 4 (1995): 164–69.

———, ed. *Encyclopedia of Television News.* Phoenix, AZ: Oryx Press, 1999.

———. "End of an Era at CBS: A Conversation with Bill Leonard." *American Journalism* 8, no. 1 (1991): 46–62.

———. "A Passion for Politics: A Conversation with Tom Brokaw." *American Journalism* 17, no. 3 (2000): 109–17.

———. "Persuasive Dimensions of *See It Now:* Report on Senator Joseph R. McCarthy." *Communications Quarterly* 24 (Fall, 1975): 13–20.

———. *The Political Performers: CBS Broadcasts in the Public Interest.* Westport, CT: Praeger, 1994.

———. "Reporting Histories' First Draft: A Conversation with Byron Pitts." *Television Quarterly* 33, no. 4 (2003): 26–33.

———. "The World of Change in TV News: A Conversation with Garrick Utley." *American Journalism* 14, no. 2 (1997): 223–30.

Murray, Michael D., and Donald G. Godfrey, eds. *Television in America: Local Station History from across the Nation.* Ames: Iowa State University Press, 1997.

Nachman, Gerald. *Raised on Radio.* New York: Pantheon, 1998.

Napoli, Philip M. "The Federal Communications Commission and Broadcast Policy-making—1966–95: A Logistic Regression Analysis of Interest Group Influence." *Communication Law & Policy* 5, no. 2 (2000): 203–33.

Nash, Francis M. *Towers over Kentucky: A History of Radio and TV in the Bluegrass State.* Lexington, KY: Host Communications, 1995.

National Aeronautics and Space Administration. *Apollo 11: Moon Landing, First on the Moon.* Documentary. Fresno: California Microfilm Co., 1969.

National Archives and Records Administration (NARA). "Electronic Records Archives." http://
www.archives.gov/electronic_records_archives/index.html.
———. "Records Management by Federal Agencies." http://www.archives.gov/about_us/
basic_laws_and_authorities/federal_agencies.html.
National Press Photographers Association. "Code of Ethics." http://www.nppa.org/professional
_development/business_practices/ethics.html.
Neilsen, Joyce McCarl, ed. *Feminist Research Methods: Exemplary Readings in the Social Sciences.*
Boulder, CO: Westview, 1990.
Nevins, Allan. "American Journalism and Its Historical Treatments." *Journalism Quarterly* 36
(Fall 1959): 411–22.
———. *The Gateway to History.* New York: D.C. Heath, 1938. Rev. ed. Chicago: Quadrangle
Books, 1963.
Newcomb, Horace, ed. *Encyclopedia of Television.* 3 vols. Chicago: Fitzroy Dearborn, 1997. 2nd
ed. 4 vols., 2005.
———. *Television: The Critical View.* 6th ed. Oxford: Oxford University Press, 2000.
Newhall, Beaumont. *The Daguerreotype in America.* 3rd ed. New York: Dover, 1976.
———. *The History of Photography.* Boston, MA: Little, Brown, 1982.
———. *Photo Journalism or Photo Fiction?* Videocassette. Produced by Kathy Nelson. Directed
by Graham Knight. Arlington, VA: Freedom Forum, 1995.
Newkirk, Pamela. *Within the Veil: Black Journalists, White Media.* New York: New York University
Press, 2000.
Newman, Mark. *Entrepreneurs of Profit and Pride: From Black-appeal to Radio Soul.* New York:
Praeger, 1988.
Nmungwun, Aaron Foisi. *Video Recording Technology: Its Impact on Media and Home Entertainment.* Hillsdale, NJ: Lawrence Erlbaum Associates, 1989.
Nord, David Paul. "Intellectual History, Social History, Cultural History, and Our History."
Journalism Quarterly 67, no. 4 (1990): 645–48.
———. "The Nature of Historical Research." In *Research Methods in Mass Communication,*
edited by Guido H. Stempel III and Bruce H. Westley. Englewood Cliffs, NJ: Prentice-Hall, 1989.
Nord, David Paul, and Harold L. Nelson. "The Logic of Historical Research." In *Research Methods in Mass Communication,* edited by Guido H. Stempel III and Bruce H. Westley.
Englewood Cliffs, NJ: Prentice-Hall, 1981.
O'Connor, John E., ed. *Image as Artifact: The Historical Analysis of Film and Television.* Malibar,
FL: Robert E. Krieger Publishing, 1990.
O'Dell, Cary. "A Station of Their Own: The Story of the Women's Auxiliary Television Technical Staff (WATTS) in World War II Chicago." *Television Quarterly* 30 (2000): 58–67.
———. *Women Pioneers in Television: Biographies of Fifteen Industry Leaders.* Jefferson, NC:
McFarland, 1997.
Oates, Stephen B., ed. *Biography as High Adventure: Life Writers Speak on Their Art.* Amherst:
University of Massachusetts Press, 1986.
Oppenheimer, Michael. "Copyright and Intellectual Property." Arizona State University, Telecommunications for Instruction. Fall 1997. http://seamonkey.ed.asu.edu/~mcisaac/emc
523/work/a8/oppen.html.
Orlik, Peter B. *Electronic Media Criticism: Applied Perspectives.* 2nd ed. Mahwah, NJ: Lawrence
Erlbaum Associates, 2002.

Overbeck, Wayne. *Major Principles of Media Law.* Belmont, CA: Wadsworth, 2004.

Page, Benjamin I., and Jason Tannenbaum. "Populist Deliberation in Talk Radio." *Journal of Communication* 46, no. 2 (1996): 33–54.

Paglin, Max D., ed. *A Legislative History of the Communications Act of 1934.* New York: Oxford University Press, 1989.

Paglin, Max D., Joel Rosenbloom, and James R. Hobson, eds. *The Communications Act: A Legislative History of the Major Amendments, 1934–1996.* Washington, DC: Pike & Fischer, 1999.

Paley, William S. *As It Happened: A Memoir.* Garden City, NY: Doubleday, 1979.

Pardun, Carol J. "An Analysis of Qualitative Research in the *Journal of Broadcasting & Electronic Media,* 1978–1998." *Journal of Broadcasting & Electronic Media* 44, no. 3 (2000): 529–35.

Paredes, Mari Castanede. "The Transformation of Spanish-Language Radio in the U.S." *Journal of Radio Studies* 10, no. 1 (2003): 5–16.

Parke, Catherine N. *Biography: Writing Lives.* New York: Twayne, 1996.

Parsons, Patrick R. *Cable Television and the First Amendment.* New York: Free Press, 1987.

Parton, James. *Life and Times of Benjamin Franklin.* New York: Mason Brothers, 1864.

Pawley, Edward. *BBC Engineering: 1922–1972.* London: British Broadcasting Corporation (BBC), 1972.

Pearl, David, Lorraine Bouthilet, and Joyce Lazar, eds. *Television and Behavior: Ten Years of Scientific Progress and Implications for the Eighties.* Washington, DC: U.S. Government Printing Office, 1982.

Pember, Don, and Clay Calvert. *Media Law, 2005–2006.* Boston, MA: McGraw-Hill, Forthcoming.

Peterson, Bernard L., Jr. *Early Black American Playwrights and Dramatic Writers: A Biographical Directory and Catalog of Plays, Films, and Broadcasting Scripts.* New York: Greenwood, 1990.

Phifer, Gregg. "The Historical Approach." In *An Introduction to Graduate Study in Speech and Theatre,* edited by Clyde Walton Dow. East Lansing: Michigan State Press, 1961, 52–80.

Phillips, Mary Alice Mayer. *CATV: A History of Community Antenna Television.* Evanston, IL: Northwestern University Press, 1972.

Phillips, Vivian J. *Early Radio Wave Detectors.* London: Peter Peregrinus, 1981.

Pike and Fischer. "Communications Regulation." http://www.pf.com/commreg.asp.

———. *Communications Regulation: Current Service.* Bethesda, MD: Pike and Fischer, 1995–.

Plutarch, Alexander. *Greek Lives,* trans. by Robin Waterfield. Oxford: Oxford University Press, 1998.

Podber, Jacob J. "Early Radio in Rural Appalachia: An Oral History." *Journal of Radio Studies* 8, no. 2 (2001): 388–410.

Pool, Ithiel de Sola, ed. *Trends in Content Analysis.* Urbana: University of Illinois Press, 1959.

Posner, Richard. "No Thanks, We Already Have Our Own Laws." *Legal Affairs.* (July–August 2004): 40–42.

Pospisil, George. "Common Rule," 45 CFR, part 46. Bethesda, MD: Oral History Association, October 2003.

Powe, Lucas A., Jr. *American Broadcasting and the First Amendment.* Berkeley: University of California Press, 1987.

Powell, Adam Clayton, III. "You Are What You Hear." *Media Studies Journal* 7, no. 3 (1993): 71–76.

Prelinger, Richard, and Celeste Hoffnar, eds. *Footage 89: North American Film and Video Sources,* index edited by Tom Damrauer. New York: Prelinger Associates, 1989.

Pride, Armistead Scott, and Clint C. Wilson II. *A History of the Black Press.* Washington, DC: Howard University Press, 1997.

Primeau, Ronald. *The Rhetoric of Television.* New York: Longman, 1979.

Public Broadcasting System. *The Gulf War,* Frontline documentary. January 1996. Available online at http://www.pbs.org/wgbh/pages/frontline/gulf/.

Puddington, Arch. *Broadcasting Freedom: The Cold War Triumph of Radio Free Europe and Radio Liberty.* Lexington: University Press of Kentucky, 2000.

Purlin, Stuart H. "Ascertainment of Community Needs by a Black-oriented Radio Station." *Journal of Broadcasting* 16, no. 4 (1972): 421–29.

Pusateri, C. Joseph. *Enterprise in Radio: WWL and the Business of Broadcasting in America.* Washington, DC: University Press of America 1980.

Raby, Ormond. *Radio's First Voice: The Story of Reginald Fessenden.* Toronto: Canadian Communications Association, 1970.

Ramirez, Ron, with Michael Prosise. *Philco Radio 1928–1942.* Atglen, PA: Schiffer, 1993.

Ray, William B. *FCC: The Ups and Downs of Radio-TV Regulation.* Ames: Iowa State University Press, 1990.

Redstone, Sumner, with Peter Knobler. *A Passion to Win.* New York: Simon & Schuster, 2001.

Rehm, Diane. "Talking Over America's Electronic Backyard Fence." *Media Studies Journal* 7, no. 3 (1993): 63–69.

Reinharz, Shulamit, with Lynn Davidman. *Feminist Methods in Social Research.* New York: Oxford University Press, 1992.

Richardson, Marilyn, ed. *Maria W. Stewart, America's First Black Woman Political Writer: Essays and Speeches.* Bloomington: Indiana University Press, 1987.

Riggins, Stephen Harold, ed. *Ethnic Minority Media: An International Perspective.* Newbury Park, CA: Sage, 1992.

Riis, Jacob. *How the Other Half Lives: Studies among the Tenements of New York.* New York: Charles Scribner's Sons, 1890. Online ed. http://www.yale.edu/amstud/inforev/riis/title .html. Paperback ed. Sam Warner, ed. London: Penguin, 1997.

Riney-Kehrberg, Pamela. "The Radio Diary of May Dyck, 1936–1955: The Listening Habits of a Kansas Farm Woman." *Journal of Radio Studies* 5, no. 2 (1998), 66–79.

Ritchie, Donald A. *Doing Oral History.* New York: Twayne Publishers, 1995.

———. "Oral History Evaluation Guidelines." Oral History Association, Pamphlet Number 3, Adopted 1989. Washington, DC: U.S. Senate Historical Office, Revised Sept. 2000.

Ritchie, Donald A., and Linda Shopes. "Application of the Department of Health and Human Services Regulations for the Protection of Human Subjects at 45 CFR Part 46, Subpart A to Oral History Interviewing." Washington, DC: Oral History Association and American Historial Association, 2003.

Rivera, Geraldo. *Exposing Myself.* New York: Bantam, 1991.

Roberto, Anthony J., Gary Myers, Amy J. Johnson, Charles K. Atkin, and Patricia K. Smith. "Promoting Gun Trigger-lock Use: Insights and Implications from a Radio-based Health Communication Intervention." *Journal of Applied Communication* 30, no. 3 (2002): 210–30.

Robinson, Thomas Porter. *Radio Networks and the Federal Government.* New York: Columbia University Press, 1943.

Rogers, Everett. *A History of Communication Study.* New York: Free Press, 1994.

Rohlfs, Jeffrey H. *Bandwagon Effects in High-technology Industries.* Cambridge, MA: MIT Press, 2001.

Rolo, Charles. *Radio Goes to War: The "Fourth Front."* New York: Putnam, 1942; London: Faber & Faber, 1943.

Roscigno, Vincent J., and William F. Danaher. *The Voice of Southern Labor: Radio, Music, and Textile Strikes, 1929–1934.* Minneapolis: University of Minnesota Press, 2004.

Rose, Brian G. *Television and the Performing Arts: A Handbook and Reference Guide to American Cultural Programming.* Westport, CT: Greenwood, 1986.

———. *TV Genres: A Handbook and Reference Guide.* Westport, CT: Greenwood, 1985.

Rosen, Philip T. *The Modern Stentors: Radio Broadcasters and the Federal Government, 1920–1934.* Westport, CT: Greenwood, 1980.

Ross, Susan Dente. *Deciding Communication Law.* Mahwah, NJ: Lawrence Erlbaum Associates, 2004.

Rosteck, Thomas. *See It Now Confronts McCarthyism: Television Documentary and the Politics of Representation.* Tuscaloosa: University of Alabama Press, 1994.

Rothenberg, Jeff. "Ensuring the Longevity of Digital Documents." *Scientific America,* January 1995, 42–47.

Rothenbuhler, Eric W. "Commercial Radio as Communication." *Journal of Communication* 46, no. 1 (1996): 125–43.

Rowe, Suzanne E. *Oregon Legal Research.* Durham, NC: Carolina Academic Press, 2003.

Rowland, Willard D. "Continuing Crisis in Public Television: A History of Disenfranchisement." *Journal of Broadcasting & Electronic Media* 30, no. 3 (1986): 251–74.

Rowland, Willard D., Jr. "The Meaning of 'the Public Interest' in Communications Policy, Part II: Its Implementation in Early Broadcast Law and Regulation." *Communication Law and Policy* 2, no. 4 (1997): 363–96.

Rowney, Don K., and James Q. Graham. *Quantitative History: Selected Readings in the Quantitative Analysis of Historical Data.* Homewood, IL: Dorsey Press, 1969.

Rubin, Alan M., and Mary M. Step. "Impact of Motivation, Attraction, and Parasocial Interaction on Talk Radio Listening." *Journal of Broadcasting & Electronic Media* 44, no. 4 (2000): 635–54.

Rubin, Bernard, ed. *Small Voices and Great Trumpets: Minorities and the Media.* New York: Praeger, 1980.

Ruffner, Marguerita Anne. "Women's Attitudes Towards Radio." *Journal of Broadcasting & Electronic Media* 17, no. 1 (1972–1973): 85–94.

Ruggiero, Greg. *Microradio & Democracy: (Low) Power to the People.* New York: Seven Stories Press, 1999.

Rumble, Fr. Leslie, and Fr. Charles M. Carty. *Radio Replies in Defence of Religion Given from the Catholic Broadcasting Station 2Sm Sydney, Australia.* 3 vols. St. Paul, MN: Radio Replies Press Society, 1938. Reprint, San Francisco, CA: Tan Books, 1979.

Runco, Mark A., and Kathy Pezdek. "The Effect of Television and Radio on Children's Creativity." *Human Communication Research* 11, no. 1 (1984): 109–20.

Ryan, Milo. "Here Are the Materials, Where Are the Scholars?" *Journal of the Association for Recorded Sound Collections* 2, no. 2/3 (1970): n.p.

———. *History in Sound.* Seattle: University of Washington Press, 1963.

———. "A Treasure House of Broadcast History." *Journal of Broadcasting* 1, no. 1 (1956–1957): 75–78.

Samorishki, Jan. *Issues in Cyberspace: Communication, Technology, Law and Society on the Internet Frontier.* Boston, MA: Allyn & Bacon, 2002.

Sampson, Henry T. *Swingin' on the Ether Waves.* Lanham, MD: Scarecrow Press, 2005.

Sanders, Marlene, and Marcia Rock. *Waiting for Prime Time: The Women of Television News.* Urbana: University of Illinois Press, 1994.

Savage, Barbara Dianne. *Broadcasting Freedom: Radio, War, and the Politics of Race, 1938–1948.* Chapel Hill: University of North Carolina Press, 1999.

Sawyer, Ben, and Ron Pronk. *Digital Camera Companion.* Scottsdale, AZ: Coriolis Group Books, n.d.

Scafella, Jeanne Swann. "Legal Research in the Hinterland." *Media Law Notes* 18 (Spring 1991): 3.

Schachter, Madeleine. *Law of Internet Speech.* 2nd ed. Durham, NC: Carolina Academic Press, 2002.

Schatzkin, Paul. *The Boy Who Invented Television: A Story of Inspiration, Persistence and Quiet Passion.* Silver Spring, MD: TeamCom Books, 2002.

Schiffer, Michael Brian. *The Portable Radio in American Life.* Tucson: University of Arizona Press, 1991. Reprint ed. Tucson: University of Arizona Press, 1992.

Schiller, Herbert I. *Mass Communications and American Empire.* New York: Augustus M. Kelley, 1970.

Schoenbrun, David. "Murrow's Boys." In University of Maryland Broadcast Pioneers Oral History Project, May 30, 1974.

Schonfeld, Reese. *Me and Ted against the World: The Unauthorized Story of the Founding of CNN.* New York: Cliff Street, 2001.

Schramm, Wilbur, Jack Lyle, and Edwin Parker. *Television in the Lives of Our Children.* Palo Alto, CA: Stanford University Press, 1961.

Schroeder, Richard. *Texas Signs On: The Early Days of Radio and Television.* College Station: Texas A&M University Press, 1998.

Schroth, Raymond A. *The American Journey of Eric Sevareid.* South Royalton, VT: Steerforth Press, 1995.

Schultze, Quentin J. "Evangelical Radio and the Rise of the Electronic Church, 1921–1948." *Journal of Broadcasting & Electronic Media* 32, no. 3 (1988): 289–306.

Schwartz, Evan I. *The Last Lone Inventor: A Tale of Genius, Deceit and the Birth of Television.* New York: HarperCollins, 2002.

Scott, Gini Graham. *Can We Talk? The Power and Influence of Talk Shows.* New York: Perseus, 1996.

Scott, Robert L., and Bernard L. Brock. *Methods of Rhetorical Criticism.* New York: Harper & Row, 1972.

Seitz, Frederick. *The Cosmic Inventor: Reginald Aubrey Fessenden (1866–1932),* transactions of the American Philosophical Society, 89. Philadelphia, PA: American Philosophical Society, 1999.

Seldon, Anthony, and Joanna Pappworth. *By Word of Mouth: Elite Oral History.* London: Methuen, 1983.

Sendall, Bernard, and Jeremy Potter. *Independent Television in Britain*. Vol. 1, *Origin and Foundation, 1946–62*. Vol. 2, *Expansion and Change, 1958–68*. Vol. 3, *Politics and Control, 1968–1980*. Vol. 4, *Companies and Programmes, 1968–1980*. London: Macmillan, 1998.

Shafer, Robert Jones, ed. *A Guide to Historical Method*. Homewood, IL: Dorsey Press, 1969. Rev. ed. 1974. 3rd ed. 1980.

———. "Using Evidence: Internal Criticism." In *A Guide to the Historical Method*, edited by Robert Jones Shafer. 3rd ed. Homewood, IL: Dorsey Press, 1980, 149–70.

Shapiro, Andrew O. *Media Access: Your Rights to Express Your Views on Radio and Television*. Boston, MA: Little, Brown, 1976.

Shapiro, Mitchell. *Radio Network Prime Time Programming, 1926–1967*. Jefferson, NC: McFarland, 2002.

———. *Television Network Daytime and Late-night Programming, 1959–1989*. Jefferson, NC: McFarland, 1990.

———. *Television Network Prime-time Programming, 1948–1988*. Jefferson, NC: McFarland, 1989.

———. *Television Network Weekend Programming, 1959–1990*. Jefferson, NC: McFarland, 1992.

Shields, Carol. *Jane Austen*. New York: Viking, 2001.

Shields, Steven O., and Robert Ogles. "Black Liberation Radio: A Case Study of Free Radio Micro-broadcasting." *Howard Journal of Communication* 5, no. 3 (1995): 173–83.

Siebert, Fred S. "Research in Legal Problems of Communications." In *An Introduction to Journalism Research*, edited by Ralph O. Nafziger and Marcus M. Wilkerson, chapter 4. Baton Rouge: Louisiana State University Press, 1949.

Siegel, Paul. *Communication Law in America*. 2nd ed. Boston, MA: Allyn & Bacon, 2002.

Siepmann, Charles A. *Radio, Television, and Society*. New York: Oxford University Press, 1950.

———. *Radio's Second Chance*. Boston, MA: Little, Brown, 1946.

Sies, Leora M., and Luther F. Sies. *The Encyclopedia of Women in Radio, 1920–1960*. Jefferson, NC: McFarland, 2003.

Sies, Luther F. *Encyclopedia of American Radio, 1920–1960*. Jefferson, NC: McFarland, 2000.

Signorielli, Nancy, ed. *Women in Communication: A Biographical Sourcebook*. Westport, CT: Greenwood, 1996.

Sillars, Malcolm O., and Bruce Gronbeck. *Communication Criticism: Rhetoric, Social Codes, Cultural Studies*. Prospect Heights, IL: Waveland Press, 2001.

Sillitoe, Linda, and Alan Roberts. *Salamander: The Story of the Mormon Forgery Murders*. Salt Lake City, UT: Signature Books, 1988.

Sisman, Adam. *Boswell's Presumptuous Task: The Making of the Life of Dr. Johnson*. New York: Farrar, Straus, and Giroux, 2001.

Slide, Anthony. *The Television Industry: A Historical Dictionary*. Westport, CT: Greenwood, 1991.

Slim, Hugo, and Paul Thomson. *Listening for a Change: Oral Testimony and Community Development*. Philadelphia, PA: New Society Publishers, 1995.

Sloan, William David. *Perspectives on Mass Communication History*. Hillsdale, NJ: Lawrence Erlbaum Associates, 1991.

Sloan, William David, and James D. Startt, eds. *The Media in America: A History*. 3rd ed. Northport, AL: Vision Press, 1996. 4th ed. 1999.

Slotten, Hugh R. *Radio and Television Regulation: Broadcast Technology in the United States, 1920–1960*. Baltimore, MD: Johns Hopkins University Press, 2000.

Small, William J. *To Kill a Messenger: Television News and the Real World*. New York: Hastings House, 1970.

Smead, Elmer E. *Freedom of Speech by Radio and Television*. Washington, DC: Public Affairs Press, 1959.

Smethers, J. Steven. "Unplugged: Developing Rural Midwestern Television Audiences Without Live Network Service, 1949–1952." *Southwestern Mass Communication Journal* 12, no. 1 (1996): 44–60.

Smethers, J. Steven, and Lee B. Jolliffe. "Homemaking Programs: The Recipe for Reaching Women Listeners on the Midwest's Local Radio." *Journalism History* 24 (Winter 1998–1999): 138–47.

———. "Singing and Selling Seeds: The Live Music Era on Rural Midwestern Radio Stations." *Journalism History* 26, no. 2 (2000): 61–70.

Smith, Allen, ed. *Directory of Oral History Collections*. Phoenix, AZ: Oryz Press, 1987.

Smith, Bruce L., and Jerry C. Brigham. "Native Radio Broadcasting in North America: An Overview of Systems in the United States and Canada." *Journal of Broadcasting & Electronic Media* 36, no. 2 (1992): 183–94.

Smith, Bruce L., and M. L. Cornette. "Eypapaha for Today: American Indian Radio in the Dakotas." *Journal of Radio Studies* 5, no. 2 (1999): 19–30.

Smith, F. Leslie. "How to Use Pike & Fischer." In *Electronic Media and Government: The Regulation of Wireless and Wired Mass Communication in the United States,* by F. Leslie Smith, Milan D. Meeske, and John W. Wright II. White Plains, NY: Longman, 1995, 13.

———. "Quelling Radio's Quacks: The FCC's First Public Interest Programming Campaign." *Journalism Quarterly* 71, no. 3 (1994): 594–608.

Smith, F. Leslie, Milan D. Meeske, and John W. Wright II. *Electronic Media and Government: The Regulation of Wireless and Wired Mass Communication in the United States*. White Plains, NY: Longman, 1995.

Smith, Mary John. *Contemporary Communication Research Methods*. Belmont, CA: Wadsworth, 1988.

Smith, MaryAnn Yodelis. "The Method of History." In *Research Methods in Mass Communication*, edited by Guido H. Stempel III and Bruce H. Westley. Englewood Cliffs, NJ: Prentice Hall, 1981. 2nd ed. 1989, 316–30.

Smith, Merritt Roe. "Technological Determinism in American Culture." In *Does Technology Drive History? The Dilemma of Technological Determinism,* edited by Merritt Roe Smith and Leo Marx. Cambridge, MA: MIT Press, 1994, 1–35.

Smith, R. Franklin. "Oldest Station in the Nation?" *Journal of Broadcasting* 4, no. 1 (1959): 44.

Smulyan, Susan. *Selling Radio: The Commercialization of American Broadcasting, 1920–1934*. Washington, DC: Smithsonian Institution Press, 1994.

Smythe, Dallas W. "Communications: Blind Spot of Western Marxism." *Canadian Journal of Political and Social Theory* 1, no. 3 (1977): 1–21.

Snyder, Robert. *Pare Lorentz and the Documentary Film*. Reno: University of Nevada Press, 1994.

Sobel, Robert. *RCA*. New York: Stein and Day, 1986.

Socolow, A. Walter. *The Law of Radio Broadcasting*. 2 vols. New York: Baker & Voorhis, 1939.

Socolow, Michael J. "Questioning Advertising's Influence over American Radio: The Blue Book Controversy of 1945–1947." *Journal of Radio Studies* 9, no. 2 (2002): 282–302.

Soley, Lawrence C. *Free Radio: Electronic Civil Disobedience.* Boulder, CO: Westview Press, 1999.

Soley, Lawrence, and George Hough, III. "Black Ownership of Community Radio Stations: An Economic Evaluation." *Journal of Broadcasting* 22, no. 4 (1982): 455–67.

Solomon, Martha M., ed. *A Voice of Their Own: The Woman Suffrage Press, 1840–1910.* Tuscaloosa: University of Alabama Press, 1991.

Soltes, Mordecai. *The Yiddish Press: An Americanizing Agency.* New York: Arno Press and *The New York Times,* 1925. Reprint, New York: Columbia University, Teachers College, 1969.

Sontag, Susan. "Foreword" to *Italy: One Hundred Years of Photography,* edited by Cesare Colombo and Susan Sontag. New York: Rizzoli International Publications, 1988.

———. *On Photography.* New York: Farrar, Straus, and Giroux, 1977.

———. *Regarding the Pain of Others.* New York: Farrar, Straus and Giroux, 2003.

Sparks, Glenn G. *Media Effects Research: A Basic Overview.* Belmont, CA: Wadsworth, 2002.

Spaulding, Norman W. *History of Black-oriented Radio in Chicago.* Master's thesis, University of Illinois at Chicago, 1974.

Sperber, Ann M. *Murrow: His Life and Times.* New York: Freundlich Books, 1986.

Squier, Susan Merrill, ed. *Communities of the Air: Radio Century, Radio Culture.* Durham, NC: Duke University Press, 2003.

Stacy, Susan M. *The Emergence of Women in American Network Television Journalism, 1948–1985.* Master's thesis, Wright State University, 1993.

Startt, James D., and William David Sloan. *Historical Methods in Mass Communication.* Hillsdale, NJ: Lawrence Erlbaum Associates, 1989. Rev. ed. Northport, AL: Vision Press, 2003.

Stashower, Daniel. *The Boy Genius and the Mogul: The Untold Story of Television.* New York: Broadway Books, 2002.

Stearns, Peter, H. "Why Study History?" American Historical Association. http://www.historians .org/pubs/Free/WhyStudyHistory.htm.

Stedman, Raymond W. *The Serials: Suspense and Drama by Installment.* 2nd ed. Norman: University of Oklahoma Press, 1977.

Stelzner, Hermann G. "War Message, December 8, 1941: An Approach to Language." *Speech Monographs* 33, no. 4 (1966): 419–37.

Stempel III, Guido H., and Bruce H. Westley. "The Systematic Study of Mass Communication." In *Mass Communication Research and Theory,* edited by Guido H. Stempel III, David H. Weaver, and G. Cleveland Wilhoit. Boston, MA: Allyn & Bacon, 2003.

Sterling, Christopher H. *Electronic Media: A Guide to Trends in Broadcasting and Newer Technologies, 1920–1983.* New York: Praeger, 1984.

———, ed. *Encyclopedia of Radio.* 3 vols. New York: Fitzroy Dearborn, 2004.

Sterling, Christopher H., and John M. Kittross. *Stay Tuned: A Concise History of American Broadcasting.* 2nd ed. Belmont, CA: Wadsworth, 1990. 3rd ed. Mahwah, NJ: Lawrence Erlbaum Associates, 2002.

Sterling, Christopher H., and George Shiers. *History of Telecommunications Technology: An Annotated Bibliography.* Lanham, MD: Scarecrow Press, 2000.

Stevens, John D., and Hazel Dickens Garcia. *Communication History.* Beverly Hills, CA: Sage, 1980.

Stielow, Frederick J. *The Management of Oral History Sound Archives.* Westport, CT: Greenwood, 1986.

Stokes, John W. *70 Years of Radio Tubes and Valves.* Vestal, NY: Vestal Press, 1982.

Stone, David M. *Nixon and the Politics of Public Television.* New York: Garland, 1985.

Storey, John. "Introduction: The Study of Popular Culture and Cultural Studies." In *Cultural Theory and Popular Culture: A Reader,* edited by John Storey. 2nd ed. Athens: University of Georgia Press, 1998, x–xviii.

Strachey, Lytton. *Eminent Victorians.* New York: Harcourt, Brace & World, 1969.

Streeter, Thomas. "The Cable Fable Revisited: Discourse, Policy, Politics and the Making of Cable Television." *Critical Studies in Mass Communication* 4, no. 2 (1987): 174–200.

———. *Selling the Air: A Critique of the Policy of Commercial Broadcasting in the United States.* Chicago, IL: University of Chicago Press, 1996.

Streitmatter, Rodger. *Raising Her Voice: African-American Women Journalists Who Changed History.* Lexington: University Press of Kentucky, 1994.

Suggs, Henry Lewis, ed. *The Black Press in the South, 1865–1979.* Westport, CT: Greenwood, 1983.

Summers, Harrison B., ed. *Radio Censorship.* New York: H.W. Wilson, 1939.

———, comp. *A Thirty-year History of Programs Carried on National Radio Networks in the United States, 1926–1956.* Columbus: Ohio State University Department of Speech, 1958. Reprint, New York: Arno Press, in the series *History of Broadcasting,* 1971.

Surlin, Stuart H. "Ascertainment of Community Needs by a Black-oriented Radio Station." *Journal of Broadcasting* 16, no. 4 (1972): 421–29.

Swain, William N. "Propaganda and Rush Limbaugh: Is the Label the Last Word?" *Journal of Radio Studies* 6, no. 1 (1999): 27–40.

Sweeney, Michael S. *Secrets of Victory: The Office of Censorship and American Press and Radio in World War II.* Chapel Hill: University of North Carolina Press, 2001.

Taylor, Robert. *Fred Allen: His Life and Wit.* Boston, MA: Little, Brown, 1989.

Tedford, Thomas L., and Dale A. Herbeck. *Freedom of Speech in the United States.* 5th ed. State College, PA: Strata, 2005.

———. *Resources for Teaching Freedom of Speech.* State College, PA: Strata , 2005.

Teeter, Dwight L., Jr., and Bill Loving. *Law of Mass Communications.* 11th ed. New York: Foundation Press, 2004.

Thomas, Isaiah. *History of Printing in America.* Worcester, MA: Isaiah Thomas, 1810.

Thomas, Laurie, and Barry Litman. "Fox Broadcasting Company, Why Now? An Economic Study of the Rise of the Fourth Broadcast Network." *Journal of Broadcasting & Electronic Media* 35, no. 2 (1991): 139–57.

Thompson, Edward P. "History and Anthropology." In *Making History: Writings on History and Culture.* New York: New Press, 1994, 199–225.

———. *The Making of the English Working Class.* New York: Pantheon, 1963.

Thompson, Paul. *The Voice of the Past: Oral History.* 2nd. ed. New York: Oxford University Press, 1988. 3rd ed. 2000.

Thyer, Bruce A. *Successful Publishing in Scholarly Journals.* Thousand Oaks, CA: Sage, 1994.

Tillinghast, Charles H. *American Broadcast Regulation and the First Amendment: Another Look.* Ames: Iowa State University Press, 2000.

Timberg, Bernard M. *Television Talk: A History of the TV Talk Show.* Austin: University of Texas Press, 2002.

Tinker, Grant, and Bud Rukeyser. *Tinker in Television: From General Sarnoff to General Electric.* New York: Simon & Schuster, 1994.

Tolles, Frederick B. "The Biographer's Craft." In *The Craft of American History: Selected Essays,* edited by A. S. Eisenstadt. New York: Harper & Row, 1954.

Toplin, Robert. *History by Hollywood: The Use and Abuse of the American Past.* Urbana: University of Illinois Press, 1996.

Torres, Sasha. *Black, White, and in Color: Television and Black Civil Rights.* Oxford: Princeton University Press, 2003.

Townsend, Sean, Cressida Chappell, and Oscar Struijvé. *Digitising History: A Guide to Creating Digital Resources from Historical Documents.* Arts and Humanities Data Service, *Guides to Good Practice* series. Oxford, England: Oxbow Books, 1999.

Trahant, Mark N. *Pictures of Our Nobler Selves: A History of Native American Contributions to News Media.* Nashville, TN: Freedom Forum First Amendment Center, 1995.

Tuchman, Barbara W. "Biography as a Prism of History." In *Biography as High Adventure: Life Writers Speak on Their Art,* edited by Stephen B. Oates. Amherst: University of Massachusetts Press, 1986.

————. *Selected Essays: Practicing History.* New York: Ballantine Books, 1981.

Tucker, Kenneth A., ed. *Business History: Selected Readings.* London: Frank Cass, 1977.

Tulloch, John, and Simon Chapman. "Experts in Crisis: The Framing of Radio Debate about the Risk of AIDS to Heterosexuals." *Discourse and Society* 3, no. 4 (1992): 437–67.

Turner, Ted. *Ted Turner Speaks: Insight from the World's Greatest Maverick.* New York: Wiley, 1999.

Tyne, Gerald F. J. *Saga of the Vacuum Tube.* Indianapolis, IN: Howard W. Sams, 1977.

Udelson, Joseph H. *The Great Television Race: A History of the American Television Industry, 1925–1941.* Tuscaloosa: University of Alabama Press, 1982.

United States. *The Constitution of the United States of America: Analysis and Interpretation.* Washington, DC: Government Printing Office, 1996.

United States Commission on Civil Rights. *Window Dressing on the Set: An Update.* Washington, DC: Government Printing Office, 1979.

————. *Window Dressing on the Set: Women and Minorities in Television.* Washington, DC: Government Printing Office, 1977.

University of California. "The Digital Millennium Copyright Act." Los Angeles, February 8, 2001. http:www.gseis.ucla.edu/iclp/dmca1.html.

Upshaw, James. "Tom Brokaw." In *Encyclopedia of Television News,* edited by Michael D. Murray. Phoenix, AZ: Oryx Press, 1999.

Urban, George R. *Radio Free Europe and the Pursuit of Democracy.* New Haven, CT: Yale University Press, 1998.

U.S. Copyright Office. "The Digital Millennium Copyright Act of 1986." http://www.copyright.gov/legislation/dmca.pdf.

VandeBerg, Leah, Larry Wenner, and Bruce Gronbeck, eds., *Critical Approaches to Television.* New York: Houghton Mifflin, 1998.

van der Reyden, Dianne. "Identifying the Real Thing." Smithsonian Center for Materials Research and Education (SCMRE), School for Scanning, sponsored by the National Park Service and managed by the Northeast Document Conservation Center, September 11–13, 1996, New York City, http://www.si.edu/scmre/relact/analysis.htm.

Vandiver, Frank E. "Biography as an Agent of Humanism." In *Biography as High Adventure: Life Writers Speak on Their Art,* edited by Stephen B. Oates. Amherst: University of Massachusetts Press, 1986.

Vargas, Lucila. *Social Uses and Radio Practices: The Use of Participatory Radio by Ethnic Minorities in Mexico.* Boulder, CO: Westview Press, 1995.

Vaz, Kim Marie. *Oral Narrative Research with Black Women.* Thousand Oaks, CA: Sage, 1997.

Veninga, James F., ed. *The Biographer's Gift: Life Histories and Humanism.* College Station: Texas A&M University Press, 1983.

Vincent, John Martin. *Historical Research.* New York: Peter Smith, 1929.

Vogel, Todd, ed. *The Black Press: New Literary and Historical Essays.* New Brunswick, NJ: Rutgers University Press, 2001.

Volokh, Eugene. *Academic Legal Writing: Law Review Articles, Student Notes, and Seminar Papers.* New York: Foundation Press, 2003.

Walker, Jesse. *Rebels of the Air: An Alternative History of Radio in America.* New York: New York University Press, 2001.

Ward, Brian. *Radio and the Struggle for Civil Rights in the South.* Gainesville: University of Florida Press, 2004.

Ward, Jean, and Kathleen A. Hansen. *Search Strategies in Mass Communication.* 3rd ed. New York: Longman, 1997.

Warner, Harry P. *Radio and Television Law.* Albany, NY: Matthew Bender, 1948.

———. *Radio and Television Rights.* Albany, NY: Matthew Bender, 1953.

Warren, Donald. *Radio Priest: Charles Coughlin, the Father of Hate Radio.* New York: Free Press, 1996.

Wasser, Frederick. *Veni, Vidi, Video: The Hollywood Empire and the VCR.* Austin: University of Texas Press, 2001.

Watkins, John J. *The Mass Media and the Law.* Englewood Cliffs, NJ: Prentice-Hall, 1990.

Watson, Mary A. *The Expanding Vista: American Television in the Kennedy Years.* New York: Oxford University Press, 1990.

Webb, Jacqueline Gales, Lex Gillespie, Sonja Williams, and Lou Rawls. "Black Radio ... Telling It Like It Was." Radio Smithsonian transcripts (series of 13). Washington, DC: Smithsonian Institution, 1996.

Weiler, Paul C. *Entertainment, Media, and the Law.* 2nd ed. St. Paul, MN: West Group, 2002.

Weinberg, Steve. *Telling the Untold Story: How Investigative Reporters Are Changing the Craft of Biography.* Columbia: University of Missouri Press, 1992.

Weinstein, David. *The Forgotten Network: Du Mont and the Birth of American Television.* Philadelphia, PA: Temple University Press, 2004.

Wershba, Joe. "The Broadcaster and the Senator." Undated manuscript, later portion published as "Murrow vs. McCarthy: 'See It Now.'" *New York Times Magazine,* March 4, 1979.

Wertheim, Arthur F. *Radio Comedy.* New York: Oxford University Press, 1979.

Werthmann, B., W. Schiller, and W. Griebenow. "Naturwissenschaftliche Aspekte der Echtheitspruefung der Songenannten 'Hitler-Tagebuecher,'" *Maltechnik-Restauro* 90, no. 94 (1984): 65–72.

Whalen, David J. "Communications Satellites: Making the Global Village Possible." National Aeronautics and Space Administration. http://www.hq.nasa.gov/office/pao/History/satcom history.html.

Wheeler, Thomas. *Phototruth or Photofiction? Ethics and Media Imagery in the Digital Age.* Mahwah, NJ: Lawrence Erlbaum Associates, 2002.

Williams, Gilbert A. *Legendary Pioneers of Black Radio.* Westport, CT: Praeger, 1998.

Williams, Huntington. *Beyond Control: ABC and the Fate of the Networks.* New York: Atheneum, 1989.

Williams, Mark J. "Considering Monty Margetts's *Cook's Corner:* Oral History and Television History." In *Television, History, and American Culture: Feminist Critical Essays,* edited by Mary Beth Haralovich and Lauren Rabinovitz. Durham, NC: Duke University Press, 1999.

———. "From Remote Possibilities to Entertaining Difference: A Regional Study of the Rise of Television Industry in Los Angeles, 1930–1952." PhD diss., University of Southern California, 1993.

Williams, Ralph. *A. Atwater Kent: The Man, The Manufacturer, and His Radios.* Chandler, AZ: Sonoran Publishing, 2002.

———. "The Atwater Kent Radios." *The Antique Wireless Association Review* 12 (1999).

Williams, Raymond. *The Long Revolution.* New York: Columbia University Press, 1961.

———. *Television: Technology and Cultural Form.* Hanover, NH: Wesleyan University Press, 1992.

Wilson, Clint C., II, Félix Gutiérrez, and Lena M. Chao. *Race, Multiculturalism, and the Media: The Rise of Class Communication in Multicultural America.* Thousand Oaks, CA: Sage, 2003.

Wimmer, Roger D., and Joseph R. Dominick. *Mass Media Research: An Introduction.* Belmont, CA: Wadsworth, 2003.

Winston, Brian. "How Are Media Born?" In *Connections: A Broadcast History Reader,* edited by Michelle Hilmes. Belmont, CA: Wadsworth, 2003, 3–18.

———. *Media Technology and Society: A History from the Telegraph to the Internet.* New York: Routledge, 1998.

Wittke, Carl. *The German-language Press in America.* Lexington: University of Kentucky Press, 1957.

Wolfe, Art. *Migrations: Wildlife in Motion.* Text by Barbara Sleeper. Hillsboro, OR: Beyond Words Publishing, 1994.

Wolseley, Roland Edgar. *Black Achievers in American Journalism.* Nashville, TN: James C. Winston Publishing, 1995.

Woodward, Bob, and Carl Bernstein. *The Final Days.* New York: Simon & Schuster, 1976.

Youm, Kyu Ho. "Editorial Rights of Public Broadcasting Stations vs. Access for Minor Political Candidates to Television Debates." *Federal Communications Law Journal* 52, no. 3 (2000): 687–725.

Yow, Valerie Raleigh. *Recording Oral History: A Practical Guide for Social Scientists.* Thousand Oaks, CA: Sage, 1994.

Zelezny, John D. *Communications Law.* 4th ed. Belmont, CA: Wadsworth, 2004.

Zettl, Herbert. *Sight, Sound, Motion: Applied Media Aesthetics.* 3rd ed. Belmont, CA: Wadsworth, 1999. 4th ed. 2004.

Zuckman, Harvey L., Robert L. Corn-Revere, Robert M. Frieden, and Charles H. Kennedy. *Modern Communication Law.* St. Paul, MN: West Group, 1999.

Index